STUDIES IN EVANGELICAL HISTORY AND THOUGHT

The Growth of the Brethren Movement

National and International Experiences

STUDIES IN EVANGELICAL HISTORY AND THOUGHT

A full listing of all titles in this series appears at the close of this book

Harold H. Rowdon

STUDIES IN EVANGELICAL HISTORY AND THOUGHT

The Growth of the Brethren Movement

National and International Experiences

Essays in Honour of Harold H. Rowdon

Edited by

Neil T.R. Dickson and Tim Grass

Wipf & Stock
PUBLISHERS
Eugene, Oregon

Wipf and Stock Publishers
199 W 8th Ave, Suite 3
Eugene, OR 97401

The Growth of the Brethren Movement: National and International Experiences
Essays in Honor of Harold H. Rowdon
Edited by Dickson, Neil T. R. and Grass, Tim

ISBN 13: 978-1-55635-117-4
ISBN 10: 1-55635-117-8
Publication date 11/27/2006
Previously published by Paternoster, 2006

STUDIES IN EVANGELICAL HISTORY AND THOUGHT

Series Preface

The Evangelical movement has been marked by its union of four emphases: on the Bible, on the cross of Christ, on conversion as the entry to the Christian life and on the responsibility of the believer to be active. The present series is designed to publish scholarly studies of any aspect of this movement in Britain or overseas. Its volumes include social analysis as well as exploration of Evangelical ideas. The books in the series consider aspects of the movement shaped by the Evangelical Revival of the eighteenth century, when the impetus to mission began to turn the popular Protestantism of the British Isles and North America into a global phenomenon. The series aims to reap some of the rich harvest of academic research about those who, over the centuries, have believed that they had a gospel to tell to the nations.

Series Editors

Contents

Contributors

D.W. Bebbington is Professor of History at the University of Stirling and the author most recently of *The Dominance of Evangelicalism: The Age of Spurgeon and Moody* (2005)

Beth Dickson is a Senior Lecturer in the Faculty of Education at Glasgow University and writes for *Partnership Perspectives*

Neil T.R. Dickson is a secondary school teacher, author of *Brethren in Scotland 1838–2000: A Social Study of an Evangelical Movement* (2002), and edits the *Brethren Archivists and Historians Network Review*

Tim Grass is an Associate Lecturer in Church History at Spurgeon's College, London, and the author of *Gathering to His Name: The Story of Brethren in Britain and Ireland* (2006)

Graham Johnson is the archivist of the Christian Brethren Archive, John Rylands University Library, Manchester

Jean M. Johnson is a retired lecturer in Chemistry

August Jung is a retired pastor who lives in Iserlohn, Germany

Jason Lim from Bethesda Hall (Ang Mo Kio) in Singapore is currently a PhD candidate at the University of Western Australia

Peter Lineham is an Associate Professor of History at Massey University, and is the author of *There We Found Brethren: A History of Assemblies of Brethren in New Zealand* (1977)

Winston G. Litchmore is a former Schools Inspector and is a full-time worker among Brethren assemblies in Jamaica

Kovina L.K. Mutenda is a full-time Christian worker and the Executive Director of the Christian Resource Centre in Zambia. He has written the *History of the Christian Brethren in Zambia (1898–1998)* (2002)

José Neto is a full-time worker among Brethren assemblies in Angola

Ian M. Randall is Senior Research Fellow at the International Baptist Theological Seminary, Prague, Czech Republic

Harold H. Rowdon is a retired lecturer in Church History, London Bible College, and is the author of *The Origins of the Brethren 1825–1850* (1967)

Roger Shuff is a research historian (freelance) and the author of *Searching for the True Church: Brethren and Evangelicals in Mid-Twentieth Century England* (2005)

Timothy C.F. Stunt is a secondary school teacher of history and author of *From Awakening to Secession: Radical Evangelicals in Switzerland and Britain 1815–35* (2000)

Neil Summerton is a retired civil servant who is the Chairman of Partnership and the author of *A Noble Task* (^{2}1994)

Pauline Summerton is a retired Hospital Chaplain and author of *Fishers of Men: The Missionary Influence of an Extended Family in Central Africa* (2003)

Gerald T. West has been for many years an elder of an assembly of Christian Brethren in London

Elisabeth Wilson is currently researching evangelical networks and international speakers in Australia, 1870s–1900, for a doctoral thesis

Introduction

Most of the essays collected in this *Festschrift* were delivered at a conference held in Redcliffe College in Gloucester in July 2003 in honour of Dr Harold Rowdon under the aegis of the Brethren Archivists and Historians Network. Harold Rowdon's *The Origins of the Brethren 1825–1850*, published in 1967, has had a seminal influence on modern Brethren historiography. There had been several excellent popular histories of the Brethren, and Roy Coad's *A History of the Brethren Movement* appeared the year after *The Origins of the Brethren*. But it was in the latter book, which was based on Rowdon's PhD thesis for the University of London, that the movement was first examined in a work of critical history. His life and work are analysed in the present book by Dr Ian Randall. Recently a number of historians, several of them contributors to the present volume, have followed in Dr Rowdon's pioneering footsteps, and several works supplementing or extending the task begun by him have appeared. It is therefore only fitting that the present generation of historians of the Brethren should pay tribute to his work as their *fons et origo*.

Dr Rowdon's significance has not only been within the field of historiography. Professor F.F. Bruce noted in his introduction to *The Origins of the Brethren* that there were two divergent tendencies contained within the early Brethren. Only one of Bruce's tendencies concerns us here, the one he described in the contemporary scene as consisting of 'independent churches enjoying evangelical freedom and liberality of communion'.[1] Dr Rowdon has worked tirelessly to further the life of such congregations by his teaching at London Bible College (now London School of Theology), his preaching, writing and editing, and through the work of the Christian Brethren Research Fellowship and its successor body, Partnership. His aims in this aspect of his life and the enthusiasm with which he has pursued them are abundantly clear in his own contribution to this volume. This *Festschrift* is thus not only a tribute to him as a significant historian of evangelicalism in the later twentieth century, but also to his importance as a servant of the church.

As well as celebrating the life and achievement of Harold Rowdon, the essays in this book cohere round the theme of the growth of the Brethren movement, offering fresh perspectives on the movement in the United Kingdom, but also examining a number of other national experiences. The history of the Brethren in the United Kingdom is the best-researched area in the field of Brethren historiography, but there are a number of areas still to be explored within it and the contributors aid this process. Thus original contributions are made to regional or local history, both in Britain and further afield, which at the same time raise wider themes and issues such as revivalism, social class or paternalism in a colonial setting. Brethren historiography receives its first systematic treatment and even in the area of origins—the subject of Dr Rowdon's own thesis—an original contribution is made in the study of the neglected figure of John Howard, while the better-known figures

1. H.H. Rowdon, *The Origins of the Brethren 1825–1850* (London, 1967), p. xii.

of A.N. Groves and George Müller are given fresh and extended treatment, the last receiving his first serious academic study through an economic analysis of his methods of funding. The essays on Angola and Jamaica are the only histories to exist in English, while the essays on other nations significantly extend Brethren historiography in these countries. The volume is rounded off by a paper on the movement in its international context by a leading historian of evangelicalism, Prof. David Bebbington, which also fittingly manages to define the characteristics of Brethrenism. The collection thus brings together two of the central interests of Harold Rowdon's life: the writing of Brethren history and his concern for the worldwide spread of the movement.

The editors would like to acknowledge the assistance of Jeremy Mudditt and Dr Anthony R. Cross at Paternoster in assisting the production of this book.

Neil T.R. Dickson
Tim Grass

PART 1

Writing Brethren History

CHAPTER 1

'To Equip and Encourage': The Life of Harold H. Rowdon

Ian M. Randall

Harold Hamlyn Rowdon was born on 26 September 1926 in Sucre, Bolivia, where his parents were Brethren missionaries linked with 'Echoes of Service'. His father, Reginald Robert Rowdon (known as 'Robert'), died at the age of forty-six of typhoid fever when Harold was only a few months old, and his mother, Alice Elsie (née Tizard), returned soon after to her home town, Christchurch, Hampshire, in order to bring up her four children. They were a close-knit family. Daily prayer and Bible study were part of the family routine, with the children taking part in prayer and discussion. The Rowdons' church was Bargates Gospel Hall, part of a strong group of Brethren assemblies in the Bournemouth area of the south coast of England. Harold experienced a meaningful childhood conversion at the age of five, on Easter Sunday 1931, literally at his mother's knee, and was baptized as a believer in May 1938. The joy of Christian experience, his sister Dorothy notes, was known by Harold from his conversion onwards.[1] He played a full part in the life of Bargates Gospel Hall, teaching in Sunday school, taking part in the typical open-air meetings and tract distribution of the period, singing bass in a young men's quartet, and commencing preaching when he was about seventeen.[2]

At home, Harold was always interested in cooking. His first attempt at cake-making, using a recipe book, was when he was eleven. His mother was at that time in a nursing home and when the cake was brought in the nurses found it hard to believe that young Harold had made it on his own. His other interests at various points have included cross-country running, walking, cricket and the historiography of Winnie the Pooh. He took some training as a cricket coach. As a boy, together with some friends, Harold edited a magazine which covered a range of topics. These included Bible teaching and cookery hints.[3] At this early stage there were indications of the way in which Harold's future career and interests would develop.

1. I am indebted for this insight to Mrs Dorothy Helmer (one of Harold's sisters) in a letter dated 26 October 2003.

2. I am grateful to Harold for providing me with a brief autobiography which has filled in a considerable number of details.

3. Dorothy Helmer to Ian Randall, 26 October 2003.

Harold was educated at Bournemouth School (1938–44) and University College, Southampton (1949–53) where he graduated BA (Hons) in Medieval and Modern History and obtained the Certificate in Education. Between 1944 and 1949, he fulfilled his national service as a conscientious objector by working as a hospital porter, and taught part-time in a preparatory school. The latter confirmed his long-standing desire to teach. At university he participated fully in the Christian Union, which had a membership of 40-50 in a college of about 900 students. This was a period of considerable vitality for the Inter-Varsity Fellowship, which linked the Christian Unions (CUs) in higher education.[4] The CU gave Harold strong links with the wider evangelical world. He served as CU prayer secretary, and then as president. About forty of those who were members of the CU at that time have kept in touch through the succeeding years. Harold edited a prayer calendar and there has been an annual reunion. About a dozen spend a few days on holiday together each year.

In his early teaching career, Harold taught history at a small country school in Gloucestershire, Chipping Campden Grammar School. In 1954 he was invited to join the teaching staff of London Bible College (LBC), which would become established as the leading interdenominational Bible college in Britain.[5] At the time, LBC was preparing students for the external examinations of London University and, in view of the new requirement for the teaching of religious knowledge in schools, was preparing students in various arts subjects, including theology, for a BA. Harold was appointed to teach history for the BA as well as church history for the BD degree. He was concerned, as he put it, to create interest in history, a subject often dismissed as dull and irrelevant.[6] After some years, it became apparent that the BD was appropriate for intending school teachers and, in any case, take-up for the BA course had been small. So LBC discontinued it, and Harold was invited to teach Christian ethics as well as church history. When LBC moved from central London to a new site in Northwood, north London, and from the London University system to the Council for National Academic Awards (CNAA), which called for more seminar work, he was able to focus on church history alone. From the 1970s onwards he played a major role in pioneering curriculum development when LBC submitted courses for the approval of the CNAA. He remained a lecturer at LBC until retirement in 1991, and was, therefore, engaged in equipping large numbers of people who became significant evangelical leaders.

After about three years at LBC, Harold was invited to become the college's resident tutor, responsible to the Principal, at that time Ernest Kevan, for the

4. Douglas Johnson, *Contending for the Faith: A history of the Evangelical Movement in the Universities and Colleges* (Leicester, 1979), p. 235. For more recent work on the IVF/UCCF, see Geraint Fielder, *Lord of the Years: Sixty Years of Student Witness* (Leicester, 1988); and Oliver Barclay, *Evangelicalism in Britain, 1935–1995* (Leicester, 1997).

5. LBC changed its name to the London School of Theology in 2004.

6. H.H. Rowdon, *London Bible College: The First Twenty-five Years* (Worthing, 1968), p. 37. For a recent history of LBC see Ian M. Randall, *Educating Evangelicalism: The Origins, Development and Impact of London Bible College* (Carlisle, 2000).

residential life of the college.[7] This continued throughout the whole of his time at LBC, under successive Principals, and it became an important part of his ministry there.[8] He received some training through Care and Counsel and spent a good deal of time with students, resolving many problems which they were facing. He was often asked by students to officiate at their weddings. Leslie Allen, a colleague and close friend of Harold's at LBC (and later Professor of Old Testament at Fuller Theological Seminary, USA), recalls that when Harold's bachelor state was pointed out on such occasions he would observe, 'The onlooker sees most of the game.'[9] Derek Tidball, Principal of LBC from 1995, and a former student of LBC, writes:

> what a valuable contribution [Harold] made as a resident tutor both in Marylebone Road days and here at Northwood where he lived in a small flat at one end of Laing Hall. He was wonderfully hospitable, perhaps a characteristic which was typical of the Brethren. Many beat a path to his door and student groups were always enjoying his coffee and even more the pavlovas he made for which he was famed. His pastoral contact with current and former students was immense and his contact with ex-students is still prodigious.[10]

The pavlova and coffee would often be preceded by another of Harold's specialities, lettuce curry!

Although Harold invested a great deal of time in ministry to individuals, this is not to say that he neglected academic research and writing. He was invited to give LBC's Annual Public Lecture in 1960 which was published as 'Puritan Church Discipline: A Critical Analysis and Evaluation'.[11] This led to an invitation to contribute articles to a forthcoming *Encyclopedia of Christianity.* He has subsequently contributed articles to a number of encyclopedias, dictionaries and Bible commentaries. In 1965 Harold was awarded the London University PhD for a fine thesis which was published the following year as *The Origins of the Brethren: 1825–1850*, and which was ground-breaking in bringing the study of Brethren history into the academic arena. Derek Tidball comments: 'He was much admired for his original research on the origins of the Brethren in days when PhDs were much rarer than they are now.'[12] This major work was followed by several smaller books. *London Bible College: The First 25 Years* was published in 1968 to commemorate LBC's silver jubilee; *Law and Grace* (1968) was one of a series of Bible study books published by Scripture Union; *Turning the Church Inside Out* (1982) represents his lifelong concern for world mission; and his book *Who are the Brethren and does it*

7. G.W. Kirby, *Ernest Kevan: Pastor and Principal* (London and Eastbourne, 1968), p. 34.

8. The Principals under whom Harold served were Ernest Kevan, Gilbert Kirby, Michael Griffiths and Peter Cotterell.

9. Leslie Allen to Ian Randall, 1 October 2003.

10. Derek Tidball to Ian Randall, 21 October 2003.

11. For Harold Rowdon's publications, see the Bibliography below.

12. Derek Tidball to Ian Randall, 21 October 2003.

matter? (1986) lies at the heart of his concern for the welfare of the Brethren movement.

Over the years from the 1960s, a significant number of important articles from Harold's pen, both scholarly and more popular in nature, have appeared in various journals as well as in symposia. Some are on historical subjects, mainly appearing in the pages of LBC's own *Vox Evangelica*, several others are on Brethren history and practice, and still others are related to world mission. Of particular significance, given Harold's Brethren commitment, was *A Bible Commentary for Today* (1979), which was a showcase for Brethren learning of the time. Harold contributed several articles to this commentary. Editorial activity has also occupied a good deal of his time. A Brethren colleague, John Baigent, writes appreciatively of Harold's personal qualities of care and encouragement in his editorial work: 'I have always found him very encouraging, patient and understanding (especially of my inability to meet deadlines!). He has a wonderful ability to persuade people to write who thought they could not or did not have the time.'[13]

Preaching and teaching at church services and midweek Bible study meetings developed with Harold's appointment to the staff of LBC. The interdenominational contacts he made meant that he preached at churches belonging to most of the major denominations. He was rarely used by the most traditional of the Brethren assemblies nor (more surprisingly) very often by the progressive causes at the opposite end of the Brethren spectrum. He was preaching most weekends and often midweek, and his ministry was always considered to be practical and relevant. Invitations also came to speak at the then-popular Saturday Brethren conferences held around the country. Getting to know many 'middle-of-the-road' Brethren assemblies enabled him to detect weaknesses that were appearing among them, and he began to address the uncertainties and unanswered questions of those occupying the centre ground. Harold also spoke at residential Brethren conferences, which from 1957 were held annually at 'The Hayes' conference centre, Swanwick, Derbyshire. In January 1953 a conference was held in London at which differing views of the Second Coming were exchanged and in September of that year there was a similar conference on the theme of the Holy Spirit.[14] At later conferences, Brethren leaders, such as Montague Goodman, F.F. Bruce and G.C.D. Howley, suggested the need for Brethren church leaders to receive training and raised the possibility of women speaking in public meetings, something unknown in assemblies at that time. Derek Tidball comments:

> I think [Harold] played a key role, along with others like F.F. Bruce, in encouraging any number of younger Brethren leaders first to be unafraid of Bible college education, and in benefiting from post-graduate research. It was however, as so often, a double-edged sword. On the one hand, it strengthened their self-confidence

---

13. John Baigent to Ian Randall, 8 September 2003.

14. See Peter Hocken, *Stream of Renewal: The Origins and Early Development of the Charismatic Movement* (Carlisle, 1997), ch. 3, for commentary on this conference.

> and sharpened their identity, on the other hand, it inevitably ran the risk that their introduction to broader horizons bred a little dissatisfaction with home.[15]

Harold also became involved in committee work for LBC and the wider Christian world. He had a gift in this area, which was recognized and eagerly utilized by others. He was invited to join the board of the Regions Beyond Missionary Union (RBMU), an interdenominational faith mission with oversight of missionary work in three continents. Later he became involved in the Andes Evangelical Mission (AEM), a task which was hard to resist in the light of his connection with Bolivia. He was delighted when the British branch of AEM joined with the Evangelical Union of South America (EUSA), but dismayed that the rest of AEM merged with another mission previously involved only with work in Africa which began to recruit missionaries for Bolivia. He played a part in the complete restructuring of EUSA, in fellowship with RBMU, to form Latin Link along lines which seemed to him to be highly relevant to contemporary mission. He also served on the council of the Bible and Medical Missionary Fellowship (now Interserve). The London council was the supreme governing body, and Harold was able to play a part in internationalizing the Fellowship. These involvements led to trips to Peru and Bolivia (which included a moving visit to his birthplace, Sucre), and India and Nepal. Harold was a supporter of the Evangelical Missionary Alliance (EMA), formed in 1958, of which Gilbert Kirby, the Evangelical Alliance General Secretary and then LBC Principal, was General Secretary.[16] Harold served as a member of the Board of Management of the EMA (later Global Connections). His desire to see more collaboration between missionary societies and a drastic reduction in their number earned him some notoriety, but he was encouraged by a limited amount of action.

Not surprisingly, Harold became more and more involved in committee and other work connected with the Brethren movement. For a number of years, he served on what was known as the Bloomsbury Committee, whose task it was to organize two series of Bible teaching meetings in central London, on the Saturday nights of February and November each year. John Baigent recalls Harold's involvement: 'I served with him on the committee that organised and planned the "Bloomsbury Meetings". I was the last chairman. Harold was a regular speaker as well as helping to plan the series… [H]e has made a tremendous contribution to the life of Brethren churches by his persistent, provocative dissemination of new and radical ideas for church life.'[17] Another Brethren venture in which Harold participated was the

---

15. Derek Tidball to Ian Randall, 21 October 2003. For Brethren and scholarship in the 1940s–50s see D.W. Bebbington, *Evangelicalism in Modern Britain: A History from the 1730s to the 1980s* (London, 1995), p. 260. Cf. also Roger Shuff, *Searching for the True Church: Brethren and Evangelicals in Mid-Twnetieth Century England* (Carlisle, 2005), pp. 69-101; and Tim Grass, *Gathering to his Name: The Story of Open Brethren in Britain and Ireland* (Milton Keynes, 2006), pp. 370-76.

16. Ian Randall and David Hilborn, *One Body in Christ: The History and Significance of the Evangelical Alliance* (Carlisle, 2001), p. 230.

17. John Baigent to Ian Randall, 8 September 2003.

magazine originally called *Harvester* and subsequently renamed *Aware*. For some years he served on the editorial committee and was part of a determined effort to make the magazine more relevant. The effort ultimately failed, possibly because it alienated too many existing subscribers and failed to attract enough new ones to make it financially viable.

For a good number of years, Harold was a member of the council of the Counties Evangelistic Work (later known simply as Counties). This was a fellowship of over thirty Brethren evangelists. Harold's period of involvement coincided with a time of far-reaching transition for the Counties work, during which many of the evangelists moved away from their traditional role of pioneering evangelism, primarily in rural areas, towards more specialized evangelistic work in prisons, schools, among ethnic minority groups and, increasingly, church planting and church development, and also in training others for evangelism. Another development was the building of mobile Bible exhibitions.[18]

The Christian Brethren Research Fellowship (CBRF) was one of a number of initiatives taken by Brethren in the 1960s to counteract the adverse publicity arising from some of the excesses of the Exclusive Brethren and the declining strength of the Open Brethren. The CBRF gained a reputation for being *avant-garde* and, although a founder member, Harold was not at first convinced that it was moving in the right direction since in the 1960s and 70s he felt that there must be a pathway between traditionalism and radicalism. He writes: 'I was at that time vainly looking for a middle way between the crippling traditionalism of some, and the radicalism of CBRF. Needless to say, I subsequently realised that there is no middle way!'[19] In the mid-1980s it became apparent that a new type of Brethren church was coming into existence and that Partnership (as CBRF was now known) was being called to support and resource such churches, and to encourage others to move in a similar direction, for example by modifying patterns of worship, allowing women to play a more active role, becoming more involved in the wider community, and appointing men and women to work full-time with a local church. It was Harold and Brian Mills who pioneered the idea and the procedures for Brethren churches to engage full time workers (later the Partnership Link Up Service [PLUS]).

Harold became deeply involved in the work of Partnership, particularly after his retirement from LBC in 1991, coinciding as this event did with the Nantwich Conference which confirmed Partnership's new direction. As its general editor, he played a crucial part in developing a quarterly magazine, *Partnership Perspectives*, as an organ of communication and inspiration dealing with aspects of church life through appropriate articles, and featuring reports from churches and book reviews. As *International Partnership Perspectives* (from 1999), the magazine has correspondents in about sixty countries. The international dimension grew out of the Lausanne II conference in Manila in 1990 when Harold met with Brethren delegates

18. For the history, see Brian Mills, *A Story to Tell: Evangelism in the Twentieth Century* (Carlisle, 1999).

19. Cf. H.H. Rowdon's 'Brethren in Britain, 1945–2000: A Personal Sketch', p. 124 below.

from about thirty countries who were attending. In the 1990s Harold was again writing more steadily, resulting in an increasing flow of books and booklets. As international secretary of Partnership, he has been involved in the development of relationships between Brethren leaders in the large number of countries (well over 100) where there are Brethren churches, many of them growing and sending missionaries to other countries. Though not a Partnership initiative, the International Brethren Conferences on Mission (IBCM) held in Singapore (1993), Rome (1996) and Serimbar, Romania (2003), have been warmly supported by Partnership. Harold has served on the international committee almost from the beginning and edited a selection of IBCM papers under the title, *The Brethren Contribution to World Mission*.

As a speaker, lecturer and writer, Harold's style has always been accessible. John Baigent suggests that perhaps the fact that, although Harold was an academic, it was as a church historian and not a professional theologian that he approached and taught the Bible, made him more accessible to the average listener. Yet Harold has been a thorough and creative scholar.[20] Derek Tidball notes that he was an early pioneer in supervising postgraduate research students.

> In the 1980s I was one of those who gained from Harold's supervision. He guided me through my MPhil, which was to lead on to teaching church history at Spurgeon's College. As a long-standing and much-loved lecturer at LBC, Harold became known for his well-worn jokes. They were passed down from year to year and were the frequent subject of comment among students. He was also well known for self-deprecating comments, such as 'I have taught you all I know and you still know nothing.'[21]

Despite his lifelong and continuing involvement in and devotion to the Brethren movement, since his retirement Harold has been part of the life of churches belonging to other denominations. Like many other evangelicals who have been nurtured in a particular tradition, his experience increasingly has been that there seems to be little difference in practice between local evangelical congregations even if they have different denominational affiliations.

Underlying all Harold's ministry has been his transparent Christian character and his deeply personal commitment to Christ. He has always recognized that spirituality is vital for ministry and that it is important for each person to develop their personal relationship with God. Leslie Allen comments: 'He was a spiritual person with high standards for himself, a bit old-fashioned—I had to encourage him to vote and come to the cinema... He [also] had a great interest in the Greek/medieval fourfold view of personality, phlegmatic, sanguine, etc. and swore he could fit everybody into one of the four types.'[22] Harold's sister Dorothy speaks of Harold's own personality as 'humorous and fun-loving', and describes him as an

---

20. John Baigent to Ian Randall, 8 September 2003.
21. Derek Tidball to Ian Randall, 21 October 2003.
22. Leslie Allen to Ian Randall, 1 October 2003.

'exemplary' son and brother. The very many people who have been helped in a wide variety of ways by Harold will echo her remark that Harold has 'worked tirelessly' throughout his life, motivated by a vision 'to equip and encourage Christian leaders'.[23]

23. Dorothy Helmer to Ian Randall, 26 October 2003.

CHAPTER 2

The Quest for Identity in British Brethren Historiography: Some Reflections from an Outsider

Tim Grass

Introduction

Histories of the Brethren movement, and in particular of the Open Brethren, are rather like London buses: it is alleged that you wait for a very long time until finally several appear at once. It is noticeable how many of the histories of the Open Brethren, whether by Open or Exclusive writers, can be grouped together: the first group appeared in the years to 1901, the second during the 1930s and the third in the 1960s. This phenomenon intrigued me, and what follows is an attempt to explain it. This paper surveys these works, exploring aspects of the relationship between historiography and the development among Brethren of a sense of their own identity and offering some suggestions for consideration by those involved in the current wave of Brethren research.

My main aim is to demonstrate that Brethren historiography reflects successive phases of the movement's quest for a sense of its own identity, and that there appears to be an upsurge of historiography at times when that identity is perceived as being in need of clarification. Each group of published histories appears to reflect factors at work in the Open Brethren movement and beyond which challenged it to a clearer understanding of its identity. As a result, certain emphases are particularly prominent in each period, and these are indicated in the section titles. I think it likely that these works have also helped to shape the movement's sense of identity, although it has not been possible to investigate this aspect of the topic. I should add that I describe myself as 'an outsider' because I have never belonged to a Brethren assembly of any type (although my father was converted among Open Brethren); however, I am engaged in research for a history of Open Brethren in Britain and Ireland.

A Survey of the Historiography of British Brethren

Welcoming the appearance of Harold Rowdon's *magnum opus*, *The Origins of the Brethren 1825–1850*, Timothy Stunt commented in a review that 'The study of Brethren history has been irregular and all too often partisan. Writers in the last century were too involved in events, while more recent studies have tended to be unobjective hagiography.'[1] Another, more recent, writer, J.P. Callahan, concluded his survey of primitivist themes in the writing of Brethren historians with the assertion that 'The effort to disenfranchise both Christendom and dissenting Brethren has characterized Brethren histories.'[2] These quotations remind us that Brethren had a great deal of emotional and theological capital invested in the writing of their movement's history.

Callahan looks at how the writers' differing theological and ecclesiastical viewpoints coloured their interpretation of the movement's early history, but I want to stand back, and look not at the events of Brethren history themselves, nor primarily at the writers' interpretations of those events, but at how the works which those writers produced reflected, and were even called forth by, what was going on within and beyond the movement at the time of writing.

Limitations of space preclude any reference to works on regional or local Brethren history; works which deal solely with Exclusive Brethren history, such as those by Dronsfield[3] (Kelly-Lowe-Glanton) or Gardiner[4] (Taylorite); works from the *Needed Truth* standpoint;[5] or the related genre of biography, individual and collective.[6]

1. T.C.F. Stunt, 'The Origins of the Brethren', *W,* 98 (1968), p. 147.

2. James Patrick Callahan, *Primitivist Piety: The Ecclesiology of the Early Plymouth Brethren* (Lanham, MD/London, 1996), p. 242.

3. W.R. Dronsfield, *The 'Brethren' since 1870* (Ramsgate, revised edn, 1993). This reflects the quest for identity in the Kelly-Lowe-Glanton section of the movement, being written to justify the reunion of the 1970s as having been achieved without surrendering fundamental principles concerning fellowship (E.N. Cross to Tim Grass, 24 June 2003). Works from an Exclusive standpoint view Brethren history in terms of developments in relationships between groups of meetings or, to put it negatively, divergences of belief and practice which resulted in schism and the formation of further such groups. This is because of their belief that like-minded gatherings should form part of a visible circle of meetings among whom intercommunion can be practised in the assurance that the gatherings so united are truly separated from evil. Each meeting is responsible to the others in its circle of fellowship, and not simply to Christ alone.

4. A.J. Gardiner, *The Recovery and Maintenance of the Truth* (Kingston-upon-Thames, [1951]; revised edn [1963]). This followed the lines laid down by George W. Ware, *A Review of Certain Contentions for the Faith (Jude 3)* ([London, c.1938]). It has been updated according to the perspective of one group of Taylorite seceders by B.W. Burton, *A Further Review of Recovery to the Truth and its Maintenance (1827–1997)* (Lancing, 1997). Many historical works by Exclusive writers in the Taylorite tradition are characterized by a refined version of the Exclusive perspective. This interprets Brethren history in terms of a succession of conflicts for the truth, and each conflict as arising from an attack by the enemy. The writers focus on the 'moral issues' at stake in each successive conflict, and therefore disavow sustained consideration of the human agents. Such an approach entailed revision each time there were major developments within Taylorite Exclusivism and its splinter-groups, so that an account of the latest conflict and the issues at stake in it could be incorporated.

5. See A.T. Doodson (ed.), *The Search for the Truth of God* (Bradford, 1947); [J.J. Park], *The Churches of God: Their Origin and Development in the 20th Century* (Leicester, [1987]).

However, I believe that closer examination of any of these would demonstrate the general applicability of my thesis.

The late Victorian Era: Responses to Critics

The first period of Open Brethren historiography was characterized by an apologetic concern to respond to the accounts of the movement's rise and development provided by its critics. (Histories of the controversies of the 1840s had displayed a similar apologetic motive, whether written by Open or Exclusive Brethren.) Critical accounts would have been slanted in the direction of warning readers against contact with the movement, so it is hardly surprising that Brethren responses were slanted in another, affirming the movement's divine origin. An examination of the dozens of critical works published during this period, and of Brethren responses to them, would show how the sense of Brethren identity was being shaped by the experience of hostility from mainstream denominations—'the sects', as Brethren often called them. Many of the published critiques of Brethrenism majored on its Exclusive manifestations; thus, when Open Brethren during this period sought to distance themselves from Exclusivism, they were, in effect, answering non-Brethren opponents as well as Exclusive Brethren.

One relevant aspect of the background was the resurgence of exclusive thinking during the late nineteenth century, possibly aided by the move of some teachers from Exclusive to Open Brethren. From about 1876, there were calls within Open Brethrenism for a more consistent and separatist approach to such matters as reception to fellowship, which ultimately resulted in the Needed Truth schism of the early 1890s. During the 1890s, too, discussions began in Britain and the United States between some Open Brethren and some groups of Exclusive Brethren in an attempt to find a way round the hindrances to fellowship presented by the 'Bethesda Question' and other such matters by shelving discussion of the movement's divisions, disclaiming the Open and Exclusive labels and seeking a united return to its first principles. These culminated in the Devonshire House conferences in London during 1906–07, themselves conducted against the background of the developing Glanton division among those Exclusive Brethren who had followed Darby, Stoney and Raven.

---

6. Although Henry Pickering's compilation, *Chief Men Among the Brethren* (London, 1918; 2nd edn, [1931]), was not a history as such, it remains one of the more significant historical works. However, many biographies within its covers are long on hagiography and short on facts. This has been a persistent problem with Brethren historiography; writers who viewed the movement as an unparalleled recovery of apostolic truth would be more concerned to point out what God did through their subjects rather than establishing all the biographical details of their careers. This genre has continued to find favour among conservative Open Brethren, with a number of collected biographies appearing in recent decades.

MILLER

Andrew Miller was a moderate Exclusive Brother who followed William Kelly when the Exclusives divided around 1880. He produced the first work of any length purporting to be a history of the movement, *The Brethren: A brief Sketch of their Origin, Progress and Testimony*.[7] In fact, this turns out to be primarily a response to critics, seeking to justify the Exclusive position over against both Open Brethren and critics of Brethrenism, and relatively little history is included—just one chapter on the early years. Two chapters on the events of 1845–48 and its results testify to the author's concern to distance Exclusive from Open Brethren and to portray the former as standing on the original ground, while another chapter is devoted to answering allegations made by non-Brethren critics. The final four chapters quote and expound Brethren teaching on issues often raised by critics, such as sanctification, the Law of God, ecclesiology and eschatology.

COLLINGWOOD

William Collingwood's slight work, *'The Brethren': A Historical Sketch*[8] focused on the early days and on the division of 1845–48, from a desire to bring to light the principles which motivated the movement's founders. He contended that Exclusive Brethren

> have taken a position as far removed from the original ground as they are separated from actual fellowship. As to either, they retain nothing in common with those they have left, except that they still have the same custom of 'breaking bread' on the Lord's-day, and an open ministry. The latter being to the popular idea the distinguishing mark of the 'Brethren,' the two classes, different as they are in all other respects, remain confounded in the minds of those who see only the external form.[9]

Such an approach has continued to influence Open perceptions of their Exclusive brethren and vice versa, although it is open to serious question, historically speaking. Collingwood also alluded to the subsequent recrudescence of exclusive thinking among Open Brethren,[10] but welcomed a recent return to something more like the original spirit of fellowship. Thus we can see how his work reflects the concerns of the 1890s noted above.

NEATBY

W. Blair Neatby's *A History of the Plymouth Brethren*[11] was the first major history of the Brethren movement. It appears that Neatby was associated with an Open Brethren assembly at Kendal at the time when he wrote, although the book gives no

---

7. London, [c.1879].
8. Glasgow, [1899].
9. Collingwood, *Brethren*, p. 22.
10. Collingwood, *Brethren*, pp. 24-25.
11. London, 1901, 2nd edn, 1902.

hint of this.[12] Although the work was not apologetic in the sense of defending the movement against its detractors, it was motivated by a concern to remedy the prevalence of inaccurate impressions concerning the movement's beliefs and practices. It majored on Darbyism, that being the most vigorous form of Brethrenism in his day in terms of literary output and, in his view, normative Brethrenism: Neatby considered that Open Brethrenism 'may be best regarded as a kind of incomplete Darbyism'.[13] In spite of its moderate tone, which contrasts with the intemperate language of many of the critics, the appearance of Neatby's work gave rise to a flurry of hostile responses from Open and Exclusive writers: here was an insider treating the movement with the critical attitude hitherto expected from outsiders—a fifth-columnist, in effect.

The Brethren responses to Neatby's work illustrate recurrent ways of thinking concerning their own history. There is a remarkable degree of homogeneity about them, given that those which I have examined came from very different quarters—the Tunbridge Wells Exclusive W.M. Sibthorpe,[14] the separatist Open brother and editor of *The Believer's Magazine*, John Ritchie, and two more moderate Open Brethren, 'S.F.B.' in *The Witness*[15] and W.H. Bennet, one of the editors of *Echoes of Service*. What stung them all was his assertion that the movement 'took shape under the influence of a delusion',[16] that of the immediate return of Christ, and his alleged failure to acknowledge any divine hand in the events of Brethren history.

It is clear that Neatby's status as an insider must have made his criticisms all the more painful to read. 'S.F.B.' even compared his action to that of Ham uncovering his father's nakedness (Genesis 9.21-27).[17] Decades later, William Hoste referred to the book as 'a work heralded with joy by all our kind detractors',[18] while Henry Pickering described it as 'Correct as to facts, unreliable as to deductions and objectionable as to title'.[19] Neatby's work failed to pass muster on several points.

12. John Ritchie, *'The Way which they call Heresy.' Remarks on Mr. W. Blair Neatby's book, 'A History of the Plymouth Brethren'* ([Kilmarnock], n.d.), p. 104 n. He later associated with Baptists and then Quakers (E.N. Cross to Tim Grass, 26 June 2003).

13. Neatby, *History*, p. 325.

14. W.M. Sibthorpe, *A Defence of the Truth: Called for by Neatby's 'History of the Plymouth Brethren'* (London, 2nd edn, 1903).

15. S.F.B., *W*, 32 (1902), pp. 82-83.

16. Neatby, *History*, p. 339. In response to critics, Neatby in his second edition added the words 'in part' after 'took shape', but refused to retract the point which he had been seeking to make.

17. Cf. the Exclusive leader F.E. Raven's description of the book as 'the work of an Edomite, not a trace of sorrow for the breakdown of that which was fair' (F.E. Raven to Dr van Someren, 8 May 1902, in *Letters of F.E. Raven and Fragments from his Ministry* [Kingston-on-Thames, 1963], p. 187).

18. William Hoste, 'The "Brethren" Movement and its Critics', *BM*, n.s. 38 (1937), p. 177.

19. Henry Pickering, 'A Concise Statement Concerning "The Brethren"', *W*, 69 (1939), p. 255.

Firstly, the book lacked any intent to edify.[20] Secondly, regarding the 'delusion', John Ritchie (himself no friend to the 'sects') pointed out that the advent hope had spread far beyond Brethrenism;[21] in any case, according to Bennet, Brethren did not insist that the Lord's return was necessarily to be expected immediately.[22] Thirdly, the main question was whether or not God had actually raised up a testimony during the nineteenth century to the nature of the church; Neatby's methodology could not answer this as it relied on worldly learning rather than divine wisdom. Bennet characterized it as 'written from a human standpoint rather than a divine',[23] in other words, making no acknowledgement of the divine hand at work in Brethren history, as did 'S.F.B.', who also criticized Neatby's reading of events in terms of a succession of divisions and not as a story of evangelistic and missionary outreach.[24]

What these responses show us is an understanding of Brethren history which sees the movement as divinely raised up, and of historiography which sees its main purpose as edification. This may explain the unease among Open Brethren at the portrayal of Brethren history as a series of controversies, since they did not make the link between these and increasing spiritual light which would be made by many Exclusive writers.

The 1930s: Defining Open Brethren in Relation to Exclusive Brethren and other Christians

In some ways, this period continues the note heard in the first period of clarifying the sense of identity of Open Brethren in response to developments in Exclusive thinking: the context was one in which there was considerable discussion about fellowship between Open and some Exclusive Brethren, complicated by the 'London' Exclusive leader James Taylor Sr's denial of the eternal sonship of Christ at Barnet in 1927, which had provoked many secessions from that branch of the movement. As well as the discussion, there appears to have been a fair amount of traffic between Open and more moderate Exclusive groupings, with a number of moderate Exclusive assemblies deciding to associate with Open Brethren. All this is reflected in the appearance of a number of publications designed to put forward each side's claims or to refute those of the other side. On the wider scene, Brethren were also seeking to clarify their distinctiveness in relation to the other evangelical groupings and agencies with whom increased co-operation was evident in certain sections of the

---

20. W.H. Bennet, *A Return to God and His Word: Remarks on Mr. W. BLAIR NEATBY'S 'History of the Plymouth Brethren'* (Glasgow, [1914]), p. 20.

21. Bennet, *Return*, pp.7,16; Ritchie, *'The Way'*, p. 87.

22. Bennet, *Return*, p. 30. In the preface to the second edition of his work, Neatby explained that the delusion to which he had referred was not that of the premillennial Second Coming, but the idea that it was to be expected within a very few years (*History*, 2nd edn, p. v). His critics had thus misread him at this point.

23. Bennet, *Return*, pp. 27-8.

24. Of course, given Neatby's focus on Exclusivism, the emphasis on division is to some extent understandable.

movement, and also to locate themselves within the sweep of Christian history. A clutch of histories of the movement were written during the 1930s: Veitch (c.1933), Noel (1936) and Beattie (1934–38, published in book form in 1940).

BROADBENT

I ought here to say something about *The Pilgrim Church*,[25] by the Brethren missionary E.H. Broadbent. This was not a history of the Brethren movement, but a reading of church history which reflected typical Brethren attitudes and which gave them a sense of their place within it. Broadbent's thesis was that throughout church history there had been a continuum of faithful groups of believers, often oppressed by organized religion or by the state (or by the amalgam of the two known as 'Christendom'). These were marked by their insistence upon the guidance of the Holy Spirit and the attempt to realize a pure fellowship comprising only true believers.

The background to this book is of particular interest. Towards the end of the First World War, Broadbent had given an address at a Missionary Study Class conference in Malvern concerning the lessons to be learnt from previous attempts to follow the New Testament pattern of church life, and Professor A. Rendle Short suggested that it should be published.[26] However, according to G.H. Lang, a major reason why the book was written was the rise of 'the doctrine of expediency' among Open Brethren:[27] both Broadbent and Lang had protested at the way that the movement was developing (and justifying) a plethora of service agencies, trust funds, and other bodies which in their opinion represented a move away from scriptural principles and imperilled the direct headship of Christ over each local assembly and each of his servants. These developments were regarded as foreshadowing the centralization and the oppression of dissidents which would characterize the ascendancy of the Beast and the False Prophet. In 1928, Broadbent had been asked to resign as an associate editor of *Echoes of Service* because of his views.

Broadbent's interpretation of church history proved highly influential, and was to have an impact upon leaders of the Restorationist or House Church Movement.[28] His presentation of earlier dissenting groups is often open to serious question, but he made the useful point that Brethrenism as a 'back to the New Testament' movement did not lack precedents. Incidentally, a forerunner of this approach was Andrew Miller's other historical work, *Short Papers on Church History*.[29] Miller's expressed

---

25. London, 1931.

26. Review in *Links of Help*, 20 (1931–32), p. 188; G.H. Lang, *Edmund Hamer Broadbent: Saint and Pioneer* (London, 1946), p. 88.

27. Lang, *Broadbent*, p. 90.

28. See Andrew Walker, *Restoring the Kingdom: The Radical Christianity of the House Church Movement* (Guildford, revised edn, 1998), p. 147.

29. 3 vols; London, 1873–78. The work was reprinted by the Open Brethren publisher Pickering & Inglis in 1928 and 1964, each time with additional chapters bringing it up to date, but the latter edition omitted Miller's conclusion.

aim was to edify,[30] and thus he focused not so much on the institutional church as on '*the silver line of God's grace in true Christians*'.[31] Such a perspective contrasts with that of an early leader at Plymouth, Henry Soltau, who in 1863 had asserted that the Brethren movement had no parallel in church history in its attempt to return to the scriptures, apart from all tradition, as its source of authority and direction.[32]

VEITCH

A Scottish solicitor, T.S. Veitch, attempted to offer an impartial perspective on Brethren history in *The Story of the Brethren Movement*.[33] A slight work, apparently intended to mark the movement's centenary, its main argument was that the succession of schisms which had shattered Exclusivism resulted from the insistence upon doctrinal and practical uniformity, which in practice was defined by one source—Park Street in London, which had been Darby's assembly. By contrast, Open Brethren represented a century's attempt to remain faithful to scripture and to offer a welcome to all sound and godly believers. It was like the next work, by Noel, in being a history of divisions, but stood the Exclusive approach on its head by arguing that each successive division represented a further move away from the truth, rather than towards it. Its contemporary relevance is evident from the preface, in which the prominent Open Brother George Goodman expressed the author's intent as being 'to tell the truth, that those who desire information and help in the confusion of Exclusivism may find it and act before the Lord'.[34]

NOEL

Napoleon Noel's two-volume *History of the Brethren*[35] is full of detail not found elsewhere, but partisan and badly organized. Although the author's expressed intent was to edify, three-quarters of the book was devoted to the 'divergences' which have disfigured Exclusive Brethren history. An apologetic motif also runs through the book, in which Open Brethren are portrayed as hopelessly divided, far more so than Exclusives. It has the merit of assembling a great deal of primary source material (though this is not always quoted with complete accuracy), and also covers later developments, especially in Exclusive circles, in greater detail than elsewhere. Noel himself was a moderate Exclusive, and so the final chapter focuses on the reunion of two moderate Exclusive groupings, the Kelly Brethren and the Lowe Brethren which

---

30. Miller, *Short Papers,* vol. 1, Preface [unpaginated].

31. Miller, *Short Papers,* vol. 1, p. 2. Such a reading of church history had been offered by the Lutheran Pietist Gottfried Arnold in his *Non-Partisan History of Church and Heresy* (1699–1700) and the Evangelical Joseph Milner's *History of the Church of Christ* (1794–1809).

32. F. Roy Coad, *A History of the Brethren Movement* (Exeter, 2nd edn, 1976), p. 92.

33. London, [1933]. No date appears in the book, but it was reviewed in *The Harvester* 10 (1933), p. 219.

34. Veitch, *History,* p. iv.

35. Denver, CO, [1936].

occurred in 1926. Here, then, we have a definition of Open Brethrenism in relation to Exclusive Brethren, but from an Exclusive standpoint.

BEATTIE

A few years later came David Beattie's *Brethren: The Story of a Great Recovery.*[36] This began life as a lengthy series of articles in *The Believer's Magazine*, which the editor, William Hoste, hoped would recall Brethren to first principles.[37] Beattie shared Broadbent's belief in a succession of faithful groups in each generation, and placed the Brethren in this line of succession. Although the work is rather hagiographic and heavily anecdotal, it covers ground which no other published work does. This is because the author sought to break away from the usual focus on Dublin, Plymouth and Bristol in order to tell the story of the movement's origins in various parts of Britain; to that end he made persistent attempts to tap local sources of information. Such a methodology reflected his interpretation of the movement in terms of the spontaneous emergence of like-minded groups throughout the British Isles and beyond. To Beattie, this was evidence that the Brethren were a movement raised up by God, and I cannot help wondering whether this was also intended to present an implied contrast with the centralization and division which characterized much contemporary Exclusivism.[38]

The 1960s: Beginnings of the 'Brethren Identity Crisis'

The late 1960s saw the appearance of major works by Harold Rowdon and Roy Coad at almost the same time, both portraying the Brethren as, among other things, an ecumenical movement. The context in which they appeared is complex and needs somewhat fuller elucidation than was the case for earlier periods. The first feature to note is the breaking down of barriers between Brethren and the wider evangelical world. Interdenominational fellowship enjoyed by men in the services, the Billy Graham crusades and the rapid growth of interdenominational evangelical agencies during the 1950s had done much to hasten this process, and it provoked some measure of questioning about the movement's identity, which was sharpened by the beginnings of a drift from assemblies to denominational churches. A second feature is the prominence of ecumenical issues in the thinking of a wide range of churches. Ecumenism was 'in the air' in the 1960s: member bodies of the British Council of Churches covenanted at Nottingham in 1964 to seek organic union by 1980; two years later, Martyn Lloyd-Jones issued his famous call to evangelicals to prioritize

36. Kilmarnock, 1940.

37. *BM*, n.s. 34 (1933), p. 283.

38. Readers may wonder why I have omitted discussion of H.A. Ironside's *A Historical Sketch of the Brethren Movement: An Account of its Inception, Progress, Principles and Failures, and its Lessons for Present Day Believers* (Grand Rapids, MI, 1942). Although his work, like others in this section, sought to locate Open Brethrenism in relation both to Exclusive Brethrenism and to wider Fundamentalism, Ironside was no longer in the movement by the time he wrote.

fellowship together above involvement in doctrinally-mixed denominations. A third feature to note is the renewed vitality, confidence and influence of evangelicalism of various shades in post-war Britain; this extended to all denominations and it meant that Brethren could no longer regard themselves as torchbearers of the truth in quite the way that they had done between the wars.

Many Open Brethren shared in the increasing readiness of evangelicals to give serious thought to such matters as ecumenism and the distinctive Brethren niche in the denominational market, as is evident from the report of the 1964 Swanwick Conference of Brethren on the theme of *Christian Unity*.[39] Both the writers in this section contributed papers to that conference, Harold Rowdon on 'Disunity, Denominationalism and the Brethren' and Roy Coad on 'The Ecumenical Movement: Evangelical Apprehensions'. Among Open Brethren, there is plenty of evidence that serious thinking was going on about what constituted the fundamental principles of Brethrenism (although many of the thinkers concerned would have disowned that label). During the late 1950s, some young men in fellowship with Open Brethren had formed a study group, which began to investigate, among other things, the origins and fundamental principles of the Brethren movement. The emergence in 1963 of the Christian Brethren Research Fellowship (later Partnership) both encouraged such research and provided a means whereby its fruits could be mediated to a wider community, including evangelicals outside the Brethren.

We should also note the spectacular success of the Young Men's Bible Teaching Conferences (1956–79) and the High Leigh and Swanwick conferences (1953–96) originally intended for more senior Brethren; all were marked by solid biblical input on a range of pertinent issues relating to Brethren belief, identity and practice. However, the movement was also experiencing a sharp increase in polarization of thought and action, manifest in the form of widely-differing reactions to this rethinking process, to the extent that we may now question whether Open Brethren are one movement or a family of movements with common historical roots. Maybe Noel had a point. What made this all the more poignant was the lurid media coverage of developments within Taylorite Exclusivism from the early 1960s. This made many Brethren reluctant to use that designation or even to allow themselves to be identified with Open Brethren as a movement, because of the way that all types of Brethren were lumped together in the perception of society at large.

COAD

One of those involved in the study group mentioned above was Roy Coad, and he delivered a paper entitled 'Notes on the Brethren Movement' at the Young Men's Bible Teaching Conference at Oxford in 1960.[40] This surveyed the movement's history and raised a whole raft of questions concerning the contemporary application of the teachings of early Brethren. The result was that he was asked to produce a book on the subject, which duly appeared eight years later: *A History of the Brethren*

---

39. Bristol, n.d.

40. A copy is preserved in the CBA, Box 13(2).

Movement.[41] Its perceptive evaluation makes it a valuable work, although it does not claim to be a complete history: Coad's focus was primarily on the nineteenth century, during which the movement's fundamental principles were established and clarified. Described by one reviewer as a 'tract for the times' which sought to recall Brethren to the freedom enjoyed and encouraged by the pioneers,[42] it supplanted Neatby as the standard general history of the Open wing of the movement. The author's wish was to provide a corrective to previous histories, which had demonstrated a preoccupation with the controversies which had racked Exclusivism.[43] This, and the attention given to answering critics of the movement, betoken something of an apologetic motif in his work.

One aspect of Coad's approach which deserves notice is his contention that the ecumenical movement needs the kind of radical perspective represented by the Brethren and other such movements. In his view, Brethren were 'one of the purest examples extant today of a strain in Christianity which has not only been recurrent from the beginning, but will continue to recur as long as the Church exists'[44]—the Bible-based, nonconforming, independent congregation, which presented a necessary corrective to the monolithic institutional bodies; such gatherings faced the challenge of maintaining their freedom while recognizing that they existed for the benefit of the whole church and not for themselves alone. Coad thus follows Broadbent in locating Brethren within a tradition of radical dissent,[45] but diverges from him in a more positive conception of the relationship of such movements to the institutional church: 'such movements are the very stuff of the Church's continual self-renewal'.[46] A major reason for this divergence may lie in the absence of the dispensationalist philosophy of history, with its gloomy prognostications concerning the future of organized Christianity, which had marked Broadbent's work.

ROWDON

The Origins of the Brethren 1825–1850 was Harold Rowdon's erudite contribution to Brethren historiography, a revision of his doctoral thesis.[47] Whilst academically objective, it is interesting that the appendix on early Brethren ecclesiology is entitled 'The Ecumenical Perspective', this being what the author contends that the authentic Open position of men such as Craik, Müller and Groves is capable of providing.[48] Even the reviewer in *The Believer's Magazine* confessed to being 'fascinated' by this

---

41. Exeter, 1968, 2nd edn, 1976.

42. T.C.F. Stunt, 'A History of the Brethren Movement', *W*, 98 (1968), p. 228.

43. Coad, *History*, pp. 7, 231. He gives minimal attention to these.

44. Coad, *History*, p. 283.

45. Chapter 7 of his work is devoted to a survey of such movements from Wyclif onwards.

46. Coad, *History*, p. 207.

47. London, 1967.

48. Rowdon, *Origins*, p. 293.

appendix, commending it as a valuable contribution to the exposition of Open Brethren principles.[49]

More recently, Rowdon's paper, 'The Problem of Brethren Identity in Historical Perspective',[50] argues that what used to be distinctively Brethren practices are now shared by other movements, and that what makes the Brethren distinct now, as it did at the beginning, is their commitment to the authority of scripture, wherever that may lead them. Thus a slavish adherence to Brethren traditions, and to the maintenance of a distinctively Brethren identity, risks negating the very principle which is the essence of Brethrenism. The same thesis is advanced in his excursus on 'The Post-war Background to Nantwich 1991' in *The Strengthening, Growth and Planting of Local Churches*,[51] the report of a major consultation sponsored by Partnership. This also argues that the choice facing assemblies is either to insist on maintaining the movement's traditions or to listen afresh to what the Spirit is saying to the churches through the scriptures; either way, the name 'Brethren' is likely to disappear, though not the emphases which marked the teaching and practice of the movement's founders. Both papers reflect the ongoing debate about Open Brethren identity, and were called forth by it.

Some Questions Arising from this Survey

What does the Historiography tell us about Brethren Views of Church History?

By way of an answer, let us take an example of a Brethren philosophy of history and the way in which it affects the writing of church history. G.H. Lang castigated most ecclesiastical historians as having 'missed the true path at the start'.[52] He interpreted history as a conflict between pagan religion (which he called 'Jezebel') and spiritual religion, and alleged that the former entered and corrupted the church early on, giving rise to the priestly system which became the official religion of the Roman Empire under Constantine, and which is now best exemplified in Catholicism and Orthodoxy. The error of most historians, said Lang, was to treat this system as Christian rather than pagan, and the great merit of Broadbent's work was its depiction of the true church in every generation as a remnant oppressed by 'Jezebel' but divinely maintained, a pilgrim body not at home in this world and characterized by submission to the written word of God.[53] A more recent work from a similar viewpoint was T.W. Carron's history of the church, *The Christian Testimony*

49. *BM,* 78 (1968), p. 155.

50. Lorenzo Giorgi and Massimo Rubboli (eds), *Piero Guicciardini 1808–1886. Un Riformatore Religioso nell'europa dell'ottocento* (Firenze, Italy, 1988), pp. 159-74.

51. Harold H. Rowdon (ed.), *The Strengthening, Growth and Planting of Local Churches* (Carlisle, 1993), pp. 127-41.

52. Lang, *Broadbent*, p. 88.

53. Lang, *Broadbent,* pp. 88-89.

through the Ages.[54] Incidentally, Carron's work includes a chapter expounding Revelation 2–3 as prophetic history depicting seven successive states of the church (a common Brethren interpretation, which provoked some discussion of whether Brethren were still in the Philadelphian age in which they had originated or now in that of Laodicea, an issue with ramifications for how they saw themselves and their role), and a concluding chapter outlining traditional Brethren thinking concerning future events as foretold in scripture. The former provides an interpretative framework for the events recounted, and the latter provides an explanation of where the historical process is heading.

The works we have surveyed reflect the post-war decline of dispensationalism as a widely-accepted philosophy of history among Brethren. The basic elements of dispensational teaching include the belief that the history of God's dealings with the earth can be divided into a series of dispensations, each marked by a particular mode in which God relates to humanity; in each, human beings fail in the responsibility committed to them, and whilst a measure of blessing or revival may be granted, the failed dispensation can never be restored. God begins over again with the faithful remnant. It is a short step from this to the perception of church history as the story of a conflict between the forces of good and evil, paganism and the true faith, and of the continuity of the true faith in spite of oppression. We noted how general church histories produced by Brethren were shaped by this outlook, but it was also there to some extent in histories of the Brethren movement: I would suspect it was implicit in those by Noel and Beattie.

What does the Historiography tell us about Brethren Views of their Place in Church History?

In the works we have examined, there are two main Brethren views of their place in church history:

1. Brethrenism represents a recovery of apostolic Christianity without parallel since New Testament days.
2. Brethrenism is a manifestation of a recurring tendency of radical dissent which seeks to cut loose from the accumulated baggage of tradition and to return to the New Testament. This view itself existed in two forms, distinguished by different attitudes to institutional Christendom. The more negative of these was founded upon dispensationalist pessimism regarding the future of the visible and institutional church.

As evangelical thinking matures on such matters as eschatology and the role played by tradition in formulating doctrinal understanding, and Brethren reflect on the

54. London/Worthing, 1956; later reprinted by Pickering & Inglis. Carron left the Taylor Brethren during the 1950s and associated with Open Brethren (E.N. Cross to Tim Grass, 26 June 2003).

extent to which they continue to constitute a discrete grouping within evangelicalism, it would seem that there is room for fresh thinking by Brethren concerning their place in church history; this may come to conclusions not dissimilar from earlier writings, but would hopefully be marked by greater sophistication and more careful handling of the evidence.

To what Extent does Brethren Historiography Represent a Search for Precedents?

Some Brethren writers looked for other movements to provide them with precedents. This desire would have affected their treatment of other early nineteenth-century radical movements, as well as of medieval dissenting movements, with the result that they appear at times to have read back their own views into earlier history. They were not the first to do so. But it is ironic that a movement which asserted the *sole*, and not merely the *supreme*, authority of scripture should feel the need to do this, and significant that so many of the works surveyed should include chapters on these earlier movements. It would be worth considering why this should be, and whether a similar need is felt among contemporary Brethren.

Current Interest in Brethren Historiography

It is curious that Brethren seem to experience a fresh upsurge of historiographical activity about every thirty years, and the current increase of interest in the movement's history fits well into that pattern. Each new generation needs to revisit not only the history, but also the question of identity—what it means to be Brethren now, rather than what it meant a generation ago. Since those Brethren with a more progressive approach to questions of church practice (which would include the churches affiliated with Partnership) presumably feel a greater need to establish a sense of their own identity, because they are less likely to be content with answers offered by previous generations, it may be that they are the ones most likely to engage in this work. On the other hand, it could be argued that those who feel an obligation to maintain the traditions might be concerned to undertake historical work in order to demonstrate the divine origin and abiding validity of those traditions.[55] Either way, the danger of pressing history into the service of ideology will need to be guarded against, perhaps through some awareness of how historiography both shapes and reflects the identity of a particular denomination.

There are certain differences which emerge from a comparison of current work with that of previous generations. Primary amongst these is the need to set research in a global context. No longer is Brethrenism a movement in which 'sending countries', mostly English-speaking, send missionaries worldwide to a number of 'receiving countries'; to an increasing extent, it is a global movement, whose centres of gravity lie in countries such as Angola, Argentina and India, and in which

---

55. Reprints of works by earlier Brethren writers, and new commentaries and doctrinal works from more conservative Brethren publishers, may fulfil a similar role.

missionaries may go from any country to any other. Research could profitably explore the movement's international dimensions, as Timothy Stunt has done.[56] For instance, it would be good to see someone investigate the missiological thinking of British workers such as Lang and Broadbent, and its impact on the assemblies with which they were involved in Romania and other parts of Central and Eastern Europe; now that primary source material is available in those countries, it would be possible to compare Western workers' perceptions of their role with the perceptions of local writers and with local records of how assemblies developed. More broadly, it would be worth considering what perspective the new generation of Brethren historians could bring to bear on the history of Christianity as a whole. The perspective of Broadbent and others may in fact be due for rehabilitation in a more sophisticated form,[57] since there is an increasing interest among Christians of many traditions in the phenomenon of radical Christian dissent. This is evident in the enormous advances made over the last six decades in the study of sixteenth-century radical movements such as Anabaptism, for example.

Secondly, the global perspective needs to be balanced by recognition of the importance of national context, especially in those nations which have gained political or ideological independence in recent decades. It is encouraging, therefore, that the importance of recording Brethren history at the national level is increasingly recognized, as histories are beginning to appear covering the development of Open Brethren in particular countries.[58] Such works are oriented towards consideration of how the movement has developed rather than the contribution made by foreign missionaries, and so they may help to shape, as well as reflect, the movement's sense of identity in those countries.

A third factor which is evident in current work is a much greater awareness of the way that Open Brethren have changed during their history. A focus on the movement's origins and early development, which I believe is related to the attempt to clarify the movement's identity, has meant that the twentieth century has usually been neglected. Yet if its identity, or its perception of this identity, changes in response to changing religious context, work on this period is just as necessary as work on the earlier period. No longer is it enough to major on delineating the principles which motivated the founding fathers, with briefer coverage of how these received expression in subsequent generations. Moreover, the movement's twentieth-century history possesses its own absorbing interest.

Fourthly, the current upsurge of historiography of the British movement is resulting in a number of works examining its development at a regional level; this phenomenon is doubtless related to the growing interest in questions of regional identity. Since significant aspects of United Kingdom Brethren history remain to be

---

56. Timothy C.F. Stunt, *From Awakening to Secession: Radical Evangelicals in Switzerland and Britain 1815–35* (Edinburgh, 2000).

57. My thanks to Gerald T. West for this suggestion.

58. For these, see David Brady, 'The Brethren a Bibliography of Secondary Sources', *BAHNR* 2.2 (2003), pp. 104-109; available online at http://rylibweb.man.ac.uk/data2/spcoll/cba/sources.html.

explored, including the history of Brethren in Wales and Ireland, this trend needs to continue. As part of this, it would be good to see more regionally-based historians emerging. This is important because of the existence of discernible regional variations in the ethos of British Open Brethrenism. A writer's geographical roots are, to a certain extent, indicative of his or her likely theological perspective and evaluation of the movement's significance. This in turn is likely to influence his or her selection and treatment of evidence. This should not be pressed too rigidly, because there are exceptions, but there does seem to be a degree of correlation between where a writer lives and what stream of Open Brethren thinking he or she espouses. For example, Partnership is stronger in the South-East than elsewhere, and this has long been the case with respect to more 'progressive' Brethren. Similarly, those Brethren who would align themselves with the approach espoused in the pages of *Precious Seed* tend to be concentrated in the South-West and South Wales. More explicitly separatist approaches, such as would be found in *Assembly Testimony*, would be more popular in the north, especially in Scotland and Ulster.

Certain regional perspectives do not appear to have found historiographical expression, a fact which may correspond to some extent with gaps in the coverage of the British movement's history. For example, there have been few Welsh writers of Brethren history, and correspondingly little treatment of the movement's history in Wales, apart from brief accounts of individual assemblies. This is in spite of the aspects of Welsh Brethren history which cry out for examination, such as the fact that Brethren and Pentecostals both experienced a remarkable degree of success in the South Wales valleys during the early twentieth century. Much recent historiography has been the production of Southerners, perhaps because they are more likely to espouse progressive views, and thus more likely to be affected by the 'identity crisis'. Perhaps, too, more conservative Brethren may not feel that historical study is important enough for them to give their attention to it; rather, what matters is faithful obedience to the teaching of scripture rather than historical analysis of how that teaching came to receive expression by Brethren. It would be worth thinking how each outlook could be encouraged to give attention to serious historical work, and how different outlooks might fertilize one another.

A final factor operative in the present situation, certainly in Britain, is the contemporary interest in local history. Histories of individual assemblies have proved invaluable to me in my attempt to get a feel for what it was like to belong to the Brethren at various stages in the movement's history,[59] but I have noticed that these works sometimes lack a sense of the wider background, both in terms of the Brethren movement itself and of its social and ecclesiastical context, and have a correspondingly undeveloped sense of Brethren identity. If future works are to overcome this tendency, perhaps consideration needs to be given to how writers of local histories (most of whom will not be professional historians) can be assisted. There is a potential source of tension here: on the one hand, much recent historiography of the wider movement has come from trained academics, but, on the

59. See my *Gathering to his Name*.

other, 'grass roots' history provides local perspectives and assists local assemblies in locating themselves within their part of the ecclesiastical landscape. Academics must, therefore, seek to encourage local writers in a sensitive manner, avoiding any intellectual version of the 'clerisy' against which early Brethren protested so unceasingly. Time and effort devoted to cultivating relationships between the two communities will be well spent.

Conclusion

At the beginning, I asserted that Brethren historiography reflects successive phases of the movement's quest for a sense of its own identity, and that there appeared to be an upsurge of historiography at times when that identity is perceived as being in need of clarification. I believe that we may view the present explosion of interest in writing Brethren history in that light.

However, historiography may shape or clarify as well as reflect the development of a sense of Brethren identity. This would be a great gain, especially in the English-speaking world, where the Open Brethren 'identity crisis' seems to be biting deeply. Traditionalists and progressives alike manifest a real sense of pain and dislocation as they seek to come to terms with the movement's changing fortunes and the implications of these for their own sense of Christian identity. The historian's task is thus all the more challenging, especially as one result of the current fragmentation is that there are four different attitudes to the movement's history current among Open Brethren. Some have no sense of belonging to the Brethren tradition and no grasp of its history. Some are aware of Brethren history and are reacting against it. Some are aware of Brethren history and seek to remain faithful to the tradition at all costs. Some are aware of Brethren history and appreciative of it, but prepared to modify their thinking and practice as appropriate. Writers need to be able to respond to each of these, without sacrificing integrity in their handling and interpretation of the evidence. In particular, they must avoid taking short-cuts which would involve concocting or perpetuating historically-inaccurate myths about the movement's origins, development and fundamental principles.

There have always been some in the movement who have displayed the ability to reflect on its history in a self-critical way, notably some of the periodical editors. But perhaps what is needed now is work which manifests a greater degree of awareness of how writers' philosophies of history shape their perception of the history of the movement to which they belong. Such work would assist Open Brethren to arrive at a clearer sense of their identity, and thus to serve God's purposes in their generation. For all its shortcomings, the movement has been greatly used by God, and there is much in its history and heritage which could provoke not only sober reflection but grateful thanksgiving, leading to a renewed sense of confidence in the calling given to assemblies as bodies of Christian believers.

CHAPTER 3

To Encourage Historians of the Christian Brethren: A Meditation[1]

Beth Dickson

Researching and writing history is a lonely affair which requires stamina and commitment. Having lived with a historian, my husband Neil, now for twenty years, I thought that at this rare occurrence, a conference of historians of the Christian Brethren, I might make so bold as to encourage you in your work for the Lord.

In the first place it seems to me that history, as much as theology, has a claim to be *primus inter pares* as a means of interpreting of God's work in the world, as the German word, *Heilsgeschichte*, or salvation history, makes clear. How can there be theology without history? In Augustine's *The City of God* there is a massive section on theology and another on philosophy, but sandwiched between the two is the section where Augustine says, 'My present duty, as it seems to me, is to defend the historical truth of the scriptural account',[2] and in short order he enunciates the principles of selection and the ends to which narratives are constructed which characterize historical writing. I remember discussions at an Evangelical Alliance conference in the 1990s about how to define an evangelical. Most of these attempted definitions were theological and were too clumsy because they were too general—they would have included any orthodox Christian from American fundamentalists to Greek Orthodox monks. The precise historical definition—conversionism, activism, biblicism, crucicentricity (formulated for us by Professor David Bebbington)[3]—did not resonate with these theological definitions, presumably because it came from another academic discourse with whose categories they were unfamiliar; yet in terms of precision it has still to be bettered. The answer is not always theological.

Such issues appear in the biblical narrative itself. The resurrection brings questions of theology and history into sharp focus. On the road to Emmaus two despairing disciples asked, 'Are you the only one living in Jerusalem who doesn't

1. This meditation was delivered at morning prayers during the conference.

2. Augustine, *Concerning the City of God against the Pagans* (trans Henry Bettenson; Harmondsworth, 2nd edn, 1984), bk 15, ch 8, p. 607.

3. D.W. Bebbington, *Evangelicalism in Modern Britain: A history from the 1730s to the 1980s* (London, 1989), pp. 2-17.

know the things that have happened there in these days?' (Lk. 24.19) The double ironies of this question show how difficult it is for human beings to catch the purpose of God even when it is happening in space and time in front of their eyes. *They* were the ones who as yet neither knew what had happened nor that the stranger they were talking to—not dead but alive in Jerusalem—was the single most amazing historical fact any human being has ever witnessed. This is not to disparage the two disciples—we would not have recognized him either until our eyes were opened. But this question, 'What happened?', is one of the foundational historical questions which human beings return to again and again in their search for meaning and purpose.

I was brought up in a meeting which taught that women were inferior to men and that they were a liability in matters spiritual.[4] When Neil's research showed that women evangelists, such as Mary Paterson and Mary Hamilton, were not victims of patriarchy or peripheral to Brethren tradition but, through their church-planting activities, movers and shapers of that very tradition, life was never the same for me again.[5] These were women who were in my tradition, whom, had I lived earlier, I might have known and talked to. If historians—and male historians at that—had not recorded this, how would I have learnt what it could mean to be a Christian woman? Feminists have shown quite clearly that to have a 'history' is something which dignifies a people, that 'enslavement becomes total when history is destroyed because solidarity with the faith and suffering of the dead is made impossible'.[6] Thus Neil's history which records and reflects on the historical agency of these generations of working women and men dignifies them not only with historical agency but also with Christian worth because God

> ...chose the lowly things of this world and the despised things—and the things that are not—to nullify the things that are... (1 Cor 1.28).[7]

If 'What happened?' is the foundational question, then 'So what?' is the next question. And for the apostles quite a lot followed from the resurrection—one of the most obvious features was a thoroughgoing revision of their history. Seeing Jesus of Nazareth as the fulfilment of the Old Testament prophecies set Stephen apart from his own people whom he addressed as 'you' not 'we' in a sermon where he described in detail the way in which God had been rejected by his own people from Abraham to the exile. Suddenly history of which a man could be proud was being turned into judgement:

---

4. Cf. Beth Dickson, *The Secret Life of an Evangelical* (Carlisle, 2005).

5. Neil Dickson, 'Modern Prophetesses: Women Preachers in the Nineteenth-century Scottish Brethren', *Records of the Scottish Church History Society* 25 (1993), pp. 89-117.

6. Elisabeth Schüssler Fiorenza, *In Memory of Her: A Feminist Theological Construction of Christian Origins* (London, 2nd edn, 1995), p. 31.

7. Bible quotations are from the New International Version (1973).

> You stiff-necked people with uncircumcised hearts and ears! You are just like your fathers: You always resist the Holy Spirit! Was there ever a prophet your fathers did not persecute? (Acts 7.51-53)

This paradigm shift expressed in such direct language led to Stephen's immediate murder.

Historians who reflect deeply (biblically, theologically and imaginatively) on the meaning of the past are not always popular. Generally, people become attached to their own version of the past and don't thank others for saying, 'Well, actually, that's not quite what happened.' Harold Rowdon's articles in the early 1980s, 'Who are the Brethren and does it matter?', had such a provocative title that many Scottish Brethren simply dismissed the articles.[8] Thus the issues that arose out of the previous thirty years (chiefly the necessity for biblical change) that Harold raised and addressed came upon them in judgement when they could have been met in grace.

The dialogue between history and reflection is the one of the utmost importance to any human community because it provides an explanation of identity. Loss of identity has been a severe problem for the UK Brethren in the second half of the twentieth century. Because of the strictures of the past, many have become so ashamed of their tradition that they have left it altogether or, have simply denied it. This is probably where we are at present in the UK. Even on Partnership Council members are wary of speaking too much about the 'Brethren' in case we raise the old ghost of Pharisaism. Yet keeping company with historians as I do, I am convinced that this fear of the past is not only misplaced but an obstacle to fulness in Christ. God was active in our history. None of us has the right to dismiss it, because if we do, we are ultimately dismissing how God worked among us. Obviously churches need to move on—and who more than me would be the loser if I were to advocate a lurch back to bygone days—but we need to move on with an understanding of the places in our tradition through which God worked: the enthusiasm for and commitment to the gospel; love for the scriptures; church-planting; evangelism among children; lay ministry; outstanding activism.

In 'Four Quartets'—a series of reflections on time and eternity—T.S. Eliot examines the difficulty mortals have in extracting sense from life:

> We had the experience but missed the meaning.[9]

Until the voice of history is listened to, the movement will continue to flounder, unable to grow as a movement with all the added strength that entails and will simply exist as independent magpie congregations taking influences from here and there but neglecting the direct, genetically-targeted, nourishment which comes from roots.

---

8. Republished as *Who are the Brethren and does it Matter?* (Exeter, 1986).

9. T.S. Eliot, 'The Dry Salvages', II, in T.S. Eliot, *Collected Poems 1909–1962* (London, 1974), p. 208.

History often contains the call of God for the future. It is my settled conviction now that there is a future for UK Brethrenism—a chastened movement and I don't suppose we'll call it that—and it comes from the recent historical interpretations. This way of being church is being called by God to a new maturity in Christ where the defining scriptures are not Acts and the Epistles but those where the prophets deal with restoration after exile:

> Comfort, comfort my people,
> Says your God
> Speak tenderly to these churches with Brethren roots
> And proclaim to them that their hard service has been completed
> That their sin has been paid for
> That they have received from the Lord's hand
> Double for all their sins. (Isaiah 40.1-2)

In God there could be a new future for these churches which would no longer be stumbled by the obstacles of modernity but with an educated and flexible membership would thrive on carrying the gospel, of which many of them now have an enlarged sense, to a lost world as their mothers and fathers did.

So, you historians, I have laid before you today your high calling as recorders, researchers and interpreters of the divine activity in our world. Through you the ephemeral decisions and actions and words of Christians of previous generations are caught and shaped and presented as full of divine activity. I don't suppose that when the two Marys, Hamilton and Paterson, went to begin a series of revival meetings in Larkhall, Lanarkshire, which were to issue in the foundation of the assembly there they ever thought that these actions would have such a resonance that we would still be talking about them today, as the gospel is preached twice—once by the women to their listeners and secondly by Robert Chapman, Larkhall assembly's first historian,[10] and Neil Dickson to subsequent generations to strengthen the faith of those who come after; not the gospel of the four spiritual laws, assuredly, but the good news of the reconciliation of God with the entire created order which includes the writing of history along with all the other forms of interaction with creation that God has blessed us with.

Although it is a high calling, I know that it is not followed without sacrifice. I know that there is not much money to be made from it; that it demands hours of concentration —a sacrifice of time offered freely by historians and their families; that you may be ill when you are writing or that you may be afflicted by suffering for any of the numerous reasons that such things occur in this broken world. When you wonder if it is all worthwhile, remember that the processes which brought much of scripture itself into being are being worked out through your agency. Along with Luke, the Gospel writers, the Old Testament historians, you are God's fellow-

10. Robert Chapman, *The Story of Hebron Hall Assembly, Larkhall, 1866–1928: A Short History of the Inception, Progress and Personalities of the Assembly* (Kilmarnock, 1929).

workers, just as surely as the men and women whose actions they recorded. In your writing is deep significance as we watch the past reveal its divine fulness. As Eliot puts it:

> So we moved, and they, in a formal pattern,
> Along the empty alley, into the box circle,
> To look down into the drained pool.
> Dry the pool, dry concrete, brown edged,
> And the pool was filled with water out of the sunlight,
> And the lotus rose, quietly, quietly,
> The surface glittered out of the heart of light,
> And they were behind us, reflected in the pool.
> Then a cloud passed, and the pool was empty.[11]

Or if Eliot is not to your taste, as Paul says in 2 Corinthians 4.16:

> Therefore we do not lose heart. Though outwardly we are wasting away, yet inwardly we are being renewed day by day. For our light and momentary troubles are achieving for us an eternal weight of glory that far outweighs them all.

Let us come before the Lord and thank him that in his mercy he has blessed us with a historical sense. Pray as you are led. Ask him for what you most deeply desire. Some of you will have reflected more deeply on these issues than I could ever do. Pray out of the fulness of your experience of God. Don't hold back. Often as evangelicals we rightly recognize the need to make our language as accessible as possible but sometimes for intelligent people this becomes a spiritual trap as we appear to have things taped when we don't. In spite of all that, pray simply, if that is how you normally pray. Come, historians, before the Lord at the limits of your strength and pray into the deep reaches of his person so that he may be authentically worshipped by his creatures and we may be blessed in all our neediness as he enables us by reflection on the past to strengthen our grasp on the vastness of the grace which has saved us.

11. T.S. Eliot, 'Burnt Norton', I, in *Collected Poems*, p. 190.

PART 2

British Brethren Experiences

CHAPTER 4

John Eliot Howard: From Friend to Brother

Gerald T. West

John Eliot Howard's Quaker Family

This paper outlines briefly John Eliot Howard's Quaker background. It describes the stages leading to his secession from the Society of Friends and his subsequent founding of the Brethren assembly in Tottenham.[1] John Eliot Howard was born on 11 November 1807 in Plaistow, a village in Essex beside the River Lea, and a few miles east of the City of London. His father was Luke Howard, a prosperous young manufacturing chemist who had burst onto the scientific scene in 1802 with a brilliant explanation and description of the different cloud formations. His reputation as the father of meteorology remains unchallenged.[2] Luke had married Mariabella, the only daughter of John Eliot, a wealthy Quaker. Mariabella's brother, John Eliot IV was the last of four generations with that name. Luke and Mariabella named their eldest son Robert after Luke's father and their second son was named John Eliot after Mariabella's father and brother.

Both families had been Friends for over three generations. If Quakers married out of the Society they were disowned. They inter-married and developed a complex network of cousins. The Howards and the Eliots had business and family connections in Plymouth.[3] The Society provided many opportunities for social intercourse[4] and Luke Howard became a national figure in touch with influential Quakers throughout the country.

---

1. G.T. West, 'From Friend to Brother: A Study of the Spiritual Migration of Luke Howard and his Family, and the Meetings of Friends and Brethren at Tottenham' (unpublished MS, 2004); a copy of this MS has been deposited in the CBA, John Rylands Library, The University of Manchester.

2. For a lively biography of Luke Howard as a scientist and meteorologist see R. Hamblyn, *The Invention of Clouds* (London 2001).

3. E. Howard, 'Fragments', pp. 1-6. This signed MS by Luke Howard's sister Elizabeth is in the Howard Archive, London Metropolitan Archive, ACC/1017/1709.

4. Particularly important were the Yearly Meetings held in London each May to which representatives and many others came.

Robert Howard married Rachel Lloyd in April 1825. She was a daughter of the banker Samuel Lloyd. John Eliot Howard married in September 1830.[5] His wife was Maria Crewdson, a cousin of Robert's wife Rachel. Their marriages put Robert and John Howard into direct relationship with important Quaker families with extensive connections in the Midlands, the North-West (Manchester and Kendal) and the South-West (including Plymouth, Wellington and Bristol).[6]

In 1813 the family moved to Tottenham, some five miles north of London. Tottenham at that time was a quiet country village and was a favourite residence for Quakers. In 1831 the population was less than 8,000. The village spread out along the main road with houses clustered around a number of Greens. West Green and Wood Green, two small hamlets to the west, were also part of the village. To the south, but outside the village, was Stamford Hill. There were some sixty families in Tottenham who were members of the Society.[7]

John was only six when he moved to Tottenham, and he lived there for the rest of his life. He began to work in his father's business in 1823. Production of quinine was about to begin. John made the study of the cinchona alkaloids, from which quinine is separated, a life-long pursuit. He was later elected a Fellow of the Royal Society.[8]

Contemporary Quaker Tensions

John Eliot Howard rejected traditional Quaker quietism and left the Society of Friends in 1836. The term quietism is often used to describe traditional eighteenth century Quakerism. This was the majority view into the 1830s. Quietists looked to the writings of the early Friends as the authoritative basis for interpreting scripture. The principal writers were George Fox, William Penn and Robert Barclay.[9] The last of these, Robert Barclay, was probably the most influential. They developed a mystical form of Christianity which stressed the 'inward light'. Quakers believed that this inner light was within all human beings, was sufficient to bring them to know and to do what is good. Evangelicals rejected this.

Quietists and evangelically-inclined Friends assigned different meanings to key words. 'Justification' meant to the Quietist an amalgam of justification and sanctification. 'Conversion' meant a change related to growing sanctification. The

5. CBA 13,665, Maria Howard, *Memorials of John Eliot Howard of Lord's Meade, Tottenham* (private circulation, 1885), p. 3.

6. T.C.F. Stunt, *Early Brethren and the Society of Friends* (CBRF Occasional Paper, 3; Pinner, 1970), pp. 10-11. For additional family connections see West, 'From Friend to Brother'.

7. Paragraph based on W. Robinson, *The History and Antiquities of the parish of Tottenham in the County of Middlesex* (2 vols; London, 1840).

8. On 4 June 1874. Maria Howard, *Memorials*, p. 49. Luke had been elected a Fellow in 1821

9. For George Fox (1624–91), William Penn (1644–1718), and Robert Barclay (1648–90) see *Oxford Dictionary of National Biography*.

gospel was the good news of the inward light. Ralph Wardlaw, the notable Scottish Congregational minister,[10] considered that this doctrine wrapped the Quaker understanding of justification in obscurity and reversed the order of salvation, putting sanctification before justification.[11]

From about 1790 evangelicalism had increased among Quakers. Robert Howard (John's grandfather) was influenced by this movement. He was a founding member of the Committee of the British and Foreign Bible Society and later, in 1813, Luke Howard replaced him.

Further evidence for the growth of Luke's evangelical faith is found in a letter he wrote in 1822. His scientific studies of cloud formation had been widely published on the Continent. As a result the German poet Goethe became an admirer of his. He wrote elegant verses in celebration of Luke's theories, and eventually asked a contact in London to seek out as much information about him as he could find. This resulted in Luke's autobiographical letter to Goethe. He explained his position in clear evangelical terms.[12]

By the mid 1820s the leading evangelical Friend was Joseph John Gurney.[13] His family were Friends. He was a gifted scholar and from 1807 onwards became increasingly evangelical in outlook. In 1811, at considerable personal cost, he adopted the distinctive Quaker style of dress and speech.[14] Later he published a series of works defending the evangelical orthodoxy of Quaker theology and he regularly defended Quaker principles. In spite of this he came to be regarded by Quietists as 'the arch-antagonist'.[15] Gurney believed he could reconcile the teaching of the early Friends with scripture, but few Quakers agreed. Nor were evangelicals such as Wardlaw convinced. Gurney was particularly influential among John Howard's generation of Quakers, encouraging them to study the scriptures and to believe Quaker belief was compatible with evangelical faith.

In 1827–28 the Society in North America was torn apart by the extreme teaching of Elias Hicks. He transgressed the boundaries acceptable even to Quietists. One

---

10. Ralph Wardlaw (1779–1853) was Professor of Systematic Theology at the Glasgow Theological Academy and Congregational Minister at West George St Chapel, Glasgow; see *Dictionary of National Biography.*

11. R.D.D. Wardlaw, *Friendly Letters to the Society of Friends on some of their distinguishing principles* (Glasgow, 1836), pp. 197-201.

12. This letter dated February 1822 is published in Douglas F.S. Scott (ed.), *Luke Howard 1772–1864: His Correspondence with Goethe and his Continental Journal of 1816* (York, 1976). See also Hamblyn, *Invention of Clouds*, 'Goethe and Constable', pp. 204-22.

13. Stephen W. Angell, 'J.J. Gurney', in Donald Lewis (ed.), *Blackwell's Dictionary of Evangelical Biography* (2 vols; Oxford, 1995), I, pp. 492-93.

14. J.B. Braithwaite, *Memoir of Joseph John Gurney* (2 vols; Norwich, 1854), I, pp. 78-88.

15. M. Grubb, 'The Beacon Separation', *Journal of the Friends Historical Society* (hereafter *JFHS*) 55.6 (1988), pp. 190-97.

third of the membership in North America followed him out of the Society.[16] In 1829 the London Yearly Meeting (YM)[17] condemned Hicks' teaching, but tension in England between the quietist and evangelical streams increased.

In January 1835 Isaac Crewdson published *A Beacon to the Society of Friends*.[18] Isaac Crewdson and William Boulton, two leaders in the Manchester Meeting of Friends, were both Maria Howard's uncles. It was an uncompromising evangelical response to the works of Hicks. It provoked within a few weeks a furious pamphlet war and acrimony and division in the Lancashire Quarterly Meeting (QM). This controversy raised fundamental questions about Quaker belief with which John Eliot Howard had been struggling. The whole Society nationally became involved. The situation in Lancashire was considered in May by the 1835 YM and a committee was appointed to help restore unity in the Lancashire QM. The Yearly Meeting Committee (YMC) included J.J. Gurney, but even though he and some others were considered 'evangelical' no member of the committee supported publication of the *Beacon*. One of the first actions of the YMC was to silence the ministry of Issac Crewdson and William Boulton. Those who looked to J.J. Gurney for leadership were confused by his apparent complicity in this action. The YMC finally 'restored unity' in November 1836 but only through the resignation of some forty-eight members of the Manchester Meeting, including Isaac Crewdson and William Boulton.

The Conversion of John Eliot Howard

Recalling the period immediately after their marriage in September 1830, Maria observes that she 'can hardly say whether at this time either of us knew ourselves safe through the precious blood of Jesus: we were Friends, and had no thought of remaining anything else but Friends, but evangelical truth was beginning to be unfolded to us'.[19] There is no record of a sudden conversion experience for any of Luke's children. In John's case it was a gradual unfolding to the mind and acceptance in the heart of evangelical truth as taught by scripture.

Luke refers to a formative spiritual experience in his youth. Robert, his older half-brother, died when Luke was about eighteen. He experienced a deathbed conversion, which deeply affected the family.[20] Some months later Luke 'gave himself to the Lord'.[21] But this experience did not immediately produce an undiluted evangelicalism. In the autumn of 1822, Luke recorded the struggle he still had in freeing himself from bondage to his Quaker background. This inhibited his ability to

16. R. Jones, *The Later Periods of Quakerism* (2 vols; London 1921), II, p. 470. This schism caused considerable intolerance, much personal tragedy, and family division.

17. In this paper YM is used for Yearly Meeting; QM for Quarterly Meeting; MM for Monthly Meeting; YMC for Yearly Meeting Committee.

18. I. Crewdson, *A Beacon to the Society of Friends* (London, 1835).

19 Howard, *Memorials*, p. 3

20 Howard, 'Fragments'. This Robert Howard died in 1791.

21 Anon., 'Obituary of Luke Howard', *The Friend* n.s. 7.41 (May, 1864), pp. 99-102.

take part in social prayer, as Quakers termed any prayer expressed in the presence of others.[22] Quietism emphasized the need for every act of ministry including any public act of prayer to be consciously inspired by the Spirit. Public prayer was virtually confined to acknowledged ministers.

Luke had just bought 'The Villa'. This was a substantial property in the small village of Ackworth near Pontefract in Yorkshire. Luke and Mariabella lived there with their daughters Rachel and Elizabeth during the summer each year until 1828 when they settled there permanently. During these years Rachel came to an evangelical faith. She was awakened to the gospel under the preaching of J.J. Gurney in 1824. Her temperament was somewhat introspective and depressive, and this led to doubt and perplexity.[23] She was under conviction of sin accompanied by deep repentance but could not find peace. Gradually this changed and in 1828 she could write 'my heart is filled with peace, through the unmerited goodness of God in Christ my Saviour'.[24] Rachel also experienced difficulty with social prayer. She was responsible for developing schools in Ackworth and Tottenham but found herself unable to pray with the mistress of her school at Ackworth. When she became involved with pastoral visits to parents and sick children she found herself inhibited in praying with them. Help, however, came through contact with the Methodists who did not require specific prompting by the Spirit before praying. She went back to scripture to find freedom.

In early 1831 John became very concerned for the spiritual condition of his younger brother Joseph who was showing serious symptoms of consumption. To clarify his own position he began an earnest study of scripture, which led to his eyes being opened to the doctrine of justification by faith. This was an essential starting point for any Quaker moving in an evangelical direction. John Howard did not consult the early Friends but scripture and Magisterial Reformation theology to clarify his understanding.

When Joseph's illness entered its final stages in early 1833 John was able to respond to him from a convinced evangelical position. On Sunday 7 April his mother told Joseph that there was no longer hope of recovery. He died on 13 June and the conversations with him, principally with John, in the weeks before his death are recorded in detail.[25] The whole experience, particularly the final few hours, made a profound impact on the family. It was particularly painful for Luke. His own spiritual experience had been formed by the deathbed conversion of his stepbrother. Now he had watched his own son dying in similar circumstances.

---

22. London Metropolitan Archive, ACC/1017/1518, Luke Howard to TR in Sunderland, 18 November 1822.

23. Howard, 'Fragments', p. 26, and L. Howard, *Memoranda of the Life and Death of Rachel Howard*, (3 parts; London, 1839), generally.

24. Howard, *Rachel Howard*, p. 139.

25. L. Howard (ed.), *Memoranda of the Last Illness and Death of Joseph Howard* (London, 1836).

The record does not describe a sudden conversion experience, but a slow and somewhat tortuous progress from unbelief to faith. In the early weeks of Joseph's final illness much of the discussion concerned the meaning of terms. Gradually there was increasing peace, and towards the end a marked sense of relief from the burden of sin. Just before he died he was able to declare 'My hope is in Christ crucified—being justified by faith.' The whole family were convinced he had fallen asleep in Jesus.

Steps to Secession

Joseph's spiritual needs had been the driving force behind John's considerable spiritual progress. Well before Joseph died, John had come to a settled evangelical faith. But this raised questions about the theological position of the Society. He therefore began a study of the writings of the early Friends. In this he had the help of notes on Robert Barclay left by his uncle John Eliot IV. He became convinced that their views were unsound. He no longer attempted to reconcile scripture with the early Friends. These researches later enabled him to give 'great assistance' in 1834 to Maria's uncle, Isaac Crewdson, in the preparation of the *Beacon*.[26]

John and Maria were moving further away from their Quaker roots. The loosening of their ties was evident in early 1833 when John and Maria took 'a very bold step'. They began daily family prayer. We have seen that Luke and Rachel both struggled with social prayer and Maria too emphasizes the difficulty this step caused them. In May of 1834 family prayers were extended into daily family worship. Maria saw this as a very serious and important step in relation to their connection with the Society.

Their next step was to challenge the Quaker view of baptism and the Lord's supper. Quietists held that no outward expression of the spiritual meaning of these ordinances was required and they should not observe them. John took the opportunity of a visit to Scotland to observe for the first time a communion service at Dr Wardlaw's chapel in Glasgow. He could not see any reason to reject the ordinance.

When the Beacon controversy broke over the Society in 1835, John stood somewhat aloof from the public debate. His name does not appear in any of the reported debates at Yearly Meetings, although Luke, Robert and Richard Ball all took a prominent part. However, John helped to publish several works. One was by Richard Ball who that summer published a pamphlet which includes an Appendix by 'his friend' John Howard on the subject of mysticism and the notes on Barclay by John Eliot IV.[27] Richard had also published in the spring a letter supporting publication of the *Beacon*.[28]

---

26. Howard, *Memorials*, p. 5.

27. R. Ball, *Holy Scripture the Test of Truth* (London, 1835), Appendix B, 'Notes on Mysticism by John Eliot Howard', and Appendix C, 'Strictures on Barclay by the late John Eliot'. Richard Ball was of a West Country Quaker family. He lived at Taunton at that time.

28. R. Ball, 'Letter to I. Crewdson', *The Evangelical Magazine* (May, 1835), pp. 197-98.

In the autumn, *The Christian Observer* published an extended review of publications connected with the Beacon controversy.[29] They included Richard Ball's letter and B.W. Newton's *Remonstrance* to the Society.[30] In this Newton, who had been brought up among Friends but was by then a leader of the Brethren in Plymouth, dealt with the writings of the early Friends. The reviewer quotes him at length and with approval. J.J. Gurney responded the following month. He attacked Newton and the reviewer responded suggesting that by quietist standards even Gurney was not a good Quaker! The controversy was beginning to cause defections. John Wilkinson, a well-known minister and evangelical, resigned in February 1836 and his letter of resignation was published.[31] This stimulated further resignations and Wilkinson was soon preaching in Upper Clapton, near Tottenham, to congregations of between eighty and a hundred.

In the early months of 1836 John Howard was writing a paper for Isaac Crewdson on the tendency of the doctrine of the inward light to deism by bringing scripture to the test of reason. The pamphlet was published in May at the time of YM.[32] Shortly afterwards John and Maria 'had much intercourse with Mr. and Mrs. B. W. Newton', who were visiting the neighbourhood. This is the first reference to direct contact between members of the Howard family and the Brethren. Newton was following the controversy in the Society closely and had probably come to London during the YM so that he could influence as many Friends as possible.

John Howard and Benjamin Newton would have no differences over the early Friends. Newton would have sensed that John and Maria were moving away from the Society and that the break point would come when they decided to be baptized. The question then would be what to do about Christian fellowship. By the summer of 1836 Brethren leaders were agreed that existing church structures were apostate. Newton would urge John not to join an existing denomination or to try to establish a new sect of evangelical Friends. As the position in the Society was still fluid all Newton could do was try to influence events as they developed. He did not have long to wait.

John and Maria were baptized on 28 July that year. Elizabeth Messer Wright, a cousin who had connections with the Wright family of Bristol, was also baptized that evening. There were many others in the neighbourhood who shared their sentiments and John did not wish to sever relationships unnecessarily. But the Tottenham meeting was watching their position and they had already received a visit from the overseers.

Writing to Richard Ball in late July, John discusses with him the question of future fellowship. Their baptism at a Baptist church did not involve joining that body, but those who have left Friends without joining a church still wish to unite in simple communion. He does not know whether this will happen. Later in August he

29. Anon., 'Review Article', *The Christian Observer* (October, 1835), pp. 629-42.

30. B.W. Newton, 'A Remonstrance to the Society of Friends' (London, 1835).

31. *The Christian Advocate* 15 February 1836.

32. J.E. Howard, *The Doctrine of the Inward Light considered in relation to The Written Word* (Tottenham, 1836).

is concerned about the influence their decision will have on others and is anxious to act in accordance with scripture. He believes the Monthly Meeting (MM) would probably not disown members for observance of the Lord's Supper and wonders whether a group of Friends and ex-Friends could meet simply to celebrate it together.

During the summer of 1836, G.V. Wigram, a wealthy leader among the Brethren in Plymouth who had been deeply influenced by J.N. Darby, sensed that Brethren prospects were developing in London. That August, he took premises in Little Portland Street, near Oxford Circus in central London, registered them as a place of worship and began the first small Brethren assembly in the capital.[33] That autumn the Beacon affair came to its final crisis. In early September, Elisha Bates was baptized. He was a prominent Friend and evangelical minister from North America, and later resigned to avoid being disowned.

Everything that was happening confirmed John's decision to resign from the Society. This could not be long delayed. His outstanding questions concerned future fellowship and the 'real' character of other Christian bodies. John and Maria tendered their resignations on 6 October 1836. A few days later they renounced Quaker garb, a painful step for them. Meanwhile a further eleven members of the Society in Tottenham had been baptized, including Mary Stacey. Some of these would join the Methodists, Independents or Baptists. Mary Stacey suffered considerably from family opposition. Her father was clerk to the YMC dealing with the Beacon affair and her baptism appeared as a clear rejection of her father's position.

John and Maria were anxious to take communion, so, together with Mary Stacey and Elizabeth Wright, they asked the local Baptist chapel for permission to do this without committing themselves to membership. This was agreed, and John considered this indicated a growing acceptance of scriptural principles of union among Christians. Although he was still in favour of developing a sect of evangelical Friends, he was also concerned to act in a way, which would preserve Christian unity. They first took communion there on 4 December.[34] But this could not be a long-term arrangement. Writing to Richard Ball at the end of December, John expresses the hope that those leaving the Society will not hastily swallow other systems.

In No-man's Land

John's position in relation to the Society was ambiguous. He was still working with those of similar mind in the Society as well as those like himself who had left. He was concerned to hold evangelically-inclined Friends together whether they were within or outside the Society. He does not finally give up this position until the summer of 1838. Meanwhile there is evidence of growing Brethren influence. At about this time J.J. Penstone met John Howard at the Brethren meeting at Little

33. London Guildhall Library, MS/9580/7, p. 221.

34. Howard, *Memorials*, p. 8.

Portland Street.[35] The subjects at a Bible study held at John's house in February 1837 included the difference of the Old and New dispensations and other related topics of interest to the Brethren. This was held on a Sunday and was followed by receiving communion together with several friends.

When Isaac Crewdson resigned from the Society in late 1836, he and William Boulton immediately formed a congregation of evangelical Friends in Manchester. Isaac Crewdson had been influenced by a Calvinist dissenting minister and seems to have imbibed some aspects of their view of the ministry. That winter Robert Howard was involved in the formation of a Bible class in London primarily for Friends, but with others welcome. John attended but was not a leader. This seems to have been an attempt to hold evangelically-inclined Friends together.

Luke Howard and Richard Ball were also attempting to hold evangelically-minded Friends together. Luke tried to get a proposition asking the YM to find a way of doing this, but his MM gave it short shrift. Richard Ball published a pamphlet arguing that evangelical Friends should stay in the Society, but if they must leave they should not join a denomination and particularly not the Established Church. He implied support for the action at Manchester and suggested that if division became inevitable they should 'come out as a secession church of Evangelical Friends'.

'In communities so formed', Richard wrote, 'the Bible would be the *only authority*. The Holy Spirit would be duly honoured by recognising *practically* the diversity of his gifts, and by permitting and encouraging their free exercise in the church... In public worship seasons of reverent silence might precede and follow the reading of the Holy Scripture, and an opportunity be thus afforded for solemn waiting upon God, and preparation for exercise of spiritual gifts, whether in the way of exhortation, invitation, or warning; and would not prayer, thanksgiving, and praise, ascend as incense from hearts touched with a live coal from off the altar?'[36] It is difficult not to see here a description of developing Brethren practice.[37] It may reflect the practice at the assembly in Wellington in the Blackdown Hills of Devon, with which Richard Ball was very probably in touch.[38] Richard's ideas were consistent with John's views at that time, but many evangelical Friends were waiting to see what would happen at the 1837 YM.

In May 1837 the YM accepted without discussion a report from the YMC that their task had been completed. The YM declined to consider a proposition asking for guidance about the action to be taken when members decided to be baptized and to take the Lord's supper. Evangelical Friends had hoped to be able to be baptized and take communion without being disowned. The tone of the discussion, confirmed by

35. J.J. Penstone, *A Caution to the readers of 'A Caution against the Darbyites'* (Oxford and London, 1867), p. 3.

36. R. Ball, *Dissuasive Considerations, more particularly in reference to joining the Established Church etc.* (London, 1837), pp 20-22 (Ball's emphasis).

37. Liberty of ministry is a theme which goes back to the earliest root of Brethren history. See the references under 'Ministry, liberty of' in the index to H.H. Rowdon, *The Origins of the Brethren 1825–1850* (London, 1967).

38. Stunt, *Early Brethren and the Society of Friends*, p. 19 n. 53.

later events, indicated that overseers were expected to maintain the traditional position and exercise discipline accordingly.

This YM marked the end of the Beacon Controversy. Immediately after it, evangelical Friends issued an address accompanied with copious scripture references setting out their theological position. James Ireland Wright of Bristol signed it.[39] He was the uncle of Elizabeth Messer Wright and had been clerk of the Somerset and Bristol QM. He was well known to Richard Ball. But it was too late!

The YM convinced Luke Howard that all hope of reform of the Society had gone and during it he decided to be baptized. Rachel, who was dying of consumption, had already asked Luke to arrange that Isaac Crewdson should baptize her. She was baptized on 19 May. [40] Luke was baptized by him on 3 June.[41] Isaac Crewdson baptized by affusion.[42] John was firmly of the opinion that immersion was the appropriate method. Luke Howard had become thoroughly disillusioned. He forthwith absented himself from the meetings of the Society, advised Pontefract MM of his actions and waited for them to disown him. When eventually they did so he published a protest.[43] John's thoughts, however, were turning to evangelism. In May 1837 he began to hold gospel services nearby at the schoolroom built by his mother at West Green. In October he took a room at Wood Green and began preaching the gospel there, too.

In August 1837 Richard Ball was baptized by B.W. Newton at Exeter. In October his wife Mary was baptized by Henry Craik at Bethesda Chapel, Bristol. They did not resign from the Society until November that year, but their baptisms link them with the Brethren and with both Plymouth and Bristol. In August, Charles and Sarah Fox of Wellington (Maria's sister and brother in law) were baptized by the Baptist minister at Tottenham.[44]

In the autumn of 1837 John Eliot Howard was busy preparing publication of a new monthly periodical. It appeared in January 1838 as *The Inquirer*. It was initially intended as an encouragement to evangelically-minded Friends, but in early 1839 was

---

39. These debates and the address are reported in *The Patriot* for 1, 5 and 12 June 1837.

40. Rachel Howard died in September 1837. She was the third of their adult children to die since June 1834. The published memorials of these children provide an insight into their spiritual development. J. Hodgkin, *Extracts from the familiar letters of the late Elizabeth Hodgkin wife of John Hodgkin, Jnr of Tottenham* (private circulation, London 1842); L. Howard, *Joseph Howard*; idem., *Rachel Howard*, p. 36

41. L. Howard, *An Appeal to the Christian Public against a Sentence of Disownment* (London, 1838), pp. 3, 9.

42. L. Danton, 'The baptism of Maria Hack, 1837', *The Journal of the Friends Historical Society* 46.2 (Autumn, 1954). pp. 67-77. This includes a description of the baptism of Maria Hack by I. Crewdson.

43. Howard, *An Appeal*. Few seceders forced their MM to disown them in this way. It indicates how deeply hurt Luke was by these events.

44. *The Inquirer* 1 (February, 1838), p. 64.

re-launched with a Brethren orientation.[45] Some historians suggest that it was an official Beaconite publication, implying that it was published in support of Isaac Crewdson and the evangelical Friends in Manchester. But this is not confirmed by Maria's account and, although this may have been the initial intention, John was moving away from Isaac Crewdson's position.

Clarity at Clifton

In June 1838 John attended the conference arranged by the Brethren at Clifton near Bristol. This conference persuaded three important individuals to associate themselves with the Brethren: W.H. Dorman of Islington Independent Chapel in London, Alexander Stewart, minister of the Presbyterian Chapel in Stafford, and John Eliot Howard of Tottenham.[46] It led John to 'adopt many of the views brought forward'. Maria is careful not to suggest he joined the Brethren. Indeed in a letter to Richard Ball a month later he makes it clear that although he does not share the general prejudice against the Plymouth Brethren, he desires to maintain entire independence of judgement and action. He never gave this up.

Following the Clifton meeting, John visited the evangelical Friends in Manchester.[47] They were resisting any suggestion that they should become a Brethren assembly and John considered the stumbling block to their progress was their attitude towards the priesthood of all believers and liberty of ministry. What he saw in Manchester confirmed the conclusion he had come to at Clifton, that formation of a new sect of evangelical Friends was not the way forward.[48]

Such a strategy was only likely to attract evangelicals who had seceded from the Quakers, but unless the sect remained loyal to some of the Quaker distinctives even they would not be attracted to them. Under Isaac Crewdson's leadership they specifically rejected Quaker distinctives and resisted pressure to become a Brethren assembly. They were an independent dissenting church with no clearly distinctive theology or practice. When he visited Manchester in the summer of 1838 John sensed that this congregation would not survive unless it developed a distinctive theological basis for its existence. This judgement proved to be correct. They were

45. He was responsible for the expenses and editorship but had able helpers in relation to the latter. [Maria Howard], *Memorials of John Eliot Howard of Lord's Meade, Tottenham* (n.pl., 1885), p. 116 n.

46. Rowdon, *Origins*, p. 176; and F. Roy Coad, *The History of the Brethren Movement* (London, 1968), pp. 75-77. The sequence of events in Stafford is still uncertain. The secession of Dorman from Islington Chapel was the direct cause of the founding of the assembly that met in Rawstorne Street, Clerkenwell, in London. This was probably the most important event in the development of Brethren assemblies in London.

47. John published a history of this congregation in *The Inquirer* 2 (February, 1839), pp. 72-77.

48. See his comments in a letter to Richard Ball dated August 1838. [Maria Howard], *Memorials*, esp. pp. 114-15.

dependent on Isaac Crewdson and when he died in May 1844 the congregation dispersed.

New Grounds for Christian Fellowship

John's new conviction resulted in a marked change of direction, with the issue of a new series of *The Inquirer* in January 1839. The Clifton meeting had helped John to develop a consistent and distinctive theological basis for Christian fellowship. He published his conclusions in an article entitled 'Christian Fellowship' in *The Inquirer* in April 1839. The article does not mention Tottenham, nor is it signed by John, but there is no reason to doubt that it was written by him.

Later he published a letter relating explicitly to the assembly at Tottenham, expressing clearly the basis on which he founded the assembly there. He argues in similar terms to his article in *The Inquirer.* Sometime in 1846, John was challenged, probably by Elizabeth Wright, to confirm the basis on which the Brook Street assembly had been formed. He had publicly denied that they had met 'simply as Christians'. He published his reply in the form of a personal open letter.[49] From the very first time they met to break bread together, which he dated in July 1838, they had grieved some because they sought to spread their views and win children of God from other communions to unite with them. Such conduct could not be justified on the basis that they met simply as Christians. They had met as Christians who had received light from God's word through the instrumentality of Brethren and they desired to teach others what they had found.

As far as he was concerned the ground of his action was closely connected with his apprehension of prophetic and dispensational truth. After long and prayerful consideration they took a position outside the camp of the church. This position acknowledged the failure in the corporate body professing the name of Christ. It was a position of weakness and blessing. They did not think of setting up the church again but they realized that where two or three meet together in the name of Jesus, he is in the midst. Their only hope was the blessed hope of the glorious appearing of our great God and Saviour Jesus Christ. They took their stand on principle when they abandoned all clericalism and recognized the Holy Spirit present in the body, dividing to every man as he will. The act of meeting around a new table in that place implied that they had new truths which were profitable for the whole church of God. They would never have met but for these distinctive truths.[50]

On this basis John decided that the time had come to form a gathering at Tottenham. He took a small room, probably in Warner Terrace, Stoneleigh South, and on 4 November 1838 a few met for the first time to break bread. This room soon became too small and another was taken, but this also was soon crowded and in the spring of 1839 he bought the land on which he built Brook Street Chapel. It was

49. J.E. Howard, *Letter from Me. I.E. Howard to Miss ——.* (London, n.d. [prob. 1846]).

50. His position is strikingly similar to that being developed around 1840 by J.N. Darby, see Rowdon, *Origins*, pp. 209-10.

opened on 9 June 1839. With its opening John Eliot Howard completed the transition from Friend to Brother.

In a letter to Richard Ball at the end of 1839 John describes the young assembly. He lists a number of couples he personally baptized that year. The first to be mentioned are Robert and Rachel Howard. They did not resign from the Society until August 1839 after Brook Street Chapel was opened.[51] By the end of 1839 the number in fellowship had grown to some thirty-four. The register of members at Brook Street, Tottenham,[52] shows John and Maria Howard, Mary Stacey, and John Ireland Wright[53] and four of his children as members in 1838. From Maria's description many more attended the meetings during these early months. Names of interest during 1839 include Robert Howard (entered in June 1839) and Luke Howard. Rachel Howard and Mariabella Howard became members in March 1840. As late as December 1839 John is anxious that his mother is the only member of the family who has not yet cut her links with the Quakers.

Quaker Influence on Brethren Thinking and Practice

It is difficult to evaluate the influence that men like John Eliot Howard, his brother Robert, and his friend Richard Ball had on the developing Brethren ethos. But John was the leading figure among those Quakers like him who had seceded and later joined the Christian Brethren. None of them were as influential as he was amongst Brethren at this period. Through his Quaker relations, John had close contacts with many of the Quakers who were influenced by Brethren. Those links were tested and strengthened by the crisis amongst the Brethren in the late 1840s when the movement divided and the Rawstorne Street assembly in London became the national centre of J.N. Darby's supporters. This conflict forged a strong Tottenham–Bristol axis whose influence in later years on Open Brethren assemblies was considerable.

The fact is that when he, and those like him, came into the Brethren, although they had rejected much of their Quaker past, they brought with them a number of distinctives which were congenial to developing Brethren practice. Richard Ball's pamphlet in early 1836 showed that some evangelical Quakers were sympathetic to the freedom to exercise spiritual gifts within scriptural boundaries. They valued both silence and liberty of ministry in the context of worship and the Lord's supper. They looked for freedom to exercise an evangelistic ministry. But Quaker insistence on the immediate leading of the Spirit as a pre-condition of any ministry had become a restrictive bondage and silence in worship became the Quaker norm. Those who

---

51. John Eliot Howard to Richard Ball, 31 December 1839. Howard, *Memorials*, pp. 119-25; London, Friends House Library, 'Tottenham MM Register'.

52. 'Members in Communion at Brook Street Tottenham'. This register is held by the assembly. It covers 1838–c.1916.

53. James Ireland Wright was from Bristol. He signed the Address issued by Evangelical Friends after the 1837 YM. He had moved to Stamford Hill shortly before he joined the Totttenham assembly but he moved back to Bristol, probably in 1840.

seceded were freed from this restriction and continued to hold to liberty of ministry under the guidance of the Holy Spirit.

Quakers were used to women's ministry. Luke Howard deplored what he considered the abuse of this by some quietist women ministers and John Howard published a number of articles in *The Inquirer* deprecating women's ministry. It may be significant that a number of the wives of seceding Friends were slow to join the Brethren and that some well-known evangelical women Friends did not secede. The most notable and influential was Anna Braithwaite, a prominent Quaker minister with decided evangelical views. In spite of these negative influences, it seems probable that Quaker sympathy towards liberty of ministry under the leading of the Holy Spirit encouraged the development of this tradition among Brethren in the early 1840s.[54]

John Howard continued to take an independent line in the various debates and controversies in the movement in the 1840s. His influence prevented the London assemblies becoming wholly dominated by Darby's followers and he kept the Tottenham assembly outside the Darbyite discipline in 1848. Looking back on his course he clearly retained an affection for the Society of Friends. He confessed that he was always glad to think that he was descended from Friends and that he continued to retain a sort of partiality towards them. He referred to himself as 'naturally and by education somewhat of a mystic' and even though this gave place to the gospel he was still conscious that he had come to the faith from quite an opposite quarter to most of his brethren. Some years later, on re-reading one of his earlier pamphlets he confesses that he feels much more 'Catholic' and much less of a 'Brother' than he did in 1848. He did not consider his theology had changed but he was much less hopeful of changing the views of Christians for the better. He is surprised that his father should have spent so many fruitless efforts trying to mend the Friends, and he supposes his own sons will look back on his efforts to do the same for the Brethren with similar compassionate pity. Nevertheless, he did not regret efforts which seemed, as far as he knew, to have borne no fruit.[55]

Whether his sons did in fact share these sentiments we do not know. But what is perhaps more significant is that most of the subsequent generations of the Howard family, and indeed of other families of Friends who seceded, did not remain within the Brethren.

---

54. Rowdon, *Origins*, pp. 227-30, reviews this development at some length.

55. In letters dated March 1869? [sic], March 1872, and December 1875. Howard, *Memorials*, pp. 190, 241, 253-55.

CHAPTER 5

George Müller and the Financing of the Scriptural Knowledge Institution

Neil Summerton

It is well known that the founding fathers of the Brethren movement—in particular, Anthony Norris Groves and George Müller—gave birth to an historically important principle when they argued that, ideally, Christian work (whether by individuals or societies) should be conducted and, especially, financed on the faith principle.[1] The principle subsequently had a major impact in evangelicalism far beyond the Brethren movement, in particular in the faith missions which burgeoned from the closing decades of the nineteenth century, as charted by Fiedler.[2]

The grip of the principle in evangelicalism has undoubtedly been weakening in recent years, at least in the USA and Britain. Consonant with general trends in the financing of charitable activity in the United Kingdom, more or less professional fundraising, whether from trusts or from the evangelical public, has become one of the principal means of funding evangelical work.

In parallel with changing practice, the principle itself has been subject to revisionist historiography. Writing largely from a theological perspective, Harold Rowdon[3] in 1995 focused on the question of whether the concept should be regarded as the biblical norm, as traditionally argued in Brethren ecclesiology. In an article prepared early in the 1990s (though published only in 1998), Timothy Larsen suggested that the mandatory and simplistic character which it assumed in Brethren tradition late in the nineteenth century and more or less throughout the twentieth

---

1. As will be seen from this paper, the 'faith principle' is capable of a variety of meanings. At its core lies the idea that Christians should not rely on the accumulation of possessions, wealth and regular income for their maintenance, but that they should divest themselves of them in the interests of others in need and rely on God to provide for their own needs, as he sees fit, through the action of others. As commonly understood, however, the focus has been on two aspects of the practical application of the principle: that Christian workers should not be salaried or employed by any body or individual, but should rely on God to cause others to meet their financial needs, without their soliciting support or drawing attention to their needs.

2. Klaus Fiedler, *The Story of Faith Missions* (Oxford, 1994).

3. Harold H. Rowdon, 'The Concept of "Living by Faith"', in Antony Billington, Tony Lane and Max Turner (eds), *Mission and Meaning: Essays Presented to Peter Cotterell* (Carlisle, 1995) pp. 339-56.

century was not to be discerned in the founding fathers: for them, the principle was an ideal which they strongly recommended to other Christians rather than a rule to be followed by all Christians in all types of Christian work.[4]

Rowdon did not, in fact, look particularly closely at the precise formulation of the principle by the founding fathers, nor at their detailed application of it. Larsen did look at the roots in the writings and practice of Groves, Müller and J.N. Darby, as a yardstick against which later formulations and practice could be measured. Apart from their advocacy of the notion as a vocation for particular individuals in particular circumstances rather than as a rule, Larsen noted the influence on Groves and Müller at least of considerations such as

> 1. the divine call to give away possessions
> 2. freedom from the control implied by the nexus of a salaried position with a society
> 3. the need for the missionary to live at the level of those being reached if the latter were to take the missionary and his message seriously
> 4. the counter-productive risk that it might be thought that the evangelist or missionary did what they did only because they were paid to do it
> 5. the socially-divisive effects of pew-rents as the source of ministerial stipends, and
> 6. in Müller's case, the desire to demonstrate to believers and unbelievers alike, in an increasingly sceptical age, that God still intervened miraculously—in particular, by providing financial means for great undertakings in response to prayer alone.

The summary illustrates how, as is so often the case, a principle is developed in response to particular circumstances, but then acquires a life of its own in subsequent generations, to a large extent divorced from those original circumstances.[5] Larsen

4. Timothy Larsen, '"Living by Faith": A Short History of Brethren Practice', *Brethren Archivists and Historians Network Review* 1.2 (Winter, 1998), pp. 67-102. Müller and his practice do seem to be capable of stirring up hostility in some: for an example, see the extended review by Stephen Rees in *The Banner of Truth* 502 (July, 2005), pp. 24-27. Rees is wrong in his assertion that Müller never provided any facts or figures, or gave information about the orphans, or made plans—they are detailed to a fault in the *Annual Reports*.

5. That the originators did not regard the original principle as mandatory is well illustrated by the case of Groves. For long periods of his missionary service, he consciously maintained himself rather than depending on gifts from others—in Baghdad, by running a school for the children of the more well-to-do citizens, and in India through a silk-growing business which quickly failed because the conditions were unsuitable. This left Groves with debts which encumbered him for a long period in the 1840s. Subsequently, he benefited from enterprises run more successfully by his sons. Further, Groves to the end of his life maintained that there was a place for a 'stated ministry', i.e., a nominated pastor, within the local church, though it is less clear whether he would have expected such a person to have been supported by a salary. See Sentinel Kulp (ed.),

also noted that Darby stated the principle more dogmatically than did Groves and Müller.

If Groves was the original author of the principle in the form pursued by the Brethren and applied it in his own missionary work in the Middle East and India, it was Müller who did most to elaborate the principle in practice and to popularize it widely in evangelicalism through the work of the Scriptural Knowledge Society for Home and Abroad which he and his collaborator, Henry Craik, founded on 5 March 1834. The purpose of this paper is to look at Müller's own formulation of the principle (or rather at the developing nexus of principles which guided him in the work), his practical application of them, and the consequential financial experience of the Institution.[6]

Memoir of the Late Anthony Norris Groves Containing Extracts from his Letters and Journals Compiled by his Widow (Sumneytown, PA, reprint, 2002).

6. George Müller, as he is usually termed in English, was born Johann Georg Friedrich Müller at Kroppenstädt, near Magdeburg, in Prussia in 1805, the son of a Prussian official. At the University at Halle in the 1820s, George Müller came into close contact with Pietist Lutherans meeting in home groups and he dated his conversion to 1825. At Halle, he could not but become familiar with the orphanage and other relief works which had been organized by August Francke (1663–1727), a leading Pietist of the first generation. Shortly after Müller's conversion, he planned to give himself to missionary service with the London Society for Promoting Christianity amongst the Jews and moved to England in 1829 for training. There, in the West Country, he came into contact with the beginnings of the Brethren movement, and in particular with Anthony Norris Groves and Henry Craik. As a result, he had increasing doubts about the limitations entailed in working with a missionary society and, in the light of a letter that Müller had written to them, the Society's committee resolved in January 1830 that they could not 'consider him as a missionary student'. (See G. Fred Bergin [ed.], *Autobiography of George Müller or A Million and A Half in Answer to Prayer* [Denton, TX, facsimile reprint edition, 2003], p. 39 [hereafter cited as *Autobiography*].) Instead, he was appointed pastor of Ebenezer Congregational Chapel in Teignmouth (1830–32), married Groves' sister, and in 1832 moved to Bristol to pastor, jointly with Henry Craik, an independent congregation, Bethesda Chapel. He remained in Bristol and a leader of the same congregation until his death in 1898. In 1834, with Craik, he founded an educational and scripture distribution work, designated The Scriptural Knowledge Society for Home and Abroad (from 1840, The Scriptural Knowledge Institution for Home and Abroad). In April 1836 they added an orphan work, initially for thirty girls, though by November 1836 a work for thirty-six male and female infant orphans was opened as well. The orphan work grew, particularly from late in the 1840s, when Müller formed the project of building large orphan houses on Ashley Down, to the north-west of Bristol city centre. By early in the 1870s, there were five such buildings, with space for some 2,050 orphans. After his second marriage, he pursued for two decades an increasingly international itinerant evangelistic and teaching ministry, the day-to-day management of the work in Bristol being in the hands of his son-in-law, James Wright, as Co-Director of the SKI. (See the annual reports of the Scriptural Knowledge Institution for Müller's own summaries of this ministry and Mrs Müller [Susannah Sangar], *The Preaching Tours and Missionary Labours of George Müller* (London, 2nd edn, 1889).)

Principles of Funding

As a preliminary, it is worth noting in an analytical way that there are in fact only a limited number of options for funding Christian work. This was as true in the first century as in the nineteenth and as at the present time.

First, there are *donations* from individuals and bodies. These can take the form of current giving or grants, or they can take the form of grants on the death of the donor (legacies). They can be solicited whether by direct approaches to individuals or bodies, i.e., fundraising, or by advertising the need in some form or another. Or at the other extreme, the individual or body can rely on divine provision, without any use of means of making the needs of the work known.

Secondly, there is the possibility of *regular subscriptions* from individuals or bodies. Normally, these must necessarily result from advertising the work and the fact that it is possible for individuals to become regular supporters.

Thirdly, Christian work can be funded by *endowment*, that is, the use of income from invested capital. Such capital must be created in the first place, of course, whether from donations, grants, legacies, trading surpluses, or reservation of investment income. The chief advantages of endowments are security and predictability of income, and reduction or avoidance altogether of the need to continue to raise additional funds whether to add to capital or for revenue spending. Investment may be in land (yielding rental income), interest-bearing securities (gilts, etc), and dividend-yielding securities (stocks and shares). Here, risk is an important consideration affecting relative yields. High-risk investment may lead to high returns, but at significant risk of reducing or losing the capital. Lower risk investment results in lower returns but with greater certainty of retaining the original capital.

Fourthly, individuals or organizations can fund the work through *trading* with the aim of providing a surplus which can be applied to the work. Historically in the medieval English church, for example, this took the form of farming the glebe lands in hand, rather than letting it to a professional tenant for the rental income. In this context, the role of subsistence farming should not be forgotten as the means of supporting Christian activities, as in the case of medieval monasteries and, more recently, pioneer missionaries in isolated locations.[7] But in modern times many Christian organizations engage in trading of different kinds (often with their own constituency, in the same way that sports clubs raise money from their fans).

---

7. Many early Brethren missionaries, for example, went to central Africa expecting to live by faith without acquiring assets, but quickly felt themselves obliged to develop mission stations not dissimilar from medieval monasteries in their farming, medical and educational activities. Examples are the stations established by Walter Fisher at Kalene Hill, Dan Crawford at Luanza, and Walter Lammond at Murchison Falls. None could have been more radical than these in their initial approach to missionary work.

Fifthly, there is the possibility of funding work by *loans*, whether or not attracting interest. As for any other enterprise, borrowing can, however, never be more than a more or less temporary expedient. Loans at less than the going rate of interest in themselves entail a form of donation. And ultimately loans must be remunerated and liquidated from one or other, or a combination, of the first four types of income already outlined.

Pace the critics of the faith principle, it is worth noticing that unless a Christian enterprise is in the happy position of being adequately endowed from the past or unless it can draw on the taxpayer, as is still possible in some European countries, *some* person or body has to have the faith that the Lord will provide financially for the work. This is so whether it is a person or a body which undertakes to pay salaries, enters into contracts with other bodies and so on, or a local church which undertakes to pay its pastor a salary, or whether faith is exercised more collectively in the enterprise, as when individual workers raise their own financial support (the enterprise concerned still has to look to God for a great many other expenses, of course). It would be a bold person who said that the faith organization has not been an astonishingly successful *modus operandi* in Christian work in the last two centuries. Those organizations might say that they prefer their way of doing the work, to other sorts of organization's way of not doing it! In the context of this paragraph, it should be noted that, as a matter of fact, Müller and the Scriptural Knowledge Institution (SKI) fell into the first of the categories, that is, it was he who exercised the faith, and normally entered into, no doubt implied, contracts of employment with the staff of SKI. Those who criticize his practice of the faith principle should take care that they have selected the right target.

This general analysis is, in my view, interesting in itself and can be used to evaluate (practically and in principle) what sorts of financial mechanisms might appropriately be used to finance particular Christian activities. But the purpose of introducing it here is to illuminate the scope of Müller's distinctive principles for funding the work of the Scriptural Knowledge Institution (as it became at the beginning of 1840).

First, it is worth noting that Müller had no scruple about using most, if not all, the possible methods of funding charitable activity. In the earliest years, the SKI was partly funded by regular subscriptions and there were collectors whose task was to bring in these subscriptions. Unused balances (which frequently existed, despite the funding crises with which we are familiar from the annual reports and the standard biographies) were put out at interest—a limited use of the endowment principle. Goods produced by the orphans were sold for cash, though this never amounted to a significant stream of income. The gardens of the orphan homes produced vegetables, etc, for consumption by the orphans and staff. In general, copies of the scriptures and tracts were sold to recipients, though they were available at discount or free to the very poor. Fees were charged for schooling, though those in need were customarily subsidized by the SKI. All these latter approaches involved the fourth principle suggested above, that of trading.[8] This trading income was not insignificant: in 1877–78, for example, sales of books, tracts and Bibles, and income from school fees, accounted for 20% of the £15,300 income for the SKI's first four objects.[9]

There was, however, little evidence of any concerted effort to build up endowment funds to maintain the work. Apart from buildings, current income was used for revenue purposes and the SKI's only assets were the significant estate of buildings which it developed, almost wholly for the orphan work. Today's charity regulator would not have been hounding Müller for building up unused financial reserves!

The annual reports demonstrate that Müller's application of the faith principle was comparatively narrow. It eschewed making specific approaches to individuals and bodies to seek money or assistance in kind—however pressing might be the need for funds at a particular moment—in order to maintain the work; nor did he advertise specific funding crises. That is, Müller did not engage in fundraising in the currently-understood sense of the term. Rather, needs were made a matter of prayer that God might move believers to give.

Even so, and it should not be a surprise, this principle took time to crystallize. The earliest formulations are interesting, if only because what they stress is separation from unbelievers and radical antipathy for the unbelieving well-to-do:

> 2. We do not mean to seek in the least the patronage of the world; i.e. we never intend to ask *unconverted* persons of rank and wealth to countenance the Society, because this we consider would be dishonourable to the Lord.
>
> 3. We do not mean to *ask* unbelievers for money...though we do not feel ourselves warranted to refuse their contributions, if they of their own accord should offer them. The Collectors of the Society have been requested to act for the Lord's sake, according to this.[10]
>
> 4. We reject altogether the help of Unbelievers in managing or carrying on the affairs of the Society...[11]

---

8. The examples given are drawn from the biannual, and from 1850 onwards, annual printed reports of the SKI.

9. Statement of the income and expenses of the Institution, 26 May 1877–26 May 1878, *Thirty-ninth Report,* 1877–78, p. 70.

10. This point may indicate that at this early stage collection was employed as a fundraising method.

11. *First Report of the Operations of the Scriptural Knowledge Society for Home and Abroad*, 7 October 1834, p. 1. The principles were included, later in slightly expanded form, up to the *Eighth Report* of 1842–44, p. 62, but were omitted thereafter. (Hereafter the annual reports are cited simply by number, with the year where appropriate. They are a copious source of information, much of which had to be omitted from successive editions of the *Autobiography*, obviously because of lack of space.)

The passage in the *First Report* dealing with 'The Manner of Supporting the Society' shows that the expectation of Müller and Craik in 1834 was that regular subscription would be the main form of income. They also went so far as to 'ask believers *in* and *out* of Bristol to help us in the Lord's work in this way'.[12] The use of collectors was expressly to facilitate donations and subscriptions even from the poor. It was only somewhat later that we see Müller arguing continually in favour of seeking the Lord rather than making requests to individuals and bodies for help in times of need. Even then, two points need to be noted about this later stage.

First, that the principle of not making specific approaches to individuals or bodies in time of need, or otherwise, did not apply in respect of the staff of the Institution. In the earlier years, it was certainly his practice to take the staff of the, at that stage, small orphan homes and Bristol schools into his confidence when funds were low—as a matter for collective prayer.[13] The practical result was that members of staff often chose to forgo payment of their wages in order to enable the Institution to make ends meet in the short term.[14] This practice continued in financial difficulties in the 1890s.[15] On other occasions, they made useful donations and loans to the Institution, including sometimes of valuable and treasured jewellery.[16] And Müller on one occasion went so far as to regard it as an answer to prayer that a member of staff had been prevented by the sickness of a relative from collecting their wages, thus reducing financial pressure on the Institution![17] It is not possible to detect that he sensed a moral difficulty with this approach. On one occasion, too, he admitted a child, in effect underwritten by her grandfather.[18]

Secondly, Müller did make the needs of the Institution extensively known in a general way. The annual reports, for example, must have had a significant role of this kind. At the peak, over 25,000 copies were being printed annually and presumably most were being distributed or there would have been no need to continue with that level of print from year to year (see Appendix chart 2). The annual reports were packed with detail. They gave full information on the number of

12. *First Report*, 1834, p. 4.

13. Journal entry, 10 September 1838, pp. 10-11, *Fourth Report*, 1836–38.

14. Journal entry, 31 August 1838, *Fourth Report*, pp. 7, 8.

15 *Fifty-third Report*, 1891–92, p. 32. In this year, expenditure on the orphan work was £1,951.7s.1d. in excess of income, not counting £1,712 of unpaid salaries to matrons, teachers and others. 'Those who were not needing money either to help relatives or for other purposes had either no salaries at all paid to them last November, February and May, or received only a part of what was due to them. All these dear fellow-labourers, however, bore the trial patiently without the least complaint; and several of them contributed to the funds, according to their ability.' (Servants, and non-resident assistants, were paid in full or nearly so. The burden was therefore borne by the upper social stratum in the SKI.)

16. Journal entries for 11 and 12 September, and 12, 15 and 17 November 1828, *Fourth Report*, 1836–38, pp. 11, 18 and 19. The entry for 13 September 1838 spoke of a sister's forgoing her salary for twelve months.

17. *Third Report*, 19 May 1835 to 19 November 1836, p. 4.

18. Journal entry 27 September 1838, *Fourth Report*, 1836–38, p. 14.

pupils at the schools, the number of orphans and the number and location of evangelists and missionaries whom the SKI (that is, Müller) was in the practice of supporting. They made clear both the scale of assistance which was needed from day to day and the frequent funding crises resulting from fluctuations in the incidence of giving. In the reports, Müller gave full prior information on his successive building projects for dramatic expansion of the orphanages. In doing so, he made clear that he had no intention of initiating each project until he had the necessary funds to hand—to have done so would have infringed his principle of not borrowing to undertake the activities of the SKI—though he did later modify his practice by beginning projects phase by phase when he had sufficient funds in hand, at the same time making clear how far additional funds were needed to complete each phase and the project overall.

Moreover, it is difficult to see that, in later life, his preaching tours at home and overseas could have failed to have had a *de facto* fundraising effect, though he insisted in his accounts of his travels in successive *Annual Reports* that he spoke on the work of the SKI only when he was specifically pressed to do so (nevertheless, he does not tell us how often that was).[19] Certainly, some people at the time made the allegation that the annual reports, and successive editions of his autobiography which was largely drawn from the reports, represented *de facto* appeals for financial support. Müller himself acknowledged in the 1860s that this charge had been made, though he sought to rebut it. In the *Twenty-fifth Report* of 1863–64, he wrote:

> how effectual this way is for the obtaining of means; for the amount, which year by year is received is large...how pleasant a way it is; for I have not to encounter unpleasant refusals...how cheap a way; for it involves none of the heavy expenses,

19. In fact, the material later in this essay suggests that funding for the SKI became increasingly erratic and more dependent on legacies during his period of travel after 1870, and a few at least thought that his long absences were *the* reason why income fell off early in the 1880s (*Forty-fourth Report*, 1882–83, p. 3). I have not had time to ascertain from the annual reports, if it can be done, whether the funding base became more international during this period. Müller's practice on his preaching tours may have evolved somewhat. Of his preaching tour in the UK in 1875–76, he wrote that it 'had no connection whatever with the Institution... Though often asked to give an account of it...I refrained...lest it should be supposed I was out collecting money.' Of his continental tour the following year, he wrote similarly but now added, 'I did not even refer to the Institution, except when specially requested so to do.' He wrote similarly of his tour in North America the year afterwards and added, 'The statements which have appeared in some public papers, that I have obtained very large sums for the Institution in America, are entirely false; for all the donations handed to me for the Institution would not meet one half of its average expenses for *one single day*...' (*Thirty-Seventh Report*, 1875–76, p. 4, 5; *Thirty-Eighth Report*, 1876–77, p. 4; and *Thirty-Ninth Report*, 1877–78, p. 6). In 1895, he admitted, however, that 'tens of thousands have been benefited by it [the SKI], which I know from the numberless letters, which I have received...and through personal intercourse with many thousands of persons on my Preaching and Missionary Tours, in forty-two countries...' (*Fifty-Sixth Report*, 1894–95, p. 7).

usually attendant on the collection of contributions: for all I do is, to make known the work in which I am engaged, by means of the Reports, which are sold for the benefit of the Orphans, and they have, generally, brought in two-thirds or three-fourths of their cost.

> But, perhaps you say, Yes, it is just these Reports, why there is nothing remarkable in the matter...now to this last statement, that the *Reports* are the means by which all the money is obtained... My reply is: There is nothing unusual in writing Reports. This is done by public Institutions generally; but the constant complaint is, that Reports are not read. Our Reports are not extraordinary as to the power of language, or as to striking appeals to feelings. They are the simple statements of facts. These Reports are not taken by me to persons, and accompanied with personal applications for means; but they are simply sent to the donors or to any other individuals who wish to have or purchase them. If they produce results, which Reports generally do not, I can only ascribe it to the Lord.[20]

There was an element of trying to have the argument both ways in this passage. In 1838, he was characteristically striving to be scrupulous on the point, for he repeatedly deferred public meetings to report on the work because 'it might have had the appearance, that we had convened the brethren for the sake of telling them about our poverty, thus to induce them to give'.[21] Even so, his position seems to have been slightly ambiguous, because from the beginning the principles of the Society stated, 'in secret prayer, God helping us, we shall carry the wants of the Society to the Lord first, and then appeal to the brethren, and act according to the success which God shall give'.[22]

It was not only the needs of the SKI, in all its ramifications, that Müller publicized in this way. From time to time, in the various disquisitions which he included in the annual reports, he referred to his own support, as, for example, in the *Twenty-seventh Report* on the year 1865–66:

> ...I repeat here again, what has been stated in the previous Reports, for the sake of those who do not know it, that in November, 1830, I was led to give up my salary in connexion with the ministry of the Gospel, and during these 35 years and 6 months I have never had any salary nor other stated income, either in connexion with the ministry of the Word, or as Director of the Scriptural Knowledge Institution for Home and Abroad. If, however, one or the other of the Readers should suppose, that, on that account, I have been the sufferer, or loser, my reply is that it has been the very reverse.[23]

---

20. *Twenty-Fifth Report*, 1863–64, pp. 50-51

21. Journal entry, 6 December 1841, *Seventh Report*, 1840–42, p. 23.

22. *First Report*, 7 October 1834, p. 1, and continued in subsequent statements of the principles.

23. Journal entry, 8 February 1866, *Twenty-Seventh Report*, 1865–66, pp. 17-18. In 1865, Müller's personal income was just over £1,365. Of this, he and his wife gave away £1,131.10s.8d. See *Autobiography*, p. 457. This was a typical proportion.

And so on, at some great length. Moreover, the diary entries which were printed at length in the annual reports frequently referred to his having been given donations specifically for his own support and that of his family. The publication of these entries was no doubt justified on the ground that he was giving evidence to the donors that he had been punctilious in observing their wishes. His longer disquisitions on the subject were evidently intended, as well, to have a teaching function. But it is difficult to see how either type of entry can have done other than to call the attention of a wide readership to the fact that he and his household needed their donations if they were to survive.

Not only did he draw attention to his own needs in this way, but he also gave prominence to the needs of others. An increasingly important object of the SKI, in the period up to 1890 at least,[24] was to channel funds to missionary workers at home and abroad who were acting on the faith principle:

> ...they are not Missionaries of the Scriptural Knowledge Institution, nor do I bind myself to give them a stated salary; for this would lead them out of the position of simple dependence upon God for the temporal supplies; but when I hear of any man of God labouring for the Lord in the Word, whether in a more public or private way, whether at Home or Abroad, who is not connected with any society, nor in the way of receiving a regular salary, and who seems to me to stand in need of help, and is working in such a spirit, as that, with a good conscience, acting in the fear of God, I could help him with the means with which Christian donors intrust me; I am glad to assist such an one.[25]

The probability is that in this way Müller gave regular help to particular individuals. In 1865–66, they amounted to 125 people, forty-four of whom were abroad and the remainder in Britain and Ireland.[26] (An interesting sidelight was the differential rate of support to Europeans as against native workers.)

Further, the orphan homes on Ashley Down also became an object of Christian tourism. Clearly, the numbers were such that the practice had to be organized. So, for example, in 1872 Müller informed his readers that each of the five orphan homes was open on one afternoon each week between Tuesday and Saturday, with three parties being shown the houses between 1 March and 31 October and two between 1 November and 28/29 February. The tours began at 2.30 pm, 3.00 pm and 3.30 pm. 'No exceptions can be made... As it takes at least one hour and a half to see the whole of each establishment, it is requested that the visitors will be pleased to make their arrangements accordingly before they come, as it would be inconvenient should one or other leave, before the whole party has seen the House.'[27] This was evidently

24. After 1870, what shortly became *Echoes of Service* became increasingly important as the channel of financial support for missionaries from Brethren circles in the UK. Müller acknowledged their work in *Fifty-Fifth Report*, 1893–94, p. 55. '...God, I rejoice to say, has greatly blessed their labours'.

25. *Twenty-seventh Report*, 1865–66, p. 62.

26. *Twenty-seventh Report*, 1865–66, pp. 48, 49.

27. *Thirty-third Report*, 1871–72, p. 94.

another significant means by which the needs of the work became known. The practice dated from the opening of the first of the New Orphan Houses on Ashley Down late in the 1840s.[28]

All this sheds light on the frequent assertion that the funds of the Institution 'came solely in answer to prayer'. There was some Gladstone-like discrimination here. It is true that each individual gift was in no way solicited from the specific individual, and the needs of the work were the subject of much prayer, often urgent and prolonged prayer in times of financial crisis. But the inevitable effect of the reports, and the reprinting of much of the text in autobiographical form in a series of editions, was to make the needs of the Institution widely known. It is evident, for example, that increasingly even Müller's daily journal was penned with a wide readership in mind, as from the mid-1830s it became his practice to include extensive passages in the annual reports, as evidence of the way in which God answered prayer—one of his main underlying motives in undertaking the work on a faith basis.[29] That the journal entries might be included in due course in an annual report and then in a further edition of the *Narrative* would increasingly have been present to his mind as he penned the entry.

No doubt, too, the growth and public success of the work had its effect on funding. It is noticeable that the *daily* trial of living on a knife-edge of provision was concentrated in the earlier years, before 1850, when the work was at its smallest. Later, particularly as the benefit of legacies began to be felt, there were often quite considerable funds in hand, as can be seen from the balances being carried forward at the year end. As an example, on 26 May 1865 there was a balance in hand for the orphan work of £7,237.7s.7d, and a year later a balance of £5,964.4s.4d.[30] As will be seen from the data to be presented shortly, the work began comparatively slowly on a small scale for a period of nearly two decades and then grew rapidly and exponentially—a normal pattern, it may be guessed, for Christian works which become well-known.

Principles of Probity

But at least as important to Müller as the principle of not approaching any individual to solicit funds was a bundle of what might be described as principles of charitable probity which he and Craik arrived at and imposed upon themselves in the 1830s as the work was first developing.

---

28. *Eleventh Report*, 1848–50, p. 62.

29. '...the work has for its *primary object* to afford to the Church at large, and to the world, an evident proof, that the Lord in these last days is as willing as in times of old to hear prayer, and show Himself mighty on the behalf of those who trust in Him.' *Fifth Report*, 1838–39, p. 2.

30. Statement of the Income and Expenditure of the Institution for the year 26 May 1865–26 May 1866, *Twenty-seventh Report*, 1865–66, p. 71.

First and foremost was the principle of not entering into debt—even of a temporary kind to fund the enormous cost of building the great orphanage buildings. As they said in 1834 at the outset, 'We intend never to enlarge the field of labour by contracting debts, Rom. Xiii. 8, and afterwards appealing to the Church of Christ for help.' This principle was kept, even during the vast expansions implied by expanding care for orphans—though Müller did choose to phase the developments though he had not originally intended to; and he initiated successive building phases when he had enough money to do so, even though he knew he did not have the funds to permit the fitting out, equipment and furnishing of the buildings. And in the early days of penury, it was concluded that they should pay their provision suppliers daily, lest they should find that at the week's end they did not have the funds in hand: 'From this day, and henceforward, whilst the Lord gives to us our supplies by the day, we purposed therefore to pay at once for every article as it was purchased, and never to buy anything, except we could pay for it at once...' (This passage is interesting because it makes clear how, at that comparatively small scale of operations, decisions were made in discussion with the team as whole.)[31]

Much later, in 1882, the importance of the principle for Müller was underlined when expenditure on the orphan work exceeded income by some £500—no small sum at the time. Müller was quick to state that the deficit was eliminated by new giving within a month of the opening of the new financial year, and that in any case the SKI had considerable property assets in the unencumbered orphan homes[32] and developable land surrounding them, so that the liability was more than covered. But in this 'entirely new' situation their consciences were not easy. Concluding that the problem lay in expenditure on the day school branch of the SKI, which was consuming most of the unrestricted giving it received, within three weeks of the year end they gave three months' notice of intention to close twenty-three of the seventy-two day schools supported by the SKI, thus making a large number of teachers and managers redundant. 'Sorrowing as we do at the necessity of this step, we are satisfied that it is the only way in which we can go on with good conscience, and so count upon the Lord's continued blessing.'[33] Perhaps the decision to shift funding priority away from day schools was all the easier because of the existence of a growing public-funded education sector under the Education Act of 1870.

A further manifestation of this strong sense of financial obligation to others was a change of practice in the 1830s with respect to rents on the buildings being used by the SKI. In the autumn of 1838, Müller concluded that it was not right for him to assume that the Lord would provide rental as a lump sum on the day that it was due; rather, it was right to set aside monies from income weekly, or even daily, so as to be certain of being in a position to pay rents when they fell due.[34] This was an example of how Müller managed tension between the faith principle and the

31. Journal entry, 14 September 1838, *Fourth Report*, 1836–38, pp. 11, 12.
32. Built at a cost of £115,000.
33. *Forty-third Report*, 1881–82, p. 59.
34. Journal entry, 29 September 1838, *Fourth Report*, 1836–38, p. 14.

principle of not being indebted: the rental obligation was not a matter to be put to the hazard of faith, as it were.

A corollary was that funds set aside for rental should be regarded as restricted and there not available to meet other needs. More generally, Müller was punctilious in distinguishing between funds which were to be regarded as restricted as to their possible use, as a result of the intentions of the donor, and those funds the use of which was at the discretion of Müller as the trustee. Throughout, the SKI had five distinct objects.[35] Annual accounting distinguished carefully between monies given for the first four objects and those given for the orphan work (the fifth). Much of the purpose of the details of the published annual reports, and the unpublished supplement for donors introduced early in the 1860s, was to demonstrate to donors that their gifts had been properly applied—that such restricted funds were used only for the purposes for which they had been given. So on one occasion of financial stress in 1838 Müller noted that he had £220 in hand which had been given for another purpose, and he was sure that he should not use it even temporarily for the orphan work, even though he considered that the donors would consent if he were to ask them.[36]

The change of name of the SKI in December 1839 itself resulted from concerns about propriety. As Craik had pointed out first in 1837, the term 'society' was inappropriate as there were neither members nor a committee responsible for the work.[37] Accordingly three years later the term 'institution' was adopted to avoid 'misapprehension' or a 'wrong impression'.[38] In these years, Craik was evidently exercised that he was little involved in the practical management of the SKI and footnotes to the reports were included to make this clear. From the eighth report in 1844, Müller alone took responsibility for the reports and the management of the Institution.

The unique responsibility for the work and the absence of any committee were given by Müller as the reason for being scrupulous to the letter in accounting for donations given, even if some donors may perhaps have been concerned that his

---

35. In summary:

1. To assist Day-schools, Sunday-schools, and Adult-schools, in which instruction is given upon scriptural principles
2. To put the children of poor persons to such Day-schools, in order that they may be truly instructed in the ways of God, beside learning those things which are necessary for this life.
3. To circulate the Holy Scriptures.
4. To aid in supplying the wants of Missionaries and Missionary Schools.
5. To establish an Orphan House, in which destitute fatherless and motherless children should be provided with food, clothes, and Scriptural education.

(The first four objects were set out in the *First Report* of October 1834. The fifth was in effect added in a printed statement of 10 December 1835 (*Third Report*, 1835–36, p. 9).)

36. Journal entry, 8 September 1838, *Fourth Report*, 1836–38, p. 9.

37. *Third Report*, 1835–36, p. 3.

practice was unscriptural and that thereby their giving might become public knowledge. Müller's concern was first scriptural, that he should 'provide for honest things, not only in the sight of the Lord, but also in the sight of men' and that 'no man should blame us in this abundance which is administered by us' (2 Cor. 8.20-21). Secondly, however, it was 'that under a cloak of religion monies are collected in our day, which never are spent for the purposes for which they are given'; and the lack of a committee.[39] For Müller, his concern to be publicly accountable clearly over-rode the concern of donors about publishing details of donations. For him the priority was 'to please the Lord in it, not the world', i.e., the demands of his conscience over-rode those of the donors, though if the latter took the initiative and asked to remain anonymous, that would be granted to them.

So Müller was scrupulous in publishing copious information annually about funding practice and the financing of the work. The annual reports become more and more extensive: the third report was twelve pages in length, the fourth thirty-seven pages, the seventh (1841–42) fifty-two pages, the twenty-fifth (1863–64) ninety-six pages, and so on. This detail was, we may surmise, a reflection of his formation in Prussian culture. Perhaps also, it was a reflection of psychological compensation for what he regarded as his inveterate dishonesty with other people's money in his teenage years before his conversion. This increase in detail was in spite of the fact that from 1840 he discontinued printing with the annual reports lists of names of individual donors. Instead, a list of donors was made available for inspection on Wednesday afternoons at the Boys' Orphan House.[40]

Throughout, the accounts were examined by three or four, or even more, individuals. The reports and accounts were sent to all donors, provided their addresses were known. In later years, a detailed (unpublished) statement of all receipts was also sent to donors. The published statements referred to many individual gifts in terms which would enable the donors to identify them to their satisfaction. Indeed, it is interesting that Müller did not really approve of anonymous donations and he did not do much to protect the identity of his donors—support came widely from the evangelical community at home and abroad, but in many instances it would have been perfectly easy to identify individual donors, and the scale of their support, from the details of initials, locations and other information which he gave in the annual reports.

More generally, and in conclusion on the question of propriety, we can say that Müller's practice in reporting on the activities and funding of his charitable work can be regarded as exemplary. Independently and voluntarily, he took many of the steps which have been required of charities by regulation in the last thirty years. Often, the concern for propriety over-rode what might have been considered the demands of the faith principle.

38. *Fifth Report*, 1838–39, p. 2.

39. *Fourth Report,* 1836–38, pp. 32-33.

40. *Sixth Report*, 1839–40, p. 43. The reports still included lists of gifts in kind which were sold to help the orphan work.

Pattern of Funding

If these were the principles, what was the actual pattern of funding of the SKI? At the end of Müller's life, those associated with the SKI noted that during his lifetime the income had been some £1.5 million—of the order of £100m in today's terms.[41] Much attention has been given to this remarkable figure. But it is worth looking at the year-by-year pattern—segregating giving for the orphans work from that for SKI's first four objects (education, circulation of the scriptures, and the support of evangelism and mission). Chart 1 (see Appendix) displays the figures year by year.[42] As might be expected, at first the work grew only gradually. It is of note that giving for the first four objects kept pace with that for orphans until the mid-1860s—indeed, in some years even in the 1850s, it exceeded it. Only from late in the 1860s did giving for orphans decisively pull ahead of that for the first four objects. Giving for the latter went into steady decline from the mid-1870s and was no more than £3,500 a year in the decade up to 1910.

The reasons for this decline are not clear: it may partly have been a growing belief on the part of the evangelical public that the SKI's work was exclusively directed to orphans. But also the growth of state-funded education, and of separate missionary support organizations in the Brethren in the UK, notably *Echoes of Service*, may also have been factors.

The level of giving for orphan work in the 1840s (at a rate of no more than about £1,500 a year) points up what a bold move it was for Müller to conceive of more than doubling the work in the first instance,[43] and then in a comparatively short space of time to add four further houses giving a total capacity of about 2,050. It is therefore not surprising that he needed to give ample publicity to his plans in the annual reports. But, excluding giving for buildings (the main need directly advertised in the annual reports), giving for the orphan work grew ten-fold between the mid-1850s and 1870, with few downward hiccups. After 1870, income varied sharply from year to year, possibly as legacies, which Müller facilitated by providing a form of words in each annual report, began to be received. Nevertheless, overall between 1870 and 1890, giving for the orphan work continued on an upward trend, though not as steep as in the two decades up to 1870. From 1890, income for the orphan

41. Between the mid-nineteenth century and today, the purchasing power of the £sterling has depreciated some seventy times, as calculated by officials of the Office of National Statistics. See Jim O'Donaghue and Louise Goulding, 'Consumer Price Inflation since 1750', *Economic Trends* 604 (March, 2004), pp. 38-46.

42. There are missing years in these data because I have not been able to trace copies of the annual report for all years. The figures in chart 1 have been adjusted into real terms at the 1834 level of prices. Inflation was low in the nineteenth century as a whole. It was significant in the Crimean and Boer Wars and during the 1860s and 1870s, but there were also times of deflation resulting typically from the opening up of cheaper sources of food from abroad. In a few later years of the century, prices were at the same level as in 1834 and occasionally below that level.

43. From about 130 places in the four rented homes in Wilson Street to 300 places in the first New Orphan Home on Ashley Down.

work shifted onto a downward trend. It is possible that there can be detected here the impact on income, first of Müller's extensive preaching tours and then of his death. It was also the case that, by the 1890s, there were somewhat fewer orphans: in March 1901, his successors were obliged, in order to fill places in the homes, to shift their policy to admitting children only one of whose parents had died.[44] This secular trend may have affected perceptions in the Christian public of the need for orphan work.

It is possible to deduce from the annual reports something about the scale of the donor base (see Appendix chart 2)—because, for reasons of accountability, from early in the 1860s the practice was introduced of preparing an unpublished, but still printed, supplement which was sent to donors as evidence of the proper use of their giving. The statement of income and expenditure recorded the number printed each year. Assuming this number is a good guide to the number of donors, the number of donors in the latter part of the 1860s was about 5,000 individuals, and a little over that number through the 1870s.[45] By any standards, this must be regarded as a very substantial number and a measure of evangelicals' interest in and knowledge of the SKI's work. After 1880, the number declined to some 3,000 in 1887–88 and 1888–89, though it recovered to 4,500 by the end of the century.

Trends in average giving to the SKI (both for orphans and the other four objects) in terms of cash per donor are given in chart 3 (see Appendix).[46] The calculation can only be approximate because it uses the number of supplements printed, as recorded in the annual reports, as a surrogate for the number of donors in the year concerned. Clearly, amounts began to be affected by legacies in the later years. But the amount given per donor showed a strong upward trend (more than doubling) in the twenty years from 1865. It plateaued in the succeeding decade and was clearly on the decline from the middle of the 1890s, reflecting perhaps the reduction in giving for the first four objects which has already been noted. These figures should be viewed in the light of the fact that average real earnings in the UK grew by some 30% between 1865 and 1885 and 55% between 1865 and 1900.[47] So the work of the SKI may, proportionately, have been drawing to itself real interest in the evangelical public, particularly in the earlier part of the period.[48]

---

44. *Sixty-third Report*, 1901–02, pp. 4, 77. The result was a swift jump in the 'load-factor', from 70% in May 1901 to 81% in May 1902.

45. See chart 2, which also gives details of the number of annual reports printed and the number sold each year for which information is available.

46 A small proportion (typically between 5 and 10%) of giving was not in cash but in shares, jewellery and other valuable items, which it was necessary for the SKI to realize. This calculation amalgamates cash given and that realized from items given.

47. According to the index published by the Wake Forest branch of Miami University (http://eh.net/hmit/ukearncpi/?CHKrealearn=on&year1=1800&year2=1900, accessed on 2 February 2006).

48. This is tentatively expressed as I am not aware of trends in giving generally in the evangelical public in this period.

It was an example of Müller's meticulous presentation of detail that from 1857 onwards the annual report gave a figure for the unit of cost of maintaining an orphan in the SKI. For the immediately preceding years the comparable cost can be calculated and compared with the cost of maintaining an orphan in 1848–49 in the four houses in Wilson Street which were used before the first New Orphan Home on Ashley Down was opened. The results are given in chart 4 (see Appendix).

In the first year in the New Orphan Home the unit cost fell by nearly a third, perhaps because of the economies of scale resulting from more than doubling the number of orphans cared for. They rose sharply the following year almost to the previous level and costs proved difficult to control in the inflationary years of the Crimean War. Thereafter for two decades they continued in real terms in the region of £11–12 per child per year (in the region of £800 in today's prices). This was not high living, but expenditure per child did rise in the remainder of the century by 25-30% with a sharp spike to 60% at the turn of the century, probably resulting from the rapidly falling number of orphans at that time and possibly also from difficulties of cost control in the inflation of the Boer War. In 1900–10, it hovered at around £14–15 per orphan.[49]

George Müller's name is commonly associated with care for orphans on a faith basis. This directs attention away from his work as a successful church leader and encourager of church planting, and also from the other four objects of the SKI. Funding of mission at home and abroad, and of education, is evidence of the wider strategic character of his mind and ministry.

From the middle of the 1840s, the annual reports provided a systematic account of Müller's deployment of monies in support of mission work, both in the UK and abroad. Chart 5 (see Appendix) uses these data to illustrate the scale of support and how it was used across the latter sixty years of the century. Once again, the activity began comparatively slowly, grew sharply to a peak across the 1870s and in the last two decades declined to some half the level of the peak. In the period up to 1865, support for work in the UK in total exceeded that for work abroad. Thereafter, support for work outside the UK exceeded that for work in the UK—very much so, if grants of £2,000 a year for schools in British Guiana, Spain, Italy and France are taken into account. Müller's pattern of evangelistic and missionary support therefore reflected the shift of focus in British evangelicalism towards foreign mission in the last thirty years of the century. By his own account, it was also influenced by what he saw and those he met in his foreign preaching tours in the period 1870–90.[50]

49. For comparison, expenditure per person on poor relief in 1905–06 was £15.16s.6d, according to the Royal Commission on the Poor Laws and Relief of Distress appointed in 1905, and net national income per head in 1905 was £41.3 (see n. 53 below for source).

50. See, e.g., his reference to the needs of India in *Forty-seventh Report*, 1885-86, p. 30, following his tour there in 1883–84.

From 1865 onwards, the annual reports began to include extensive quotation from letters to Müller from workers, particularly from abroad.[51]

The level of support given by the SKI was significant, both in terms of numbers of workers helped and the average level of support (support varied according to Müller's perceptions of the needs of the worker, and possibly of the significance of what they were doing). The data on those helped are given in chart 6 (see Appendix). In the heyday, 160-190 individuals (whom he described variously as 'labourers in the Word and doctrine', 'Preachers of the Gospel', and 'labouring for the Lord in the Word') were being assisted at home and abroad—slightly more abroad than at home. That he was supporting as many as seventy to eighty workers in the UK can scarcely have been unrelated to the rapid growth of the Brethren in these decades.[52]

If we turn to the average level of support per head (Appendix chart 7), we find that between 1855 and 1875 those working in the UK were supported at an average of £30–40 a year. In the same period, average support for those working overseas was in the range of £50–70 a year. (There could, of course, be a greater expectation that those working at home would also have received support from others. Probably, that would have been less likely to be the case for those working abroad.) After 1875, levels of support per worker fell significantly, to half of those in the earlier years, or even less. These figures can be viewed in the light of the fact that net national income per head has been calculated to be, in current prices, £27.5 in 1865 and £42.5 in 1900.[53] Of course, typically, those whom the SKI supported would have had spouses and families. Nevertheless, the donations to those working in the UK were significant in relation to average incomes at the time. The workers concerned must have depended on the SKI's support to a considerable extent, and it is not surprising that Müller said that he received many hundreds of letters each year from those who were supported.

Müller's principle in supporting these individuals has already been cited above and was stated in every annual report: the individuals were not missionaries of the SKI, nor did they receive a salary from it, but they needed to be depending on the Lord, not connected with any society or receiving a regular salary. It is obvious from the data in the reports, however, that while he did sometimes give occasional help to particular individuals, many were supported on a regular and substantial basis from year to year. The SKI's support must have been important in maintaining them in the work in their chosen location. It is clear, too, that Müller's approach was strategic: both at home and abroad his inclination was to focus in particular areas.

51. These are possibly an untapped source of Brethren mission history, e.g., on the early years of Brethren work in a number of European countries, including particularly Italy and Spain.

52. For this growth, see my appendix 1 in Peter Brierley *et al.*, *The Christian Brethren as the Nineties began* (Carlisle, 1993), pp. 83-94; and Neil Dickson, *Brethren in Scotland 1838–2000: A Social Study of an Evangelical Movement* (Carlisle, 2002), pp. 59-133 and 381-84.

53. Data from Appendix 1, Table 9, in Peter Mathias, *The First Industrial Nation: The Economic History of Britain 1700–1914* (London, 2nd edn, 2001), p. 423.

Thus, in England, while he did support an individual or two in a broad spread of counties, his support was focused on London, Birmingham and the Bristol area (growing urban areas)[54] and on Devon (to the extent of supporting over thirty workers in that county at one stage—it is perhaps not surprising that there were well over 100 assemblies in Devon at the peak of their numbers). Abroad, the pattern was of consistent support for particular individuals in a wide range of countries. But his interests, in terms of numbers of workers supported, clearly focused on British Guiana, India, China, Italy, Spain and France. And from late in the 1860s, the work in British Guiana, India, Italy, Spain and to a lesser extent France was reinforced by substantial grants to support schools. Personal connection was important here: his knowledge of Hudson Taylor and his venture in China led him to be an early and consistent financial supporter of individuals working with what became the China Inland Mission;[55] and his contact with Count Piero Guicciardini during the latter's exile in England in the 1850s led him to give consistent support to Guicciardini's work, and those associated with him, once Guicciardini returned to Italy after the success of the *Risorgimento*. The focus on Spain, and on schools work there, may also have been inspired by strategic perception; its beginning certainly coincided with the brief flowering of religious freedom following the republican revolution there in 1868.[56] All this demonstrates the extent to which the SKI was *de facto* both a home and a foreign mission for the Open Brethren in the nineteenth century. It is interesting that the foundation of the Counties Evangelistic Work more or less coincided with Müller's death—though the practice of the SKI in supporting workers at home and abroad continued well into the twentieth century. Nor did Müller seem to be perturbed by the growth of *Echoes of Service*'s work: for in 1894 he wrote, 'Within the last fifteen or twenty years, it has been laid on the hearts of several brethren, to act in a similar way, and God, I rejoice to say, has greatly blessed their labours.'[57]

54. This is a deduction drawn from the numbers supported who were stated as 'labouring in' Middlesex, Warwickshire, Gloucestershire, and Somerset. In the 1870s, the SKI was supporting up to five workers in Warwickshire, ten in Middlesex (plus three in Hertfordshire and four in Kent), ten to twelve in Gloucestershire, eight to nine in Somerset, and up to thirty-two in Devon. (Analysis of information given in successive *Reports*.)

55. See Müller's account of how and why he came to focus support on workers in China in *Fifty-fifth Report*, 1893–94, p. 45: 'As soon as I heard of him, I helped him year after year... After a number of years a band of devoted servants of Christ gathered round Mr. Tayler (*sic*)... Of these Missionaries I sought to assist, year by year, 10, 15, or more, asking God's blessing on their labours, and waiting on Him for money to send to them'.

56. See Raymond Carr, *Spain 1808–1939* (Oxford, 1966), pp. 350-52.

57. *Fifty-fifth Report*, 1893–94, p. 55.

Christian education was from the beginning the first object of the SKI:

> 1. To *assist* Day-Schools, Sunday-Schools, and Adult-Schools, in which Instruction is given upon *Scriptural principles*, and, as far as the Lord may graciously give the means and supply us with suitable teachers, to *establish* Schools of this kind.

In practice, however, it remained a comparatively minor aspect of the SKI's operations for the first three decades and more of its existence (see Appendix Table 1). Four full-time day schools were maintained in Bristol with some 200 to 300 pupils; it was only in the 1860s that two schools were added, one in Callington, Cornwall, and the other in Kenilworth. In parallel, a fully-supported Sunday School was maintained in Bristol (possibly associated with Bethesda Chapel), and an adult evening school with some fifty to a hundred pupils. In addition, a growing number of day schools and Sunday schools were given assistance, but in the earlier years this amounted to gifts of Bibles and other books. Annual expenditure on the education object remained in the region of £400–500. At the end of the 1860s, however, the decision was taken dramatically to expand the SKI's educational work. The expansion was both at home and abroad. The opportunity in Spain, which attracted spending of £1,000 a year or more for a period, has already been noted. The reasoning for the expansion at home was, by Müller's own account, partly that, having completed the expansion of the orphan homes, he was looking for a new challenge (in his mid-sixties!):

> We have of late years given ourselves especially to the enlargement of the School Department of the Institution, as formerly to that of the Orphan Work, because we judged it so deeply important, that young persons should be well grounded in the truth from their earliest days, as now the efforts of Satan are so great to put aside the Word of God.[58]

Probably, this last was a reference to the Victorian intellectual crisis of faith. But it, and the expansion at home, may also have been fuelled by fears of the consequences of state education being introduced for the first time under Forster's Education Act of 1870.

Whatever the motivation, the expansion was dramatic. From fully-supporting six day schools in the 1860s, the number increased to sixty in 1873–74, and to seventy-seven at the peak in 1877–78 (some twenty-five of them overseas, as has already been noted). The number of fully-supported Sunday schools peaked at forty-four in 1882–83, and the number of adult schools at eleven in 1871–72. The partial assistance expanded *pari passu* in the day school and Sunday school categories. At the peak there were 5,900 pupils in fully-supported day schools in England and Wales (and a further 1,800 in such schools abroad), and nearly 3,200 in fully-

58. *Thirty-fifth Report*, 1873–74, p. 33.

supported Sunday schools at home.[59] The schools were scattered across southern England and Wales[60]—there were five in Cardiff with 904 pupils, established because 'On account of the popish influence at Cardiff, which is made to bear upon the children, to lead them early into idolatry, I had been again and again requested to establish a school in Cardiff on Scriptural principles.'[61] Inevitably, this meant an increase in the number of the SKI's employees, including the appointment of a Schools Inspector.[62] Each school clearly had to provide an annual report to SKI. For their part, the H.M. Inspectors of Schools seem frequently to have found the SKI's schools 'creditable'[63] in their performance.

The aim was very definitely both evangelical and evangelistic. The day schools, for example, were subject to three criteria: that the teachers should be believers, that the way of salvation should be scripturally pointed out, and that no instruction should be given which was opposed to the principles of the gospel. Both teachers and Sunday school superintendents knew that what their masters in Bristol wanted to hear was about conversions, baptisms and spiritual growth among their pupils, and about the moral tone of the schools. Some of the schools, like the assemblies to which they were often related, had to content themselves with the occasional response, while a few others saw significant numbers of conversions among the pupils. In the case of one recently-formed Cardiff school, 'There are now about 26 boys and 37 girls, who profess to have found peace in Jesus, through believing' and within a few weeks the total was eighty;[64] and on 27 December 1878 the master of Clayhidon School could remember forty children who had made professions of faith.[65] By contrast, in 1871–72 the master of the Howle Hill School wrote, 'I have no conversions to report this year. This is matter of concern and of deep sorrow',[66]

---

59. The schools which merely received financial assistance were not asked to report numbers or other details.

60. The schools supported in 1877 were in: Bristol (4); Callington, Cornwall; Kenilworth; Howle Hill, Ross on Wye; Walham Green, nr London (2); Blackdown Hills (3); Barnstaple (4); Exeter (3); Purton (2); Cubitt Town, London; Saul, Gloucestershire; Yeovil; Bishopswood, Somerset; North End, nr London; Chittlehamholt, Devon; Hopton, Suffolk; Cardiff (5); Kilburn, London (3); High Bickington, Devon; Plympton, Devon (2); Portsmouth; Stroud; Ludlow (2); East Brent; Brentford; Plympton Underwood; Bow, Devon; Shaftesbury; and King's Stanley. The twenty-eight schools abroad were distributed between Spain (16); India (4); Italy (2); and British Guiana (6).

61. *Thirty-sixth Report*, 1872–73, pp. 30-31.

62. Evidently, school masters and mistresses regularly reported to the SKI's Schools Inspector rather than to Müller or James Wright.

63. For example, of one of the Purton schools, HM Inspector reported in 1886, 'The School is doing its work with creditable efficiency', *Forty-seventh Report*, 1885–86, p. 24.

64. *Forty-seventh Report*, 1885–86, p. 30

65. *Fortieth Report*, 1878–79, p. 39.

66. *Thirty-fifth Report*, 1871–72, p. 32.

though in 1882 he or a successor was able to say that sixteen had given evidence of having been converted in the year.[67]

Yet, in 1892 the schools work at home collapsed dramatically. There was a longstanding financial problem at its heart. As Müller explained, at no stage were donors giving specifically for the educational arm of the SKI. They did not catch the vision or emotion of it in the way that the orphan work moved them. As a result, Müller was obliged to expand the work by using monies given to the SKI for no stated purpose. The scale of the expansion meant that virtually all such monies were being applied to the schools work, and none were available should a deficit arise in the orphans account. The problem was foreshadowed in the unprecedented £500 deficit in 1882 which has already been referred to and which led to the immediate closure of twenty-three schools in the UK. The second, much larger deficit of 1891–92 wiped out the rest of the day schools in the UK, with the exception of two at Purton in Gloucestershire, which survived because the SKI owned the school buildings.[68] By 1893 only these two schools and thirteen fully-supported Sunday schools survived as the SKI's educational department. In the final analysis, the donating public did not catch Müller's educational vision, and his and their priority was the orphan work (chronologically, the last of the 'Objects'). His success in promoting that work obscured the other components of his vision.

Conclusion

Whatever opinions may be of aspects of his thought and practice, George Müller's life and achievements were remarkable. He was a church leader whose ministry was rooted in a single church, yet his interests, concerns, and eventually his preaching, had great geographical scope. The material in this essay shows how he sought to encourage evangelism and the growth of the church across southern England and to a lesser extent in the North, Scotland, Wales and Ireland. He was critical in supporting the growth of the Open Brethren in its southern heartlands. It also shows how he took the lead in the UK in the support of overseas missionary endeavour from the Open Brethren. That too was geographically focused, while not neglecting to add a measure of support in many places. While the growth of the movement both in the UK and overseas was the work of countless individuals and some prominent leaders, evangelists and missionaries, his enterprise in Bristol and elsewhere, and the publicity given to it through the annual reports and successive editions of the *Narrative*,[69] ensured that his thought and practice were immensely influential in the development of the Open Brethren in his lifetime and afterwards. The material has also shown that he was not only a leader in showing how the faith principle could be applied in great undertakings in an industrial society, but also that he was in the lead in demonstrating how a great, and personal, charitable activity could and should be

67. *Forty-third Report,* 1881–82, p. 38.

68. See the explanation in *Fifty-fourth Report*, 1892–93, p. 40.

69. Which eventually became the *Autobiography*.

conducted with integrity. So transparently did he report his experience and practice that there is inevitably the evidence with which his character and stewardship may be criticized.

Appendix

Chart 1

Scripture Knowledge Institution Income 1834–1910
(At constant (1834) prices)

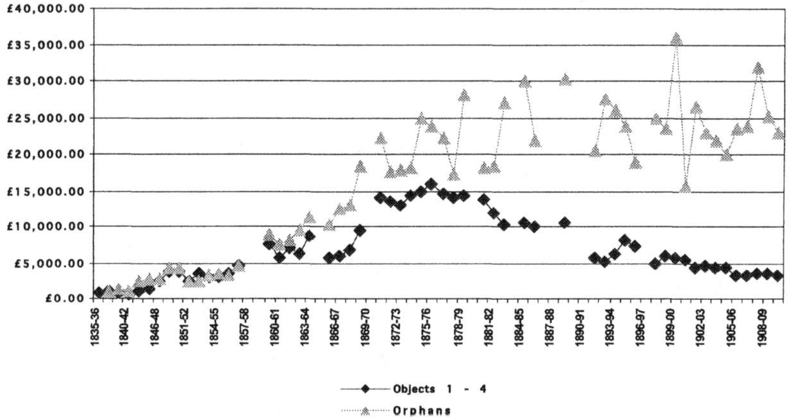

Chart 2

SKI Annual Reports: Print Runs and Sales

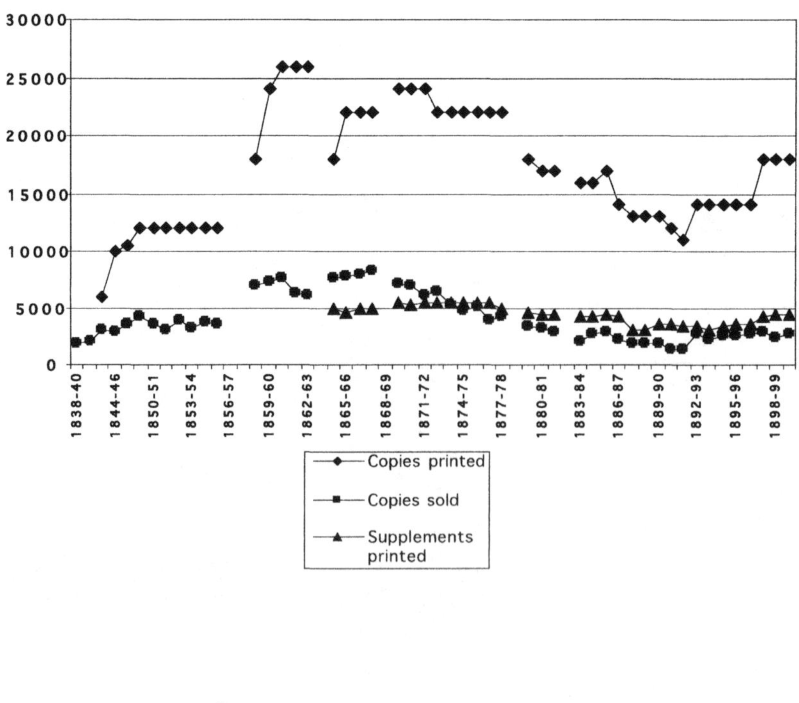

Chart 3

SKI: Approximate revenue giving per donor in cash terms 1865–1900

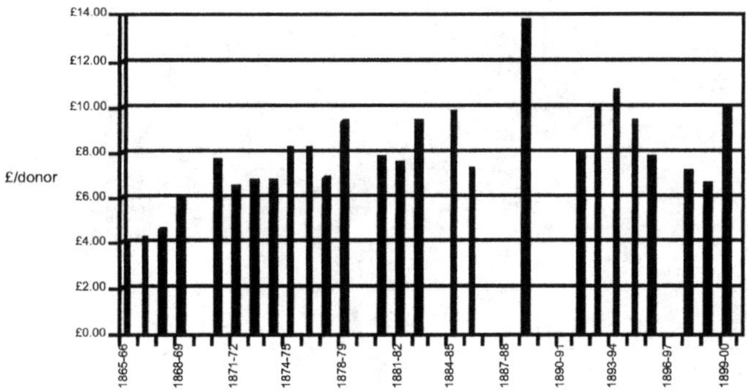

Chart 4

SKI: Annual expenditure per orphan 1848–1910

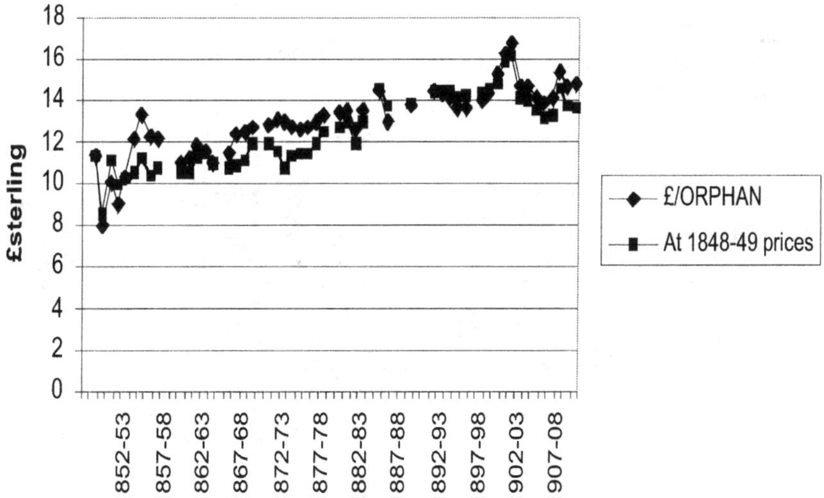

Chart 5

SKI: Expenditure on missionary purposes 1838–96

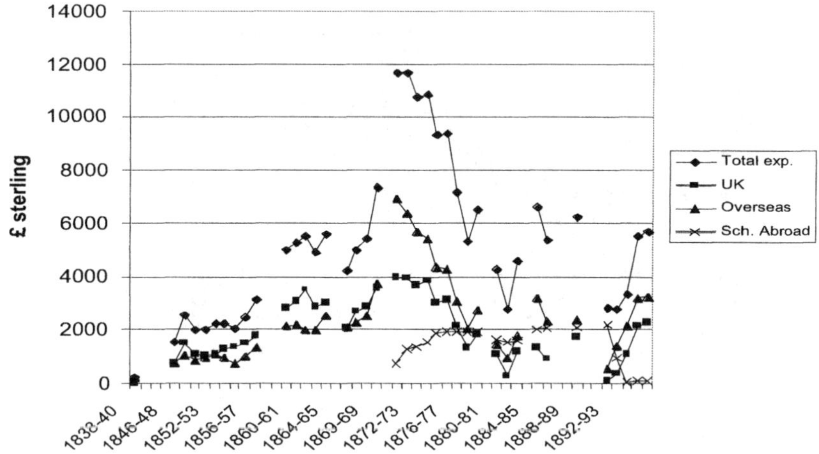

Chart 6

SKI: Numbers of workers supported at home and abroad 1838–1896

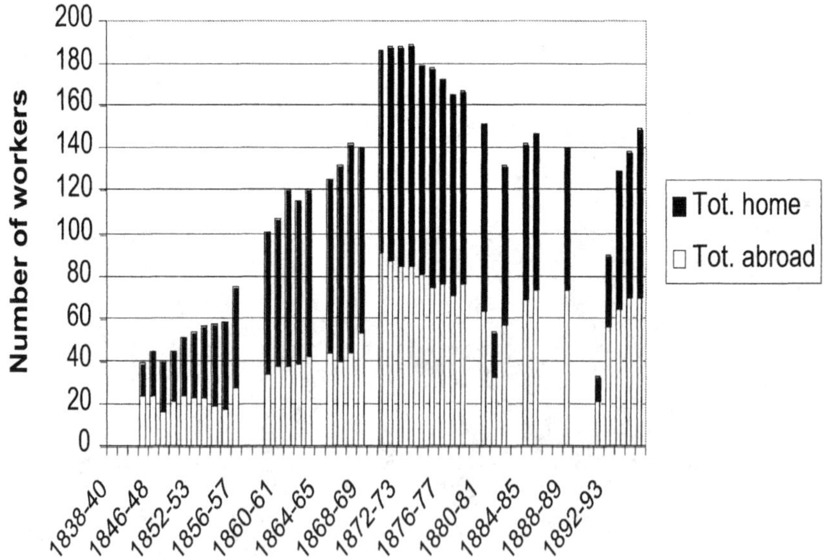

Chart 7

SKI: Average grant per worker 1844–1896

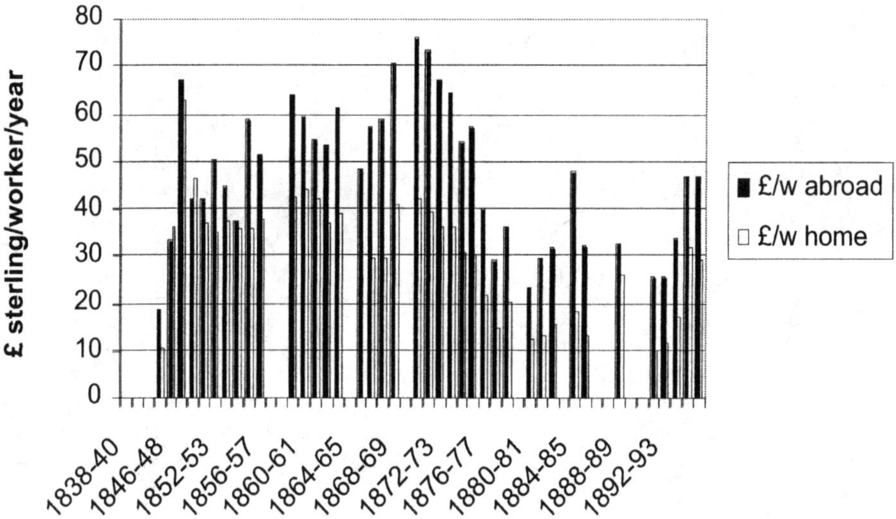

Table 1: Scriptural Knowledge Institution Educational Activities up to the Death of George Müller

	DAY SCHOOLS				SUNDAY SCHOOLS			
	Fully supported by SKI		Pupils	Assisted	Fully supported by SKI			Assisted by
	Total	in UK	in UK	by SKI	Total	in UK	Pupils	SKI
1840-42		5	363					
1842-44		6	338					
1844-46		4	278					
1846-48		6	330					
1848-50		5	329		1		168	
1850-51		4	466	3	1		397	2
1851-52		4	248	3	1		473	2
1852-53		4	235		1		430	3
1853-54		4	202		1		437	3
1854-55		4	184		1		558	7
1855-56		4	203		1		158	8
1856-57		4	181	6	1		175	6
1857-58		4	339	10	1		160	7
1858-59								
1859-60								
1860-61		4	302	11	1		177	13
1861-62		4	320	10	1		164	12
1862-63		4	321	6	1		160	13
1863-64		6	516	9	1		146	5
1864-65								
1865-66		6	450		1		150	4
1866-67		6	425	9	1		150	8
1867-68		6	415	17	1		194	18
1868-69		6	398	14	1		182	11
1869-70								
1870-71	32	17	2665	19	10		1084	27
1871-72	40	20	2955	8	14	9	1372	13
1872-73	52	31	3836	5	23	16	2452	11
1873-74	60	37	4852	11	28	16	3163	15
1874-75	70	44	4846	7	27	15	2631	15
1875-76	75	49	5422	3	29	16	2444	22
1876-77	75	49	5396	8	33	16	2487	34
1877-78	77	49	5908	4	39	16	2721	29
1878-79	76	50	5718	5	36	16	2409	16
1879-80								
1880-81	76	50	5394	2	37	18	2629	19
1881-82	72	47	5340	2	38	20	2696	22
1882-83	40	14	1242	3	44	18	2988	15
1883-84								
1884-85	39	14	1206	2	43	20	2745	25
1885-86	37	14	1281	1	29	12	2261	20
1886-87								
1887-88								

ADULT SCHOOLS			TOTAL EXPENDITURE
Fully supported	A Sch pup	Assisted	£
	80		772
	60		629
1	108		886
1	106		851
1	90		380
1	120		360
1	103		350
			360
1	133		338
1	158		348
1	72	2	386
1	48		515
1	34		484
1	34		498
1	48	2	537
2	76		587
2	40		663
2	32		687
2	40		787
2	27		686
9	339		1909
11	420		2284
8	332		2920
7	483		3328
8	316		4857
6	360		5502
6	166		6653
6	102		7273
6	96		7201
6	97		7348
6	97		7621
7	80		4272
3	68		2240
2	28		2305

	DAY SCHOOLS				SUNDAY SCHOOLS			
	Fully supported by SKI		Pupils	Assisted	Fully supported by SKI			Assisted by
	Total	in UK	in UK	by SKI	Total	in UK	Pupils	SKI
1888-89	36	13	1201		29		1921	20
1889-90								
1890-91								
1891-92	35	10	795		36	14	1831	21
1892-93	Day schools largely closed							
1893-94	2				13	13	1691	

	ADULT SCHOOLS			TOTAL EXPENDITURE
	Fully supported	A Sch pup	Assisted	£
1888-89	1	16		2276
1889-90				
1890-91				
1891-92				1968
1892-93				
1893-94				498

CHAPTER 6

Revivalism and the Limits of Cooperation: Brethren Origins in Orkney in the 1860s

Neil T.R. Dickson

Harold Rowdon epitomizes the ecumenism of the Brethren movement. His landmark work for Brethren historiography, *The Origins of the Brethren* (1967), possesses a lengthy appendix which claims that 'the movement may be regarded as an "Ecumenical Movement" of a unique character', and the appendix concludes that those who historically 'did all in their power to minimise the differences between themselves and other believers, at the same time maintaining their own somewhat distinctive positions' stood for 'the authentic "open" Brethren position which is still capable of providing a valid evangelical ecumenical perspective'.[1] That Harold was writing these words at a time when there was a sense of urgency about visible institutional church unity among mainline British denominations might partly explain the tone and vocabulary of his comments. But those familiar with the historiography of the movement will know that *The Origins of the Brethren* represented the latest work in a major strand of interpretation of the history of the movement, albeit argued with greater academic rigour than it had received until then. Open Brethren have often been comfortable with the transdenominationalism of evangelicalism, and again Harold has exemplified this in his work at the London Bible College. But equally there have been other Open Brethren, uncomfortable with the loose boundaries of such interdenominationalism, who pursued a different line of historical argument, and this group has been particularly strong in Scotland. The Scottish movement largely emerged out of mid-Victorian revivalism, and often different forces were at work within it than there were in the movement in Ireland and England of some thirty years earlier which had been the subject of Harold's seminal study.[2] Was 'the authentic "open" Brethren position' different in Scotland? In this paper I want to examine a key episode for answering that question: Brethren origins in the Orkney islands.

Orkney is an archipelago of some ninety islands which lies between the Atlantic Ocean and the North Sea and is twenty miles off the northern Scottish coastline. The

1. Harold H. Rowdon, *The Origins of the Brethren 1825–1850* (London, 1967), pp. 267, 293.

2. Neil T.R. Dickson, *Brethren in Scotland: a social study of an evangelical movement 1838–2000* (Carlisle, 2003).

largest island is known as the Mainland and it has Orkney's only two towns, Kirkwall, the administrative capital, in the east and Stromness in the west. Other districts in the Mainland are designated by the name of the parish. The islands possess a distinctive sub-culture within Scotland. They were among the first areas of the British Isles to receive the impact of the Viking invasions of the ninth century AD and they were ruled by the King of Denmark until 1468 when they were transferred to the kingdom of Scotland. In the mid-nineteenth century the islanders were predominantly engaged in agriculture and they spoke a distinctive dialect of Scots with a mixture of some Norse elements. The linguistic point is an important one for the growth of the Brethren in the islands. Unlike the Highlands, where the lack of Gaelic among Brethren itinerants was a severe handicap to the spread of the movement, the use of English in Orkney did not irreparably alienate the audience. Orkney schoolteachers in this period, many of them from outside the islands, also inculcated a belief in the superiority of the southern tongue.[3] By 1861 Orkney had achieved its highest recorded population of 32,225. However, the agricultural improvements which came after 1848 disturbed the traditional patterns and small cottars were cleared to make way for larger economic units. Although the strains of the alteration were not on the scale of the Highland clearances—they happened sporadically and over a period of time—it was a complete transition. 'No event', writes the islands' most recent historian of the agricultural changes, 'ever had such a profound effect on the landscape and on the way of life of Orkney people.'[4]

Christianity in the islands had been planted among the earlier Pictish inhabitants by the missionaries of the Celtic church, although it was forcibly reintroduced in 995 upon the conversion of the Viking ruler. From the last decade of the eighteenth century dissenting churches had begun to appear among those who sought relief from the prevailing Moderatism of the established Presbyterian Church of Scotland in Orkney and who desired a 'Gospel ministry'.[5] Some historians have also seen the conflicts between the lairds and larger farmers and the smaller crofters as a factor. Religious Dissent, it is argued, was also a social protest against the landlords and their associates, the Established church ministers, by the crofters and independent tradesman and craftsmen among whom Dissent took root.[6] Non-Presbyterian Dissent in Orkney owed its origins to the preaching tours of James Haldane, the Scottish lay itinerant evangelist of independent means. Haldane first preached in Orkney in 1797 and eventually Congregational churches came into existence in the northern isles of Westray and Shapinsay and on the Mainland at Kirkwall and the north-west parishes of Sandwick, Harray and Rendall.[7] In 1810 the Westray congregation followed

---

3. William P.L. Thomson, *History of Orkney* (Edinburgh, 1987), p. 239.

4. Thomson, *History of Orkney*, p. 199.

5. John Paterson, *Memoir of Robert Paterson, D.D. Kirkwall* (Edinburgh, 1874), pp. 10-15.

6. Thomson, *History of Orkney*, p. 236; Frank D. Bardgett, *Two Millennia of Church and Community in Orkney* (Bishop Auckland, 2000), p. 106.

7. William D. McNaughton, *Early Congregational Independency in Orkney* (forthcoming).

Haldane's acceptance of believer's baptism, and by 1827 it had succeeded in planting two more Baptist churches on other islands.[8] It was these small non-Presbyterian dissenting bodies which were to receive the full impact of the arrival of the Brethren movement in Orkney.

The individual who primarily was responsible for bringing the movement to Orkney was Rice Thomas Hopkins. Hopkins, the son of a Welsh Congregationalist solicitor, had been converted in 1858, and was, by the time of his first visit to Orkney, living in Ipswich. Along with his friend Samuel Blow, later also to become a Brethren evangelist, he had been baptized by C.H. Spurgeon and had become a student at Spurgeon's College before leaving to be a free itinerant preacher.[9] He first came to Scotland in August 1866, when he was only twenty-four, to meet the prominent Scottish revivalist Duncan Matheson at the Perth Conference, the annual convention held by those associated with the contemporary awakenings in Scotland. Afterwards Hopkins remained in the north to preach with Matheson and other of the revival evangelists.[10] Matheson had been invited to Orkney by Thomas Wingate, the Established minister in Stromness, and Matheson had intended taking Hopkins with him. Because of a sudden illness, however, Matheson sent in his own place Donald Munro of the North-East Coast Mission, a nondenominational body active among the fishing communities.[11]

In late 1866 Hopkins was already on the north island of Westray.[12] By the 1860s Orkney was open to the type of revivalism which had been affecting Scottish churches on the mainland. Revival, too, can be linked with social and economic change.[13] The agricultural changes had demonstrated that progress meant rejecting traditional practises, and there was an assumption in other areas of life that the new was better.[14] In addition, the evictions were at their height on Westray in the early 1860s as an analysis of Orkney Sheriff Court processes from 1858 until 1870

---

8. D.W. Bebbington (ed), *The Baptists in Scotland: A History* (Glasgow, 1988), pp. 317-20.

9. Chadstone, Australia, Mr Ian McDowell's collection, W.H. Hopkins, untitled typescript biography of the early life of R.T. Hopkins (undated); see also Ian McDowell, 'Rice Thomas Hopkins 1842–1916: an open brother', *BAHNR* 1 (1997–98), pp. 24-30; Fred Bresnen, 'Rice Thomas Hopkins (1842–1916)', in idem, *Assemblies of Christians in the Wirral* (privately printed, 2002), pp. 149-77.

10. John MacPherson, *Duncan Matheson: the Scottish Evangelist* (London [1871]), pp. 234-36.

11. 'Mr Wingate and the Cairstone Presbytery', *The Orkney Herald* [hereafter *OH*], 30 April 1867.

12. Rice F[sic]. Hopkins, 'Awakening in the Orkneys', *The Revival* [hereafter *R*], 16 (March, 1867), p. 173; 'Evangelical Services', *The Orcadian* [hereafter *O*] 25 December 1866.

13. Kenneth S. Jeffrey, *When the Lord Walked the Land: the 1858–62 Revival in the North-East of Scotland* (Carlisle, 2002), pp. 28-31.

14. William P.L. Thomson, *The Little General and the Rousay Crofters: crisis and conflict on an Orkney estate* (Edinburgh, 2nd edn, 2000), pp. 85-86.

shows.[15] Westray had already had a revival in 1860 and all three Westray churches—the Established Church, the United Presbyterian Church and the Baptist Church—had cooperated in it. When the itinerant evangelist Harrison Ord, also a Brethren member, had visited the island in 1865, he reported in the interdenominational publication *The Revival*, 'the love of Christ triumphing over the miserable sectarian spirit which prevails alas! too often'.[16] On Westray, Hopkins already had an introduction through Robert Lennie, the son-in-law of Henry Harcus, the Baptist minister. Lennie was a native of Kirkwall who had been a fellow student of Hopkins at Spurgeon's College, and it was possibly this connection which brought him to the islands ahead of the mission with Wingate.[17] It was assumed that Hopkins was still a Baptist, but probably his ecclesiastical views were in a transitional stage at this point. While evangelizing in his native Plymouth in 1865, Hopkins had received support from the Brethren,[18] and when he arrived on Orkney in late 1866 he probably regarded himself as a nondenominational evangelist as he kept his denominational connection quiet.[19] Before his arrival there were already expectations of revival in Westray, and Hopkins reported:

> The third night I spoke in the Baptist chapel; several were weeping aloud, and from that time, large numbers remained behind to all the after meetings. The second week, so many stayed, I scarcely knew where to begin; men and women, in every part of the place bowed beneath the power of the Word.[20]

In January 1867 Hopkins joined Munro in Stromness, where Hopkins was described as having 'a fine powerful voice, and could make himself heard by a large

15. Kirkwall, Orkney Archive [hereafter OA], Orkney Sheriff Court Records, SCll/5 1856/37; SCll/5 1858/29; SCll/5 1858/41; SCll/5 1859/32; SCll/5 1860/45; SCll/5 1861/42; SCll/5 1862/8; SCll/5 1862/27; SCll/5 1863/21; SCll/5 1863/28; SCll/5 1864/42; SCll/5 1865/12; SCll/5 1866/13; SCll/5 1868/39; SCll/5 1868/40; SCll/5 1871/27; SCll/5 1873/28. It is probable that SCll/5 1865/39 and SCll/5 1868/40 were not agricultural clearances as the evictions were being carried out against merchants.

16. *R*, 13 (December, 1865), p. 331; however, it is possible that Ord was not a member of the Brethren by this year.

17. Robert Lennie to the editor, 16 May 1916, *OH*, 21 June 1916; Henry Harcus, *The History of the Orkney Baptist Churches* (Ayr, 1898), p. 92; Harrison Ord is another connection between Hopkins and Westray as the two men had already evangelised together. Later, in Australia, they were to separate when Ord stayed with his ecumenical views and Hopkins took a separatist position.

18. Samuel Blow, *Reminiscences of Thirty Years' Gospel Work and Revival Times* (Glasgow, 1988 [c.1903]), pp. 65-67. Blow, who accompanied Hopkins, incorrectly dated the visit to Plymouth as 1866; it happened in fact in the previous year, cf. *R*, 13 (August, 1865), p. 91.

19. Jas Stephen, 'Remarkable early days in Orkney', *The Believer's Pathway* (April 1916); reprinted in John Gray (ed.), *Topics, Truth, Tales* (Glasgow, [1916]), p. 57; 'Meeting of Cairstone Presbytery', *OH*, 30 April 1867.

20. *The Latter Rain* [hereafter *LR*], 1 (1867), p. 68.

concourse'.[21] On the second week in January they commenced services which continued for two weeks in the Harray Congregational Church, another congregation which had been affected in 1860, and this time the effects were to be felt into the next year by which time a 'goodly number' had been added to the church.[22] The Sandwick Congregational Church, too, was affected, and revivalist scenes were repeated elsewhere in Orkney, the people sometimes walking through heavy snow to get to the services. There were exceptional occurrences such as are associated with revivals. William Corriegall, a member of the Harray Congregational Church, who in his youth had heard James Haldane preaching, had a vision of two strangers bringing revival to the islands, and he later recognized Hopkins as one of the men in the dream.[23] Although Hopkins and Munro, then a member of the Free Church of Scotland, again kept their ecclesiastical affiliations quiet, strains between the two evangelists and many of the Orkney churches were soon apparent. There was opposition to the two men who were typical products of the British revivalist network: evangelistically aggressive, lay-oriented and anti-institutional. They used contemporary revivalist techniques, such as hymns (a novelty in Scotland), after meetings for the anxious which sometimes went on into the early hours of the morning and preaching of 'instant salvation' and assurance as the essence of faith. As a result, they were accused of making 'desperate efforts to get up sensation meetings'.[24] Hopkins for his part claimed that only six men in Stromness on the Orkney Mainland could pray publicly, the implication being that these were the only true Christians, and a widely reported remark of Hopkins' was that hell was paved with the skulls of ministers.[25] Some suspected that the two evangelists were Plymouth Brethren,[26] probably because of their doctrine of salvation which was that which was associated with the Brethren. In addition, an identification was increasingly being made throughout Britain between lay revivalists and the Brethren, for many of the most prominent were already members or had become members of the movement as they found its theology and ethos congenial: not only was Hopkins a later member, but so too was Munro. After they had left, Wingate had to undergo a thorough cross-examination from his presbytery, and he undertook not to have any preachers unqualified by the Church taking part in his regular services.[27] Again, evidently to discredit them, attempts were made to establish if the evangelists were Brethren.[28]

---

21. 'Religious services', *OH*, 12 February 1867.

22. *Annual Report of the Congregational Union of Scotland* (Edinburgh, 1867), p. 10, quoted in McNaughton, *Independency in Orkney*, p. 57.

23. Hopkins, untitled biography, p. 8; William Corriegall was to become Brethren and his descendants were among the leading members of the Harray assembly.

24. 'Peripatetic preacher', *OH*, 19 February 1867.

25. 'Meeting of Cairstone Presbytery', *OH*, 30 April 1867.

26. 'A Friend of Presbyterian Union' to the editor, *OH*, 8 March 1867.

27. 'Meeting of Cairstone Presbytery', *OH*, 14 May 1867.

28. 'Meeting of Cairstone Presbytery', *OH*, 30 April 1867.

When Hopkins first visited Orkney he had done so through his contacts among fellow evangelicals. His criticisms of the Orkney churches, however, had not been entirely fair even from the perspective of his evangelicalism. The small non-Presbyterian dissenting bodies were evangelical. The Harray Congregational Church, for example, maintained 'that *personal* interest in Christ is essential in order to church membership'.[29] The minister, Donald McCorkindale, took pride in this gathered church stance, noting 'I am more and more convinced how necessary it is that we should have a cause here, where discipline and purity of communion are strictly adhered to.'[30] Evangelicalism also certainly existed among the Orkney Established Church congregations. Stromness was in Cairstone presbytery and Moderatism was apparently strong in it, but even Wingate had told Hopkins that his claims about the state of Stromness religion had been exaggerated. Evangelicalism was present in the Cairstone presbytery too.[31] In addition, by the later nineteenth century, two evangelical Presbyterian churches, the Free Church of Scotland and the United Presbyterian Church, were dominant in seven of the nine Mainland parishes. The latter church also became preeminent in several other islands making Orkney the only area of Scotland where it was the single largest denomination.[32] In the Victorian era this body in the islands was under the spiritual leadership of the energetic Robert Paterson, minister of its large Kirkwall congregation, and he was decidedly in favour of revivals—a pattern that was to continue in the Kirkwall United Presbyterian Church until the turn of the century at least, as the experience of the poet Edwin Muir demonstrates.[33]

The definite parting of the ways between Hopkins and his fellow evangelicals came in 1868 when he returned to the islands in June of that year for a longer visit accompanied by John Albert Boswell, a member of the Ayrshire family to which Dr Johnson's biographer had belonged and a convert of the 1859 Revival.[34] During the intervening year since his previous visit to Orkney, Hopkins had become more fully convinced of Brethren practices.[35] It was probably in the autumn of 1867, prior to his return to Orkney, that he and Blow had helped found an assembly in Aberdeen, the one to which all subsequent Open Brethren meetings in the city owed their

29 *Annual Report of the Congregational Union of Scotland* (Edinburgh, 1866), p. 12, quoted in McNaughton, *Independency in Orkney*, p. 57.

30. *Annual Report of the Congregational Union of Scotland* (Edinburgh, 1868), p. 10, quoted in McNaughton, *Independency in Orkney*, p. 58.

31. J.W. to the editor, *OH*, 2 May 1867; *OH*, 7 May 1867; cf. the portrait of Dr William Logie, a nineteenth-century Kirkwall parish minister, in Bardgett, *Church and Community in Orkney*, pp. 129-36.

32. Callum G. Brown, *The Social History of Religion in Scotland Since 1730* (London, 1987), pp. 68-70.

33. Edwin Muir, *An Autobiography* (London, 1987 [1954]), ch. 2, pp. 84-85.

34. [J.J. Park], *The Churches of God: their Origin and Development in the 20th Century* (Leicester, 1987), pp. 86-87.

35. James Stephen to the editor, *OH*, 19 July 1916, p. 3.

origins.[36] Boswell had already assisted in the formation of the assembly in Lerwick, Shetland, in 1864.[37] He, too, was becoming more fully Brethren, and during 1867 he had helped found an assembly in Iver, Buckinghamshire, where he then lived.[38] The opposition in Orkney was prepared, and Hopkins in return was deeply critical of many of the churches. 'There are a few Christians in earnest', he wrote of Kirkwall. 'It is a sad state of things here with many unconverted ministers; some are saying, It's all [i.e. Hopkins' preaching] the devil's work.'[39] Relationships between Hopkins and the churches were additionally strained when these comments, written for *The Latter Rain*, a nondenominational journal edited by the Brethren member Russell Hurditch, was republished in a local newspaper under the title of 'Shocking Account of the Religious State of Orkney'.[40] Hopkins was identified this time as being 'a champion of Plymouthism'. Archer Fortesque, the English laird of Swannibister in the Mainland parish of Orphir, who was known for his high-handed treatment of his tenants, forbad his employees from attending their services on pain of dismissal. Instead he obtained Dr Samuel Traill, the Harray and Birsay parish minister (and a later moderator of the General Assembly) who had already shown himself hostile to Thomas Wingate, to deliver a lecture on 'Plymouthism'. In the course of his address Traill opined of the Brethren that 'whatever means they may choose to adopt, they are not entitled to the name of Christians'[41]—a sentiment that Hopkins and Boswell would have doubtless reciprocated.

In private meetings and discussions with converts and supporters the two evangelists taught believer's baptism and Brethren ecclesiology.[42] The first baptisms took place in August on the Mainland in Rendall, with converts present from other north-west parishes. Again the preachers alienated the mainstream churches, Hopkins calling infant baptism a 'delusion of the devil',[43] and it was alleged that he preached close to the churches on the communion Sabbath, a day particularly revered in the Scottish Church.[44] On Westray the Baptists once more identified with the revivalism of the evangelists, although both men were careful to leave the building when the Lord's supper was being commemorated, apparently to signify that they were not

36. Donald Munro in C.W. R[oss]. (ed.), *Donald Ross* (Kilmarnock, [1904)), p. 115; *R*, 16 (1867), p. 591, reports Blow and Hopkins in Aberdeen together; however, 'John Bendelow', *BM*, 18 (February 1908), end pp, dates the formation of the Aberdeen assembly to 1868. Nevertheless, if it were formed during the latter year after Hopkins' visit to Orkney, then this still shows his increased predisposition to gather his converts into assemblies at the time of his second Orcadian trip.

37. [George Peterson], *A Century of Witness in Ebenezer Hall, Lerwick 1885–1985* (Lerwick, 1985), p. 1.

38. 'Jonathan Marks', *W*, 55 (April, 1925), p. 79.

39. R. Hopkins to the editor, *LR*, 1 (1868), p. 199.

40. 'Shocking Account of the Religious State of Orkney', *OH*, 14 April 1868.

41. 'Address on the new gospel', *O*, 23 June 1868.

42. [John Ritchie], *Donald Munro* (Kilmarnock, n.d.; reprinted Glasgow, 1987), pp. 40-41.

43. 'Rendall', *O*, 18 August 1868.

44. A.F. to the editor, *O*, 11 August 1868.

Baptists.[45] The two men discovered that there was dissatisfaction in the Westray congregation at the erosion of the Scotch Baptist practice of mutual exhortation from among the members.[46] Hopkins and Boswell visited many of the members in their homes and by the time Harcus realized what was happening he felt a faction already existed. After the evangelists left, the private meetings continued, assisted by the twenty-six year-old James Logie, a native of Westray who attended the Baptist ministerial training institution in Glasgow where he had come in contact with the Brethren.[47] Robert Lennie, again present on the island in the summer of 1868, identified the views being discussed as 'thoroughly Plymouthistic' and he preached a sermon against them the following Sunday attempting to show their 'inconsistency with the Word of God'.[48]

The unfavourable reputation the Brethren were getting in Scotland was obviously a factor in Orkney.[49] In 1810 when the congregation on Westray was debating believer's baptism, the members had waited on one another until they were virtually unanimous, but in 1868 no such time for mutual consultation was allowed for. A split was inevitable and some two-thirds of the church—about 150 individuals—left to form a Brethren assembly.[50] A gospel hall was built for the new meeting, but the remainder of the Baptist congregation was unable to sustain their financial burden and soon afterwards Harcus emigrated. Those who seceded felt that they had a divine command to leave and that Harcus 'would not bow to the Word of God'.[51] Amid much opposition assemblies also came into existence in a number of other places in Orkney. On the Mainland assemblies were formed in Stromness and in the north-west parishes of Harray and Evie and one was also formed on the island of South Ronaldsay. In the 1870s Kirkwall (c.1873)[52] and the island of Eday (1876)[53] also had meetings formed in them.[54] The new assembly in Kirkwall drew its membership

45. James Stephen, *OH*, 19 July 1916.

46. J.A. Boswell to the editor, *LR*, 2 (September 1869), p. 323.

47. Harcus, *Orkney Baptist Churches*, p. 94; James Logie was identified through oral information from Jack Oddie, Kirkwall, August 1989; his age has been calculated from the Westray Census, 1881.

48. Harcus, *Orkney Baptist Churches*, pp. 94, 302.

49. Crawford Gribben, '"The worst sect a Christian man can meet": opposition to the Plymouth Brethren in Ireland and Scotland, 1859–1900', *Scottish Studies Review* 3 (2002), pp. 34-53.

50. J.A. Boswell to the editor, *LR*, 2 (September 1869), p. 323.

51. 'One Who Ought To Know' to the editor, *OH*, 10 February 1897.

52. *Northern Assemblies*, No. 9 (September 1873), p. 36; 'William Reid', *W*, 58 (1928), p. 288.

53. 'William Peace', *W*, 56 (1926), p. 279.

54. Additional Open Brethren assemblies were founded later on Sanday (1887), Papa Westray (1933), and Shapinsay (1935); cf. the assemblies listed in Alex Goodfellow, 'Death of the Founder of the "Hopkinites" in Orkney', *O*, 29 April 1916, p. 3. The Exclusive Brethren had by the early 1880s formed assemblies in Kirkwall, Shapinsay, South Ronaldsay and Westray, *References (January 1884)* (n.pl., 1884); these were probably formed some time in the previous decade. They were more short-lived than the

largely from the town's Haldanite Congregational church, and in the adjacent parishes of Harray and Rendall the Congregational churches were severely depleted. In the opinion of one turn-of-the-century Orkney church historian (a fair-minded evangelical parish church minister), it led to their eventual closure.[55] Although the denominational magazine, *The Scottish Congregationalist,* was to note that the Harray Church 'suffered from the blighting effects of Plymouthism' for a period after 1868,[56] the labours of Donald McCorkindale, its minister until 1870, had apparently accomplished much. Unlike the Rendall Church which died out in the later nineteenth century, it survived into the early twentieth century.[57] Doubtless the Brethren secessions were a factor in the decline of both congregations, though there were probably other causes at work. The Baptist congregation on Westray recovered itself, but in a small island community a legacy of bitterness was left between it and the assembly.[58] The new gospel hall was built about a hundred yards down the track from the Baptist chapel, and there were suspicions that the Brethren were going to build a wall to block access.[59]

Few of the participants emerge out of the formation of Brethren in Orkney with unblemished reputations. Many within the Established Church reacted intemperately to the appearance of revivalism among them, and Hopkins and Boswell lacked transparency in their dealings with the churches. Even the Westray Baptists have been criticized for not pausing to learn from the new movement's church structure.[60] Later writers speculated that Hopkins's actions stemmed from the impetuosity of youth. Attractive as this charitable excuse might be, his later history does not lend it support. Both he and Boswell went on to become leaders within the Open Brethren of the emerging *Needed Truth* party, a grouping of more rigorous, sectarian separatists (nicknamed after its journal) that held any association with other Christian denominations to be 'evil' and which eventually issued in the schism of the Churches of God in 1892–94. Hopkins was recognized for a while, in England at least, as the leader of the new party and he had a seminal role in formulating the doctrine which was used to represent assemblies as a privileged fellowship.[61] By the

---

Open Brethren assemblies discussed in this essay, having all been discontinued by the mid-twentieth century.

55. Goodfellow, 'Death of the Founder'; cf. *idem*, *Birsay Church History* (Kirkwall, 1903), pp. 274-75.

56. *The Scottish Congregationalist* (1889), p. 313, quoted in McNaughton, *Independency in Orkney*, p. 58.

57. The last minister of Harray died in 1900, and the Church closed c.1912; the Rendall Church was dissolved in 1882: William D. McNaughton, *The Scottish Congregationalist Ministry 1794–1993* (Glasgow, 1993), pp. 149, 448.

58. See correspondence in *OH*, February to April 1897 and 19 April, 21 June, and 19 July 1916; and *O*, 29 April, 1 July and 22 July 1916; cf. Neil Dickson, 'Brethren and Baptists in Scotland', *Baptist Quarterly*, 33 (October, 1990), pp. 376, 378.

59. 'A Native of Westray' to the editor, *OH*, 3 March 1897.

60. Bebbington (ed.), *Baptists in Scotland*, p. 321.

61. Dickson, *Brethren in Scotland*, pp. 161-69.

time of the formal schism he had emigrated to Australia and he did not follow the secessionists initially, but later, with his brother Gordon Hopkins, he became the founder of a separate circle of equally rigorous assemblies informally known as the 'Hopkins' or 'Hopkinite' Brethren.[62] In Orkney, too, the Brethren were known locally as 'Hopkinites'.[63] He became a separatist marked by his exclusive attitude to other Christian bodies.

Ironically, the exodus into the Brethren in Orkney had been deepest among those evangelical congregations which had been most open to them. Hopkins and Boswell had been finding interdenominational cooperation difficult, and events there came at a key stage in their development. An article appeared in *The Revival* in July 1868 critical of their actions in preaching against ministers and stating that their task was to preach the gospel only.[64] Thereafter it ceased reporting their activities, doubtless because the two men stopped sending reports of their movements to it.[65] It was probably individuals such as them (and possibly the events in Orkney) that Duncan Matheson was criticizing when in his last address to the Perth conference in September 1868 he stated:

> With all my heart I protest what I have known—men received with all warmth of simplicity, and quietly leading unsuspecting ones away to their peculiar views, leaving afterwards a leaven of division injurious in its results. Let men be honest.[66]

Such reactions from those inclined to remain undenominational undoubtedly was one factor in the severing of ties. Brethren evangelists had found interdenominational revivalism congenial because of their lack of a developed institutional sense, their concept of an unsophisticated unity based on the essential evangelical message, and the urgent priority which they gave to evangelism. Brethren assemblies had formalized these features, along with several other emphases, into an ecclesiology, but in the years immediately after the 1859 Revival cooperation with fellow evangelicals had marked the Brethren in Scotland. Events in Orkney, however, brought Hopkins and Boswell to the dilemma faced by those who engage in interdenominational evangelism: whether to give greater weight to ecclesiological factors or a shared evangelicalism. It was a dilemma faced by James Haldane himself,

62. K.J. Newton, 'A History of the Brethren in Australia with Particular Reference to the Open Brethren', Dallas Theological Seminary PhD dissertation, 1990, pp. 115-21.

63. Stephen, 'Remarkable Early Days'.

64. 'Cross Purposes', *R*, 17 (1868), p. 400.

65. Intriguingly, a bound multi-volume copy issued by the publishers of *The Latter Rain*, which the present writer has seen, omits the page with Boswell's letter describing the secessions from Westray Baptist Church (see n. 48 above). Did Hurditch, on the ecumenical wing of the Brethren, disapprove when the effects of the event become known and omit the relevant page when binding the multi-volume reprint?

66. Macpherson, *Duncan Matheson*, p. 235; the proximity of this statement to events in Orkney may preclude it being Hopkins and Boswell to whom reference is being made; but more probably, as the critical comments in *The Revival* indicate (see n. 62 above), they were in the forefront of his mind.

whose critique of Orkney religion and its Moderate ministers in his *Journal of a Tour through the Northern Counties of Scotland and the Orkney Isles* (1798) parallel those of Hopkins, and he too had opted for a more separatist stance.[67] Duncan Matheson was determinedly an interdenominational evangelist to the last. Boswell was undoubtedly the 'Mr B.' to whom he said, 'We have nothing to do with the bagging of the game.'[68] But Hopkins and Boswell were brought to a position of separation partly by their pastoral concern for those captured by their message at a time when they were assessing the spiritual state of the existing churches negatively; but more significantly they were also increasingly feeling that only by adopting Brethren practices were Christians truly faithful to the New Testament. To belong to an existing denomination—even an evangelical one—was regarded as being sectarian, as belonging to a party, but paradoxically it could only be avoided by completely dissociating from all other churches and belonging to an assembly alone. The actions of the two men in Orkney, at a time when there were few assemblies in Scotland, represented a turning point for the movement in the country. The acerbic reaction to existing churches which was latent in mid-Victorian revivalism, reinforced by earlier Brethren criticisms of mainline denominations, would henceforth explicitly exist alongside the ecumenism of the earlier 1860s and would eventually predominate over it within Scottish Open Brethren until the later twentieth century. Soon the increasingly more separatist attitudes of Hopkins and Boswell, first seen so starkly in Orkney, would be spread throughout the whole British Brethren movement and transmitted by their influence to the rest of the English-speaking world.[69] There had been an early pre-sectarian phase of the movement in Scotland, but by the later 1860s it was being superseded. Ironically, those who regretted its passing in Scotland cited the interdenominational preaching of Hopkins and Boswell in Orkney as the ideal.[70]

The tension between evangelical ecumenism and separatism would also mark the later history of the Orkney Brethren. By the early twentieth century, emigration had greatly diminished Brethren numbers in Orkney and the assemblies were thereafter to remain small.[71] However, Thomas Groat, an interdenominational colporteur in

---

67. Deryck E. Lovegrove, 'Unity and separation: contrasting elements in the thought and practice of Robert and James Alexander Haldane', in Keith Robbins (ed.), *Studies in Church History: Subsidia*, 7 (Oxford, 1990), pp. 153-77.

68. Duncan Matheson quoted in [Alexander Marshall], *Wandering Lights: a stricture on the doctrines and methods of Brethrenism. A review by A.M.* (Glasgow, 3rd edn, n.d.), p. 17; 'Mr. B.' is reported as later becoming Brethren. For the association between the Matheson and Boswell see Macpherson, *Matheson*, pp. 177-79; and J.A. Boswell, 'The Open position', *Needed Truth*, 12 (1900), p. 74.

69. For Alexander Marshall's account of this transmission see CBA 2409, Alexander Marshall to P.F. Bruce 12 October [n.d.]; there is a note at the end in Professor F.F. Bruce's handwriting, 'From Alexander Marshall to P.F Bruce—1926 or 27 I reckon'.

70. J.R. Caldwell to Alexander Marshall, 30 August 1909, quoted in John Hawthorn, *Alexander Marshall: evangelist, author and pioneer* (Glasgow, [1929]), pp. 137-38.

71. James Stephen to the editor, *OH*, 19 July 1916.

Orkney in this period, felt that the Christian Brethren were 'exceedingly kind, and zealous in its encouragement of all evangelistic work'.[72] The Kirkwall assembly in the first half of the twentieth century accepted to the Lord's supper evangelicals from other Christian bodies, including, at a time when there was no Baptist church in the town, members of that denomination.[73] In the poet Robert Rendall the assembly possessed during this period an individual who was supremely integrated with both Orcadian evangelicalism and the general culture.[74] The delicacy of the balance among Scottish Brethren, however, can once more be seen in Westray. In the winter of 1903–04 revival again came to the island, and the Brethren initially joined in the services with the Baptists, only to dissociate themselves when the minister leading them asked specific individuals to pray, thereby, in Brethren eyes, suppressing the Spirit.[75] Once again, revival had united evangelicals; once again church procedure had separated them. For most Scottish Brethren, ecclesiological rectitude tended to triumph over a shared gospel.[76]

---

72. Thomas Groat, *Thirty Years a Colporteur* (Kirkwall, 1939), p. 38; Groat was for a while a member of the assembly in Kirkwall.

73. OA, D27/6/1, Robert Rendall to G.C.D. Howley, 9 April 1956.

74. Neil Dickson (ed.), *An Island Shore: the life and work of Robert Rendall* (Kirkwall, 1990).

75. Oral information from Jack Oddie, Kirkwall, August 1989.

76. The help of Mrs Katherine M. Gordon, Mr Ian McDowell, the Revd Dr William D. McNaughton, the late Mr Jack Oddie and the archivists of the Orkney Archive in compiling this paper is gratefully acknowledged. Interpretations advanced in the paper are, of course, the writer's own.

CHAPTER 7

Brethren in Bearwood: The Earliest Days[1]

Jean M. Johnson

Introduction

This study aims to assess objectively some available primary source material from the Victorian era relating to the Bearwood assembly founded by Swaine Bourne in Birmingham, a large West Midlands conurbation.[2] Additionally, it uses comparative material from accounts of two nineteenth-century assemblies: Edmund Gosse's jaundiced account of his Brethren upbringing from his birth in 1849 until 1870, in *Father and Son* (1907) which is widely cited as evidence of Brethren worship and practice in the Victorian era;[3] and from the Barnstaple assembly in the time of Robert Chapman, a prominent figure in the congregation which was founded just before Gosse's birth. Coincidentally Barnstaple is, like Gosse's assembly, in Devon, and until his death in 1923, Swaine Bourne, the leading brother at Bearwood, had close links with Barnstaple through Chapman: Bourne attended his funeral and led the memorial service.[4]

This study analyses the class composition of the Bearwood assembly and the role of women, and examines whether the nature and model of leadership or ministry presented is typical of assemblies in this period. The practice of worship, including baptismal practice, and of theology, is considered. Finally, the depiction of missionary activity is assessed. These central questions are addressed using evidence from Bearwood with some comparisons to Barnstaple and Gosse's St Marychurch.

---

1. This work is dedicated to the memory of my father, John Edwin Johnson, a lifelong, loyal worker in the Manchester assemblies.

2. [Swaine Bourne] 'Records of Bearwood Meeting Room 1881–1897' and 'Records of Bearwood Meeting Room 1898–1915'; 'Bearwood Road Meeting Room, Ledger No. 2, 1913–22'

3. For a discussion of the reliability of Gosse's account, see Timothy C.F. Stunt, 'Brethren or Philistine?', *BAHNR* 2.1 (2000), pp. 13-16.

4. *North Devon Journal*, 19 and 26 June 1902.

Background

The earliest known assembly in Birmingham was at Waterloo Street, near the Town Hall. The Quaker banker Sampson Lloyd founded it in 1838, and was joined after two years by his father Samuel, a prominent Quaker minister;[5] Peter Greenhill Anderson, a Scottish schoolmaster appears to have been active in it by 1839.[6] Anderson was 'a great friend' of Chapman.[7] No records from this assembly survive, but Leonard Barton[8] recounts how Swaine Bourne met Susan Bridgman, who had been baptized by Chapman at Barnstaple, at the Central Hall, Great Charles Street, which dated from the mid-nineteenth century. This was very near to Waterloo Street. Bourne's granddaughter, Susie, recalled the story that, once he set eyes on Susan, Swaine determined to marry her![9] Having married in 1871, they lived in Edgbaston, but joined Edward Palser and others in nearby Bearwood for the Lord's Supper in 1879, in a rented upper room. The Bearwood Old Meeting Room opened in January 1881. A new building in Bearwood Road, whose plans were commissioned by the Bournes in celebration of their Silver Wedding, opened in June 1896. Barton's account is valuable for its use of minutes of oversight meetings (which I was unable to trace), and his list of baptisms,[10] but he does not reference sources. The later centenary history[11] is especially valuable for the wealth of primary sources cited. There are centenary publications for several Birmingham assemblies,[12] but only Bearwood has detailed records. Those from Camp Hill, demolished when the ring road was built in the 1950s, were stolen, and other assemblies appear not to have kept records until recent times.

Leaving central Birmingham in a westerly direction, one travels along the Hagley Road, where the Bournes lived. This, and an area mainly to the south of it, is in the prosperous Edgbaston suburb. About three miles from the centre, Bearwood Road branches off to the north. Bearwood was inhabited by 1278 and a Bear Inn has existed since the late seventeenth century. The area was still extensive woodland until the late nineteenth century,[13] when the rural population was 1,200. The area around the Inn included an ironmonger's, a boot and shoe shop, a boot repairer and wine merchants. This was where Bourne built the first place of worship, ten years before

5. Tim Grass, *Gathering to His Name: the Story of Brethren in Britain and Ireland* (Carlisle, 2006), p. 57.

6. Neil T. R. Dickson, *Brethren in Scotland 1838–2000* (Carlisle, 2003) p. 35 n. 50.

7. Hy. Pickering, *Chief Men Among The Brethren* (Glasgow, 1931) p. 36.

8. Leonard G. Barton, *Bearwood Chapel: one hundred years of witness 1879–1979* (Halesowen, 1979).

9. Miss Susie Bourne was interviewed in 10 September 2001; she died early in 2005.

10. Barton, *Bearwood Chapel*, pp. 3, 38-39.

11. [Anon] *Bearwood Chapel Centenary, 1896–1996* (n.pl., n.d.).

12. Anon., *Camp Hill Gospel Hall, Bordesley Centenary Year 1881–1981* (n.pl., n.d.); Anon., *Tiverton Christian Fellowship (1893–1993)* (n.pl., n.d.).

13. Tim Cookin, *The Staffordshire Encyclopaedia* (n.pl., n.d.), p. 38.

the nearby Anglican church was built.[14] At the time, 'Bearwood Road was little more than a lane with very tall trees.'[15]

Primary Sources

An extensive manuscript source is available for Bearwood assembly.[16] It was started by Swaine Bourne and continued by his son, and provides a wealth of information, easily accessible to scholars since it is now in the Christian Brethren Archive in the John Rylands University Library, Manchester. Detailed weekly records allow analysis of attendance at the Breaking of Bread to be made. Gospel meeting preachers are named and their text and theme given. Their addresses are included. Since this source is extensive, analysis primarily relates to 1881 and 1891, so as to correspond with census returns consulted. The records have been scanned for other relevant material, such as special services, baptisms, visiting preachers and missionary references. There is no address list of members, but a proportion can be traced in censuses through Christian names and spouse or children. The addresses of preachers were altered frequently, presumably giving an 1897 address at the end of volume one; this also made tracing difficult. Nevertheless, these and the Bourne marriage certificate, reproduced in the *Bearwood Chapel Centenary*, provide useful evidence on occupations of assembly members or preachers.

The monthly journals of *The Missionary Echo* consist mainly of invaluable letters from missionaries. Summaries of missionary giving are useful. Unfortunately, the first publication was not until 1872. The first two years were examined for Barnstaple missionaries, then 1881 and 1891 issues used (as for Bourne's records) for both Bearwood and Barnstaple along with checks for information on missionaries named elsewhere. The centenary record of Brethren missionary endeavour is useful for a crosscheck on other missionary accounts, such as that of Vine,[17] for its extensive index and lists, and for records of missionary gifts.[18]

14. David Winters, 'Chapel marks 100 years of worship', *Smethwick Telephone*, 21 June 1979.

15. W. Ellery Jephcott, 'Origin of Bearwood', *Smethwick Telephone*, 1 December 1951.

16. [Bourne], 'Records...1881–1897', and 'Records...1898–1915'.

17. William E. Vine, *Some Birmingham missionaries in God's great harvest field* (Birmingham, 1914).

18. W.T. Stunt *et al.*, *Turning the world upside down: a century of missionary endeavour* (Bath, 1972), pp. 30-31, 603.

Early Brethren in Bearwood

Vocabulary

Primary sources copied or cited in the Bearwood centenary publication[19] give ample evidence of a distinctively Brethren vocabulary. The form certifying a 'Place of Meeting for Religious Worship', completed by Swaine Bourne as 'Proprietor' on 17 August 1896, identifies those meeting as 'Brethren', whilst the poster advertising the opening Services on 16 January 1881 refers to 'Bearwood Road Meeting Room.' An article in *The Smethwick Telephone* in August 1896 also called it a 'Meeting Room'; the 'principles...maintained...are known as those of "Brethren" who meet for "fellowship and the Breaking of Bread every Lord's Day morning" and "evening Gospel services"'. When registered for marriages in 1913, the building was named as 'Meeting Room'; Bourne, who died in 1923, made provision in his will for trustees of the 'New Meeting Room' (i.e., the 1896 building) 'for the preaching of the Gospel according to the doctrines of the Brethren known as "Open" Brethren'. The 1881 poster describes 'Lord's day' services as 'Morning at 11, for worship and Breaking of Bread' and 'Evening at 6.30, Preaching the Gospel'.

Bourne[20] prefaces all dated Sundays as 'Lord's Day'. He records 'Worship and the Breaking of Bread' and 'Preaching of the Gospel'. Those who 'joined in fellowship' in 'the breaking of Bread' included 'brothers' and 'sisters'. His opening pages refer to 'prayer dedicating the work to God' and a 'Fellowship Tea' on Saturday 15 January 1881 at the 'Bearwood Meeting Room'. He states 'Room registered as a place for Religious Worship for Christians No. of Register 25606'.

This vocabulary is echoed in the literature of Chapman and Gosse. Holmes[21] refers to 'the new chapel' erected in Grosvenor Street, Barnstaple, which 'had no special name, but was usually referred to as "The Room"—a common term among the early brethren'. Ware called it 'Bear Street Meeting House' and Chapman 'Bear Street Chapel'. Later it was named Grosvenor Street Chapel. Chapman's correspondence referred to 'Christians assembled at Bear Street'. In *Choice Sayings*,[22] Chapman refers to 'brothers' and 'sisters', also called 'saints', whilst this term is also used in his hymns, such as 'No more seek we a resting place...';[23] Gosse is faithful to tradition in most of his vocabulary, such as 'saints', 'believers', 'brothers' and 'sisters', and 'the Lord's Day'.[24] Primary sources are more explicit on the exact titles of Sunday services, and prefer the term 'Breaking of Bread' for the communion service. The term 'vestry'[25] is never used, and there is variety in terms used for the

---

19. *Bearwood Chapel Centenary.*

20. [Bourne], 'Records'.

21. Frank Holmes, *Brother Indeed: the life of Robert Cleaver Chapman* (London, 1956), pp. 48-50.

22. Holmes, *Chapman*, Selection, pp. 112-14.

23. Echoes of Service, *Hymns of Light and Love* (Bath, n.d.), No. 595.

24. Edmund Gosse, *Father and Son*, pp. 12 and 68, 167, 87 and 165 respectively. All references to are to the Penguin edition (London, 1970).

25. Gosse, *Father and Son*, p. 131.

place of worship: 'Meeting Room' is used consistently at Bearwood and sometimes at Barnstaple.

Class Composition

Both Bourne's profession—artist in stained glass—as identified on his marriage certificate,[26] and Chapman's—solicitor—correspond with Gosse's professional background. Bourne's wife, Susan, had no named occupation but their fathers were, respectively, a 'farmer' and an 'assistant overseer'. In dress, the Bournes appear cultivated as is shown from extant photographs of them,[27] whilst the description of Bourne's stained glass composition, now displayed in the foyer of Grosvenor Church, Barnstaple, says he is a 'stained glass manufacturer'. Bourne, a native of Kingsbury, Warwickshire, founded his stained glass manufacturing firm in Birmingham in 1868,[28] and among his commissions he produced the stained glass for Halesowen Parish Church and various churches in Devon.[29] His stained glass occupied a door panel in Susie's house until recently, and the family retain an amateur interest in stained glass.

Tables 1 and 2 summarize attendance at Bearwood. Eight people were present at the first Breaking of Bread in the Meeting Room on 16 January 1881, and another three are recorded within the first month. Additionally, Ann, wife of William Parkes, was received into fellowship on 24 July 1881. Of these twelve people, the two Bournes are recorded in the Warwickshire Census for Edgbaston, Birmingham, then, as now, in the more affluent part of the city. Six of the remaining ten were traced in the Staffordshire Census, in the Bearwood village part of Smethwick. Harriet Pullinger, aged eighteen, daughter of Br[other]. Pullinger, lived in as domestic servant to the Bournes. Details of another seven believers were traced in the 1891 Staffordshire Census. Four lived close to the assembly, and another three in nearby Smethwick. Apart from the Bournes, the occupations of the believers in 1881 were broadly similar to those given by Gosse, but the picture had changed by 1891, showing some occupations better described as artisan.

26. *Bearwood Chapel Centenary.*

27. For example, see <http://www.qlhs.org.uk/oracle/the-poplars/the-poplars.htm> [accessed 25 December 2005].

28 SAGB, 'Kendrick Swaine Bourne 1872–1960', *The Journal of Stained Glass* 13.4 (1962–63), p. 590.

29. Conversation with Miss Susie Bourne, 10 September 2001.

Table 1: Bearwood Meeting Room: believers in fellowship, 16 January–6 February 1881

Name	Age	Occupation	Address
Swaine Bourne	36	Artist in stained glass	174 Hagley Rd, Edgbaston
Susan Bourne	39		174 Hagley Rd, Edgbaston
Hannah Harrison	63	Laundress	Cottage on left, Bearwood Rd
Br. Horton			Could not identify
Br. Newton			Could not identify
Edward Palser	51	General draper	366 Bearwood Rd
Elizabeth Palser	52	General draper	366 Bearwood Rd
William Parkes*	38	Carpenter	331 Bearwood Rd
Ann Parkes	30	Laundress	331 Bearwood Rd
John Pickman	33	Gardener/domestic servant	336 Bearwood Rd
Br. Pullinger			Could not identify
Sr. Whiston			Could not identify

* Father, John, at 333 Bearwood Road, was a master carpenter.
Source: 1881 Census.

Table 2: Bearwood Meeting Room: additional believers in fellowship, 1891

Name	Age	Occupation	Address
Charles Alexander	26	Brass bedstead fitter	58 Baldwin St
Kate Alexander	27		58 Baldwin St
John Carless	49	Screw machine fitter	42 Tiverton Rd
Frank Fowler	48	Warehouse Clerk	246 Bearwood Rd
Elijah Madeley	39	Gardener	113 Three Shires Oak Rd
Walter Vennells	39	Station Master	360 Bearwood Rd
Jane Vennells	52		360 Bearwood Rd

Source: 1891 Census.

Apart from Bourne, three other preachers were traced in the 1891 Census. Whereas members lived very close to the assembly, these came from the Warwickshire Census area, living in the more prosperous Edgbaston district of Birmingham or nearby Sutton Coldfield. Samuel Chase was a traveller, staying with Leonard Wall, who was a bank clerk, but by 1891 had become a bank cashier. George Inchley's occupation as 'Stationery B.O.' is unclear, but these preachers were certainly not 'peasants'.[30] No Barnstaple occupations could be verified, but Holmes[31] refers to William Hake as a 'cultured man' who 'carried on a school' in Bideford in the 1840s. Henry Heath had talents demanding 'something better than a village schoolmastership' but moved to Hackney in 1848, becoming a 'gifted and consecrated teacher' in the assembly of Gosse's young days. One of his hymns is still used today.[32] There is evidence of some 'cultured' or professional people in both assemblies, then, with a broad cross-section of the working classes, including artisans. Certainly, by 1891 Bearwood was by no means an 'essentially lower-class gathering'[33] with what Gosse called 'peasants' or 'pious rustics'.[34]

Role of Women

Five of the first twelve believers at Bearwood were women. Bourne[35] gave detailed weekly attendance charts, by gender, for the Breaking of Bread, from 1884. An analysis for the first quarter of 1884 and of 1891 is given in Table 3.

Table 3: Weekly attendance by gender for the Breaking of Bread, 1884 and 1891

Year	1884			1891		
	Number	Average present	% attendance	Number	Average present	% attendance
Brothers	8	5.8	73	6	4.3	72
Sisters	15	7.2	48	7	4.2	59

Source: [Swaine Bourne], 'Records'.

Numbers of each gender attending weekly were similar because women attended less frequently, perhaps because of family commitments. There is no evening attendance record. All preachers were male. Susan Bourne was a musician and probably accompanied on occasion, such as when Swaine sang 'Blessed be the fountain of blood'[36] on 15 March 1891. Gertie Cook, who attended Tiverton Road assembly, Birmingham, from 1897, recalls that in the early days she played the violin there, and her sister the organ.[37] Missionary records show that couples often went out together; on occasion, the wife wrote the letter to *Echoes of Service*. Both Miss Lancaster (1894) and Miss Wakelin (1895) went out as missionaries from

30. Gosse, *Father and Son*, p. 87.
31. Holmes, *Chapman*, p. 44.
32. *Hymns of Light and Love* ([Bath, 1900], No. 20.
33. John Wolffe, 'Evangelicals, women and community in nineteenth-century Britain, Study Guide' (Open University module A425; Milton Keynes, 1994), p. 67.
34. Gosse, *Father and Son*, p. 87.
35. [Bourne], 'Records'.
36. [Bourne], 'Records'.
37. Miss Gertie Cook, interview, 21 June 2001.

Birmingham, but subsequently married overseas believers.[38] Primary sources confirm that women undertook 'pastoral work'[39] and may have made musical contributions. Their attendance rate was lower than men.

The role of women may not be fully recorded. At Chapman's funeral, the principal male mourners are named, but 'A large number of ladies joined in the procession';[40] however, no names are given! Nevertheless, Elizabeth Paget had moved to Barnstaple in the late 1830s, where she founded a Sunday School,[41] and she 'played a leading part' in activities 'for the benefit of the poor', including a 'soup kitchen'.[42] She later assisted Chapman with hospitality at New Buildings. Gosse's mother, Emily, was a writer who published a number of religious tracts and pious poetry.[43]

Leadership and Ministry

Bourne was clearly the leading brother in Bearwood: his records for 1881 and 1891 show that in both years he preached eight times, whilst others, like Inchley, preached no more than two or three times annually. Evangelists, such as Captain Kramer in January 1883, Ratcliffe in April 1891, and Lawes in March 1894, preached every evening for a week or more, sometimes, as on 15 March 1891, at the Gaiety Concert Hall. Thus, there is no evidence of 'one man ministry'.

There is no evidence of a 'minister', such as Gosse implies,[44] but some Brethren, such as Chapman, exerted individual, unpaid leadership assisted by others. Chapman led at Barnstaple, but received no payment, often not even having money for provisions for guests, commenting, 'We must pray about it.'[45] Writing in 1890 of Hake, whom he worked with for almost thirty years, Chapman described him as 'my loved yoke-fellow',[46] so it appears that he shared responsibility. All three of his biographers assert that he did not exert sole ministry, and worked with elders or 'oversight'.[47] Bearwood records show he found time to visit in 1883, 1885 (with Hake) and 1888, sometimes, but not always, preaching. At Barnstaple, even at age ninety-seven, he preached for an hour or more, although 'other brethren took turns with the Gospel service'.[48]

---

38. Vine, *Birmingham Missionaries*, pp. 7, 9.
39. Gosse, *Father and Son*, pp. 92-93.
40. *North Devon Journal*, 19 June 1902.
41. Robert L. Petersen, *Robert Chapman: a biography* (Neptune, NJ, 1995), p. 77.
42. Holmes, *Chapman*, p. 55.
43. For examples of her work see the extracts in Robert Boyd, *Emily Gosse: a life of faith and works* (Inverness, 2004).
44. Gosse, *Father and Son*, pp. 91, 129.
45. Holmes, *Chapman*, p. 38.
46. Petersen, *Chapman*, p. 38.
47. Holmes, *Chapman*, p. 73.
48. Holmes, *Chapman*, pp. 50, 104.

Baptismal Practice

Gosse refers[49] to adult baptism, whether indoors or out, but his own baptism, aged ten, was unusually early. In some cases, baptism was despite parental opposition; in others, it followed soon after conversion, prior to Breaking Bread. The dramatic story of Susan Bourne (née Bridgman) being baptized in the River Taw by Chapman, against her Anglican parents' wishes, was confirmed to me by her granddaughters. Neither the early premises at Barnstaple nor Bearwood had a baptistery, so Bearwood baptisms prior to 1896 took place at Great Charles Street, or Tiverton Road, Selly Oak, south Birmingham.[50] Gertie Cook recalls her baptism there in 1908, when she was fifteen. Kendrick Swaine Bourne, baptized in 1888, would have been a similar age.[51] No baptisms below this age are recorded. In some cases, baptism followed on rapidly from conversion: on Monday 5 March 1894, at the Bearwood evangelistic service conducted by A. Lawes, 'Mrs Alexander and her daughter found blessing through faith in believing.' An address to Christians on 'believers' Baptism' followed on 7 March, and on 19 March, at Tiverton Road, Lawes baptized Charles and Kate Alexander, along with four others. They broke Bread for the first time on 25 March.

Worship and Theology

Sunday worship included the Breaking of Bread and gospel preaching. Chapman composed many hymns for worship; all those used at his funeral and memorial service, led by Bourne, were his own composition.[52] Sunday schools were also a significant part of Sundays, and one was commenced in Bearwood on 1 October 1893, with seventeen children, rising to seventy a year later.[53] In the summer months, open air preaching followed the gospel service. This is recorded annually from 1882 in Bearwood, mainly in July and August. Preachers included Bourne, Pickman and Vennells. An extant photograph shows Chapman preaching at an open-air service,[54] as he did, for example, in Bearwood on 23 August 1885. A Bearwood poster advertising the opening of the Bearwood Road Meeting Room on 16 January 1881 reproduced in the centenary history[55] also advertises 'Reading and Study of the Scripture' on Wednesday evening. This poster has scriptural references relevant to each service, for example Acts 4.12 and 10.43 for the gospel service, and it states: 'Seats are free'; similarly, at Barnstaple, seats were 'purchased by no worldly pew-

49. Gosse, *Father and Son*, pp. 125-28, 132.
50. Barton, *Bearwood Chapel*, p. 38.
51. [Bourne], 'Records', and 1881 Census.
52. *North Devon Journal*, 19 and 26 June 1902.
53. [Bourne], 'Records'.
54. Holmes, *Chapman*, facing p. 73.
55. *Bearwood Chapel Centenary*

rent'.[56] Sunday prayer meetings are attested, and larger gatherings of Brethren were held on occasion, for example at Leominster in 1882.[57]

Controversies regarding prophecy occurred within the Brethren movement, and a letter from B.W. Newton states that for years Chapman 'rejected the idea of the Millennium altogether'.[58] In 1881, about half the gospel texts at Bearwood were from the Gospels or Acts, seven from the Old Testament and the remainder, all but two, from Pauline Epistles or Hebrews; the two exceptions were from Revelation 22 and refer neither to millennial teaching, nor to Rome! Presumably, such teaching when given was to believers. The preaching on 25 December 1881 was on Galatians 6.7, with no mention of Christmas. However, there was a fellowship tea on 28 December 1885. Gosse, therefore, is certainly correct in presenting Sunday as a busy day.[59] His accounts of worship appear reliable, including non-observance of Christmas,[60] but it would seem that teaching on prophecy and 'the so-called Church of Rome'[61] was rarely given at gospel services, at least in Bearwood.

Missionaries

The *Missionary Echo* was published monthly from 1872. However, Brethren missionary activity commenced, with A.N. Groves, much earlier. In 1834, George Müller founded the Scriptural Knowledge Institution.[62] It aimed 'To aid in supplying the wants of missionaries and missionary schools'. By 1872, over £116,000 had been collected.[63] In 1836, through Chapman's encouragement, George Beer, a shoemaker, and William Bowden, a stonemason, went to India with their wives, labouring until death in 1853 and 1874 respectively. Apart from missionary activity, they gave medical help during epidemics and Mrs Beer ran both a boarding school for caste girls and a co-educational school.[64] The enormous Brethren commitment to missionary work is not adequately identified by Gosse. Moreover, foremost activity in the movement at the time of which he wrote was not 'among horrid tropical niggers',[65] as Gosse alleged, but in Roman Catholic countries and in Asia.

Chapman had great missionary interest, visiting Spain four times between 1834 and 1871. Walking around Ireland in 1848, he wrote, 'I found in Spain indifference and scorn; here is a vexed and troubled conscience seeking rest and not knowing how

56. Holmes, *Chapman*, p. 49.

57. Petersen, *Chapman*, p. 115.

58. Petersen, *Chapman*, p. 108.

59. Gosse, *Father and Son*, pp. 165-67.

60. Gosse, *Father and Son*, pp. 38, 63, 72, 83, 102-103.

61. Gosse, *Father and Son*, pp. 65-67.

62. See Neil Summerton, 'George Müller and the Financing of the Scriptural Knowledge Institution', ch. 5 above.

63. Stunt *et al.*, *Witnessing*, pp. 30, 603.

64. Stunt *et al.*, *Witnessing*, pp. 24, 91-92.

65. Gosse, *Father and Son*, p. 100.

to obtain it.'[66] This highlights concern to take the gospel to Roman Catholics; Spain received many Brethren missionaries. Out of the twenty-one countries with Brethren missionaries in 1872, the annual *Echoes* report shows seven in Europe and the remainder mainly in Asia. Only South Africa and British Guiana could have had black-skinned inhabitants. The 1881 reports have letters most months from Barnstaple missionaries: Albert Fenn and his wife in Spain, Charles Faithfull in France, Henry Payne in Spain, and Henry Soltau in China. Gifts from Barnstaple are recorded most months, and on five occasions from Birmingham assemblies.

By 1891, Albert Fenn and Charles Faithfull were still sending reports; H.S. Turrall and Miss Hillis from Birmingham were in the work in Spain, and Miss Wakelin joined them in 1895. Gifts from both Bearwood and Barnstaple are recorded. However, it is with the Kinghams, from Moseley, that Bearwood interest is clearest. In the months before he went to China, Harry Kingham preached there about every three weeks, and wrote a farewell message in Swaine Bourne's record after his valedictory service on 16 October 1894. Tragically, he and his wife and daughter were martyred in China in 1906.

Conclusion

Study of early Brethren is hampered by failure of many assemblies to keep records or deposit documents in the Brethren resource, or other library. However, the exception of Bearwood, supplemented by references to the literature of Chapman and Gosse, presents us with a picture of Victorian assembly life. Gosse perhaps under-represents the role of women, and over-emphasizes prophecy, at least in relation to gospel preaching. Whilst Chapman seemed to have a similar role to that of Gosse's father, Bourne's less central role at Bearwood may have been more typical of assemblies. Gosse considerably under-represents Brethren missionary activity.

The pattern of assembly life seen in Bearwood evidently continued into the later twentieth century. My initial interest in this study arose because my father, who was active in the assemblies of Manchester from the mid- to the late-twentieth century, repeatedly said that 'one man ministry' was against assembly principles. Bourne's role at Bearwood would have been acceptable to my father; he may have justified Chapman's greater prominence by noting that he was unpaid. We always spoke of our assembly as 'the meeting' and talked even of 'the morning meeting'. This terminology is in line with use of 'Meeting Room' at Bearwood. Bourne's evident generosity in commissioning a new building to coincide with his silver wedding celebration is in line with my father's oft-repeated 'If he is not Lord of all, then he is not Lord at all.' Preaching the gospel was central to my father's life, whether on Sunday night, in the open air, or at tent meetings. All of these were a feature of the Bearwood assembly. The most exciting event of our year was attendance at the Easter missionary conference. This shows continuing Brethren commitment to worldwide mission. The message, and the ultimate aim of the Brethren, whether in Manchester

66. Petersen, *Chapman*, pp. 12, 96.

or Bearwood, was, as was often written behind the platform, ‘We preach Christ, and him crucified.’

CHAPTER 8

A Bulwark of Evangelicalism: Brethren as a Lay Movement in England in the 1930s[1]

Roger Shuff

Undergirding any worthwhile study of the subsequent development of the Brethren movement must lie a thorough and perceptive understanding of Brethren beginnings. Here at once I gratefully acknowledge the seminal role of Harold Rowdon's *The Origins of the Brethren 1825–1850*; a work that represented a new benchmark in Brethren studies. With this firm foundation in place the present paper moves us forward in time to examine the mature movement in England in the 1930s.[2] It comprised—as it had done since the schism of 1848—two main streams. One of these had become widely known as 'Open Brethren' and was distinguished by the insistence on the independence of each local assembly or meeting (as Brethren churches were known). The other stream had initially been led by John Nelson Darby (1800–82) and was, by contrast, connexional, in the sense that there was a high degree of interdependence between assemblies. This strand of the movement suffered a number of schisms in the late nineteenth and early twentieth centuries, and has been popularly dubbed 'Exclusive Brethren'.[3] For the sake of clarity the Open Brethren stream will be identified hereafter as 'independent Brethren', and the Exclusive stream as 'connexional Brethren', since an open communion table was, in practice, neither a universal characteristic of Open Brethren, nor wholly unknown among Exclusive Brethren.

As an indication of strength there were 1,182 congregations of independent Brethren recorded in England and Wales in 1933, the highest figure to that date, representing a probable membership in the region of 50,000.[4] Unlike independent

---

1. The original version of this paper was presented at a conference on the laity within Protestant evangelicalism at St Andrews University in 1999. It draws upon research undertaken for the opening chapters of the present writer's *Searching for the True Church: Brethren and evangelicals in mid-twentieth century England* (Carlisle, 2005).

2. This paper does not seek to comment on Brethrenism in other parts of the United Kingdom: Northern Ireland, Scotland or Wales.

3. Cf. Roger Shuff, 'Open to closed: the growth of Exclusivism among Brethren in Britain 1848–1953', *BAHNR*, 1 (1997), pp. 10-23.

4. Neil Summerton, *Local Churches for a New Century* (London, 1996), p. 23; Peter Brierley, Graham Brown, *et al, The Christian Brethren as the Nineties Began* (Carlisle, 1993), pp. 89, 90; *Whitaker's Almanac 1935* estimated total Brethren strength at 80,000

Brethren, the connexional stream of the movement was made up of a number of distinct factions, each functioning as a self-contained network of assemblies. The combined membership of the four principal networks in the 1930s was estimated in the region of 30,000 in more than 800 congregations.[5] The largest of these networks was the 'Taylor Brethren', a worldwide network under the leadership of James Taylor (1870–1953) of New York, with 463 meetings in England and Wales recorded in 1933.[6] The 'Kelly-Lowe Brethren' were a network which was formed by the amalgamation in 1926 of the two groups formed through schism in the late nineteenth century by the followers of William Kelly (1821–1906) and W.J. Lowe (1839–1927). In England and Wales this combined network had around 140 meetings in 1939.[7] The 'Glanton Brethren' had their origins in an early twentieth century controversy among Taylor Brethren over the meeting in the Northumberland town of that name, and, in England and Wales, numbered around 130 meetings.[8] These three groups shared a common heritage in the stream of Brethren which had followed J.N. Darby in the division of 1848. The fourth main grouping, the Churches of God, usually known as 'Needed Truth Brethren' (so-called after the journal of this name which promulgated their views), emerged in the late nineteenth century from among independent Brethren, the opponents of Darby. Having abandoned the principle of the independency of the local assembly they established in its place a universal structure of church life and government. It is, therefore, appropriate to regard this group as connexional Brethren, notwithstanding their origins. With the number of Churches of God assemblies in England estimated at around fifty, they represented a small but distinctive attempt by Brethren to demonstrate the reality of collective church fellowship.[9]

Foremost among the unifying characteristics of the Brethren movement as a whole was the centrality of the celebration of the Lord's supper. 'No Assembly of Believers, desiring to worship as the Church of the first century worshipped, can place the communion service...anywhere but in the central position', held P.W. Petter, a teacher among independent Brethren.[10] The Lord's Supper was equally the ecclesiological touchstone of the networks of connexional Brethren. Speaking of the Supper, a leader among Taylor Brethren declared, 'I know nothing greater than this remembrance of the Lord Jesus.' Reflecting on its defining significance for the Brethren movement, the 'recovery of the supper', he held, represented the 'greatest event in the nineteenth century', when 'little groups of believers learnt to assemble,

---

of which Open Brethren represented five eighths, i.e. 50,000. No membership records are available for Brethren congregations and other statistical information is fragmentary.

5. *Whitaker's Almanac 1935*.

6. W.B. Turpin (compiler), *List of Meetings June 1933* (Southampton, 1933).

7. Edwin Cross [a member of the Kelly-Lowe-Glanton group] to the author, 17 July 1998.

8. Lists of meetings indicate 149 in 1925, falling to 96 in 1953.

9. Approximated from *List of Assemblies,* 1898, 1901; and interview with former member, 23 March 1998.

10. P.W. Petter, *Assembly Service* (London, [1930]), p. 47.

meeting together in simplicity in barns, in houses, in out-of-the-way places to remember the Lord in breaking of bread'.[11] This ecclesiological emphasis set Brethren as a movement apart from wider evangelicalism, where it was unusual to give central place to the regular observance of a sacrament.[12] 'Alone among the Protestant sects, this little body has made the chief point of its Sunday worship the Breaking of Bread', noted an Anglo-Catholic reviewer in *The Church Times*.[13]

The Brethren's weekly communion service epitomized the lay ethos which pervaded every aspect of Brethren life and witness. Across each stream and grouping of the movement there was concern for freedom and spontaneity in worship at the Lord's supper, with as many male members of the congregation as possible encouraged to contribute. This was regarded as evidence of the liberty of the Holy Spirit, under whose direction worship was to proceed. 'The principles of the New Testament demand', wrote a contributor to the Kelly-Lowe magazine *Words of Help,* 'that every brother in the assembly (who is not otherwise disqualified) be open or at liberty to be used by the SPIRIT to give out a hymn, engage in prayer, or give thanks, etc.'[14] The open nature of the communion service provided a blueprint which, given regard to individual gifting and gender, dictated that opportunities for public ministry in the widest sense were open to every member of Brethren. The notion of a lay–clerical distinction was thus the complete antithesis of this universal Brethren precept. As regards the promulgation and out-working of this fundamental tenet, there were a variety of emphases to be found across the Brethren movement. For this reason the absolute laity of Brethrenism served in different ways to sustain and reinforce the broader evangelical witness in England prior to the Second World War, a time that has been regarded as its leanest period.[15]

Connexional Brethren, although the smaller section of the movement, were not without significance within evangelicalism as they represented a distinctive way of being church. Here alone in Christendom, it was claimed, could be found an expression of the true church consistent with the New Testament. They appeared an attractive haven in the midst of an evangelical world under threat from the continuing inroads of 'rationalism and ritualism'—as Brethren traditionally labelled the twin

---

11. *Words of Grace and Comfort* [hereafter *WGC*], 14 (1938), p. 70.

12. Neil Dickson, 'Shut in with Thee: the morning meeting among Scottish Open Brethren, 1830s–1960s', in R.N. Swanson (ed.), *Continuity and Change in Christian Worship: Studies in Church History*, 35 (Woodbridge, 1999), p. 289; Neil Summerton, 'The practice of worship', *Christian Brethren Review* 39 (1988), p. 54.

13. Cited by the editor, *Harvester* [hereafter *H*], 16 (1937), p. 121. This somewhat sweeping observation could be qualified by reference to the emerging Pentecostal movement which, influenced to some extent by Brethren, also focused its worship around the Supper.

14. *Words of Help* [hereafter *WH*], 28 (1935), pp. 214-15; cf. *BM*, 49 (1939), pp. 150, 151.

15. David Bebbington holds that evangelicalism in Britain was at its weakest around 1940: Bebbington, *Evangelicalism in Modern Britain: a history from the 1730s to the 1980s* (London, 1989), p. 252.

foes of conservative truth.[16] All groups of connexional Brethren maintained a vehement critique of clericalism and organized worship, which made no distinction between the practice of evangelicals and other traditions in the mainline denominations. For these Brethren untrained leadership was a mark of proud demarcation from the rest of Christendom. It was no shame that Brethren teaching and leadership were in the hands of 'unlikely persons', who nevertheless, in the words of an eminent leader, 'know more than all the [religious] teachers at the present time'. 'Let no one be haughty and turn away from one who may seem...an ignoramus as to religious matters', exhorted James Taylor, leader of Taylor Brethren.[17] Christian truth was the subject of 'spiritual revelation' and could not be established 'by debate', propagated by 'philosophy', or interpreted 'by logic'. This was certainly true of typology, the highly allegorical style of biblical exegesis applied by Brethren particularly to the Old Testament. As a contributor to the Glanton magazine *Scripture Truth* aptly observed, 'Where is your worldly-wise man who would have found the "church" in Adam's rib...or living saints in the boards of the Tabernacle...and a thousand other types, but "God hath revealed them unto *us* by His Spirit".'[18] While Glanton Brethren were glad to acknowledge the continuing existence of evangelists, pastors and teachers, 'it is not that they are trained in colleges', stressed one of their leaders, for theological training was superfluous to the instruction of the Holy Spirit. Their distance from the academic world of theological thought had enabled Brethren across the board to remain largely insulated from critical and theological trends. The dispensational scheme of biblical interpretation which Darby had developed, and the Scofield Reference Bible had popularized, provided Brethren of all shades with a system of biblical understanding which had virtually no point of contact with other approaches to biblical interpretation. It is to Harold Rowdon that I am indebted for the insight that by adhering staunchly to dispensationalism, which was effectively beyond reach of attack by critical scholarship, lay Brethren teaching played a role in preserving core aspects of evangelical thought.[19]

Fundamental to the rejection of clericalism in the minds of connexional Brethren was the belief that, being human and earthly in origin, it ousted Christ and hindered the operation of the Holy Spirit. 'Christian Fellowship knows no other head [than Christ]'; thus, held a well-known teacher with Taylor Brethren, 'giving place to man and to preachers or man-made priests instead of Christ' demonstrates that 'the will of man has place, and Christ as Head and Lord is virtually shut out'. A fellowship where man rules and has the pre-eminent place could not 'be regarded as Christian fellowship'.[20] 'The appointment of a minister, or any attempt to arrange the service

---

16. *Mutual Comfort,* 1 (1908), p. 110.

17. *WGC,* 15 (1939), p. 310.

18. *Scripture Truth* [hereafter *ST*], 27 (1935), p. 188.

19. Harold Rowdon to the author, 12 April 1999. For dispensationalism see E.R. Sandeen, *The Roots of Fundamentalism: British and American Millenarianism, 1830–1930* (Chicago, 1970).

20. H.D'A.C[hampney]., *Christian Fell*owship (Newport, n.d.), p. 7.

or worship of God', taught M.W. Biggs of Taylor Brethren, 'must greatly grieve the Holy Spirit', since it was the 'setting aside practically of the liberty of the Spirit'.[21] For Needed Truth Brethren, 'clerisy' elevated 'one man to do all the praying and preaching for the whole congregation', which was 'baneful to spiritual growth, and grieves the Holy Spirit...'.[22] 'However excellent the persons may be who carry it on, or however good their motives', held Biggs, 'the setting up of a *church order*, or a kind of *service*' which forbade or restricted liberty was iniquitous even if it was done 'in ignorance or inadvertently', since it was 'contrary to the divine commandment'.[23] Clericalism was the hallmark of an 'earthly system of religion' which 'is to be left', declared a Glanton teacher.[24]

A further factor exacerbating the Brethren distaste for everything clerical was the endorsement by many Protestant clergy of so-called '"modernist" teaching'. For a Needed Truth writer, when coupled with 'flagrant departure from the apostolic pattern' in 'matters of organisation and ritual' the effect was to put Protestant movements on a par with Catholicism.[25] Moreover, it was a growing trend, as a contributor to the Taylor Brethren journal, *Words of Grace and Comfort,* lamented: 'What is called progress and enlightenment, aided by education, seems to be steadily victorious, while those who take the place of ministers...are steadily retreating... Once the truth was defended by such, when challenged; now great religious leaders take the lead in weakening the very foundations of truth in men's souls, and in denying the authority and accuracy of the holy Scriptures.'[26] Taylor, using characteristic typological exposition, cast liberal-minded clergy in the role of Absalom (2 Samuel 14); they were men who 'are hostile to Christ yet clothed in a Christian garb. They deny his divinity, deny the atonement, deny foundations of the truth, and yet are clothed in the garb of ministers of Christ... The whole truth of Christianity is being destroyed by these returned murderers...they would kiss the king but hate him; they are preparing for Antichrist and the fabric of Christianity is being destroyed'.[27]

Clericalism was the *bête noire* of all these groups of Brethren, yet there could be inconsistency between principle and practice. Those with a wider outlook could mention clergymen on the contemporary scene, such as the Baptist Keswick speaker Graham Scroggie, with approval.[28] In addition, when a correspondent, identified as 'A Clergyman', wrote a laudatory letter commending a remarkably earthy article on marriage and parenthood in *Words of Help,* the gratification felt by the editor was

---

21. M.W. Biggs, *The Christian's Path in Days of Difficulty* (Hampton Wick, n.d.), p. 42.

22. *Needed Truth,* 42 (1935), p. 235.

23. Biggs, *Christian's Path,* p. 14.

24. *ST,* 28 (1936), p. 130.

25. T.M. Hyland, *Churches of God: New Testament Pattern* (Hayes, n.d.), p. 24.

26. A.E. Myles, 'Good and evil', *WGC,* 15 (1939), p. 254.

27. *WGC,* 14 (1938), pp. 9, 10.

28. *ST,* 29 (1937), p. 178.

almost tangible.[29] However unacceptable the principle of clerisy might be, Brethren in practice were not immune from the adulation of those with such status. For evangelicals outside the movement, the way in which these Brethren dismissed *all* 'earthly' systems of worship, evangelical or otherwise, as displacing Christ and denying the role of Holy Spirit seemed to cast doubt on their own ecclesiastical position, a sensation intensified by the all too apparent departure from conservative truth by many clergy within evangelicalism. Feeling the need to find a purer and more biblical pattern of church life, a number found their way into the several networks of connexional Brethren.[30]

In the later years of the inter-war period it was, however, the autonomous local assemblies of independent Brethren, to be seen meeting in halls and chapels throughout England, which constituted the more familiar face of the Brethren movement in the evangelical world. Characterized by a separatism often noticeably less severe than that of connexional Brethren, independent Brethren had traditionally been a little less damning in their attitude to the wider evangelical scene.[31] Nevertheless, the absence of an ordained ministry was a key factor which set independent Brethren apart, in their own minds, from other denominations, evangelical or otherwise, and was one of the reasons why it was believed that no churches could be found 'nearer the Scriptural pattern' than their own assemblies.[32] Clericalism, it was declared, epitomized the apostasy of 'the religious systems of Christendom' where 'the establishment of an ecclesiastical class of priests was 'flagrantly contrary' to 'the divinely-inspired and authoritative teaching that all believers are priests'.[33] The independent Brethren scholar, F.F. Bruce, recalled hearing the aphorism, 'Clerisy is the sin of sins Godward, as socialism is manward'; a reflection also of the political preoccupations of the time.[34] The evil of clerisy in practice, held the prominent teacher George Goodman, was that it led 'those not clerics to regard themselves as excused from responsibility' so that they become 'mere pew-sitters'.[35]

There was an energy and motivation among independent Brethren in the pre-war years which was fuelled by continuing results in evangelism and church planting. This owed much to the fact that independent Brethren applied the principle of the priesthood of all believers in a way which provided almost unique opportunities for gifted and enthusiastic lay people and dispensed with the need to rely on formally

---

29. *WH,* 28 (1939), p. 181.

30. See, e.g., C. Wood, *Exclusive By-Path* (Evesham, 1976).

31. For the development of the independent wing of the movement, see F. Roy Coad, *A History of the Brethren Movement* (Exeter, 2nd edn, 1976).

32. H. Lowman, 'Why I joined the Brethren', *Journal of the Christian Brethren Research Fellowship* [hereafter *JCBRF*], 10 (1965), p. 14; F.F. Bruce, *In Retrospect* (London, 2nd edn, 1993), p. 316.

33. *BM*, 48 (1938), p. 10.

34. Bruce, *In Retrospect*, p. 26.

35. G. Goodman, *God's Principles of Gathering* (London, n.d.), p. 54.

trained or ordained leaders to spearhead their endeavours.[36] An editorial early in 1938 by Henry Pickering of *The Witness*, the widely-read independent Brethren journal, reflected the upbeat mood at this time:

> Brethren (so-called)...have never increased at the rate at which they do today. Numerous new halls have been built, Assemblies are being started in many places, young folks are increasing in most meetings. One main cause is, they cleave to the Fundamentals of the Faith.[37]

By contrast, commented F.A. Tatford in the same issue, 'denominational bodies are deploring empty churches and the lack of interest on the part of the younger generation'.[38] The conversionism of independent Brethren remained a potent force at a time when mainstream churches were often content merely to compete in the provision of secular leisure, rather than preach the gospel.[39] 'The Church is not commissioned to "amuse" the unconverted masses', remarked *The Witness*, noting with disdain that even the Salvation Army was organizing '*debating societies, literary and dramatic societies, and cultural games*'.[40]

The basic evangelistic tool remained the Sunday evening gospel service, but mission work reached beyond the immediate vicinity of the 'Gospel Hall', as many independent Brethren buildings were appropriately designated. A particular target was the virgin territory of the new housing estates which spread rapidly in the inter-war years.[41] The fruit of a range of evangelistic activity in new areas was regularly in evidence as *The Witness* recorded the opening of new assemblies 'as a result of S[unday] S[chool] and Gospel Work', 'open-air work', 'pioneer work', or 'tent work'.[42] There was an openness to new methods, ranging from the use of loud-speakers in the open-air, to the suggestion that the BBC 'might be approached with a view to speakers being drawn from assemblies' in order to redress the 'weakness of the evangelistic appeal' in religious programmes.[43] But not all were enthralled by the tone of this evangelistic advance. There were complaints that young men were, in fact, no longer preaching the gospel with such fervent appeal, and that the tendency was to *teach* the gospel, rather than *preach* it, at meetings for the unsaved.[44]

While the witness of connexional Brethren for the cause of laity was stridently anti-clerical in tone, many independent Brethren could strike a less trenchant note. Notwithstanding the universal denunciation by independent Brethren of the principal of clericalism, a number of prominent evangelical clergymen were held by them in

36. Neil Summerton to the author, 1 January 1999.

37. *W*, 68 (1938), p. 43.

38. *W*, 68 (1938), p. 29.

39. Cf. Neil T.R. Dickson, *Brethren in Scotland 1838–2000: a social study of an evangelical movement* (Carlisle, 2003), pp. 193-94.

40. *W*, 68 (1938), p. 113.

41. *W*, 66 (1936), p. 112; *BM*, 49 (1939), p. 147.

42. *W*, 65 (1935), pp. 216, 240; *W*, 66 (1936), pp. 144, 264.

43. *BM*, 49 (1939), p. 147; *H*, 16 (1939), p. 49.

44. *BM*, 48 (1938), pp. 158, 320; *W*, 65 (1935), p. 5.

high regard.[45] Notable among these was the Anglican clergyman, Stuart Holden, chairman of the Keswick Convention, who, *The Witness* noted following his death in 1934, had Brethren connections in his early days. Subsequently, although charged with being a modernist and holding 'non-Eternity'—the view that unbelievers will be annihilated—Holden had personally assured the editor of *The Witness* 'that he had no sympathy with Modernism, and never had a modernist in his pulpit'.[46] In Brethren eyes, Holden represented the breed of sound and godly evangelical Anglican or Nonconformist clergyman that they genuinely admired, but which was, alas, fast disappearing. After the death of the Methodist Dinsdale Young of Westminster Central Hall in 1938, the editor of *The Witness* noted that, of the great evangelical preachers in London, only the Baptist Graham Scroggie at the Metropolitan Tabernacle, with 'a few lesser lights', remained.[47] *The Witness* lamented that those who still stood by conservative truths had little chance of advancement in the Church of England, 'when such "deniers" as Bishop Barnes, Dean Inge, Dr Shepherd [sic] and others are promoted'.[48] 'It seems', bemoaned the editor, 'that the more bold the denial of Scripture and even of Creed, the quicker the advancement. A worm is at the root—and decay is sure.'[49] Yet Christian courtesy was maintained even toward 'deniers': 'What a beautiful voice, a kindly heart, a courteous smile', wrote Pickering in *The Witness*, recording the sudden death of Dick Sheppard, the unconventional vicar of St Martin-in-the-Fields in Trafalgar Square, in 1937. Praise from these quarters was, however, faint and somewhat damning: 'We always looked upon his messages as aiming more at "helping lame dogs over stiles", than that of "the glorious Gospel of the blessed God".'[50]

It is possible to detect a perceptible shift in attitude among independent Brethren in the pre-war years, as a positive stance towards inter-denominational activity began to emerge alongside the much stricter separatism which had dominated the Brethren movement as a whole. This process was evidenced in developing relations between Brethren and the wider evangelical witness, which created a broader awareness of core Brethren values, including the refusal to recognize lay–clerical distinctions. It also provided opportunities for gifted Brethren laymen to contribute to the evangelical cause at a time of unprecedented weakness for evangelicalism. Despite the affinities between the holiness ethos of Keswick Convention and Brethren views of sanctification, it was not until the late 1920s that Brethren became directly involved with the Keswick scene, when respected Brethren leaders began to appear on the

45. *BM*, 48 (1938), pp. 10-13; *H*, 14 (1937), p. 153.

46. *W*, 65 (1935), p. 33.

47. *W*, 68 (1938), p. 65.

48. E.W. Barnes was Bishop of Birmingham; W.R. Inge was Dean of St Paul's; and Dr Dick Sheppard was vicar of St Martin-in-the-Fields, London (for the last, see below).

49. *W*, 65 (1935), p. 40.

50. *W*, 67 (1937), p. 281.

Keswick platform for the first time.[51] In doing so they broke the clerical domination of the Keswick platform in place since the founding of the Convention in 1875. During the 1930s Brethren interest and involvement in Keswick increased. By 1938, 700 out of the 5,000 attending the July Convention week were Brethren, compared to just 200 twelve years earlier.[52] There was a glow of pride in the announcement in 1936 that George Goodman had 'been favoured with a invitation to give the Special Bible Addresses to the 5,000 intelligent Christians who will (DV) assemble at Keswick'.[53] Reports of the Conventions in *The Witness* were enthusiastic, none more so than when in 1939 an editorial heading proclaimed, 'Two of our Writers at Keswick'. These were Harry A. Ironside of Chicago and Montague Goodman, a teacher and evangelist, and younger brother of George Goodman. That neither were, as *The Witness* put it, 'what may be called "clergymen" or "trained ministers"' was seen as an acknowledgement of the validity of Brethren's lay ethos.[54] The Keswick platform, under its non-denominational motto, 'All one in Christ Jesus', provided Brethren with an important opportunity to promote their ecclesiology on a much broader stage, yet in an environment which was sympathetically non-sectarian.

It was their lay strength, coupled with a lack of concern for denominational boundaries, that fitted independent Brethren to play a crucial role in another key conservative evangelical initiative, the Inter-Varsity Fellowship of Evangelical Unions (the IVF). In 1937 *The Harvester*, an independent Brethren magazine with an evangelistic focus, found it 'reassuring to know that in most universities there is now a local Christian Union which seeks to bind together Christian students for mutual help and encouragement, and which also arranges evangelistic services'.[55] Independent Brethren, along with evangelical Anglicanism, provided many of the student leaders of these often small but determined groups of evangelical undergraduates.[56] Furthermore, they enjoyed the support of Brethren figures who carried considerable weight in their professional field, including Professor A. Rendle Short, a Bristol surgeon who was a mentor to Douglas Johnson, the dynamic secretary of IVF who also came from an independent Brethren background.[57] Rendle Short exercised a wide and effective ministry in the field of apologetics, publishing several works of considerable help to thinking evangelicals when such material was rare.[58] In 1938 F.F. Bruce, then a lecturer in classics, was appointed to Leeds

---

51. Bebbington, *Evangelicalism*, pp. 158-59; Ian M. Randall, *Evangelical Experiences: a study in the spirituality of English Evangelicalism 1918–1939* (Carlisle, 1999), p. 156.

52. Randall, *Evangelical Experiences*, p. 156.

53. *W*, 66 (1936), p. 139.

54. *W*, 69 (1939), p. 210.

55. *H*, 14 (1937), p. 217.

56. Oliver Barclay, *Evangelicalism in Britain 1935–1995* (Leicester, 1997), p. 24.

57. I am indebted to Dr Norman James for information concerning Douglas Johnson's church background; see W.M. Capper and D. Johnson, *Arthur Rendle Short: Surgeon & Christian* (London, 1954), and D.J. Johnson, *Contending for the Faith* (Leicester, 1979).

58. Barclay, *Evangelicalism in Britain*, pp. 20, 30.

University, where he was 'a major help' to the struggling Christian Union.[59] The IVF circle proved to be a vital seedbed for the post-war renaissance in evangelical scholarship which was presaged by the formation by Johnson in 1938 of the IVF Biblical Research Committee in which Brethren scholars, Bruce, and the Old Testament expert, W.J. Martin of Liverpool University, became involved.[60] Other channels for the evangelical fervour of progressively minded independent Brethren included the Children's Special Service Mission (CSSM) and Scripture Union. The renowned children's evangelist R. Hudson Pope was on the permanent staff of CSSM, while George Goodman and his brother Montague, both lawyers, were also prominent in its work.[61] George Goodman also wrote *Daily Notes* for the Scripture Union's Bible readings.[62] Montague Goodman's devotional writings were acclaimed beyond the confines of Brethren, and along with many other Brethren, including the building contractor John Laing (later Sir John), he was also active in the non-denominational Crusader organization for young people. In common with the parallel Covenanter movement in which Laing was again a key figure, Crusaders owed much to Brethren for its development in this period.[63]

As evangelical life in England declined to its lowest ebb around the outbreak of World War II, the Brethren movement represented a bulwark of evangelicalism in the decade preceding the Second World War. Connexional Brethren asserted with confidence their claim to represent authentic church life, untainted by the Spirit-hindering principal of clericalism. Here was a spiritual refuge free from the terminal decline which was purported to be engulfing wider evangelicalism, under the influence of clerics adrift from their theological moorings. Notwithstanding the negative tenor of their separatism, these lay circles of fellowship played a part in preserving the evangelical faith, not least through their dogged adherence to evangelical truth, albeit in its dispensational guise, and their ability to draw to themselves disillusioned evangelicals from the mixed denominations. The role played by independent Brethren on the evangelical stage was growing more significant. The evangelistic fervour and upbeat tone of these lay evangelicals were rare commodities in the hard-pressed world of pre-war evangelicalism. Continuing, if hard-earned, results in home mission drew in new converts, a rare event elsewhere. Their strident but not wholly undiscerning critique of contemporary religion chimed with the

59. Oliver Barclay, 'F.F. Bruce and the Inter-Varsity Fellowship', *CBRFJ*, 22 (1971), p. 20.

60. Johnson, *Contending for the Faith*, pp. 209-11; Bruce, *In Retrospect*, pp. 110-11.

61. Nigel Sylvester, *God's Word in a Young World: the story of Scripture Union* (London, 1984), pp. 49, 92, 93.

62. *W*, 66 (1936), p. 139.

63. See the endorsement by *The Christian* of Montague Goodman's book, *The Comforter*, in an advertisement, *H*, 16 (1939), p. 23; Barclay, *Evangelicalism in Britain*, p. 24; Summerton, *Local Churches*, p. 4; Jack Watford, *Yesterday and Today: a history of Crusaders* (St Albans, 1995), pp. 80, 87, 88; *H*, 57 (1980), pp. 46-49; for Laing, see [F.] Roy Coad, *Laing* (London, 1979).

stirrings of discontent in the minds of many in mainstream denominations who, in common with Brethren, saw it as their calling to cleave to the fundamentals of the faith. A significant number transferred their allegiance, the attraction for some being undoubtedly the far greater scope among Brethren for lay people to be involved in ministry.[64] Those who remained loyal to their own denomination were, nevertheless, often nourished by the devotional warmth, biblical knowledge and confident tones of lay Brethren speakers, writers and youth leaders, as the most dynamic and out-going members of the movement gained increasing recognition in the evangelical world.

64. Timothy C.F. Stunt to author, 14 February 1999.

CHAPTER 9

Brethren in Britain, 1945–2000: A Personal Sketch

Harold H. Rowdon

Towards the end of my time at London Bible College (LBC), where I taught church history for thirty-seven years, when students were less inhibited than they once were, some of them said of me, 'Of course he knows a thing or two about church history—he's lived through most of it!' Certainly I have lived through the period under review in this paper, and have been involved in some of the developments that have taken place. I would like to start with a few sweeping generalizations which I will attempt to substantiate as I proceed.

The period 1945–2000 witnessed the decline of a movement which had played a not inconsiderable part in preserving evangelical faith and practice in the UK against the assaults of rationalism and sacerdotalism during the first half of the twentieth century. It was a movement, totally convinced of the validity of its highly distinctive emphases, which was looking forward to exploiting the opportunities afforded by post-war reconstruction and was making great strides towards achieving this goal, when its hopes began to crumble, and gradual but steady decline set in.

I believe that this happened largely because the movement had become captive to a tradition, which was fondly imagined to be thoroughly biblical but was in fact a man-made interpretation of biblical data, heavily influenced by cultural factors, impervious to the breaking forth of yet more truth from God's holy word, and unserviceable for the needs of a rapidly changing world.

But new life began to appear throughout the period, especially during the last few decades, some of which fed into other branches of the church but much remained, though in a radically different form.

On the Crest of the Wave (c.1945–60)

Before the end of the war, when post-war reconstruction was already under discussion, Brethren laid their own plans. Meetings were held in London, some arranged by leading men in the London assemblies, others by the editors of the influential missionary magazine, *Echoes of Service* (whose knuckles were rapped by some for their pains). Similar meetings were held in some other parts of the country. There was no shortage of ideas for seizing the opportunities afforded by what was currently called 'post-war reconstruction'.

But what actually happened? In the absence of effective denominational machinery, everything depended on initiatives taken by individuals or local churches. This was both a strength and a weakness. On the one hand, there was no need to wait for action or to seek authorization from denominational officials. On the other hand, action by local churches could be crippled by the traditional insistence on unanimity before making any significant change, and by the fact that, with the absence of younger men in the forces, many assemblies were dominated by elderly men who were often set in their ways.

Evangelism

As might be expected, one area in which action was widely taken was that of evangelism. (Brethren, broadly speaking, have a congenital weakness for evangelism!) Here are a few examples:

1. Following the influx of immigrants from Eastern Europe, fleeing from communism, energetic steps were taken to evangelize them. Under the banner of 'The Gospel to Britain's Guests', men like Ransome Cooper distributed Christian literature, held meetings, and engaged in personal evangelism with some degree of success.

2. Young evangelists, many of them ex-servicemen, like Squadron Leader Bob Pettifer, engaged in evangelism. Some were to become household names, like Stephen Olford, son of a Brethren missionary, who was later to become pastor of Calvary Baptist Church, New York. I have memories of a very effective evangelistic campaign led by him and a senior missionary to the West Indies, Harold Wildish, held in a huge tent pitched on a strategic site in the centre of Bournemouth, during which over 300 professions of faith were made. Later, after the heady days of the early Billy Graham Crusades (at which about one quarter of the counsellors were said to be Brethren), first Eric Hutchings and then Dick Saunders gained national recognition as evangelists who used radio as well as traditional evangelistic crusades to spread the gospel.

3. The post-war boom in house building provided golden opportunities for evangelism and church-planting which Brethren were not slow to seize. Indeed, their efforts probably preceded and exceeded those of other groups. One great advantage they enjoyed was the support of John Laing whose rapidly growing construction firm was erecting new housing estates in various parts of the country. It was Laing's policy to set aside a strategic site for a church building, and he helped to finance the construction of many a new building (and later the refurbishment of many an old one).

Usually commencing with work among children, groups of people from existing assemblies were able to plant new churches without the formalities that often shackled the church-building plans of others. Very often, the nucleus consisted of the more progressive elements of the parent church (freeing them from the frustrations they might have experienced in the mother church, but leaving it in a potentially parlous condition).

In retrospect, a common defect in such church plants was that they were almost always undertaken by middle-class people who rarely if ever gave a thought to the cultural difference between them and the residents of the usually working-class estates in which they faithfully served. Little wonder that many of the churches they planted have not survived.

4. Another area of post-war evangelistic expansion was the holding of summer camps for children. In itself, this was not an innovation since, before the war, Brethren in London had established the Climping Camps near Littlehampton, Sussex, to provide children from deprived areas of London with a holiday by the sea in a Christian environment.

Now, even before the end of the war, tented camps were set up in the summer, mainly for boys, and private schools were hired for girls, where they could spend a week on holiday in a Christian environment. The main purpose was not recreation but evangelism. I was a camper at one of the earliest ones—the Hants and Dorset Christian Youth Camps—set up by a committee of Brethren in the Bournemouth area. Later, I returned as a tent officer and, for a number of years, as commandant of the camp for junior boys. (Incidentally, I have often wondered why military terminology was used—even including the term 'padre'. Perhaps it was because it all began during wartime.)

Similar camps were held in an increasing number of counties, or group of counties, and some evangelists organized their own, with the help of their supporters. Many young people were converted, or helped forward in their Christian lives. Almost inevitably, the atmosphere could become that of a spiritual hothouse, and the number of young people who, year after year, confessed to having fallen away from the Lord during the previous year raises questions; but that is not to deny that much spiritual fruit was harvested at these camps.

As a by-product they also provided opportunities for 'officers' from assemblies which they found frustrating to share their concerns. We used to do so at what we called 'cookhouse conferences' from the venue where they took place. Though such camps continue to this day, they have not succeeded in halting the decline in the strength of Brethren churches which marked the decades after 1960. I wonder how many of the officers compared the opportunities for uninhibited evangelism and unfettered discussion at camp with the situation in their home churches, and became disillusioned.[1]

5. Using modern technology, some Brethren in London equipped a vehicle with loudspeaker equipment and launched the first Evangelistic Mobile Unit (EMU). This enabled groups of men (for the most part) to be conveyed to centres of population, such as new housing estates, where they could broadcast the gospel, as well as distribute evangelistic literature, gather children together for an illustrated talk, and engage in personal evangelism. At weekends, forays could be made into more distant

1. For the Merseyside camps, see D. Porter, *'So Much More': Camp! 40 years of history* (Warrington, 1986). For the Devon camps, see R. Steer, *Canvas Conversations* (Copplestone, Devon, 1995).

areas of population. Once a year permission was secured for an evangelistic rally to be held in the heart of London, at Trafalgar Square (a practice which continues to this day). Eventually there were EMUs in each corner of London—and beyond (e.g. in Reading for the Thames Valley area). It was a development of the longstanding idea of 'village evangelism' traditionally conducted by groups of younger people on bicycles or motor cars.

6. Even more ambitious were the sustained efforts made notably by W.H. Clare to secure the airing of Brethren services on the BBC. Eventually, these efforts were crowned with success, and for a number of years services were broadcast several times a year, mainly as regional but sometimes as national broadcasts. Though overt evangelism was not possible, the main purpose was clearly evangelistic.

Counties Evangelistic Work

Throughout the post-war period, conventional forms of evangelism continued. Ever since 1899, groups of evangelists had evangelized in rural areas in southern England where there was little or no evangelistic witness. Using first horse-drawn, then motor-drawn caravans, they would spend the summer months visiting villages and hamlets where they pitched large tents in which evangelistic meetings for children and adults were held. In 1928, the various groups came together under the term 'Counties Evangelistic Work'. Its activities continued apace after the war. Each year, supporters gathered in considerable numbers in the spring to commission the evangelists for the season's work, and in the autumn to hear them report on their activities. During the 1980s the report meetings were held in London's Westminster Central Hall, where they attracted attendances of up to 2,500.[2]

Overseas Mission

Like John Wesley, Brethren have always regarded the world as their 'parish' and overseas missionary work continued apace after the war, in part stimulated by it. The number of missionaries grew, and every year, several days of meetings for reports were held in London, which, incidentally but importantly, fulfilled many of the functions of a denominational national assembly. The Great Hall of Westminster Central Hall proved too small for the numbers who came from all over the country and for a number of years specialist meetings were held in the smaller halls simultaneously with the main meetings.

Similar, but of course much smaller, annual meetings were held in many areas and I well remember the excitement of attending the 'missionary meetings' which were held for three days in Bournemouth. Everybody seemed to be there, and there was an atmosphere that could be 'electric' when a particularly gifted missionary was making his appeal.

---

2. For a lively account of the work of these 'Counties' evangelists, see Brian Mills, *A Story to Tell: evangelism in the twentieth century* (Carlisle, 1999).

Interdenominational and Parachurch Activities

Brethren involvement in interdenominational and parachurch activites, though no new phenomenon, gathered momentum in post-war years. A surprisingly large number of Brethren attended the Keswick Convention[3] and, very occasionally, some took part as speakers. One of the first was George Goodman, brother of the better-known Montague Goodman who was deeply involved in the activities of the Crusader Movement (he also wrote a series of books for boys under the title of *The Wantoknow Books*) and served as chairman of the board and then president of the LBC. Another who played a key role in the development of LBC was John Laing whose business acumen and financial resources proved invaluable as they did to the Inter-Varsity Fellowship of Evangelical Students and its Tyndale Fellowship for Biblical Research. John Laird, originally from New Zealand, not only served on the board of LBC but played a key role in the post-war development of Scripture Union, particularly its transformation into a fully international movement.

Several Brethren were key figures in the remarkable post-war resurgence of biblical research. Among them were F.F. Bruce, whose commentary on the Greek text of *Acts*, published in 1951, is often regarded as a turning point for evangelical biblical scholarship, and W.J. Martin of Liverpool University. Bruce went on to publish a score or more of volumes on the Old Testament, the inter-testamental period, the New Testament (particularly) and the history of the English Bible. Bruce held the John Rylands Chair of Biblical Criticism and Exegesis at Manchester University, widely regarded as the leading position of its kind in the UK, from 1959 to 1978. He is said to have supervised more PhD students in biblical studies than any other scholar of his generation.[4] Though a meticulous Old Testament scholar, Martin published little, probably because he was something of a perfectionist! Another who rose to prominence in this period was Donald J. Wiseman, a leading Assyriologist who was to become Professor of Assyriology in the University of London and edited the Old Testament series of Tyndale Commentaries. They were to be followed by a steady stream of Brethren who achieved wide recognition in scholarly circles as biblical scholars, particularly in the field of Old Testament. Included among them are Alan Millard, Rankin Professor of Hebrew and Ancient Semitic Languages at Liverpool University; David Gooding of Queen's University, Belfast; Robert Gordon, Professor of Hebrew at Cambridge University; and Hugh Williamson, Regius Professor of Hebrew at the University of Oxford. (I have often wondered why so many Brethren focused on the Old Testament; perhaps it is related to the attention paid in Brethren circles to that part of the Bible.)

---

3. According to Charles Price and Ian Randall, *Transforming Keswick* (Carlisle, 2000), p. 121, at least 800 Brethren attended the 1952 convention. Up to 700 had attended the Brethren breaking of bread meeting held at Keswick during the convention weeks in the 1930s: *Transforming Keswick*, p. 98.

4. According to Ward Gasque, in Timothy Larsen (ed.), *Biographical Dictionary of Evangelicals* (Leicester, 2003), pp. 85-88.

Training

One of the needs that was perceived albeit somewhat dimly by those Brethren who indulged in planning for the post-war period was training. Traditionally, it was believed, and is still believed by many, that all the training that is required for any kind of Christian service is, or should be, found within the normal routine of assembly life, aided of course by personal devotions and study. Nevertheless, the Brethren leaders who met in London to discuss post-war needs came to the conclusion that additional training was needed and a series of training courses was initiated, meeting in the Orange Street Congregational Church in central London. These continued for some years, but eventually lapsed and the attempt to revive them, made in the 1960s, was short lived.

More momentous—for evangelicalism as well as for the Brethren—was the founding of Matlock Bible College, Derbyshire, in 1948. The brainchild of an evangelist, David Clifford, the original intention was to train young men for evangelism. It grew in numbers, raised its academic standards, admitted women, moved to larger premises in Devon (changing its name from Matlock to Moorlands Bible College) and, after some ups and downs, widened its sights to become a fully interdenominational and international college (now known as Moorlands College) with a good reputation for theological training with a strong practical bias.[5]

It is highly significant that so much of the vibrant life of post-war Brethren in the UK expressed itself outside local assemblies. Within them, things continued much as they had done before the war. The breaking of bread remained the central point, if not the sum and substance, of their spiritual life. Bible teaching was provided by the weekly conversational Bible reading, supplemented by the Saturday fellowship meetings which every assembly worth its salt held as its annual celebration. If you lived in an area where there were numerous assemblies, many of your Saturdays provided feasts of biblical teaching as well as tea and cakes! In the Bournemouth area, where I was brought up, there were also annual 'May Meetings' when for several days, visiting Bible teachers presided over morning Bible readings and gave Bible addresses each afternoon and evening. On top of all this, every few years, most assemblies invited an itinerant Bible teacher for a week or more of teaching.

Evangelism revolved around the Sunday evening gospel meeting, open-air meeting, tract distribution and the occasional week-long mission (sometimes extended to a fortnight) conducted by a visiting evangelist. Afternoon meetings for women (I recall them described as 'Mothers' Meetings') while they had an unintended social function, were primarily evangelistic in nature. So too were the meetings for children held on a midweek evening, as well as the traditional Sunday school.

Very little changed in these areas (or, for that matter, in the weekly mid-week prayer meeting), except in the activities for children. A purely recreational element was introduced and the term 'youth centre' (said to have originated in Scotland) was

5. The story of Moorlands has been engagingly told by Alison Notman, *Faith & Vision* (Christchurch, Dorset, n.d.). Only a brief reference is made to its Brethren origin, on p. 10.

used. Physical training, games and craftwork were included—as well as the mandatory epilogue. When our youth centre commenced, we invited a local brother to give the epilogue after an evening of recreational activity, and he solemnly expounded the verse which begins 'Bodily exercise profiteth *little*'!

The Emergence of Fault Lines (c.1960–70)

Despite appearances, all was not well with the Brethren in Britain. Reasons for this are not far to seek. Some lay deep down; others were closer to the surface; and some swept in from outside, with the force of a tornado. Here, I believe, are some of them.

1. At rock bottom, it seems to me, was the fact that Brethren had been taught by men of ability and conviction that the last word had been said on a range of issues. All that was needed was to proclaim these truths, including those relating to the church, without alteration or equivocation. In short, a Brethren tradition had been created which, in theory, was derived from scripture alone and posed no threat to its authority but which, in practice, constituted a second authority not merely alongside scripture but above it (since it acted as a filter through which any new understanding of scripture must be able to pass if it were to be accepted as scriptural truth).

That this is the case was illustrated for me when an elderly brother, admittedly in the heat of the moment, exclaimed to me when I was marshalling scripture in support of my contention, 'I don't mind what scripture says, I believe...' (repeating the Brethren dictum that I was questioning).

2. Two circumstantial factors undermined the fundamental Brethren tenet which, put rather bluntly and without qualification, asserted that Brethren alone held the full truth about the gospel and could expect divine blessing on their endeavours. Young men who were called up for military service during and just after the war, and young people who went away to college or university during the post-war expansion of higher education, soon discovered among their colleagues fellow-believers who were not Brethren and, in many cases, they benefited from the ministrations of non-Brethren evangelical churches. As a result, some felt they had been misled, and lost confidence in their Brethren teachers, feeling that, if they had been wrong on this point, they might be wrong on others.

3. The fact was that, contrary to the expectation common, if not universal, among Brethren that the liberal theology and sacerdotal churchmanship rampant pre-war would develop into universal infidelity leading up to the rapture of the church and the Second Coming of Christ, something approaching an evangelical revival was taking place. What is more, it was emerging most strongly in the very areas where Brethren least expected it —the Established Church against which early Brethren had inveighed so strongly and which their successors (conveniently overlooking men of the spiritual stature of Bishops J.C. Ryle and Handley Moule) had regarded as impervious to biblical truth, on the one hand, and the Charismatic Movement which grew so strongly in the 1960s and 70s, on the other. (Sometimes the two coalesced!)

4. The emergence of the Charismatic Movement posed more than one problem for Brethren. Ironically, this movement, which used to be thought to have originated (in

the UK) in the Church of England has been shown by the researches of Andrew Walker and Peter Hocken[6] to have been initiated by men who were Brethren—Arthur Wallis and David Lillie—and to have been strengthened by the constant addition of others from the same source.

Brethren tradition was almost unanimous in believing that some of the spiritual gifts mentioned in 1 Corinthians 12 and elsewhere in the New Testament were intended only for the foundational period of the church's history, and that any claim to have received them since was a delusion of either fleshly or demonic origin. Now, a small but increasing number of Brethren came to the conclusion that God did not share Brethren inhibitions about either the Church of England or the Charismatic Movement and their confidence in the Brethren movement was further eroded. Many of these left the Brethren.

5. One other background factor must be mentioned, though lack of space forbids exploration to the extent that it deserves. I refer to the happenings among the Taylorite Brethren which I would regard as external to the 'Open' Brethren we are concerned with, though some maintain that they are an integral part of a single 'Brethren' movement. (I fail to understand how a movement which divided into two hermetically-sealed entities one and a half centuries ago can still be regarded as a single entity.)

When the Brethren hit the headlines in the mass media, the journalists who were reporting the events proved totally incapable of distinguishing between 'Open' and 'Exclusive' Brethren. Nor could the wider public. To make matters worse, the 'Open' Brethren possessed no central organs from which information could be sought, apart from the editors of magazines, such as G.C.D. Howley of *The Witness* (who did his best to make the situation clear). For some reason, I was invited to explain who Brethren were by one newspaper—I think it was *The Sunday Citizen*—which has long since ceased publication.

The sensational events that were reported as happening among Exclusive Brethren following the total banning of table fellowship between believers and unbelievers, including alleged instances of suicide, did incalculable harm to the 'Open' Brethren. As soon as people heard the name 'Brethren' they thought of what they had read in the papers. An attempt was made to counter this by using the term 'Christian Brethren', but to the uninitiated 'Brethren' were 'Brethren'. Before long, the term was virtually unusable, especially by those who were moving away from Brethren traditions that had outlasted their usefulness, thus hastening the fragmentation and loss of any sense of common identity which have been so characteristic of the last few decades.

6. One final factor of crucial importance was the difficulty of bringing about change in a typical Brethren assembly. Of course, change usually presents difficulties in any context, and the Brethren have the advantage of not possessing any formal denominational structures that might inhibit change. But, on the other hand, the

6. Andrew Walker, *Restoring the Kingdom* (London, 2nd edn, 1988); Peter Hocken, *Streams of Renewal* (Carlisle, 1997)

insistence on unanimity before taking action placed a heavy premium on continuity and facilitated what came to be described as 'minority rule'.[7]

So, with anyone known to indulge in charismatic practices (such as speaking in tongues) almost automatically disfellowshipped, a single dissentient voice (particularly at leadership level) being sufficient to prevent change taking place, and the natural reluctance of many people (particularly those older in years) to embrace change, it is hardly surprising that those who felt strongly that change was needed became restless, and a steady stream of people left their assemblies. Many became ministers of Baptist, FIEC and even Anglican churches, and a considerable number became deacons of Baptist churches. (At one time it was said that Upton Vale Baptist Church, Torquay, was the largest Brethren church in Devon!)

Attempts to Stem the Tide (c.1960–80)

What was done to stem the tide and with what success? In brief, the answer is: a great deal, but with little permanent effect. I will try to be brief because I have written at some length about this elsewhere.[8]

1. The Swanwick Conferences. As early as January 1953, a private conference was held in a London hotel at which conflicting views of the Second Coming were exchanged with candour but also respect. A second private conference followed in September that year on the Holy Spirit, and then further conferences of a public character were held at High Leigh Conference Centre. Men like Montague Goodman, F.F. Bruce and G.C.D. Howley discreetly suggested that there was need for church leaders to receive training and that there was no absolute scriptural bar on women raising their voices in public meetings. Open discussion enabled men to share their concerns. The conference became an annual event which in 1957 moved to a larger Conference Centre at Swanwick, Derbyshire. I attended many of them—and spoke at some. My distinct impression was that the Swanwick Conferences soon largely lost their cutting edge—though on occasions they spoke out clearly—and largely ceased to be an effective agent of change.

2. The Oxford Young Men's Bible Teaching Conference. Whereas the Swanwick Conferences were directed towards church leaders in particular and thoughtful adults in general (though at first, men only!), the Oxford Young Men's Bible Teaching Conferences were specifically designed for young men who might develop into church leaders. The formative influence on these conferences was James Houston, at that time lecturer in geography at the University of Oxford and bursar of Hertford College. They were held annually over a weekend during the Easter vacation at various Oxford colleges. Each year an aspect of Christian doctrine was taught,

7. The tradition goes back to the honoured Brethren patriarch, Robert Chapman, who insisted on unanimity before initiating change (though, even so, a minor secession followed the introduction of the change in question which, however, was healed in time).

8. See my survey in Harold H. Rowdon (ed), *The Strengthening, Growth and Planting of Local Churches: The report of a Partnership consultation, 11-13 July 1991* (Carlisle, 1993), pp. 127-41.

together with biblical and practical material (e.g. homiletics). Among the lecturers were F.F. Bruce, H.L. Ellison, an outstanding teacher of the Old Testament with an impish delight in setting off theological fireworks, full-time Bible teachers like G.C.D. Howley, a shrewd and farsighted man who, if he had possessed a thicker skin, might have been the leader of a neo-Brethren movement, and professional men such as the accountant, Arnold Pickering, blessed with a keen sense of humour, and the dentist, K.G. Hyland, who was to become influential in the south-west of England, where he launched a number of Bible teaching and other conferences, one of which, the Devon Bible Teaching Conference, continues to this day. And, of course, there was James Houston himself.

The conferences attracted attendance of 300 and more—all men, though not all young men—as the conference photographs reveal! When Houston moved to Canada as founding principal of Regent College, Vancouver, the conference moved venue to King Alfred's College, Winchester. But its best days were over and despite becoming co-educational (as the phrase went in those days), numbers declined, and the annual conferences ceased.

The Oxford Conference spawned broadly similar conferences in various parts of the country, from Devon to Durham; and weekend conferences for women made their appearance and became popular. The conferences for women met a real need. One regular attender claimed that they provided her with the only opportunity during the year of expressing an opinion! Several of them continue to this day, attracting large attendances and regarding themselves as interdenominational.

3. One very significant by-product of the Oxford Conference was the Christian Brethren Research Fellowship (CBRF), which was founded in 1963, with Roy Coad its prime mover. Its original purpose was threefold: as its name implies, to encourage research into Brethren history; to provide a point of reference for people enquiring into the nature of the Brethren Movement; and, most importantly, to provide a forum in which younger people in particular could freely exchange their opinions. A journal and a range of booklets were published, some good historical research was produced and a decennial survey of Brethren churches was regularly undertaken by Graham Brown (one has recently seen the light of day).[9] Conferences were held, some of which were well attended—notably one addressed by Malcolm Muggeridge and another on the role of women in church at which F.F. Bruce gave a powerful paper.

But suspicions were aroused by the fact that members had to be sponsored by an existing member and the cyclostyled journal was originally headed 'confidential'. (I confess that I myself, though a founder member, was ambivalent about CBRF in the '60s and early '70s, since I was at that time vainly looking for a middle way between the crippling traditionalism of some, and the radicalism of CBRF. Needless to say, I subsequently realized that there is no middle way!)

---

9. Graham Brown, *Whatever Happened to the Brethren? A Survey of Local Churches in 1998–1999* (Carlisle, 2003).

4. Something which, at the time, I thought would do a great deal towards giving Brethren a sense of achievement was the publication in 1969 of *A New Testament Commentary*, edited by F.F. Bruce, H.L. Ellison and G.C.D. Howley (the last being the prime mover), followed in 1979 by a complete Bible Commentary. Written almost entirely by Brethren authors, many of them with academic credentials, and edited with skill and sensitivity, the commentary circulated beyond its primary Brethren constituency. Originally based on the RSV, it was later revised by Andrew Gray to match the increasingly popular NIV version. Though it was widely used and helped many to a better understanding of scripture, I doubt whether it achieved to any significant extent its other purpose of giving confidence to the Brethren.

5. Something must be said about developments within the very important field of Brethren periodical literature. Magazines at the traditional end of the spectrum (notably *Assembly Testimony*, founded in 1954, and the older *Believer's Magazine*) remain largely unchanged. A new magazine, located well to the right of centre, *Precious Seed,* launched in 1945, presented traditional views in a positive way, and also included news from the regions. Under the enlightened editorship of G.C.D. Howley, *The Witness* enjoyed a radical change of format, and its content moved a good way left of centre, without becoming in any sense radical. The regular articles written by 'Touchstone' (the editor) raised a wide range of issues and sometimes hinted at radical solutions. The other major magazine, *The Harvester*, founded in the 1920s to report the burgeoning evangelism of that period, had become a general magazine under the editorial guidance of F.A. Tatford who managed to combine a traditional stance on theological (especially dispensational) issues with a fairly radical position on ecclesiastical matters. Falling circulation of both *Witness* and *Harvester* (a sign of the times, if ever there was one) necessitated a merger, which was latterly issued under the name *Aware*. But neither a new format, nor skilful editing by editors of the calibre of Roy Coad, Jonathan Lamb, Jonathan Ingleby and John Allan, nor content relevant to the times, sufficed to ensure its survival.

How successful were these attempts to stem the tide of decline? What influence did they have upon the local churches which constituted the heart of the Brethren in the UK?

On the one hand, a number of churches, particularly some situated in the suburbs of London and other cities and large towns, introduced significant changes. In the area of teaching and preaching, the practice (by no means universal) of reserving time after the breaking of bread on Sunday morning for ministry of the word was insisted upon—and developed in new ways. A syllabus of subjects would be drawn up, with a rota of previously invited speakers (who were not necessarily members of the church in question). Instead of the ritual of gospel preaching on Sunday evenings, whether or not those in need of it were likely to be present, what was often described as a 'teaching gospel' would be expounded, covering over a period of time Bible exposition, teaching of doctrine, etc. The mid-week 'conversational Bible reading' which had sometimes degenerated into what was cruelly described as a 'pooling of ignorance' often went the same way, attempts being made to cover a balanced programme of biblical, doctrinal, ethical and sometimes even historical subjects.

Alongside all this went other changes, such as more ambitious activities for young people, women and, sometimes, men; more imaginative missionary weekends and Saturday conferences; and, almost always, increasing emphasis on the necessity to clearly recognize church leaders, especially elders, and to submit to their authority. Sometimes, a new category of church leader, with a biblical pedigree, made its appearance in the form of men (rarely, if ever, in those days, women) whose role, as deacons, differed from that of the elders and whose authority ranked below theirs.

While changes such as these came about in a number of churches, most of them settled into a new pattern which became fixed and almost as difficult to change again as the traditional pattern had been (and continued to be in those churches which had retained it).

I sometimes wonder whether, in one sense, the advocacy of change in conferences, publications and personal ministry may not have been counter-productive. What I mean by that is that many people were brought to see the need for change, but were unable to achieve it in their own assemblies. As a result, they became disillusioned and often migrated to churches outside the Brethren fold where there seemed to be more spiritual vitality than in their stick-in-the-mud assemblies. Anecdotal evidence certainly bears this out.

Nantwich and Beyond (1991–Present)

By the mid-1980s, there was a strong feeling in the council of Partnership (as CBRF had renamed itself) that it had done all it could to revitalize the Brethren in Britain. It was on the verge of disbanding, trusting the Lord to raise up a new instrument for the task if such were required, when it felt a strong constraint to re-tool itself for a new phase of its work. We realized that, up and down the country, changes were taking place that were far more radical than previous changes had been. They included the adoption of Sunday morning family services to replace the effete Sunday evening gospel meetings as a first point of contact with interested non-Christians; the gradual opening up of opportunities for women to take part in public services; the appointment of men—and sometimes women—as full-time youth, community or pastoral workers; and, in a few but increasing number of churches, changes in worship involving the use of modern worship songs and even a wider range of spiritual gifts. Not surprisingly, such churches were usually shunned by more traditional ones, and were in danger of becoming isolated churches without links with other churches beyond their immediate neighbourhood (where they usually enjoyed good relationships with other evangelical churches). Partnership felt the call of God to do what it could to resource such churches and to serve as a means of providing links of fellowship between them.

In order to test this conviction, a weekend residential conference was held in Nantwich, Cheshire, from 11-13 July 1991. There is a degree of significance in the date, since it was ten years, almost to the day, since the last of a series of conferences held in London, between 1974 and 1981, to consider the state of the assemblies, and the prospect for their revival. These were mostly small, private, one-day conferences which did little more than bemoan the situation and propose measures that might be taken. The last, however, held 9-11 July 1981 at the LBC was more ambitious both in duration, size, and seriousness. Thanks to Neil Summerton, it was superbly organized. Each morning, for example, participants received a digest of the previous day's proceedings, a summary of specific suggestions for future action extending to twenty-one items was drawn up at the conclusion, and a working party was set up, not to take action but to make representations to existing bodies to do so. This led to the setting up by CBRF of two sets of advisory panels, one to provide pastoral care for missionaries at home, the other to advise potential missionaries, and also to considerable changes in the magazine, *The Harvester*.

Though convened rather hurriedly, the Nantwich conference was attended by 140 leaders from about eighty churches. The opening session, which consisted of regional reports on the state of Brethren churches around the country, painted such a dark picture that some felt there was little point in continuing the conference! The steering committee decided to allow time next morning for a period of waiting upon God. During that time, a number felt moved by the Lord to give words of encouragement, and the conference continued, as planned. The concluding session, which looked for a way forward, was somewhat inconclusive beyond making it clear that, if anything was to happen, it must be done by those who had been present at the conference and by Partnership. And it was![10]

On the way home, several carloads of people, including some from Scotland, Yorkshire and Essex, decided to do something in their areas, and regional conferences followed in a growing number of areas, bringing together church leaders and others to consider matters of common interest. The term 'activist' (usually associated with political agitation) came into use and in 2000, Dr Bob Tripney, a recently retired GP who had long been involved in Partnership (and CBRF) was appointed regional co-ordinator with a brief to promote more regional activities. These are now held in upwards of a dozen parts of the UK, taking the forms of seminars or forums for church leaders, 'roadshows' of a more public nature, 'retreats' for full-time church staff and, now, training sessions which have been pioneered by Mark Thomas, Graham Poland and others.

In 1992, I was invited to edit a new series of 'Partnership Newsletters' which in November 1995 developed into a sizeable, quarterly magazine, *Partnership Perspectives*. Each issue, apart from one each year which was entitled *International Partnership Perspectives* and served the international aims of Partnership, focused on an aspect of church life with appropriate articles, reports from churches, book reviews, etc. The flow of publications, which had almost dried up, began to flow again, though not always as steadily as we would have liked. Among these publications have been *Declare His Glory* (1998), a symposium on worship; *Don't Muzzle the Ox* (1997), a ground-breaking collection of papers on the role of people

10. On Nantwich, see Rowdon (ed), *The Strengthening, Growth and Planting of Local Churches*.

working full-time in churches; *Ten Changing Churches* (1999), the stories of ten churches which had changed significantly in recent years; *Guide to God's Family* (2000), a readable introduction to what it means to be a church member, and *Sharing the Good News in C21* (2002), a well-informed call to evangelism, both written by Stephen McQuoid; and *Church Leaders Handbook* (2002), a substantial volume, written by forty-four authors on fifty-one aspects of church life, which had to be reprinted within a few months of publication.

Partnership devised a simple mechanism, called Partnership Link-Up Service (PLUS), to help churches find suitable people to work with them full-time. Originally the brainchild of Brian Mills, I managed to keep it going on a small scale while I was teaching at LBC, but it was Alan Batchelor who really got it off the ground and faithfully served it for thirteen years (1989–2003). It is now in the safe hands of Keith Barnard whom Partnership was able to appoint as part-time assistant executive director and secretary of PLUS in 2002. Two-day midweek conferences for full-time and other church leaders have been an important feature in PLUS's calendar since July 1995. Held in alternate years, they have provided spiritual, mental and personal refreshment for between fifty and eighty people.

Finally, in this brief survey of Partnership's activities, the international dimension has not been neglected. For a few years in the 1980s, as mentioned above, Partnership operated a system of advisory panels designed to provide pastoral care of missionaries, particularly after retiral, and advice to people seeking guidance regarding opportunities for missionary work in other countries. In 1987, Partnership arranged a consultation on world mission which was attended by nearly 100, including a few from Germany, Italy, France, Spain, New Zealand and Zambia. In 1992, a European Missionary Conference was organized for the year of the UK's entry into the European Union—not to stimulate missionary work within Europe, but to promote missionary work from European countries. About forty individuals from a dozen European countries attended. The Partnership national conference held at Swanwick in 1998 brought together about fifty people from European, North American and a few African countries, as well as many from the UK, and an extra day was added to the conference specifically for the non-British and a few specially invited Britishers to confer together.

Ever since 1990 when I met with Brethren delegates from about thirty countries who were attending the Lausanne II conference in Manila, I have edited an annual newsletter with correspondents in a growing number of countries—currently about sixty. In 2000, this was expanded into *International Partnership Perspectives*, a substantial magazine which now contains articles and news items, as well as the requests for praise and prayer which constituted the original newsletter.

Though not a Partnership initiative, the International Brethren Conferences on Mission (ICBM) held in Singapore (1993), Rome (1996) and Serimbar, Romania (2003) have been warmly supported by Partnership. I served on the international committee almost from the beginning and, having retired from LBC and been invited to teach at Discipleship Training Centre in Singapore in 1993, I was able to serve on the local planning committee for IBCM 1, as well as to give a paper at the conference and, for good measure to edit a selection of the papers given at the conference under the title *The Brethren Contribution to World Mission.* Neil Summerton has borne the brunt of the organizing of the recent IBCM 3 conference.

Prospects

The decline in the number of Brethren assemblies in the UK continues unabated. I estimate that as many as one-third have closed already and that another third are heading for closure within the next few decades.[11] Most of this third continue as if nothing amiss had happened. The magazines they read are virtually unchanged (though *Precious Seed* has a new, more attractive format, and a recent issue drew attention to Brethren decline). The conferences they attend appear to have changed very little, and their assemblies remain firmly wedded to the past.

Of the remaining third, 150 are currently associated with Partnership, where they may well be joined by another hundred or so during the next few years. An indeterminate number, perhaps between fifty and 100, have linked up with the FIEC or one of the charismatic groups such as Icthus or New Frontiers International; others may follow. A few have changed radically but decline any association with other churches, apart from evangelical ones in their immediate locality, and have effectively become single independent churches. I shall be surprised if more than a very few of those who continue rigidly to follow the old paths will serve any useful purpose in the future, other than providing a spiritual home for elderly or conservatively-minded believers who love the Lord and his word, but find it impossible to embrace change.

Conclusion

What is there to show for the movement whose steady decline I have been describing and whose ultimate fall (in Britain) seems inevitable? Strange though it may seem, the answer is: 'A great deal'!

So I conclude with a summary of some of the things which the Brethren movement in Britain has contributed to the onward march of the kingdom.

1. A multitude of people have been brought to faith in Christ, many of them at times when very few, apart from the Brethren, were faithfully proclaiming the evangelical gospel. Though there are probably many fewer freelance evangelists now than used to be the case, 'Counties' has never been stronger—or more innovative.

2. Brethren churches have been planted, first in Western Europe, then in British colonies, then across the world, until today, there are churches in well over 100 countries (some say as many as 130) and that number is increasing as we speak.

11. Roy Hill, who compiles the UK assembly address lists, estimates that 'in the last few years assemblies have been closing at the rate of about one per week, and the numbers in some of those remaining are very small indeed', with a drop of 36% in the number of assemblies in the last forty years and 60% in members: R. Hill, 'What is happening to UK Assemblies?', *Believer's Magazine* 114 (April, 2004), p. 107.

That statement, I know, is an over-simplification (since not all Brethren churches in other countries owed their beginnings exclusively to British missionaries). But even so, it represents an achievement. At one time, something like one per cent of total 'membership' must have been working overseas, and even today the proportion is probably not much less (if we include the substantial number who go out with interdenominational missionary societies).

3. Bible teaching has been prolific and the contribution Brethren have made to the serious study of the Bible has been very considerable. Like their missionary contribution, it has been out of all proportion to their numbers. As well as Bible teachers at grassroots level, Brethren have produced a very considerable number of biblical scholars at the academic level (including, as we have seen, not only F.F. Bruce, but current professors of Hebrew at both Oxford and Cambridge).

4. Brethren anticipated, by well over a century, the current search for ways of applying New Testament principles to church life that would provide team leadership and 'body ministry'. However partial their success, at least Brethren led the way (though I am not persuaded that current attempts have drawn directly upon their experience).

5. Finally, Brethren have exported considerable numbers of gifted men to other denominations where they have served as church ministers, leaders and faithful members. Cecil Howley used to assure me that this was a God-given role, but I pointed out (whether to him or later, I do not remember) that this could not go on forever!

While, like any group of Christian churches throughout Christian history, Brethren have much to regret, they have also much for which to be grateful. And, while the UK scene is bleak in many respects, we should never forget that in numerous other countries, the scene is bright. Perhaps the time has come for us to recognize that the baton has been handed on to others who will carry it further and more effectively than we did.

Addendum

No mention has been made of dispensationalism—a way of interpreting scripture which was virtually devised by Brethren, characterized them for a very long time and has had considerable influence on evangelicalism, particularly in the US and areas of the world influenced by American theology.

The reason for this is that a largely silent revolution has taken place in the UK. Traditional Brethren still adhere to it, but it has been quietly dropped by most of those who have questioned other aspects of Brethren tradition (and by most of the non-Brethren evangelicals in the UK who once promoted it) without a great deal of commotion. This seems to have happened as the result, not of open hostility towards it but of steady erosion as the Bible has been expounded without recourse to it (and perhaps as a result of the decline of interest in the details of the Second Advent).

Part 3

Worldwide Brethren Experiences

CHAPTER 10

Julius Anton von Poseck (1816–1898) and Brethren Origins in Germany

August Jung

On the Lamb our souls are resting,
What His love no tongue can say;
All our sins, so great, so many,
In His blood are washed away.

Sweetest rest and peace have filled us,
Sweeter praise than tongue can tell;
God is satisfied with Jesus,
We are satisfied as well.

Conscience now no more condemns us,
For His own most precious blood
Once for all has washed and cleansed us,
Cleansed us in the sight of God.

Filled with this sweet peace for ever,
On we go, through strife and care,
Till we find that peace around us
In the Lamb's high glory there.

On the living Lord believing,
We have righteousness and peace.
By the Holy Spirit given,
We have joys that never cease.[1]

One day Julius Anton von Poseck visited the old abbey church in Werden, near Essen (founded around 800, burnt down and reconstructed; consecrated by St Albertus Magnus in 1275). Looking at the church steeple he saw a lamb carved in the stone. When he asked for the meaning of this stone figure he was told the following story:

1. *Hymns and Spiritual Songs for the Little Flock* (Kingston-upon-Thames, 1962/1973), No. 410.

> A long time ago a roofer was just putting new shingles on the church steeple. People stopped in the street to watch the brave workman. Meanwhile a shepherd and his flock passed along the main street of Werden. But how astonished the shepherd was when the whole flock suddenly stopped in front of the abbey church and refused to move from the spot. Then suddenly!—a scream from the crowd. The roofer had slipped and fallen from the high church steeple. Everybody thought the poor man would be lying with broken bones in the front of the church. But when people rushed to the scene, they found the roofer pale, but uninjured. Under him lay a dead sheep, which had broken the force of his fall. To express their thankfulness the stone figure of the lamb was cut in the church facade, where it can still be seen to this day.[2]

This story reminded von Poseck of what is written about Jesus in John 1.29: 'Behold the Lamb of God, who takes away the sin of the world!'. And so he wrote the above-quoted verses: 'On the Lamb our souls are resting.' The significance of this hymn is proved by the fact that it is sung today in many assemblies in Germany, England, the Netherlands and Switzerland. What follows is designed to revive the nearly forgotten memory of its author, who was also the first founder of Brethren assemblies in Germany.[3]

Ancient Nobility from the Vogtland

Julius Anton von Poseck came from the fourteenth generation of an ancient noble family of the Vogtland, dating back to the fourteenth century. Initially the von Posecks were peasants. They acquired considerable tracts of land. At the Reformation they became Lutherans. By the end of the sixteenth century they gradually uprooted themselves and entered the service of their royal rulers as officers in the army of the Elector of Saxony. When the Elector Augustus the Strong (1670–1733) became a Catholic for the sake of the Polish royal crown, his wife, Christiana Eberhardine von Ansbach-Bayreuth (1671–1727) remained a faithful Lutheran. Her bodyguard was led by the Cavalry Captain Johann Konrad von Poseck (1677–1722, Julius Anton's great-great-grandfather). He was married to the Baroness Sophia Eleonare von Saiza and died at the early age of fifty-six leaving his widow and a six-year-old son. His son, Anton Günther von Poseck (1716–84, Julius Anton's great-grandfather) also became an army officer and later Commandant of the episcopal town of Paderborn. This made his conversion to the Catholic Church necessary, because his 'employer' was no less than the Elector of Cologne, Klemens August (1700–61). From then on the von Poseck children became either priests or officers. The eldest of many children, Franz Anton Friedrich von Poseck (1747–1817, Julius Anton.'s grandfather) became an officer and served as Lieutenant-Colonel in a Münster regiment, the *Saltza, 1812*.

2. Wolfgang Schulze, *Das große Essener Sagenbuch* [n.pl., n.d.], pp. 180ff.

3. Cf. the detailed 175-page biography by August Jung, *Julius Anton von Poseck. Ein Gründervater der Brüderbewegung* (Wuppertal, 2002).

One of his sons, Bernhard Anton Franz von Poseck (1781–1852, Julius Anton's father) also became an officer, while the others went into the church. As an officer he saw a lot of the world. Napoleon (1769–1821) had overrun the whole of Europe, including the region of Greifenberg (now Gryfice in Poland), where a Prussian cavalry regiment was stationed. There Cavalry Captain von Poseck met the twenty-two-year-old landowner Helene von Zitzewitz, who had just been widowed. They were married in 1810 according to the Lutheran rite in the mother church of Zirkwitz (now Cirkvice in Poland), whose patron was the king himself. The young couple came to live on the estate. In 1811 the eldest son was born, in 1812 a daughter and on 2 September 1816 our Julius Anton. All three children were baptized as Lutherans in the mother church of Zirkwitz.

In 1818 the family moved to the town of Rheine. Here the cavalry captain, now retired, found a post as a customs officer. His wife and the three children were the first Protestants in that small town, which was otherwise 100 per cent Catholic. Hard times came upon them and things became even harder in that three more children were born here and were all of course baptized as Catholics.

When Julius Anton was eleven years old, his father and family were transferred in 1827 to the other end of Prussia to the border town of Saarbrücken, where he was put in charge of the main customs office. Here (in contrast to Rheine) people were good Lutherans. The Protestant Ludwigsgymnasium (grammar school) left its intellectual mark on Julius Anton. He received a thorough education there in the humanities, learning Hebrew, Greek, Latin and French

In 1833 they moved again, this time to Duisburg, where the father took over the administration of the municipal finances. In the meantime there had also been a remarkable change in the family's religious views. With their father's permission the three younger children, who had been baptized as Catholics, became Protestant. However, this seemed to be only a superficial conversion to the gospel; publicly the mother pretended to be five years, Theresia three years and Ferdinandine two years younger than their birth certificates warranted. Julius Anton was accepted into the 'Prima' (the eighth and ninth years) of the Protestant grammar school, where he, strangely enough, stayed for three years. The reason was that because of his extra-ordinary knowledge he was allowed to teach the lower classes of the school, something that happened quite often at that time because of a shortage of teachers.

At the age of twenty Julius Anton went to Münster to the Catholic Theological and Philosophical Academy. But why did the Protestant Julius Anton choose to study Catholic theology? It seems that Catholic relatives in Paderborn and Rheine had put so much pressure on his father to make sure that at least one member of the family should continue the clerical tradition that he finally agreed and 'made' Julius Anton a Catholic. He could do so because at that time sons did not come of age until twenty-four. Julius Anton did indeed register in Münster, but he disregarded his father's will and it can be proved that he did not attend any theological lecture. Instead he threw himself into the most remote areas of philosophy such as logic, physics, medieval history, the writings of Sophocles and Plato, psychology, atmospheric studies, and the Gnostic aspects of astrology. His teachers testified to his extraordinary diligence.

Then he started studying philology in Berlin. There he met a researcher who, unlike anyone else in his time, was studying the Greek text of the New Testament: Professor Karl Lachmann (1793–1851), the founder of philological textual criticism and editor of a scholarly text of the Greek New Testament (1831). He testified to the very diligent attendance of his student, J.A. von Poseck. Here von Poseck acquired the tools that he was to need later for his translation of the New Testament. In the winter semester of 1838–39 he suddenly transferred without any obvious reason to the Faculty of Law, where he studied for six full semesters. Again and again his teachers testified that he was 'very diligent' and 'extraordinarily diligent'.

But one more story must certainly be mentioned. At the age of twenty-two he was called up, like all the others of his age, for compulsory military service in the Prussian army. His father could indeed have bought him out or sent a replacement, but he did not dream of doing that. As he had already failed to make a priest of his son, he wanted him to become at least a proper officer. So from 1839 to 1840 Julius Anton, steeped in the humanities, reluctantly went (when he had no lectures) to the First Company of the Royal Guards Battalion in Berlin.

And then a strange event occurred, which W.B. Neatby called 'an interesting story'.[4] He, whose great-great-grandfather, great-grandfather, grandfather, and father had been officers, declared himself to be a pacifist and refused for 'religious reasons' to do military service. Thus he was the first conscientious objector on religious grounds in Prussia! The result was that he was sent to prison for three-and-a-half days. From there he sent to his king, Friedrich Wilhelm IV, a number of Darbyist papers with which he sought to justify his refusal.[5] In fact, at that time in England many senior officers resigned from the services after they had been converted and justified their decision before an astonished public with the help of the Bible. Having read the papers the king found the objector to be indeed 'harmless', but decreed that he would have to leave Prussia. This happened after his successful graduation in 1841. He then disappeared for six years, and no information at all has been found as to his whereabouts.

His parents moved from Duisburg to Düsseldorf in 1847, at which time their 'prodigal son'—as if by pre-arrangement—returned to the parental home. With his leaving certificates from the Faculty of Law dated 1841 he applied to the Royal District Court and at the age of thirty-one was taken on as a trainee. But only half a year later he abandoned his legal career. What had happened?

Turning Point

In 1848 his momentous journey with God started. He found faith in Jesus Christ—and in an exceptional way. While he was participating that year in the 600th

4. W.B. Neatby, *A History of the Plymouth Brethren* (London, [1901]), p. 256.

5. It is not known who gave the papers to von Poseck.

anniversary celebrations of the laying of the foundation stone of Cologne Cathedral, a stone came off the parapet of the cathedral, fell down and killed a girl who had been standing exactly on the spot from which he had just been pushed away by the crowd. This shook him so severely that he suffered great anguish of soul. His elder sister and her parish priest, Karl Krafft of Düsseldorf, helped him to a firm belief in the Protestant faith. Through the missionary preacher Heinrich Werth he met with independent Christian groups, which later developed into Free Evangelical Churches.[6] He had nearly become one of their forefathers.

But things turned out differently. In the autumn of 1848 Willam Henry Darby (1790–1880), the elder brother of John Nelson Darby (1800–82), came to Düsseldorf. He was the rich heir of his father's estate at Leap Castle, King's County, Ireland. Unlike John Nelson he was financially independent and—what was still more important—he brought Brethrenism to Germany.

But why did W.H. Darby come to Düsseldorf of all places? Did von Poseck call on him to come so as to set up together with him a Brethren mission in the Rhineland? Whatever the explanation, he abandoned the legal career which he had just started upon and entered into the full-time-service of the gospel within the Brethren movement. He could afford to do this because he also was a 'Particular', that is, a man who could live off his fortune without holding a public office. And so, being independent of anybody's goodwill, he could throw himself wholeheartedly into his new work, which was the translation of a vast number of J.N. Darby's papers.

Besides his translations Julius Anton still found time for evangelistic service. He combined preaching and literature distribution, taking many of Darby's papers and tracts with him and giving them to people free of charge. So for example, at Jüchen-Kelsenberg,

> In the beginning he was well received by meetings attended by hundreds and thousands of Protestants and Catholics until, however, the meetings were soon declared to be against the law of protective custody because of the danger to his life. Von Poseck's followers rejected as Babel etc. infant baptism and everything connected with it: the great number of nominal adherents, the most secularised national church and the sacraments. They themselves claimed, in an extremely brusque manner, to be completely sinless and holy.[7]

Of course, John Nelson Darby had heard of this somewhat dubious missionary activity. That is why many letters flew back and forth between London and Düsseldorf—at a time when Carl Brockhaus (1822–99) showed no interest at all in Darby's teaching.[8] This, indeed, is the new discovery: the real founder of Brethren

6. August Jung, *Als die Väter noch Freunde waren* (Wuppertal, 1999), pp. 15ff.

7. Max Goebbel, 'Der Brüderverein und der Baptismus am Niederrhein', *Bonner Monatsschrift* 13 (1854), 2nd part, pp.190ff.

8. Rolf-Edgar Gerlach, *Carl Brockhaus—ein Leben für Gott und die Brüder* (Wuppertal, 1994).

assemblies in Germany was not Carl Brockhaus but J.A. von Poseck. True, Brethren historians still tell a different story. From the beginning, after all, their fathers kept silent about von Poseck as a rival to Brockhaus. In 1851 Darby wrote in his first letter to von Poseck:

> I have received your translations of the Epistles to the Romans and Hebrews, which now constrains me to write to you to acknowledge the same, and testify to you my Christian affection, and all the interest I feel in your labour...
>
> My brother has kept me somewhat *au courant* as to your labour, and my soul is much interested in it...
>
> Greet affectionately all our dear brethren, though I do not know them. It matters not. We are one in Jesus. But my brother has mentioned to me some of their names. May God help them and lead them by His Spirit in all their ways. Peace be unto you. If I have to make any remarks as to your translations, I will write to you when I have examined them...
>
> I still have some hope of seeing you in the summer. But all depends upon the will of our God. May the Lord come! This would fulfil our highest desires.[9]

Darby wrote six further letters to von Poseck. They were printed in the three-volume edition of the *Letters* but the editor, William Kelly (1821–1906), had deleted all the names of places and recipients in order to prevent identification. With the assistance of Edwin Cross in London it has now been possible to name von Poseck as the original addressee of seven of Darby's letters. In these letters Darby discussed the recently discovered 'Bergische Taufbewegung' (a baptismal movement in a former German duchy) and warned against insisting on a particular mode of baptism.[10] Indeed he himself baptized infants. Also he praised von Poseck for his resolute stand against the priests, who called his work 'separatist' and complained about him to the church authorities in Koblenz. Darby also mentioned von Poseck's temporary imprisonment and comforted him by explaining that similar incidents were taking place in France.

Von Poseck had withdrawn from the Jülich area some time previously. In the meantime he had founded the first Darbyite assemblies in the area between Düsseldorf and Barmen. There the Evangelischer Brüderverein (Evangelical Brethren Association) was also active. Some of their preachers heard Darby's strange new teachings and followed them. Finally Brockhaus joined them as well. This led to the crisis in the assembly.[11] In December 1852 Brockhaus and seven teaching brothers left, and at the beginning of 1853 he founded an assembly on Elberfeld lines, which was in fellowship with Darby.

---

9. J.N. Darby, *Letters* (Winschoten, Netherlands, 1971), vol. 3, p. 269 (London, [1851]]).

10. August Jung, *Als die Väter noch Freunde waren* (Wuppertal, 1999), pp. 70ff.

11. Jung, *Als die Väter*, pp. 92ff.

However, von Poseck, who had started the work years before, did not consider cooperating with Brockhaus. Instead, he consolidated 'his' assemblies by a concerted withdrawal from the Lutheran Church, the acceptance of a creed, and the publication of a small collection of sixteen hymns: *Lieder für Kinder Gothes* (*Songs for the Children of God*). It included among others 'Auf dem Lamm ruht meine Seele' (see the opening of this chapter for the English version). Brockhaus responded by publishing for his Elberfeld Brethren a book of eighty-three hymns: *Kleine Sammlung geistlicher Lieder* (*A Small Collection of Spiritual Songs*)—a sign that the two founding fathers did not understand each other. Von Poseck, high-born and university educated, could not cooperate with Brockhaus, the bourgeois elementary schoolteacher, nor vice versa.

Darby was aware of this discord. He looked for a solution and found it in this idea: the two men should be put to work for several months in close proximity on an important task. This led to the translation of the New Testament in the years 1854–55. Darby, von Poseck, and Brockhaus (who had meanwhile given up his teaching career and was living on the donations of his brothers and sisters in the assembly) occupied themselves with the Greek text. Brockhaus, who knew very little Greek, had no choice but to write down what the two experts dictated. One of Darby's letters explained the atmosphere among the translators:

> Dear brother, I am here [in Elberfeld] and speak broken German with the dear brothers, whom God has so richly blessed through the well-known difficulties of a Christian work. Indeed, we have outstanding workers, but we still have our difficulties. One brother, whom my brother supported, worked amongst them and had the means to revive several of them; but it seems he has not created much confidence among the brothers as to the depth of his godliness. He is keen, self-confident and talented. Relationships are difficult; not for me, except as far as my efforts are concerned to improve them, but in their own field of activity both of them are much blessed.[12]

In November 1854, some brothers in Elberfeld expressed distrust of von Poseck. They said that his piety was not deep enough. They were annoyed that he sometimes quoted Sophocles and Goethe; that he used foreign words; that in the assembly he would translate directly from the Hebrew and Greek text; that he quoted whole passages by heart from the original; that he understood the script, the meaning and the context better than the others and so—instinctively—he corrected and confused the simple brothers. Did not his continual know-all manner indicate a lack of humility and a superficial piety? When one further remembers that the first generation of German Brethren came from the petit bourgeois world of workers, craftsmen and small shopkeepers, who anyway thought of university studies as worldly, then it was obvious why they reproached him with a lack of godliness. For them, it was as if von Poseck had come from a different world. He was felt to be a stranger who could not fit in with their petit-bourgeois revivalist piety. Darby, who

12. *Le Messager Evangélique* 40 (1899), p. 57.

himself came from a rich and influential family, had no problems with him. After all, they were both cast in the same mould; but Darby advised him to come to England, as it were to his own kind.

As soon as the translation was completed (1855) von Poseck moved to Hilden, where as early as 1851 he had founded the really first sizeable Brethren assembly. There he again snubbed Brockhaus by publishing an enlarged hymnbook without taking into account the existing one by Brockhaus, whereupon the latter enlarged to 116 hymns his *Kleine Sammlung geistlicher Lieder*. At that time von Poseck was the undisputed leader of 'his' assemblies. But why did he in 1857 leave his German homeland to go to England? It may be assumed that Darby had got to know his two German brothers thoroughly in the six months that they had worked together on the translation. Therefore it is a fair supposition that, in an effort to dispel the differences between the two men, he invited von Poseck to come to England. The early Darby biographer Ischebeck wrote that von Poseck 'was taken to England to get him away from the battle. He was too scholarly for the Elberfeld Brethren and they did not get on with him.'[13] Or—quite another and much more plausible possibility—could it be that a very charming person, Christiana Wilson, was in London expecting to become his wife?

A New Home

When Julius Anton von Poseck came from Düsseldorf to London in 1857, he did not feel much at home there except with his betrothed. A dispute of historic proportions had in 1848 split the early Brethren movement into Exclusive Brethren and Open Brethren. Von Poseck had heard of this dispute when a young Christian in Düsseldorf. However, he had heard only Darby's point of view, which had influenced him to follow faithfully in his leader's footsteps.

Von Poseck 'was justly esteemed as an interesting and original preacher'.[14] He also became well-known as a writer on edification. His first book appeared in 1874 under the title *Green Pastures and Still Waters, for the Flock of God*. With much allegorical interpretation and disregarding the grammatical and historical aspects he applied the whole of Psalm 23 to the celebration of the Lord's Supper. One has to admire his deep piety when he confessed in the (somewhat amended) words of the hymn by Isaac Watts:

> Before that Cross I bow my poor head into the dust, not to reason about it, but to muse and worship before it.
> Whene'er I muse upon the Cross,
> On which the Lord of Glory died,
> My richest gain I count but loss

13. Gustav Ischebeck, 'Blätter aus vergangenen Tagen', *Der Gärtner* (Witten, 1919), p. 82.

14. Neatby, *Plymouth Brethren*, p. 256.

And pour contempt on all my pride.[15]

His other book, *Light in our Dwellings* (1875), was directed at the Christian family. He saw families troubled by the spirit of revolution. Theologically he held here to the 'gap theory' of creation and to dispensationalism; he also advocated withdrawal from the world, warning against university studies and secular literature. He called for paternal authority, the subservience of women, who should have their heads covered in the services, and for the obedience of children. Later, after the painful schism between Darby and Kelly in 1881, he published several magazines such as *Die christliche Laufbahn* (*The Christian Walk*) and *Worte der Wahrheit in Liebe* (*Words of Truth in Love*).

At first, he always sided with Darby's party in church disputes. He belonged also to the leading group which Darby had appointed from among his chief followers in London and which had to take decisions on matters of dispute. But after some years he had his first doubts about the dictatorial teaching of his master. For example, in 1866 it was Darby of all people, his great theological teacher, who was accused of promoting false doctrine: it was said that he had expressed ideas in a paper on 'The sufferings of Christ' (1858), for which he had in 1848 condemned Benjamin Wills Newton (1807–99). Indeed, for his teaching on the three classes of Christ's sufferings, he took large parts of his argument from the Psalms and other Old Testament passages, and he used these texts as if they were historical reports. At the head of those who opposed Darby at this time was his former comrade-in-arms, William Henry Dorman (1802–78). He accused Darby of spreading the same Newtonian nonsense that they had previously fought against together. Now he would have to weigh him in the same scales and measure him with the same measure as had once been applied to Newton. Dorman had concluded that Darby had raised the question of ecclesiastical power even in the dispute on Christology. He said,

> At first, of course, all this was pursued as necessary to the maintenance of purity of doctrine and of 'a true Christ'...and I honestly thought it so myself. But this guise is now utterly and rudely stripped away... What...correspondence is there between a company of Christians meeting simply in the name of Christ...and that of an immense ecclesiastical ramification, which is everywhere subject, and in all things, as to its order, doctrine, and discipline, to Mr D.'s decrees? enforced by a ubiquitous, unseen, spiritual supervision, from which, as there is no escape, so is there no appeal?... [The latter is] as narrow and sectarian, and as hard also, as the domination of man can desire it.[16]

Dorman was not alone in his criticism. This time, von Poseck also refused to follow Darby. Where the person of Jesus Christ was concerned, speculations were suspect for him. But his opposition did not last long. 'Some time after his secession he

15. J.A. von Poseck, *Green Pastures and Still Waters for the Flock of God* (Addison, Illinois, 1874), p. 230.

16. Neatby, *Plymouth Brethren*, p. 255.

returned to his allegiance, I believe under Darby's personal influence'[17] and remained also a loyal follower. However, the foundations had already been laid for his later complete rejection of Darby's high church exclusivism when in 1881 such a split occurred that brotherly relations between the two leaders were severed. Something must now be said about this. It concerns the Park Street crisis.

Park Street in London was the assembly to which Darby belonged and, as far as questions of order and doctrine were concerned, for years theirs had been the last word. And this applied to Ramsgate, 120 kilometres away from London, where one assembly had split so that two had been formed. However, as there may be only one assembly in any one place, which was the right one? After much to-ing and fro-ing, it was Darby himself who finally decided to recognize the new assembly and reject the old one. But that was not the worst. The worst was that Darby, now an old man, required all the assemblies in the whole world—even the farthest islands—to bow to his decision. Kelly, von Poseck and many longstanding friends could not accept this all too human principle—and they were expelled as opponents. As a result of this deplorable affair, von Poseck wrote to the well-known C.H. Mackintosh in a private circular, 'Just put one letter before your favourite word (evil), and you will get the root of the matter (devil).'[18] A short time before that, von Poseck had sent an alarming brochure to his German brothers in Elberfeld. It contained these prophetic sentences:

> Here we are on the direct road to Rome! The only difference is that instead of an infallible Pope, we have an infallible assembly. The Word of God is set aside and the resolutions of the church take its place! Where have things got to with us? The sectarian tree of 'Darbyism' and 'Brethrenism' has grown to such a height that under the dark and poisonous shade of this upas-tree the precious sheep and lambs of God's flock, for whom the Good Shepherd suffered and died, are robbed of heavenly fight and healthy nourishment. They lose all power and discernment and so become an easy prey to the attack of the ravening wolf and the serpent that corrupts the sense and spoils the simplicity of Christ.[19]

When the Darbyite Elberfelder Brethren read these sentences they were appalled. Was this not proof that von Poseck had always been a heretical teacher? He opposed Darby! Carl Brockhaus called him 'a wolf in sheep's clothing'. His judgement caused all the Exclusive assemblies in Germany (as in England) to refuse to have fellowship with him. So, on his fairly frequent visits from England, von Poseck now turned more and more to the Free Evangelical Churches, among whose predecessors he had once been at home. Chiefly, he came to Düsseldorf, where he had found faith in God, and to Witten, where the young preacher Friedrich Fries (1856–1926) quite often invited him to preach. To this period of his life belonged also the above-mentioned

17. Neatby, *Plymouth Brethren*, p. 256.

18. J.A. von Poseck, *The Word of God or Private Revelations. Which?* (Lewisham, 1881), p. 2.

19. J.A. von Poseck, *Christus oder Park Street? Gottes Wort oder Menschenwort? Eine Stimme der Warnung an meine Brüder deutscher Zunge* (London, 1882), pp. 74ff.

magazines, *Die christliche Laufbahn* and *Worte der Wahrheit in Liebe*. In these he endeavoured with deep piety to win back his separated brethren.

Having written once again in 1882 against the seeming liberalism of the 'Open Brethren', he published in Kelly's *Bible Treasury* for 1888–89 some detailed 'Lectures on the Book of Jonah'. Finally in 1890–03 he published 'The Gospel and the Church', a work following Kelly's line of teaching. This was his real and detailed life's work.

Regrettably, there is almost no information about his wife. In their old age both were looked after by their daughter, Helene. Julius Anton von Poseck died on 6 July 1898, a little more than two months after his wife Christiana, who had died on 20 April. His was a life full of conflict and victory. His daughter Helene said, 'Among his last words were these: "Lord, you are ready for me and I am ready for you. Praise the Lord."'[20] Kelly wrote about the funeral, at which he had given the address for his friend,

> Dear Mr von P[oseck]. fell away rapidly since the departure of his wife and a run-over he sustained which seemed to affect him little at the time. He died at 2 A.M. on last Monday; and the funeral took place yesterday afternoon at Lewisham Cemetery a little before 4. There was a goodly company from all parts of London and from the country, North and South, especially from the meetings in his own neighbourhood. W. of Lewisham gave out hymn 316, 'We are by Christ redeemed', at the grave (to which we at once repaired without using the chapel) and I prayed and read 1 Cor. XV.55-57., and spoke to the saints and sinners accordingly. Another brother gave out hymn 266, 'Christ the Lord will come again', and W. prayed. A benediction was then said at the close before we broke up. Miss von P[oseck]. was there, and many sisters. All was as happy as such an occasion admits of, as our beloved brother was departing to be with Christ.[21]

Appendix: Helene von Poseck

It seems that Helene von Poseck had felt in her heart for quite a long time the call to missionary service. But as long as her old parents were alive she felt it was her duty to take care of them. Shortly before his death her father had given her his blessing for missionary work. Only now that he had died did she feel free to follow her vocation. So at the age of thirty-seven she became a missionary to China. Apparently this was a well-considered decision for Kelly writes something about the beginnings of the Kellyite Brethren mission. First of all, there is the following note:

> You will be interested in hearing that Miss von P[oseck]. goes D.V. to China with Mr. and Mrs. H[uttonl. in October next, her dear father heartily concurring with this

20. Abraham Meister, 'Einiges aus der Geschichte der Brüder', *Die Botschaft* (1939), p. 158.

21. William Kelly, letter of 11 July 1896, in the Archive of Edwin Cross held at Chapter Two, London.

> her desire a little before his death. As she has no income, any more than the H[utton]. family, they will be the more laid on our hearts. It is quite a different thing from working in the West Indies or Demerara where there are already many hundreds of saints and a considerable number of meeting rooms. Our dear friends go to a far more distant and heathen land with not one as yet in fellowship. But they go with joy, hope, and godly confidence.[22]

A few months later Kelly reports:

> We had an excellent and full meeting on Tuesday evening in commending to the Lord the H[utton].'s and Miss von P[oseck]. They go amply provided for in every way, and with faith and love on the part of many to hold them up.[23]

At the end of 1896 they set out together for China: Helene von Poseck and Thomas Hutton and his family. They got to Hsin-Huan, where Thomas Hutton preached the gospel and the women taught the Chinese children to read, write, and sing, since contemporary theology did not allow them to do anything else. In March 1899, a good two years after their departure, Kelly could report this about them:

> The H[utton].'s and Miss von P[oseck]. go on undisturbed by the unsettled state of China. He craves for young English brothers; but I fear a sort of college. I urged his looking to the Lord for native converts to help in due time, far more efficiently than foreigners.
>
> He might also look for missionaries, like himself, to learn 'a more excellent way'. We must beware of the religious world abroad and at home.[24]

Helene von Poseck was also well-known as the writer of many much-loved hymns. Ten of them can be found in the Exclusive Brethren hymnbook, *Hymns Selected and Revised* (1928).[25] Only two were published also by the Open Brethren: 'Father divine, in grateful love' and 'Once more around Thy table'.[26] She also wrote a remarkable children's book, *Adrift in Naples* (1896), in which she describes the story of the Neapolitan boy Little Joe who was healed from his illness after he had prayed to God and who from that time followed Jesus. She it was also who, at the beginning of the twentieth century, when German researchers wanted to know more about her father Julius Anton von Poseck, sent them some—unfortunately imprecise—information. When she finally died in 1951, aged ninety-two, the name 'von Poseck' died with her, but not sincere thankfulness for Julius Anton von Poseck.

---

22. Kelly, letter of 11 July 1896.
23. Kelly to H, 1 October 1896.
24. Kelly, letter of March 1899.
25. Nos. 58, 148, 191, 248, 279, 287, 292, 303, 321, 330.
26. In the *Mitchley Supplement* to *Hymns of Faith* (London, 1967), Nos 701, 782.

CHAPTER 11

The Early Years of a New Assembly: Bethesda Gospel Hall, Singapore, 1864–1914

Jason Lim

Introduction

The Brethren movement began in Singapore when four believers met to break bread in a place known simply as the Mission Rooms on 3 July 1864. It is not clear how these four people met, but their act in remembering the Lord Jesus Christ that Sunday was significant in that they met simply as believers, as a 'non-sectarian' assembly. While the only other places where the Lord was remembered were the denominational churches that had their own buildings, these four believers met in a little room at 108 Bencoolen Street on the outskirts of the city.

These four believers were Philip Robinson and his wife, and William Macdonald and his wife. Little is known about William Macdonald, other than that he was a bookkeeper, and that when the Brethren had their own building for the first time in 1866 he was one of the original trustees of the new building. Robinson, on the other hand, was a merchant who left Tewkesbury, England, for Melbourne in the late 1840s, and arrived in Singapore in 1857. He started a company with a partner in 1858, but when the partner left the next year, the business was renamed Robinsons & Company. It still exists today.[1]

The choice of the name 'Mission Rooms' is significant. The name perhaps represented the hopes of those in the assembly that the gospel of the Lord Jesus Christ be propagated among the people on the island through the preaching and evangelical services in the new assembly. In the early years, however, the assembly remained very small. A head count of those who attended the Breaking of Bread service on 11 March 1866 revealed only eighteen believers present—and this was the highest attendance for the Mission Rooms. The first deacons—J.L. Wheatley and a Mr Sausunan—were appointed to attend to the 'temporal affairs' of the assembly

1. Tong Suit Chee, *The Bethesda Legacy* (Singapore, 2004), pp. 125-29; Jason Lim, 'Assumptions and evidence: the case of Philip Robinson (1830–1886)', *BAHNR*, 3.1 (2004), pp. 18-47.

only on 4 March 1866.[2] There was no mention about the appointment of an oversight for the assembly, but Robinson and MacDonald preached frequently in the evening service of the assembly.

A decision was reached on 5 August 1866 to build a new building for the assembly. On that day, a total of $34.15 was collected for the building fund. Two days later, a contractor was employed to build the new building in fifty days for $260. The contractor must have met his deadline, as the last meeting in the Mission Rooms was held on 28 September. The new building, 'called Bethesda', nearby at 77 Bras Basah Road, was opened on 30 September with prayer and ten believers attended its first Breaking of Bread at 9 a.m.[3]

The Early Years

The new building was not without its problems. On 30 December 1866, the assembly met to discuss the need to raise funds for the building to be lit by gas. It is indeed noticeable that when the assembly met in the Mission Rooms, there was no indication of evening services. The first evening service commenced in the new Bethesda building the very day it was opened with prayer—on 30 September 1866. One can only imagine how dark the interior of the building must have been during the evening for that first year, that there was a need to light it by gas! An entry was recorded in the assembly record book, the principal source for events within the assembly, that Bethesda Free Meeting House (note the new name) was lit with gas from 20 January 1867.

Another matter that was planned by the new Bethesda Free Meeting House was drafting a trust deed in the event that attendance in the assembly might dwindle to the point that it would have to be dissolved. A draft of the trust deed was passed around the assembly on 31 March 1867 for the members to ponder over the following week. On that day, too, the assembly agreed to purchase a small plot of land in front of the building, and this piece of land would be included in the trust deed. No mention was made of any further discussion, but a copy of the trust deed can be found at the back of the assembly record book.

The trust deed nominated both Robinson and Macdonald as the trustees of the assembly building. Furthermore, it stipulated that should membership in the assembly be reduced to only two, the building and its assets would be handed over to George Müller or whoever was the Director of the Scriptural Knowledge Institution (SKI) in Bristol 'for missionary operations in the Colony of the Straits Settlements'.[4] Over the years the trustees of the assembly building had to be changed. Macdonald had settled in Johore Bahru in July 1866 (before the Bethesda Free Meeting House was opened). Robinson died in London on 14 February 1886,

---

2. Unless otherwise stated, the source for events in this paper is the assembly record book, a register kept at Bethesda Gospel Hall chronicling major events in the assembly from 1864 to 1934.

3. Assembly Record Book, p. 41.

4. Assembly Record Book, pp. 451-54.

and Macdonald was asked by the assembly to resign his trusteeship in May 1886. Three other men—Philip Hocquard, Andrew Koenitz and C.F. Moore—were appointed the new trustees. Moore resigned on 4 February 1895, and was replaced by a British missionary named W.G. Honywill.

Coming of Resident Missionaries

When believers met in the Mission Rooms there were no known missionaries (defined by people who had been called to work full-time preaching the gospel to unbelievers) associated with the assembly. The first known Brethren missionary to arrive in Singapore and Malaya was John Chapman from Bristol. Through his efforts, Farquhar Street Mission Chapel was started in Penang in 1860. Chapman also made an effort to study the Malay language in order to preach the gospel to the Malays in their own tongue. In 1868, however, on account of his wife's poor health due to the local climate, Chapman and his family left for Melbourne.[5]

Chapman first visited Bethesda Gospel Hall in April 1867 and probably stayed in the assembly premises until June. The assembly record book noted that he preached nearly every Sunday evening from 28 April to 23 June. Indeed, a farewell tea meeting was arranged at Bethesda Gospel Hall for the Chapmans on 26 June. During his stay at Bethesda Gospel Hall, he baptized Tan See Boo and five other Chinese men on 8 May. This was another important development in the history of the Brethren movement in Singapore, as Tan See Boo subsequently left the Presbyterian Church and started the first Chinese Brethren assembly in Singapore, known as the Hock-Im-Koan (Chinese Gospel Hall), in late 1867.

On 11 August 1867, Alexander Grant and his wife moved to Singapore from Penang where he became the first resident missionary in association with Bethesda Gospel Hall. Grant was a Scottish missionary with the English Presbyterian Church who joined the Brethren over this period, having learned of the movement's manner of commemorating the Lord's Supper in China.[6] The Grants had intended to work among the Chinese and European communities in Singapore. Indeed Grant's first task was to preach at the Sailors' Home the very afternoon of the day he arrived in Singapore.

Beginnings of Mission House

On 6 September 1878, a special church meeting was held at Bethesda Gospel Hall to consider the desirability of providing a home for missionaries passing through the port, either needing rest or temporary accommodation. The matter could not have been timelier, as Hudson Taylor and a party of missionaries *en route* to China arrived in Singapore on 7 April 1879, and stayed for a few days on the island. As the

5. N. Thiran, 'The Christian Brethren of Malaysia: Our Heritage', paper presented at the Assembly Leaders' Conference at Highlands Christian Centre, Cameron Highlands, Malaysia, 26 April 1990, pp. 23-24.

6. J.W.J., 'Alexander Grant', *The Believer's Pathway*, 35 (May 1914), pp. 70-71.

assembly had no accommodation for them, Taylor and his colleagues had to stay at the home of J.L. Wheatley, an assembly deacon.

Wheatley applied to the colonial authorities in Singapore for a piece of land to build a Mission House on 27 April 1879. The assembly was of the opinion that the site granted by the government was more eligible for a Mission House than that of Bethesda Gospel Hall. The assembly was finally given permission to occupy the ground for a Mission House on 14 November, before Wheatley and his family moved to Madras (now Chennai) in India. Nothing is known about what happened during the time when Wheatley was in India, as no account was kept in the assembly record book of persons who met at the morning meetings until early 1880. An entry in the assembly record book finally appeared on 27 March 1881 with Wheatley reporting that he had received a contribution from the Chinese believers at Penang toward the expenses for the building of the Mission House. The building was completed on 20 July 1882, and the first missionary to occupy the new Mission House was Alexander Grant. This Mission House at 92 Neil Road (later 417 New Bridge Road) was to prove to be a haven for missionaries from many countries. It was certainly a needful retreat for those who were driven out of China during the Boxer Rebellion in 1900. An adjoining house was rented for use later as a Gospel Hall and the Sunday School was transferred from the Mission House.

Grant was instrumental in planning and conducting evangelistic tours of Malaya, the Dutch East Indies and even China. Between 2 June and 21 July 1883 he worked in Java. In June 1885, however, Grant left for Britain, returning to Bethesda Chapel (a new name was given in the assembly record book in January 1898) on 29 March 1899. He did not stay long, and left for Penang in June. Four months later, he was in Singapore but departed for China on 15 October. Returning to Singapore on 3 June 1901, he continued on with a tour of Penang, leaving for Britain finally in December 1902.

Other Early Resident Missionaries

Another early missionary at Bethesda Gospel Hall was Philip Hocquard. He arrived on 2 March 1884 from China. Initially, life could have been difficult for him and his wife was called home on 30 April 1885. But the assembly record book noted that Hocquard continued to play active roles in the assembly and the mission field. Two people were baptized by him at the Chinese Gospel Hall in late 1885. On 1 February 1886, Hocquard married Sarah Ann Casterveld and left Singapore the next month for an evangelistic tour of Malaya, returning from Perak only on 28 April. Hocquard eventually left for England on 26 February 1898 on account of his poor health, and was called home on 13 October 1899.

On 4 January 1890, the ‘SS Breconshire’ arrived in Singapore, bringing a group of missionaries who were to remain active until the early years of the twentieth century. Within this group of missionaries were two men who would play important preaching and evangelistic roles at Bethesda—W.G. Honywill and Alfred Thoburn. Honywill was the assembly’s baptizer throughout 1890. That year also saw the assembly making plans for a new building of brick and no wood. Honywill was involved in the project, and he obtained an estimate of $2,140 for the cost of a new building in May 1890. The new building took the whole year of 1891 to complete, as iron beams ordered for the building were sent to Hong Kong by mistake. Eventually, the building was completed and opened on 17 January 1892. Honywill did not stay very long with Bethesda—he left for England with his wife in November 1896. But by that time, the financial state of the assembly was good, and Honywill reported a surplus of income from voluntary offerings, as well as special offerings made to the Building Fund. Honywill died of typhoid fever in Italy on 17 August 1907.

Alfred Thoburn arrived with Honywill in 1890, but whereas Honywill concentrated on working among the English-speaking assembly of Bethesda, Thoburn left soon after to learn the Southern Hokkien dialect in Amoy. Returning from his work in Penang, Thoburn and two other brothers were given the task of speaking at gospel meetings on Sunday evenings, a decision made at a church meeting on 23 September 1892. He remained active at Bethesda Gospel Hall and on 22 February 1911 he became a member of the assembly oversight. He left for England on 6 June 1912.

Upon Honywill's departure, W.D. Ashdown arrived to work at Bethesda Gospel Hall. It seems that, from this moment on, a missionary would be sent from England to replace one who had left. A year later, in December 1897, another two missionaries—A.E. Green and T. Angus—arrived from Britain. Ashdown left for Penang on 17 January 1898, and his work in the assembly accounts was handed over to Green. A month later, J.C.M. Dawson arrived with his family to work in the assembly. As early as May 1898, both Green and Dawson spoke on the teaching of scripture concerning believer's baptism. Another missionary, George Wilson, arrived from England with E. Hill from Taipeng on 1 March 1899, and four weeks later Alexander Grant returned to the assembly before departing for Penang.

In late 1899, however, Dawson became critically ill and was ordered by a doctor to return to England. Grant had already gone to China. It was only on 3 January 1900 that J.R. Angus arrived from China en route to Kuala Lumpur. Considering the lack of people doing God's work in the assembly, Angus decided to stay and help the assembly until someone else arrived to replace him. He did not wait very long. Miss Hankins, a New Zealander who had worked in Penang, arrived in Singapore on 19 May. She did not live long as she died suddenly on 11 November. On 30 July, Charles G. Roberts arrived from Weihaiwei in China in the wake of the Boxer Rebellion. He would be joined by E. Eagger and his family in September, so it was, therefore, the right time for Angus to move on with God's work at Kuala Lumpur, and he left on 11 October.

Another missionary, named Tom Baird, arrived from Britain on 25 April 1901, and straightaway he took over the work at the assembly from Eagger, who had returned to Britain three days before. Baird was to suffer much pain when his son Harry died aged eight months and one week, on 22 August 1903. Yet Baird was not the only one to have suffered the loss of a child at Bethesda Gospel Hall. The entry in the assembly record book that recorded the death of Harry Baird also included the sad statement, 'Every child that has lived in this house has been taken.' Baird, his wife and two surviving children eventually left Singapore to return to Britain for their health's sake on 2 April 1906.

From 1890 to 1914, several missionaries came to Singapore and worked in the Bethesda Chapel in quick succession. One such person was Alfred Green, who arrived from England on 9 December 1897, and the assembly accounts were passed to him the following month. In April 1899, he left for Kuala Lumpur and his wife joined him in May. It was not known when he returned to England, but the assembly record book recorded the Greens' return to Singapore on 16 December 1904. It seemed their last departure from the island was on 28 March 1910. Green was Director of the George Müller Foundation in Bristol from 1930 to 1940.

Upon Green's departure, James Teskey came to Singapore with his wife on 22 November 1910. Commended from Christians in Somerset, Teskey had worked as an evangelist in England, and now he had come to minister to the needs of the English-speaking assembly. He left in 1932 for the West Indies. Other missionaries included H.C. Bowen (who laboured from 1914 to 1919), Handley Bird (who worked at the chapel for nine months in 1914) and J. Burns from New Zealand (who arrived in November 1914 and left for Penang in March 1915).

Deaths in the Assembly

Life for believers in the first fifty years of the assembly was difficult. Reading through the entries of the assembly record book, one keeps finding that many believers had to return to Britain or temporarily suspend their activities at the Bethesda Free Meeting House on account of ill-health. Epidemics may affect the work of the assembly, and an entry in the assembly record book on 31 December 1873 noted that the assembly was preserved during an outbreak of cholera.

The assembly record book also recorded that on 27 August 1876 one Mrs Jallent was admitted into fellowship after a 'long and severe' illness, although the record did not mentioned exactly what the illness was. On 19 November 1877, C.F. Moore left for Calcutta in India as his health was 'failing'. He returned to the assembly only on 25 February 1878.

On 5 January 1899, Mrs Green contracted smallpox, and so it was announced that all assembly services from 13 to 17 January would be held at the Town Hall instead. Further tragedy befell the assembly when the infant son of J.W. Moore passed away on 15 April 1900. Nine days later, one Mrs Mansfield left for England 'in a delicate state of health'.

The weather was a source of great discomfort to the early missionaries. Miss Alice Emmerson from New Zealand recorded that she was 'somewhat run down through overwork'.[7] Eventually she left Singapore in April 1903 after nine years

---

7. *The New Zealand Treasury*, 2 (1900), p. 158.

service to go to England for 'a change in climate'.[8] Miss E. McIntosh wrote that she was run down with the constant heat in Bangalore, India, and yet she felt that the city had an advantage over Singapore in that it had 'two or three months of cold weather'.[9] Miss McIntosh was to record in early 1914 that there was 'excessively hot weather' in Singapore for the last five weeks, 'and there has been much sickness, and many laid aside with fever and several cases of cholera'.[10]

Miss Jessie Koenitz died of typhoid fever on 13 May 1902 and was buried at Bukit Timah Cemetery. Two weeks later, it was announced that Mrs J.W. Moore had died in the Moore's houseboat on the river in North Borneo (now Sabah) after nine years of service for the Lord. It was also recorded that on 10 July 1906 the infant child of Mr and Mrs Fish died. From these records, one can understand that it was not easy for the missionaries to leave the comforts of home and travel and work in Singapore.

Problems in Early Years

Part of the assembly work includes assembly discipline and the need to protect itself from doctrinal errors. The assembly record book faithfully recorded several instances when the assembly had to gather together and act upon those who had deliberately twisted the word of God to suit themselves. The assembly also practised biblical separation, by calling its members to dissociate themselves from those who had wilfully fallen into sin and were unrepentant.

On 25 July 1867, one Miss O'Callaghan visited the new assembly. She was originally from Malacca, but she was accepted into fellowship with Bethesda Free Meeting House and began preaching frequently to sailors and at tea meetings. However, she left for the Cape of Good Hope suddenly on 17 February 1870. It seemed that she had been led to believe that there was a place called 'The City of God' and that the church in South Africa would be the one to which God would be speaking. This belief had been propounded by a Dutch couple from South Africa known only as the Grenwolds, who had arrived at Bethesda in January 1870. Mr Grenwold even preached in an evening service and a prayer meeting in early February. But within a month, Miss O'Callaghan, one of the main assembly workers, had been influenced by their erroneous teachings. Even worse, the assembly later learned from a Dutch missionary from South Africa named Leiopoldt that the Dutch Missionary Society had dissociated itself from Grenwold due to his strange views, and that the woman introduced as Mrs Grenwold was not his wife. His real wife was alive but separated from him due to his cruelty towards her. But Bethesda Free Meeting House took this setback in the Lord's work as a valuable lesson for them from the Lord. The assembly record book did not express any frustration with the Grenwolds or Miss O'Callaghan, but instead chose to record that 'we praise and

8. *The New Zealand Treasury*, 6 (1904), p. 21.
9. *Missionary Tidings*, 1.1 (January 1910), p. 4.
10. *Australian Missionary Tidings*, 1 August 1914.

bless God that He has sent this brother [that is, Leiopoldt] in our midst to assure our hearts and to teach us a lesson—may we profit thereby'.[11]

The record from early years of the new assembly also showed that it expected its members to exercise spiritual discipline. As early as 17 June 1866, before a congregation of just eight people, Robinson observed that some members had questionable conduct. He also mentioned the names of three people who had been avoiding assembly services in connection with such questionable conduct. By the end of the month, two of them were expelled from the assembly, probably because they refused to repent. The third person's case was shelved for a week due to the death of his wife. Eventually he was suspended from the assembly.

Occasionally, visitors to the assembly would ask if they could be identified with the assembly in fellowship. Several of them had to be rejected on various grounds. On 23 February 1868, one Mrs Mitchell wanted to identify herself with the assembly, but she was not accepted into fellowship due to an 'appearance of evil' in her.[12] The assembly, however, agreed to accept her later on 14 March 1869, and she was baptized with her daughter in May. She left for England on 14 May 1882.

Letters of commendation were common even in the early days of the assembly. No one knew anything about a man named Peter Alexander Clarino who joined the assembly on 13 June 1869. However, within a week, a letter arrived from Malacca saying that he was guilty of deceit and lying and it urged Bethesda not to allow him to take part in the Breaking of Bread service. Nothing more was recorded about Clarino—he probably left the assembly.

There was also a case where a minor dispute affected the assembly. In June 1884, one John Haffenden wrote a letter to the assembly calling for the discontinuation of using ordinary red wine during the Breaking of Bread. He suggested unfermented grape juice be used instead, a well-known demand of Temperance campaigners. On 16 June, a special service had to be convened in order to give Haffenden the occasion to bring his case before the assembly. He urged the use of infused raisins rather than 'intoxicating' wine, and threatened to withdraw himself, his wife and their two sons from the assembly if his wishes were not met. Nothing was mentioned in subsequent records until ten years later. To a question posed on Christmas Eve 1894 on whether Haffenden could rejoin Bethesda, the assembly felt that it could not agree to the use of only unfermented grape juice. On 4 February 1895, a letter was written from Hocquard to the assembly to put aside Haffenden's demand for the time being. There were no record since then of Haffenden ever rejoining the assembly, and indeed, until today, wine is still used at Bethesda Hall (Ang Mo Kio), the successor to Bethesda Free Meeting House after the latter was demolished.

There are few records extant on whether non-believers resisted the attempts by the assembly to spread the gospel throughout Singapore. There are, however, records which suggest that the work of the missionaries was not easy. Miss Emmerson wrote in *The New Zealand Treasury* that 'we have a very good hall and a good

11. Assembly Record Book, pp. 102-103.
12. Assembly Record Book, p. 65.

attendance at the Gospel meetings, but the conversions are very few on the whole'. She continued to record that the Seventh-Day Adventists were very active in Singapore, and 'I am sorry to say that a good number have been won by them.'[13]

Conclusion

Bethesda Gospel Hall between 1864 and 1914 was a growing assembly. This paper has mentioned the role it played even in the founding of the first Chinese assembly in Singapore in 1867. As the congregation grew, the assembly building itself needed expansion and a new home for resident missionaries had to be built by Bethesda Gospel Hall.

Yet the early years of Bethesda Gospel Hall were also years of struggle. Missionaries who came, stayed and worked in the new assembly had to face uphill challenges in bringing new members into fellowship in the assembly. But the missionaries also faced uncomfortable conditions, sickness and even death of their loved ones.

Another challenge for the new assembly in its first fifty years was to ensure that believers in fellowship in the assembly would not be influenced by the many 'winds of doctrine'. Letters of commendation may help prevent people with erroneous doctrines from identifying themselves with the assembly, but the assembly record book showed that there were cases of people within the assembly bringing up issues that were divisive.

May the Lord's name be praised even as we consider his work among assembly believers in Singapore!

13. *The New Zealand Treasury*, 8 (1906), p. 95.

CHAPTER 12

Brethren Revivalism: A Second Look at New Zealand

Peter Lineham

The Brethren achieved an impact in New Zealand that was paralleled only in some of the African mission settings. The explanation for this lay in a huge impact that they made in the rural communities. It is remarkable how to this day significant proportions of the current Brethren trace their Christian roots to a small number of communities, Rongotea, Waverley, Maxwell, Ngaere, Te Kopuru and Maharahara in particular. These tiny communities (absent from almost all modern maps) are the heartland of the Brethren community, and they are so because in the 1870s, 1880s and 1890s they were the scene of remarkable community-wide revivals. In this paper I want to explore the notion that I presented some thirty years ago about Brethren revivalism, and I also want to ponder how the Brethren became a significant part of some rural communities in New Zealand.[1] Over the years I have accumulated a large number of comments and corrections to what I wrote at that time, and it is timely to reflect on the story and to clarify the ways in which the Brethren were changed by their involvement with the revivalist tradition.

Several key issues emerged in the course of my study. I was puzzled to understand why the Brethren flourished in the countryside rather than the cities of the colony, in contrast to most other churches, particularly the 'new' churches, and perhaps in contrast to their patterns in the United Kingdom. It seemed to me that part of the answer lay in the close link between the Brethren and revivalism—a phenomenon which had never been studied in New Zealand before my work. Yet this revivalism seemed anything but Brethren, and seemingly bore little resemblance to the rather sectarian characteristics of the Brethren as they later developed. I puzzled to understand this. Were there, I wondered, any distinctly Brethren elements to this revivalism or was it an 'imported' product? And I wondered if any of these trends were particular to New Zealand. This paper seeks to answer these questions.

The revivalism that emerged in New Zealand was in evidence throughout the English-speaking world, and fruitful comparisons can be made with patterns in

1. Peter J. Lineham, *There we found Brethren: a history of assemblies of Brethren in New Zealand* (Palmerston North, NZ, 1977).

Australia and Canada.[2] It was deeply inspired by the transatlantic revivalists, who have been the focus of work by Carwardine and Kent and many others.[3] Since I wrote thirty years ago we have a much better understanding of revivalism as a historic phenomenon. It fits in as a phase in the history of popular Christianity, and took a very precise form which needs to be recognized.

The Emergence of Revivalism

There is a particular shape and form to late nineteenth-century revivalism. It precedes the Fundamentalist age, and represents an ebullient populist Christianity. It is different from the eighteenth-century revivalism, for it is much more a lay movement, an interdenominational movement, and has moved away from the paternalism and sectarian structure of the eighteenth-century movement. Nineteenth-century revivalism, shaped by the contributions of Dow, McGready, Caughey, Finney, the Primitive Methodists and the American camp meetings, was conversionist, premillennial and 'higher-life' in theology and comfortable with movements of social change and societal transformation. The revivalist tradition was 'fixed' by Finney, whose ideas and whose lectures on revivalism were widely circulated.

How Revival Gained Currency in New Zealand

In terms of significant evangelistic movements, the missionary work among Maori in the 1820s to the 1840s was by far the most successful example in New Zealand history. But particularly the Church Missionary Society placed its emphasis on traditional methods of catechism and moral instruction, and did not encourage waves of religious excitement. The Wesleyan mission was somewhat different, and given the West Country origin of some of the missionaries there must have been a

2. There is a very rich literature on the Canadian tradition of revivalism, for example in G.A. Rawlyk (ed.), *The Canadian Protestant Experience 1760–1990* (Burlington, ON, 1990). I have attempted to make the Canadian comparison in my article, Peter J. Lineham, 'When the Roll Is Called Up Yonder, Who'll Be There? An analysis of nineteenth century trans-Atlantic revivalism in New Zealand and Canada', in Douglas Pratt (ed.), *'Rescue the Perishing': comparative perspectives on evangelism and revivalism* (Waikato Studies in Religion, 1; Auckland, 1989), pp. 1-22. Comparison with Australia would be useful, and a beginning was made by Hugh R. Jackson, *Churches and People in Australia and New Zealand 1860–1930* (Wellington, 1987); and for Australia, see Mark Hutchinson, Edmund Campion and Stuart Piggin (eds), *Reviving Australia: essays on the history and experience of revival and revivalism in Australia* (Sydney, 1994). For New Zealand, see Robert Evans and Roy McKenzie, *Evangelical Revivals in New Zealand: a history of evangelical revivals in New Zealand and an outline of some basic principles of revivals* (Paihia, NZ, 1999), although this is weak on historical analysis.

3. Richard Carwardine, *Transatlantic Revivalism* (Westport, CT, 1978); John Kent, *Holding the Fort: studies in Victorian revivalism* (London, 1978).

measure of revivalist expectations, but they saw relatively little fruit. The introduction of revivalistic methods to the colony was by an American Methodist evangelist, William 'California' Taylor in 1864–65, during his visit to Australasia.[4] But at this stage most other denominations looked on somewhat cautiously.

Then in the 1870s interest in revivalism rose sharply, and there is every reason to attribute this to reports about Moody's impact in England. Moody's status and approach gave him an appeal which was symbolically inclusive. Moody's great mission to England in 1873–76 was of immense significance for New Zealand religious life. Geoffrey Troughton argues that the first report of this mission came in a Presbyterian magazine in February 1874.[5] The Wesleyan magazine also published accounts of Moody's English revivalism in August 1874.[6] The extensive reports of the London campaign were the object of much discussion and debate in 1875 particularly.[7] J.H. Twentyman lectured on Moody in 1875 in Christchurch, doubtless reflecting much newspaper comment about his English campaigns.[8] There was a proposal at the 1876 Wesleyan Conference that Moody and Sankey should be invited to New Zealand, but some newspaper writers vehemently opposed this because it undermined the respectability of the colony.[9]

Now the 1870s are crucial for the development of New Zealand as a whole, because it was the decade in which huge numbers of assisted immigrants doubled the European population of the colony from 256,000 to 489,000 people. At this time came the first examples of attempts to 'get up a revival' in New Zealand. In April 1874 the Wellington Presbytery urged prayer for revival in New Zealand, and John Elmslie, moderator of the presbytery and minister of St Paul's Wanganui, was keenly interested. The Wesleyans in Wanganui were also sympathetic, and special meetings were held early in 1875, and again in the second half of 1875 very large numbers gathered in the small town week after week for the special meetings.[10] It was the first major case of revival in the post-1859 sense in the colony. There were significant numbers of converts and new church members.

From then on and for the next thirty years, revivalism formed a major theme in New Zealand religious history, although a theme ignored by more institutional approaches to church history. The most dramatic beginnings were of the Salvation

---

4. See Bryan Gilling, 'Rushing into the Kingdom of Heaven: William "California" Taylor and New Zealand revivalism', *Stimulus* 12.1 (2004), pp. 7-12.

5. Geoffrey M. Troughton, 'Christianity and Community: aspects of religious life and attitudes in the Wanganui-Manawatu Region, 1870–1885' (MA thesis, Massey University, 1995), p. 82; idem, 'Moody and Sankey Down-Under. A case study in "Trans-Atlantic" revivalism in nineteenth century New Zealand', *Journal of Religious History* 29.2 (2005), pp. 146-47.

6. *New Zealand Wesleyan* (1 August 1874), pp. 135-36.

7. See, e.g., *Lyttleton Times* (14 July 1875), p. 3.

8. *Press*, Christchurch (1 June 1875), p. 2, and (19 July 1875), p. 2.

9. *Otago Witness* (29 January 1876), p. 15.

10. Troughton, 'Christianity and Community', pp. 85-93; 'Moody and Sankey Down-Under', *passim*.

Army which arrived with two soldiers in Dunedin in 1883 at the end of the revivalist era, and had spectacular success in the major towns of the colony and a few of the smaller towns as well. Research has suggested that the Salvationists attracted poorer townspeople through their style of confrontation with middle class respectable values.[11] But other denominations were also associated with revivalism, including some Baptists and Presbyterians and Methodists, but also three other new denominations, the Campbellite Churches of Christ, the Seventh-day Adventists and the Brethren.

An Example of a Brethren Revival

The Brethren had a distinctive part in this history because, unusually, their revivalist activities were almost entirely in rural districts. It may help to convey the flavour of these revivals by looking at a specific community. Any number of examples could be cited. I will consider a minor case, just north of Wanganui on the west coast of the North Island. The revival began at Waverley, a small town north of Wanganui which supported a Presbyterian church (there were strong concentrations of Scots in the outskirts of Wanganui) and had monthly Wesleyan services. To this township, fresh from extraordinary revival scenes in Taranaki, and before that from an extraordinary revival in Campbelltown (later Rongotea) in the Manawatu, came Edwin Moyse, a preacher from Tasmania, and with him 'in training', a young Manawatu man, C.H. Hinman, identified as a budding preacher, who had served his apprenticeship in the Taranaki preaching. The order of the Presbyterian congregation was disrupted by what happened in that revival, and many of the congregation transferred, including the sexton, who would ring the bell and then run off to the town hall.[12] The minister was Rev. Ralph J. Allsworth, a Scot who had ministered in the area from his induction in 1861, apart from a pastorate in Victoria, Australia, from 1869 to 1876.[13] The converts included whole families and groups of families, including the Aiken, Milner and Dickie families. The Dickies were from Scotland,

11. See Cyril R. Bradwell, *Fight the Good Fight: the story of the Salvation Army in New Zealand 1883–1983* (Wellington, 1982). There is a fine recent local study of the Salvation Army in a small town in Michael F. Hay, '"Onward Christian Soldiers": the Salvation Army in Milton 1884–1894', in John Stenhouse and Jane Thomson (eds), *Building God's Own Country: historical essays on religions in New Zealand* (Dunedin, 2004), pp. 113-23.

12. J. Dickson, *History of the Presbyterian Church of New Zealand* (Dunedin, 1899), p. 517; C.H. Hinman, *Lectures on the Tabernacle in the Wilderness, with a short account of the life of the author* (Palmerston North, 1923), p. 6. (The 'Short Account' was by Franklin Ferguson.)

13. See the Register of Ministers, online at the Presbyterian Archives, <http://www.archives.presbyterian.org.nz/Page146.htm>, consulted 7 October 2005. It is curious that this church had a Bible Class founded in the same year, 1883; perhaps an attempt to hold those who had not deserted? See M.N. Garing, '"Foursquare for Christ" The Presbyterian Bible Class Movement' (MA thesis, Victoria University of Wellington, 1985), p. 45.

and the senior member, James Dickie, born in 1849, had been converted in A.N. Somerville's Presbyterian evangelistic meetings in Wanganui in 1878, so he was well experienced in Moody-style evangelism.[14] Dickie almost immediately became a preacher and gospel tract distributor, so we may assume that he was already waiting for the revival. He must have been delighted at the new church of some 100 members that was established as a result of the preaching. Even in 1891 there were fifty people 'in fellowship' in the assembly.[15]

The preaching at that time impacted other little towns in the vicinity, and some converts came from these areas; most of them sawmillers and dairy farmers, for in the 1870s there was a rapid opening up of the countryside to new settlers and farms had to be cut out of the bush.[16]

Close to the epicentre of the first revival another occurred eleven years later. In the winter of 1891 two or three preachers from Waverley spoke in the little community of Maxwelltown, on the road from Waverley to Wanganui, and it became a frenzy of excitement through the work of Brethren evangelists. James Dickie of Waverley had been faithfully preaching and distributing tracts in the area and he was now joined by James Chrystall, another Scot who had been commended as a preacher by the Rongotea Assembly that had commended C.H. Hinman. This preaching led to the conversion of the local shopkeeper, Alfred Brown, as well as the Luty, Derbyshire and Bunting families, twenty people in all, and another smaller assembly was formed here.[17] More people were converted here in 1894, particularly young people.[18] Dickie's tract distribution certainly paid off; he told a story to an English magazine in 1896 about a man from another adjacent settlement of Waitotera:

> In Wairotaea [sic] I had a few meetings, and one was brought under conviction. I kept giving him tracts when I had the opportunity. About 12 months after he was convicted I met him on the road driving a team of horses. He jumped off his drag [dray] and gave me a warm shake of the hand and said he was a new man in Christ. He then gave me a sovereign, 'This is to buy more tracts for they have been used in my conversion.'[19]

It seemed like an area sensitized to revival, and revival preaching was frequent in the area, for in 1900 Franklin Ferguson from Napier, newly commended as a full-time evangelist, held nine months of meetings in the district, and there were thirty

---

14. *Treasury* 27 (1925), p. 31; 35 (1933), p. 111; 45 (1943), p. 88; A.H. Taylor to P.J. Lineham, 10 July 1974.

15. *Echoes of Service* No. 247 (October 1891, part one), p. 232.

16. See Rollo Arnold, *The Farthest Promised Land: English villages, New Zealand immigrants of the 1870s* (Wellington, 1981).

17. Lineham, *There we found Brethren*, p. 86; *Treasury* 20 (1918), p. 15; 28 (1926), p. 79; 32 (1930), p. 127; *Echoes of Service* No. 247 (October, 1891, part one), pp. 232-33.

18. *The Witness* [hereafter *W*], n.s. 4 (1894), p. 101.

19. *W*, n.s. 6 (March 1896), [cover].

converts, doubling the size of the Maxwell assembly. One of the converts was Alfred Perkins, who became a highly respected Brethren missionary.[20]

Overseas Evangelists

Now strikingly there was no outside leader of the Wanganui revival of 1875, just the co-operation of two local pastors. In the case of the Salvation Army, the evangelists were young Englishmen with a minimum of preaching experience. In the Waverley and Maxwell revivals, the initial preachers were colonial itinerant evangelists who responded to James Dickie's requests for revival preaching. These are instructive indications of the receptivity to revivalism.

How far did international English speaking revivalists influence the revivalistic trends in the colony? Already by the 1870s, New Zealand was one port of call for revivalist preachers, who had sprung up particularly in the wake of the 1859 Revival, some of them denominational, others non-denominational, and others Brethren or Adventist. These visiting evangelists included Dr A.N. Somerville of the Glasgow Evangelical Band in 1878, Henry Varley in 1879, Mrs Margaret Hampson in 1881–82, George Grubb for Keswick in 1890–91 and again in 1892, Thomas Cook the Methodist, in 1894–95, and finally the famous American, R.A. Torrey, in 1906.[21] Such visitors came on entrepreneurial ventures; they usually linked up with local ministers or sympathizers who would organize a meeting, and then depending on the response, they would stay or move on.

It is clear that New Zealand had finally become involved in the revivalistic pattern of preaching and the 'international sawdust trail' in the wake of the 1858–59 Revival. But these revivalists were not the only agents of revival. The significant community religious awakenings seem to have been somewhat independent of the quality or fame of the preachers.

Many of these evangelists were influenced by Brethren ideas. Because of the timing of his visit in 1878–79,[22] Henry Varley was one of the most significant visitors. Varley was a well-known independent evangelist with strong Keswick and premillenial views. He visited New Zealand again in 1890, and ended up as a resident

20. F. Ferguson, *Reminiscences of Christian Experience and Service in New Zealand from Very Early Days* (Palmerston North, 1938), pp. 41, 49-50; *The Believer's Magazine* n.s. 1 (June 1900), p. iv; n.s. 1 (August, 1900), p. iv; n.s. 1 (October, 1900), p. iv; n.s. 2 (March 1901), p. iv.

21. For lists and details of these overseas evangelists, see Troughton, 'Moody and Sankey Down-Under', pp. 159-60; Evans and McKenzie, *Evangelical Revivals*, *passim*; the subsequent story may be traced in Bryan D. Gilling, 'Retelling the Old Old Story: a study of six mass evangelistic missions in twentieth century New Zealand' (PhD thesis, University of Waikato, 1990).

22. Evans and McKenzie, *Evangelical Revivals*, pp. 57-58.

of Melbourne.[23] His son Frank was resident in New Zealand and made a significant contribution to its Christian culture. Darryl Paproth comments that, 'Though usually regarded as one of the Brethren, he eschewed church affiliation, his independence masking a barely concealed separatism.'[24] Frank was associated with an independent quasi-Brethren mission chapel, York Place Hall, and many of Henry's converts ended up as members of the Brethren.[25] So Varley is representative of a group of independent revivalists who nevertheless fed the Brethren movement.

There is also an interested group of self-consciously Brethren evangelists, including Harrison Ord, Edward Moyse, Douglas Russell, and W. Corrie Johnson, although in saying this, one should recognize the very considerable freedom of the Brethren evangelist, answerable only in a very loose way to their 'commending assembly'. Moyse is a curious example, for he had settled in Tasmania in the 1870s, moving between Australia and New Zealand, a preacher of some forcefulness, who did not move exclusively in Brethren circles, and was very active in New Zealand especially in Taranaki, accompanying C.H. Hinman on his pioneer trip to Taranaki and then to Waverley, as we have seen.[26] He was later accused of homosexual behaviour with his fellow evangelist Donleavy while they were in Christchurch, and this brought their ministry to an end.[27] Harrison Ord was a very well known Brethren evangelist in Britain, who moved to Australia in 1876, aged forty-three, and who ministered in New Zealand in 1877–78 and again in 1899.[28] The most eccentric of the Brethren preachers was W. Corrie Johnson, who worked as an evangelist in Melbourne and later in New Zealand, and was for a time associated with the Brethren, but eventually fell out with them.[29]

The Brethren participation in revivalism may seem paradoxical, for their early focus lay on the restoration of the 'original' pattern of the church, not on mass conversion. Yet the 1859–60 Revival in America, Ireland and Scotland, as Ross

23. See Henry Varley [Jr], *Henry Varley's Life Story* (London, 1913); Darryl Paproth, 'Henry Varley and the Melbourne Evangelicals', *Journal of Religious History* 25.2 (June, 2001), pp. 171-87.

24. D. Paproth, 'Varley, Henry', in Timothy Larsen (ed.), *Biographical Dictionary of Evangelicals* (Leicester, 2003), p. 685. See *Missionary Echoes* (1878), p. 80, for his Brethren links.

25. E.g. Samuel T. Wood, *Gospel Ambassador* (1915).

26. See Stephenson, *Pioneering with Christ*, p. 73, for his preaching in the Churches of Christ. For his Brethren work in New Zealand, see Lineham, *There We Found Brethren*, pp. 67-69, and see also Kenneth John Newton, *A History of the Brethren in Australia with Particular Reference to the Open Brethren* (Gailes, Qld: Aberdeen Desktop, based on 1990 Fuller Seminary DPhil thesis, 1999), pp. 17-18.

27. Elisabeth Wilson, '"Do the next thing": Henry Lewis Garrett and the evolution of the Hobart Brethren assembly', ch. 13 below.

28. Pickering, *Chief Men among the Brethren*, p. 165; Newton, *A History of the Brethren in Australia*, p. 19; *Treasury* 1 (1899), p. 62.

29. *Treasury* 12 (1910), p. 130; Lineham, *There we found Brethren*, pp. 107-108; see also his magazine, *Truth and Words of Grace* (1892); and book, W. Corrie Johnson, *Echoes of Grace* (Melbourne, 1880).

McLaren has argued, profoundly reshaped the second phase of the Brethren.[30] As he argues, the original patterns linked with Darby on the one hand and Groves on the other were thereafter complemented with a third part of the 'triple tradition'. Evangelists who had fallen out with the Free Church developed a new emphasis on 'patternism' as they instructed converts in what the church should be. Nevertheless the impact of the Scottish evangelists associated with Donald Ross took some time to penetrate New Zealand.

Revivalism and Methodism

To understand why revivalism flourished, we need to recognize the strength and the character of Methodism in New Zealand, especially among the settlers of the 1870s. By 1900 over 10% of all settlers were Methodist adherents. Methodism was in the background of a significant proportion of the assisted immigrants of the 1870s, drawn from the poorer countryside, and Methodist churches were often very open to revivalist preaching. Indeed it played a huge role in the very early years of the denomination in New Zealand. The success of 'California' Taylor in 1864–65 was due to his use of Finneyite methods, which led to many conversions, especially in Christchurch.[31] It is not uncommon to read of Methodist congregations for example at Apiti in the Manawatu in the 1890s, where the general tone was revivalist.[32] Yet Methodism had an ambiguous relationship with revivalism, both in England and in New Zealand.[33] The local Methodist Conference was concerned about this trend in undermining their churches.[34] The Methodist magazine as early as 1874 cited the American minister, H.W. Beecher, on 'objections to revivals', including an accusation that they led to fanaticism.[35] The magazine's editor was enthusiastic when large numbers of young people were converted, but hoped that 'no-one bearing the peculiar designation of "Revivalist" had been employed' by their churches as a preacher.[36] There was a debate in the Methodist newspaper between J.L. Wilson and Alexander Reid, who was one of the great ministers of the denomination in the nineteenth century, and criticized the kind of revival that disturbed the church. He rejected as legend the common tale that 'California' Taylor's evangelism had

30. Ross H. McLaren, 'The Triple Tradition: the Origin and Development of the Open Brethren in America' (MA thesis, Vanderbilt University, 1982); published as Ross Howlett McLaren, 'The Triple Tradition: The Origin and Development of the Open Brethren in North America', *Emmaus Journal* 4 (1995), pp. 169-208; 5 (1996), pp. 67-87, 161-203; 6, (1997), pp. 129-50.

31. Gilling, 'Rushing into the Kingdom of Heaven', pp. 7-12.

32. H.M. Miller, 'Apiti Reminiscences' (personal communication).

33. For the English context, see W.R. Ward (ed.), *Early Victorian Methodism: the correspondence of Jabez Bunting 1830–1858* (Oxford, 1976), *passim.*

34. Wesleyan Methodist Church, *Minutes of Annual Conference* (1876), pp. 31, 74.

35. *New Zealand Wesleyan* (2 March 1874), pp. 33-34.

36. *New Zealand Wesleyan* (1 March 1876), p. 58.

transformed the numbers of the church.[37] Others complained that in Methodism 'order takes the place of enthusiasm',[38] but that was very much the preference of Wesleyan ministers. They did not reject all revivalism, but they preferred a kind of institutionalized and in-house revivalism, for example special meetings to recruit Sunday school leavers, trying carefully to control popular approaches to religion.[39]

Revivalist preachers were at risk from this nervousness among Methodist officials. One example is Walter Douglas, the American converted in London in 1863 before he emigrated to Christchurch, who began outdoor preaching in the city in 1865, presumably inspired by the work of William Taylor. The result was that he was banned from preaching in Methodist chapels on account of his 'disorderly' behaviour. The Methodists were very anxious for a sober and respectful tone in revival, keeping it safely indoors like Taylor, and so they were very unhappy at Douglas' approach.[40] Douglas went to Melbourne in 1866 and by 1869 was preaching in Launceston and Hobart, and Douglas was arrested for singing hymns in the street in Hobart. His meetings led to the formation of Brethren assemblies in Tasmania, but Douglas was probably still independent in outlook and went on to live and preach in the United States.[41] It is significant that those Methodists who were rejected for their revivalistic tendencies found a home among the Brethren. The drain from Methodists to the Brethren was a matter of concern in Methodist circuit meetings.[42]

The Primitive Methodists were a special case. They were a very small denomination in New Zealand, but a significant proportion of immigrants of the 1870s had Primitive Methodist links from Britain. This is not surprising considering the extent to which the immigration of the 1870s was based on close work with the Agricultural Labourers Union in the Midlands, where the Primitives were strong.[43] So there were many 'ranters' in the land; indeed the census returns show a quite

37. The debate began with an article by Reid in *New Zealand Wesleyan* 3.29 (June, 1873), pp. 81-83, critical of Taylor. Wilson responded in *New Zealand Wesleyan* 3.31 (August, 1873), p. 119; Reid and others responded in *New Zealand Wesleyan* 3.32 (September, 1873), pp. 132-33.

38. *New Zealand Wesleyan* 3.32 (September 1873), p. 133.

39. Peter J. Lineham, *New Zealanders and the Methodist Evangel: an interpretation of the policies and performance of the Methodist Church of New Zealand, Wesley Historical Society (N.Z.) Proceedings*, 42 (Auckland, 1983), p. 8.

40. *Lyttleton Times* (31 January 1865); *Press*, Christchurch (5 September 1866), p. 5; Newton, *A History of the Brethren in Australia*, p. 15. citing *Lifted Up: the life of Walter Douglas* (London, [1868]), pp. 12, 17.

41. Newton, *A History of the Brethren in Australia*, pp. 11-12, citing *Lifted Up: the life of Walter Douglas*, p. 91. See also W.T. Blight, *A House not Made with Hands*, (Christchurch, 1964), p. 21; Elizabeth Wilson, 'Do the next thing', p. 176; Michael P. Grimshaw, '"Fouling the Nest": the conflict between the 'Church Party' and settler society during the New Zealand Wars 1860–1865.' (PhD thesis, University of Otago, 1999), p. 239.

42. See Evans and McKenzie, *Evangelical Revivals*, p. 37.

43. See Arnold, *The Farthest Promised Land.*

substantial group of Primitives, rising from 1883 in 1871 to 4,643 by 1881, and then jumping to 7,041 in 1896, 10,143 in 1901, and to an astonishing level of 21,796 in 1906 and 27,445 in 1911, while the Wesleyans during this period remained more or less unchanged at 63,000 from 1896. In 1913 an official merger of Wesleyan and Primitive Methodists took place, other minor Methodists having merged in 1893. By the time of the merger Wesleyans had declined from their high point of 9.2% of the population in 1901 to 6.3% while the Primitives had risen from 1.3% in 1901 to 2.7% of the population. After the merger between the Wesleyans and the Primitives in 1913, there were many complaints among the Wesleyans that the numbers of Primitive Methodists were greatly exaggerated. But perhaps the explanation was that despite continuing to call themselves Primitives in the census they were attending services in sympathetic churches if there was no Primitive church nearby. William and James Coppin in 1878 formed what became a Brethren assembly at Kakahu near Geraldine in South Canterbury because there was no Primitive Methodist church in the district.[44] Some of the so-called Primitive Methodist adherents recorded in the censuses of the period 1890 to 1911 may have been protesting against growing Wesleyan formality, because they preferred revivalistic Methodism. In 1913 a number of local preachers left the 'Prims' and joined the Brethren, among them Norman Hyde, who had a significant influence in challenging Brethren sectarianism.[45]

The flavour of lay Methodist interest in revivalism is conveyed in a marvellous diary by Charles Henry Lord of Papakura Valley in South Auckland from 1882 to 1885. It tells the story of a young Wesleyan settler increasingly exercised to 'go out as an evangelist'. In the process he several times visited Auckland for a round of revivalist meetings and locally attended an eclectic range of meetings in the district, including preaching by Baptists, the conditionalist, William Brown, the overseas preacher Thomas Holness, and local tent meetings. He was very excited when Brother Parker (a Methodist local preacher) took him along to a week's revival meetings. Acknowledging that 'there will be some who will cry out against it and will call it excitement', he was convinced that it was worthwhile, despite the community hostility it aroused, when four people were converted. No wonder he ended up in the Salvation Army. It is clear that revivalism could provide a full social life for those who were committed Protestants, and it is clear that it often led people to change denominations.[46]

The Tone of Revivalism

Many nineteenth-century pioneers looked on at the impact of revivalism with some concern, believing that the churches' priority was to build institutions, and

44. Lineham, *There we found Brethren*, p. 73.

45. Lineham, *There we found Brethren*, pp. 126-27.

46. Journal of Charles Henry Lord, entries for 1-9 November 1884; 4 January 1885; 29 September 1885; 7 December 1885. (Diary in private hands, Wanganui). There is a biographical entry at the conclusion.

revivalistic activity was misdirected. There was widespread comment in the community that this kind of revivalism was unhealthy.[47]

Revivalism in the first instance was undenominational, and attracted people from all Protestant churches. So in Dunedin in 1874, all the denominations except Anglicans and Catholics attended combined meetings in the Masonic Hall, and Alfred Brunton of the first Brethren assembly participated, singing one of Sankey's hymns.[48] Similarly in Christchurch in 1872 there were combined meetings in the Canterbury Museum Hall on Sunday evening, attended by some 250 people, using a variety of lay and ordained speakers.[49]

Music probably did more to extend revivalism and to create a common milieu than anything else. The style of music was that of the music hall. The introduction of Sankey's hymns was a key aspect to the Wanganui revival in 1875.[50] In Frank Bullen's conversion, 'another burst of song, quite unaccompanied but wonderfully sweet' played a crucial role.[51] The tunes and the words became universally known, and they were hymns for singing and for personal and mutual exhortation. The hymns were absorbed into popular culture; in 1882 an atheist candidate for Parliament in the Grey Electorate provoked a sharp reaction, and members of the audience cried out 'hold the fort', the text of a well known Sankey hymn.[52] The standardization of revival hymnbooks must have been very important. Brethren sang the revival hymns, and moreover the Brethren service allowed people to choose the songs they wanted. In the Brethren, frequent 'all-day meetings' gave great opportunity for singing. Compared to the Brethren in England, they had little of the introverted devotional tone; visitors from Britain often remarked that the Open Brethren in New Zealand had replaced the biblicism of the English Brethren with enthusiastic singing; 'too much little book, not enough big book' was the common comment in later years. The hymnody of Brethren in the United States has been described as reflecting Moodyite values, with little evidence of the reflective spirituality of the 1820s, and the description would suit the New Zealand case as well.

The primary location of the revivalism in the colonial world was the small towns which were the boosters, promoters and conduits of money and development for the colony. Compared to the caution of close country communities, there was more revivalism in the towns, and the towns, though small, provided reasonable audiences for visiting evangelists like Henry Varley. Nevertheless such revivalism had to compete with a wider range of colonial entertainments, for even these small towns

---

47. See, e.g., James O'Brien Hoare, *Our Father's Church* (Christchurch, 1892), p. 74; Alison Drummond (ed.), *The Thames Journals of Vicesimus Lush 1868–82* (Christchurch, 1975) pp. 11ff.

48. *New Zealand Wesleyan* (1 August 1874), p. 134.

49. *Lyttleton Times* (22 July 1872), p. 2.

50. Troughton, 'Christianity and Community', p. 95.

51. F.T. Bullen, With *Christ at Sea: a Religious Autobiography* (London, [1900]), pp. 86-94.

52. *Echo*, Dunedin (16 December 1882), p. 3.

had active leisure industries. The Salvation Army was effective in the towns because they provided a high level of entertainment beside preaching with their striking methods and styles. Other evangelists mostly spoke in existing churches or in public halls. Some like the Wanganui revival of 1874, broke out of denominational moulds; some like Mrs Hampson offered the additional interest of a female preacher.[53] These are the factors in ordinary revivalism; the Brethren rural revivals clearly defy these trends.

The growth of colonial revivalism may be explained at several levels. Reports of the revivalists and their sermons were in demand among keener Protestants, perhaps because the story was so much more vibrant than the stories of denominational developments. News of evangelists was spread through denominational and secular newspapers. There was a huge amount of literature distributed about revivalism in the colonies. This certainly helped the Adventists.[54] The distribution of the *War Cry* by the Salvation Army in the public houses helped increase knowledge of this new religious language.

Revivalism revalued the role of the laity, and it was on the laity that New Zealand Christianity had to depend; yet very little Christianity had been part of the settlers' baggage. Revivalism placed religion in the life of the laity and in their homes. So we should recognize the role of the cottage meeting as the first step towards the Brethren and other lay-based churches. Some Christians had long been concerned at the contrast between the formal side of the colony and the roughness of colonial life. They felt that the churches failed to reach out, and they supported revivalism because it defied this pattern. One local Christian magazine described the 1859 Revival as 'times of refreshing', urging a less formal church, and longed for the same kind of developments in New Zealand.[55] The Dunedin Christian magazine, *The Evangelist*, felt that the Presbyterian Church was failing, 'without any general or remarkable outpouring of the Holy Spirit, of which we feel deeply, she stands in need'.[56]

Revivalism and Sectarianism

We need to set revivalism in the context of sectarian debates, for undoubtedly the revivalist world was full of these. These debates did the tradition no good, but much of the appeal of revivalism lay in its claim to be non-denominational, a value shared by all colonists, and this stance had great appeal with many colonists. I have explored the emergence of Adventism from 1885 as another example of a sectarian movement that gained a following by appearing to be a movement for Christian

53. See Troughton, 'Moody and Sankey Down-under', pp. 145-62.

54. Peter J. Lineham, 'Adventism and the sawdust trail in late nineteenth century New Zealand', in Peter H. Ballis (ed.), *In and Out of the World: Seventh-Day Adventists in New Zealand* (Palmerston North, 1985), pp. 34-35.

55. *Christian Messenger* 4.41 (February, 1873), pp. 13-14; 5.6 (June, 1874), pp. 42-43.

56. *Evangelist* 4.1 (January, 1872), p. 23.

unity.[57] The same case could be made for the growth of the Campbellite Churches of Christ in the same era; they were a restorationist movement that flourished in the wake of revival movements.[58]

The revivalists frequently voiced concern at heresies in other churches, especially among the Wesleyans in 1893 with C.H. Garland's sermon on the human element in the Bible, which seems to have provoked a conservative reaction from among Methodists that benefited the revivalists. The revivalists were instinctive conservatives. They were democrats, in the sense that Nathan Hatch describes them in American context, for democrats and backwoodsmen can be very conservative in theology.[59]

Eschatological concerns probably affected the revivalist atmosphere to quite a large extent. Premillennial views and an expectation of the return of Christ heightened the sense that evangelism was of critical importance. The Adventists benefited from intense discussion on millennial themes. These were hot issues in the late nineteenth century. The independent Baptist preacher Samuel Edger was querying the doctrine of hell through the 1870s, and the Life and Advent school under the Rev. George Brown and then George Aldridge, advocated 'soul sleep' and conditionalism in the 1880s.[60] The Adventists took this up. Then in the late 1880s a controversial book by a professor at the first University, William Salmond's *Reign of Grace*, raised the issue of the reality of hell, and provoked intense discussion about Christian beliefs.[61] Prophecies and concern about the antichrist had a wide circulation in New Zealand.[62] Many of the visiting evangelists were 'futurists' including George Grubb, George Soltau and Henry Varley.[63] The Brethren futurist interpretation of Revelation provoked a great deal of interest, although their belief in hell was not popular with settlers.[64] A correspondent from Maxwell wrote to a Brethren magazine asking for guidance to keep people out of the trap of the Prohibition Movement. He noted,

> There is a small gathering of believers most of whom have not known the Lord very long, but are now rejoicing. There is great excitement all through this country at present on account of the general election, votes for or anti prohibition. Many dear Christians are greatly taken up with the matter, not seeing that the 'one man one vote' will not accomplish much until...the Man of Lawlessness appears.

57. Lineham, 'Adventism', pp. 32-51, especially p. 34.
58. See Troughton, 'Christianity and Community', p. 102, for evidence of this in Wanganui.
59. Nathan O. Hatch, *The Democratisation of American Christianity* (New Haven, CT, 1989).
60. Lineham 'Adventism', p. 39.
61. Lineham, 'Adventism', p 40.
62. Lineham, 'Adventism', p. 41.
63. Lineham, 'Adventism', p. 42.
64. See *Echoes of Service* No. 352 (February, 1896 part 2), p. 64.

Christendom without Christians will flourish for a while and then receive judgement.[65]

There is an economic factor in the revivalist age to do with the Great Depression of the 1880s. This cut back the level of activity of the established churches just after the decade of the greatest growth of the New Zealand population, with the Vogel-assisted immigrants of the 1870s, most of whom settled on farms being shaped out of the 'great bush' of the West Coast.

In the colonies denominational loyalties were weakened. People visited churches of other denominations regularly, and many country church services were alternated between denominations in joint-use properties, community halls, schools or community-owned churches. This ecumenical outlook was important for revivalism. It is interesting that J. Norman Case, after visiting Brethren in Australia and New Zealand, explained the strength of the New Zealand Brethren compared to the Australians by referring to the debates on ecclesiology among Australian Brethren which did not much occur in New Zealand and the focus on gospel preaching in New Zealand, which was much less common in Australian Brethren.[66] This focus on evangelism led to complaints by those seeking to build up the denominations in the colony. The Rev. J. Berry declared that 'a great deal of harm was done by strolling evangelists, who only stirred up the people, raised disfavour in them against their pastors, and ended by scooping up a potful of money, leaving the door open for the next'.[67] But the strolling evangelists came to people who were used to the itinerant pattern of preaching.

Revivalism also took an effective stance against the debate over the de-Christianization of nineteenth century society. It is striking to look at the contest between Spiritualists and Freethinkers on the one hand and revivalists on the other for the soul of New Zealand. The Freethinkers had a great deal of fun at the expense of the revivalists, but this probably reflected a deadly combat going on in the popular world. A Taranaki freethinker cited revivalism's campaigns as 'impediments that impede our march' and they mocked the preaching in their meetings, the preachers pacing up and down, the loud tones and frantic gesticulations, the emotional hymns sung to Christy-minstrel tunes.[68]

The Pattern of the Rural Revival

Revivalism is not revival. Yet as we have seen in the countryside there were significant instances of profound religious movements on a scale which is proportionately the same as American revivals. The most striking revivals that touched the New Zealand Brethren were in communities where Christian identity was

65. *W*, n.s. 7 (February 1897), p. 42.

66. J. Norman Case in *W*, n.s. 10 (1901), p. 65.

67. T.F. Robertson, *Patriotic Church Union and Co-operation* (Auckland, 1891), p. 8.

68. *Freethought Review* 1.6 (March, 1884), p. 13; 2.1 (January, 1885), pp. 3-4; 2.18 (March, 1885), p. 1.

in crisis and churches were in short supply. The Rongotea revival of 1881 reflects a new community finding its identity through spiritual events.[69] Revival and persecution travelled in sequence, and the sequence turned the 'assembly truths' into a guardian of the revival's values. The road through the dairying districts from Rongotea to New Plymouth led through a series of small communities (including Maxwell and Waverley) with other profound revivals at Ngaere in South Taranaki and at Kent Road near New Plymouth. To a very significant degree the leaders of today's Open Brethren can be traced to these small communities and their broad awakenings.

The Brethren flourished precisely in the backblocks, where small holdings were characteristic, particularly in the bush country where trees had to be felled to create farms, encouraging a more independent approach to life and one where the established church had less credibility. The co-operative shops and the co-operative dairy factory and strong neighbourly concerns gave this world a 'tight' sense of community.[70] In theory Methodists should have done well in such areas too, and in general they did, but their increasingly liberal and urban stance lost them credibility. Other revivals, nothing to do with the Brethren, for example that of Waikaka far in the south of New Zealand, had roughly the same social context.

The timing of revival in the annual routines of the community was probably significant. Troughton cites received knowledge that revivals occurred most frequently in winter.[71] This was particularly relevant in dairying regions. For when the cows were 'dry', it was possible to prolong religious services, and allow the emotions to overwhelm the sense of routine in a manner impossible in urban areas. In non-dairying areas this was also possible, so long as the farmers were not employees of large sheep stations. George Grove, a visiting evangelist from Tasmania, reported on a series of meetings at Kakahu near Geraldine in the South Island:

> at Kakohoo which is quite in the bush, among the sheep runs, there were meetings for 6 days, the mud hut meeting house was quite packed, people remaining till 10 o'clock, when an after meeting was held. The weather was cold and rough; on one occasion people from Geraldine could not get back and stayed the night in the cottage praying and praising God. 16 were converted, 8 of them in one night, and they were still happy when he passed back.[72]

So rural revivalism clearly has some differences from town revivalism. The numbers attending were small, but the whole community would attend, for lack of other

69. See Lineham, *There we found Brethren*, pp. 63-66.

70. Rollo Arnold, *New Zealand's Burning: the settlers' world in the mid 1880s* (Wellington, 1994), takes one position in this debate against Miles Fairburn, *The Ideal Society and its Enemies: the foundations of modern New Zealand society 1850-1900* (Auckland, 1989).

71. Troughton, 'Moody and Sankey Down-Under', p. 151.

72. *Echoes of Service* No. 260, (April, 1892, part 2), p. 99.

entertainment, and consequently the impact was greater. The number and solidity of the conversions was remarkable. When such revivalism faced opposition from the existing churches, it is little wonder that informal Brethren assemblies, with their minimalistic and 'do-it-yourself' structure, emerged. One may compare it to the Charismatic renewal of the 1960s. The evangelists were not necessarily planning to plant churches, but their independence and the hostility of the existing churches made church planting inevitable.

Gradually a tradition of revivalist religion developed in local communities. It is easy enough to see how this occurred. Firstly, lay preachers and occasional services provided the only source of religion for settlers many of whom had a Methodist background. Increasingly other churches recognized the force of this tradition, and the Presbyterian Church established an order of home missionaries to 'work' the backblocks. The concept of the 'bush Baptist' was important, especially as there were virtually no actual Baptists in the New Zealand countryside. Yet in these small and isolated localities, religious excitement could not be contained; it overwhelmed small districts, creating a 'burned-over district', in the aftermath of which, Brethren made a significant impact.

Although it might be reasonably easy for an evangelist to get an audience in the countryside, long-term credibility had to be established through the reputation of local converts. If this took place, then people would attend heterodox meetings quite willingly, and perhaps there was a greater chance of a deep impact.[73] A Freethinker once drew a perceptive contrast between the Salvation Army's work in New Plymouth and Brethren preachers in Ngaere and Kent Road:

> In our chief town, New Plymouth, may be seen Salvation Barracks and placards about such cheerful and refreshing matters as Redhot Shot, Blood, Hell, Hell-fire, and Damnation, and lads who would run away at the cocking of a toy pistol, 'fight the good fight', put on the armour of righteousness and the breastplate of something else, and generally get into the same pot-valiant state that Mr. Winkle did when he was about to make his renowned attack on the small boy.
>
> On our country roads the religious monomania seems to take another form, the rustic population does not go in for uniforms, cornet blowing, and parading, but it resorts to mud-holes and creeks, and gets dipped by three or four gentlemen who kindly stay among the settlers, live in their best parlors, sleep in their best beds, and eat up all their superfluous hams, jams, pickles, cream, and honey. They do not take money from anyone, only One Pound a head for each person when dipped and any stray five pound notes the well-to-do converts can be persuaded to give them. They have no particular religious doctrine except that you must either be 'dipped or damned', and that you should not play music or read newspapers. There are about four of these Evangelistic teachers or preachers, and they succeed best apparently amongst settlers who live on muddy roads and swampy places where low fevers occasionly [sic] make their appearance. During the late cold winter, vehicles loaded

73. Lineham, 'Adventism', p. 35.

> with dripping wet human beings were to be seen taking them back to their homes, huddled together, and some have suffered from severe illnesses in consequence.[74]

This account suggests that bold sectarianism did the preachers no harm. The 'bush Baptist' mode made a deep impact in the community. Neutral spaces and community spaces were often part of the philosophy of the revivalist mindset. So common-use chapels, which were extremely common as a first provision of churches, often were host to revivalist lay sermons which the denominations would not have allowed. Tent meetings were the key feature of Adventism from 1886. As David Hempton has said, apropos of early Methodism, in 'small communities the denominational label counted for less than the simplicity of the religious forms and the social bonds of the membership'.[75]

From the Brethren point of view, their participation in revivals was more significant in very specific circumstances. First, it took place where the other churches were weak or non-existent. There was, we may deduce, a certain reserve in the community about attending services by Brethren preachers, because of their sectarian reputation. In isolated places the combination of absence of choice and the stronger aspects of community—knowing your neighbours—would have made the Brethren form of revivalist church more acceptable. So when C.H. Hinman gave advice on how to reach a community he emphasized taking time, not preaching hell too much, delaying before baptizing, and ensuring that the preacher had a positive reputation.[76]

Revivals in rural areas did not necessarily have a Brethren character. Waikaka in South Otago is a particularly interesting case of a revival in an isolated valley.[77] Otago had been settled by members of the Free Church of Scotland from 1848, and Presbyterians dominated this isolated district of the province. A manuscript history of the church by A.J. Nichol makes clear that the revival picked up and transformed the existing forms of religion. The key figure in this revival movement was a certain James Dickie (not the Brethren one), who had purchased a block of land in the Waikaka Valley in 1875, and was converted in 1882 through reading his Bible. Over the next couple of years a fervent revival atmosphere resulted in many conversions and some remarkable transformations of lives. Out of this revival came a remarkable group of missionaries, and servants of churches. The work continued long after the initial fervour had subsided. Dickie was a home missionary with the Presbyterian

74. Thomas Drake to Editor, *Freethought Review* 2.15 (December, 1884), p. 7, cited in Allan K. Davidson and Peter J. Lineham (eds), *Transplanted Christianity: Documents Illustrating Aspects of New Zealand Church History* (Auckland, 1987), and subsequent editions, document 4.16.

75. David Hempton, *The Religion of the People: Methodism and popular religion c.1750–1900* (London, 1996), p. 54.

76. C.H. Hinman in *Echoes of Service* No. 362 (July, 1896, part 2), p. 222.

77. There is a useful account of this in Evans and McKenzie, *Evangelical Revivals*, pp. 58-61, but I am indebted to copies of notes by C. M. McNamara provided by Ian Hyslop.

Church in 1898, but left the church because of his beliefs on baptism, and joined the Baptist Church although his links with the Presbyterian Church continued.[78] Dickie had a huge impact in the Waikaka Valley, and his preaching was clearly heightened by his sense of 'the imminent return of Christ'. He was unprepared for his wife's death because he expected them both to be 'caught up to Christ in heaven'.[79] Many years later in 1920 Dickie continued to have influence in the Otago and Southland region, when he provoked a new round of conversions and baptisms at Waikaka.[80] So in this very different case there was a similar recurrence of revival movements in a very localized setting.

Ali Clarke, in a number of recent articles, has described the conservatism of the Otago and Southland region where this southern revival occurred, and the way it preserved Scottish and Presbyterian traditions.[81] Yet there is another side to this story in the appeal of revivalism in this area. Religion was a dominating cultural force, but the community was open to changes in religious life, despite its resistance to other cultural challenges.

Brethren Dependence on Revival

Although the Waikaka revival did not involve the Brethren it cannot be seen as a completely isolated from it because Houlton Forlong, son of Gordon Forlong, came from this area and commenced his missionary work in the New Hebrides (Vanuatu) with William McKenzie, mentioned above.[82] Moreover, William McKenzie, following the death of his first wife in the New Hebrides, returned to Scotland where he became an itinerant Brethren evangelist in the Highlands, working with the father of the great Brethren scholar F.F. Bruce.[83] This suggests that revival movements throughout New Zealand were never fully isolated from one another. While there is no record of any Brethren work in the area in that decade, in the early 1890s there was extensive evangelism by very conservative Scottish evangelists in the local community, and preachers like the Northern Irish evangelist John Blair called people

---

78. Notes by C.M. McNamara.

79. Georgina McDonald, *The Flame Unquenched: being a history of the Presbyterian Church in Southland in the years 1856–1956* (Christchurch, 1956), pp. 59-60; notes by C.M. McNamara.

80. Notes by C.M. McNamara.

81. Alison Clarke, '"Days of Heaven on Earth": Presbyterian communion seasons in nineteenth-century Otago', *Journal of Religious History* 26.3 (2002), pp. 274-97; idem, 'A Godly Rhythm: Keeping the Sabbath in Otago, 1870–1890', in John Stenhouse and Jane Thomson (eds), *Building God's Own Country: historical essays on religions in New Zealand* (Dunedin, 2004), pp. 46-59.

82. *W*, n.s. 12 (1902), p. 65.

83. F.F. Bruce, *In Retrospect: remembrance of things past* (London, 1980), p. 14; D.J. Beattie, *Brethren: the story of a great recovery* (Kilmarnock, [1940]), p. 270. I owe these references to John Hitchen.

to separate from the 'church systems'.[84] We may speculate that Brethren came in the aftermath of the key revival era, and benefited from the discontent of some of the converts. Something of the same may be evident in the activity of the Brethren in Wanganui in the aftermath of the 1875 revival, for the Presbyterian minister and pro-revivalist, John Elmslie, attacked the Brethren in a lecture in January 1876, just after the revival meetings had ended.[85] Baptist and Methodist attacks occurred at the same time, and their arguments were that Brethren had exploited revivalism for sectarian ends, and also used revivalist values to upset traditional Nonconformist values.[86]

There was a certain conflict in New Zealand between the interdenominational and the denominational forms it took. The Brethren represented this tension in the extreme. In Scotland the Brethren had been beneficiaries in the open rebellion with the formality of the Free Church during the 1859 rebellion, and yet this had produced a very sectarian church pattern, as Neil Dickson notes.[87] So the revivalist age encouraged a restorationist approach to the church, and the first generation of Open Brethren gave way to a different tone in the revivalist generation. Gordon Forlong was one of the interdenominational 'gentlemen evangelists' of the 1860s in Scotland before he came to New Zealand, but he had not been a sectarian there, any more than he was in New Zealand, always seeking freedom to move from one group to another.[88] George Müller, one of the original Open Brethren, visited New Zealand in 1888 and his open attitude of broad contact with people from different denominational outlooks reflected the approach of Gordon Forlong and Alfred Brunton, but was in sharp contrast to the narrowness of the Brethren converted in the revival.

The predecessors to the Open Brethren in New Zealand had been a group of urban churches, often combinations of Brethren and Baptist traditions, genuinely open and undenominational. They were in effect independent evangelical congregations, with a strong diet of revivalism as their flavour. It was through the sponsorship of the largest such group, in Dunedin, that the Port Chalmers Seamen's Mission developed, for example (the setting for the conversion of the noted gospel writer, Frank Bullen).[89] It is little wonder that they had a rather uncomfortable relationship with the new country assemblies, despite sharing a revivalistic flavour.

Many notable early Brethren were converted in interdenominational revivalist campaigns and then moved into the Brethren. Albert Brown and James Dickie (the

---

84. Lineham, *There we found Brethren*, p. 97.

85. *Weekly Herald* (29 January 1876), p. 9.

86. For the Baptist attack in 1878, see Tonson, *A Handful of Grain*, p. 47.

87. Neil T.R. Dickson, *Brethren in Scotland 1838–2000: a social study of an evangelical movement* (Carlisle, 2002), pp. 69-73; see also Neil T.R. Dickson, 'Revivalism and the Limits of Cooperation: Brethren Origins in Orkney in the 1860s', ch. 6 above.

88. See Dickson, *Brethren in Scotland*, pp. 61, 63, 73, 79; 'The Late Mr Gordon Forlong', *W*, n.s. 18 (1908), p. 180.

89. Bullen, With *Christ at Sea, passim.*

Brethren Dickie) were converted through Somerville.[90] It was not unknown for ministers of other churches to attend and enjoy revival preachers at the Brethren.[91] Abraham Honoré, the erstwhile Lutheran missionary who became a Presbyterian missionary to the Maori in the lower North Island, came into increasing contact with the Brethren. The British Brethren magazine, *Missionary Echoes*, supported his work, and he was probably also attracted because his spirituality was the kind of undenominational valuing of spiritual life which was characteristic of the Brethren.[92]

How did a very conservative Brethren movement emerge out of such an inter-denominational network? The numbers show that the growth of the Brethren in the 1870s and 1880s was not great. When they first appeared on the census count in 1871 there were 483 people calling themselves Brethren. During a period of huge population growth in the 1870s, this number increased modestly to 1,348 in 1878 and to 1,967 in 1881. Then came a very large jump in Brethren numbers to 3,179 in 1886 at a time when the population had scarcely grown, and another large jump to 5,035 in 1896 and 7,484 in 1901. The next big growth was to 9,758 in 1916 after the Primitive Methodist merger with the Wesleyans. However, it should be noted that these figures of growth are modest compared to the emergence of the Salvation Army, which began with 5,276 adherents in 1886 and climbed further to 9,383 in 1891, although after 1896 its figures were static or in decline. Brethren did not outnumber Salvationists until 1926.[93] There was a huge increase in the number of churches in that era, from twenty to ninety assemblies, with some thirty full-time evangelists by 1905.[94]

The Brethren benefited most profoundly from revivalism in the Manawatu and Taranaki, because of the way in which Brethren-dominated revivalism gave shape to Christian community in the relative religious vacuum of the Manawatu area. Their combination of lay preaching, cottage meetings, intense community and distinctive theology gave them a profound appeal. They were the very essence of revivalism. On the other hand they were very much taken with Adventism; futurist eschatology was the mark which enabled them to re-programme some of those who had been part of the earlier revivals.

There was a sense in which the Brethren were the equivalent of the 'enthusiasts' that so troubled Jonathan Edwards in the early 1740s. Their willingness to preach, their lack of moderation, their preparedness to shame 'half-hearted' Christians very much suggests people who maintain spiritual life by extremist zeal. None of us would probably want to meet James Chrystall in the street and be ordered to stand up

---

90. *Treasury* 45 (1943), p. 32, and 26 (1924), p. 88.

91. See the *Bible Hammer* (Hastings Methodist Church) 1.1 (July, 1896), p. 6.

92. See Lineham, *There we found Brethren*, pp. 33-36; Troughton, 'Christianity and Community', p. 116.

93. All census figures from the Department of Statistics Quinquennial Census of Population, which are reprinted in Davidson and Lineham (eds), *Transplanted Christianity*, documents 4.1, 5.1.

94. *Treasury* 7 (1905), p. 13; *W*, n.s. 8 (1898), p. 166; Case, 'The Lord's work in Tasmania and New Zealand', *W*, n.s. 10 (1900), p. 65.

and give our testimony.[95] Curiously the later Brethren became exceedingly dull, so cautious when those early Brethren were bold extremists. Perhaps the explanation is the sense of pioneering apostolicity of those early evangelists, who were indebted to nobody, for whom revivalism was a passion, where their children and grand children made it a technique, indeed a highly stereotyped 'gospel meeting'. The first evangelists shaped communities, but they were also quite independent of those communities, and would simply march off to new communities 'as the Lord led them'. Some of these evangelists had ups and downs in their experience; few were as extravagant as James Davenport in the great awakening, but there were a few moral derelicts among them. But the churches they left behind were defined by what they had discovered, and became sectarian preservers of it.

In some senses the Brethren never were just revivalists, however, because the churches that became established quickly developed a strong sense of identity expressed in warm-hearted community and steady evangelistic efforts. Sometimes these churches did see new phases of revival, for example the Maharahara revival, where circumstances not dissimilar to those that began Jonathan Edwards' revival in New England—a sudden death of a young person, the electrifying of a place of decaying religious tradition—created a religious sensation in the community which was transformative.[96] More and more as the New Zealand community matured, however, these events occurred in ever more remote parts of the 'backblocks'. I spoke when I was researching *There we found Brethren* to an elderly man who had been converted in a revival in an extremely isolated community at Maerewhenua. It was a revival I had never heard of before then and it made only a sentence or two in printed sources, but it had left a very significant impact on him and his family into extreme old age.

There was an aspect of 'primitivism' among the pioneering work of the Brethren which had a particular impact in colonial society, especially those parts of the society which were shaped by small independent freeholders. In many respects the immigrants of the 1870s were small peasant farmers, for whom establishing a new reality of life was a difficult but vital task. It was from this that the 'do-it-yourself' or 'number eight wire' culture of New Zealand emerged. In many respects the restorationism of the Brethren, the attempt to make a new beginning of the church, made a great deal of sense to colonists, and had a particular social appeal. But this would have never been shaped into a distinctive movement, had the Brethren not participated so extensively in the phenomenon of revival movements, and had not the Brethren been a locus for and a beneficiary of particular revivals.

The affinity of Brethren for revival was not unique. Many of the new small denominations in New Zealand found their initial identity in the values of revival, although only denominations with a sectarian appeal survived for any length of time. There were Exclusive Brethren involved in the same way. The key significance does not lie in the Brethren themselves; it lies in the spread of popular lay Christianity

95. See Lineham, *There we found Brethren*, p. 79.

96. Lineham, *There we found Brethren*, p. 93.

opposed to the formalism of the church among the Primitive Methodists and other 'bush Baptists' in particular, and it lies in the huge impact of the Moody and Sankey ministry in Great Britain, which began a new wave of revival in certain respects deeper than that which took place in their urban setting. It left the Brethren in some parts of New Zealand as a powerful and significant part of the religious landscape, and in turn they have contributed to a whole variety of aspects of New Zealand's religious culture.

CHAPTER 13

'Do the next thing': Henry Lewis Garrett and the Evolution of the Hobart Brethren Assembly

Elisabeth Wilson

Brethren meetings were established in Australia by the 1850s. It seems that there was an assembly in Melbourne at this stage, which grew into a large and dynamic fellowship by the 1870s, and there was possibly one in Sydney begun in the 1850s also. In 1866 William Brown, Walter Douglas and Charles Perrin (all from the United Kingdom) came to Tasmania, following the impetus of the 1859 Revival. Brown and Perrin, and also Edward Moyse who arrived soon after, took meetings along the north-west and north-east coasts, resulting in what has been called a revival in several centres—particularly Scottsdale and Kentish (now Sheffield). During the 1870s active assemblies were planted in many parts of the state—Scottsdale, Circular Head, Table Cape, Launceston, Sheffield, and the Huon.[1]

In late 1869 Douglas, an American who had been converted in London, held dynamic and controversial citywide evangelistic missions in Launceston and Hobart, the two principal cities in Tasmania.[2] As a result of the conversions which followed a fellowship of new Christians was formed which met in the People's Hall on the fringe of the central business district of Hobart.[3] With the arrival of another evangelist, Edward Moyse, and a retired Indian Army officer, Colonel Henry Shelton and his wife, this fellowship evolved into the first Brethren assembly in the south of Tasmania. Henry (Harry) Lewis Garrett's diaries shed invaluable light on this process, with the added interest of them also recording Garrett's passage to the Brethren from his earlier committed Anglicanism.[4]

---

1. Alan Dyer, 'The movement that shook Tasmania', *Assembly Challenge* (December 1987–January 1988), p. 14. The north-west coast has still, proportionately, a high number of Brethren assemblies.

2. K.J. Newton, 'A History of the Brethren in Australia with particular reference to the Open Brethren' (PhD thesis, Fuller Theological Seminary, 1990), pp. 41-42.

3. The People's Hall was demolished in the 1960s.

4. I would like to thank Harry Garrett's descendants, in particular his grand-daughter, Mrs Betty Cramp, and his great-grand-daughters, Mrs Jennifer Atkinson and Mrs Mary Farnell, for their permission to use the diaries, which are in the keeping of the family.

Harry Garrett was born in 1847, the youngest of ten children of Alfred, a merchant and importer, later an accountant,[5] and Catherine Garrett. Educated at the Hutchins School,[6] one of Australia's oldest independent schools for boys, in 1863 he gained an Associate of Arts certificate.[7] He became an accountant and later (1882) actuary of the Hobart Savings Bank, and in 1871 he married Martha Fisher (b.1843). They had five children between 1873 and 1886. The Garretts lived at Battery Point for the first few years and then moved to Sandy Bay—both suburbs within walking distance of the centre of the city.

The diaries run from 1877 (when Garrett finally made the break with the Church of England) to 1893, and are written in a clear, flowing script, with a week to each double page. They do not record many personal emotions, apart from some spiritual aspirations, and family doings probably consist of about one-third of the material. Garrett used them as a way to record partly his spiritual journey, but mainly to note events and people in the group of Christians with whom he associated. Baptisms are noted, and also lists of people at picnics, people welcomed into fellowship, magazine subscribers, places of meetings (houses, etc.), and sometimes, cryptically, controversies. He also noted in the right margin those with whom he had corresponded, and those to whom he had sent money—making it easy for him to glance back and check. On every single day he wrote there is a left marginal reference to the weather—'lovely day', 'showery', 'snow on mountain', 'fine', etc.[8] In a society where walking was the chief means of transport, the weather was clearly of paramount importance. In 1886 Martha Garrett wrote nearly all the entries, 1887 is blank, and there are no diaries for 1888–90. Also extant is a collection of letters to Garrett about assembly or related matters, or from assembly members, relatives, and a few interstate contacts.

Harry was clearly an energetic, cheerful person. There are numerous references to walks, both for pleasure and necessity. He usually walked into town to the bank, and three or four times a week walked home for tea then back to town or even New Town, about four kilometres from Hobart, for a Bible reading or prayer meeting, or to South Hobart, about three kilometres from Hobart towards Mount Wellington. In a couple of his diaries there are lists of names by location—perhaps to enable him to plan his pastoral calls more efficiently. He usually finished at the bank at 3 p.m. so on many days he visited people on his way home. These people are named in the diary.

Numerous references attest to Garrett's enthusiasm for gardening. He could sing well and possibly played an instrument, as on a couple of occasions he was asked to

5. Harold Garrett, 'Notes for the Garrett family centenary', 1935. The Garretts arrived in Hobart on 15 November 1835, on *The Brothers* (Captain Robert Towns). Archives Office of Tasmania [henceforth AOT], reference MB 2/39/2, p. 396.

6. Hutchins was established in 1846 under the auspices of the Church of England, Alison Alexander (ed.), *The Companion to Tasmanian History* (Hobart, 2005), p. 186.

7. Legislative Council Journals Vol, X, 1864, Report no. 4 (Council of Education Examiners' Report 1863), p. 8. Harry had been an Exhibitioner in 1860.

8. Several times meetings were cancelled or given up early because it was so wet.

join in practices for evangelistic missions. In March 1878 he 'played all day in the Hutchins cricket match. We had a glorious day.'[9]

An affectionate father, Harry twice refers to his children as 'the chicks'. Despite the constant demands of paid work, and his commitment to Christian activities, over the years there are references to walks (often from their home to Long Beach, about two kilometres down the river, and back 'through the bush'[10]), kite-flying, cricket and rounders, painting or scrapbooking with them on a wet day, reading, visits to the museum, a 'ramble on the rocks' at Kingston on their holiday, and one picnic at Mountain Lake of which he wrote, 'happy day with the children all enjoying themselves very much'. A favourite family activity was taking a boat over to one of the bays on the opposite side of the Derwent River.

The Garretts had at least two servants at any time, probably live-in, as quite often both Harry and Martha went to a meeting at night, presumably leaving the children in their care. There are references to Eliza and Jane and others, and their days off. They seem to have been Christian girls, held in some affection. At least twice Harry mentions the family having dinner with one of them, albeit in the kitchen, as it was her birthday.[11] The walk to Brown's River mentioned above was with Eliza, and she is named on some of the lists of Christians at picnics or outings.

Celebrations in general are interesting. His own birthday, Martha's, and their anniversary (usually 'our wedding day'), are nearly always mentioned, and on his own (7 April) he is usually touched by people's thoughtfulness and affection, and grateful for the mercies of God. A typical entry is 'My birthday 37. "Give thanks to the Lord for He is good and His mercy endureth forever." Received many tokens of love and kindness from all the dear children of God, from Marth and the children and the girls [i.e. maids]. "Praise the Lord."'[12]

Christmas Day was not observed with much ceremony. There is little evidence from the diary that the Garretts had a special meal; sometimes they visited family, or held a meeting at Cascades. On Boxing Day there was often a picnic or bushwalk, either as a family or with friends from the meeting.

Harry's work at the bank, growing in responsibility when he was promoted ('Praise the Lord') to cashier at £400 per annum,[13] meant he could usually leave at 3 p.m., but when the bank staff were balancing this could be much later. In the earlier years he worked every Saturday night ('bank as usual in evening'), though not generally during that day.

There is no clear indication in the diaries as to what, precisely, led this well-brought-up young Anglican man to seek Christian fellowship elsewhere. Evidently he had a strong religious commitment from at least young adulthood, as a letter to the bishop in 1868 seeks his blessing for an 'Association for Promoting a Mission to the Working Classes of Hobart Town'—Harry writing as the secretary. An

9. 21 March 1878.

10. Now covered with houses in the much expanded suburb of Sandy Bay.

11. E.g. 7 November 1883.

12. 7 April 1884.

13. 4 September 1882.

affectionate letter in 1874 from his former rector at St John the Baptist in West Hobart (F.H. Cox, who had returned to England[14]) mentions his meetings at the Cascades, and says, 'I am sorry you cannot "feel at home" at any church—however it must be better to persevere in an act of duty, even though it seems to bring no reward.' Cox urges him to 'speak to Mr Banks Smith [the evangelical rector of St George's, Battery Point[15]] [and] tell him candidly what you miss & what you want'.[16] It is curious that Harry could not settle at St George's, as 'the Canon [Banks Smith] maintained a stolid adherence to pre-Oxford Movement Evangelical principles'.[17]

There are also some letters from A.W. Garrett (Harry's older brother Willie), arguing with some sophistication and cogency for a generous Roman Catholicism—in particular suggesting that reliance on the Bible alone, without using the teaching and traditions of the church, was dangerous.[18] There is a draft of at least one reply from Harry, writing firmly yet with courtesy that 'I feel constrained to say that while I have never entertained any strong sentiments on the subject of R.C.s nor ever had sympathy with the party of Protestantism, the result of your letters and handling of Scripture has been to cause a deep sense in my mind of the utter corruption and Godlessness of the whole system which perpetuates such [doctrines?] as the RC church puts forth and holds.'[19] This correspondence is interesting, coming as it does the year after the controversial ex-Catholic priest Father Charles Chiniquy visited Hobart: his Hobart meetings had caused such uproar that the Tasmanian Volunteers were called out to help keep order.[20] The tone of these

---

14. Frederick Holdship Cox (1821–1906), vicar of St John the Baptist Church, Buckland, Warden of Christ College, rector of St John the Baptist, West Hobart, first Dean of Hobart 1872, and first editor of *Church News,* before his return to England in 1874: G. Stephens, *The Anglican Church in Tasmania* (Hobart, 1991), p. 84. His memorial plaque from St John the Baptist (now displayed in the church hall at St Peter's Sandy Bay) attests to his 'energy and influence...signal piety and talent...firmness, justice and purity of life'.

15. The Rev. Canon George Banks Smith (1826/7–1902): Stephens, *Anglican Church,* p. 257. He was rector from 1859–1902.

16. Letter addressed from Tilney Vicarage, Lynn [Norfolk], dated 28 October 1874. Cox himself had obviously struggled with his own situation in Tasmania: 'desponding & miserable...as I was...at St David's...a state of things in which I had well-nigh lost hope'. Stephens says he 'strove for peace in the ecclesiastical debates of the 1850s'. Stephens, *Anglican Church*, p. 84.

17. *St George's Battery Point* (Battery Point, n.d. [c.1961]), [p. 5].

18. William had a Tasmanian Scholarship to Oxford, where he gained a BA degree. While there he joined the Roman Catholic Church, to the grief of his family. He became an Inspector of Schools in India, and later an Inspector in the Education Department in Tasmania, also engaging in scholarly and literary work, Harold Garrett, 'Notes for the Garrett family centenary', 1935.

19. Letter dated 18 May 1880.

20. See Susan Warne, 'Sectarianism in Hobart: The Chiniquy Disturbances of 1879' (BA honours thesis, University of Tasmania, 1977). As far as one can tell from the diary,

letters is far otherwise: both brothers assure each other of ongoing respect and love, and express some of the pain it gives them to disagree on such fundamental issues, while holding firmly to their respective viewpoints.

St George's was an evangelical, 'low church' outpost (amid much controversy the Tasmanian diocese tended to higher churchmanship), and both Harry and his slightly older close friend Charles Crosby[21] experienced an evangelical conversion through meetings there led by the Rev. Hussey Burgh Macartney, an Anglican clergyman from Caulfield, Melbourne,[22] with wide evangelical and interdenominational contacts. Macartney often spoke on prophetic topics and the 'higher Christian life', and he was in Hobart in December 1876 and March 1877.[23] Crosby and Garrett were thereafter dissatisfied by what they perceived as the deadness of the established churches, and attracted by the warmth of fellowship they experienced with like-minded Christians through these meetings. Macartney apparently told Garrett that he might find happier fellowship with the group of Christians meeting at the People's Hall.[24]

The move to a new fellowship was by no means sudden and there does not seem to have been a once-for-all severance of connections. Some idea of the transitional stages of Harry's allegiance may be gained from entries in the first week in the diary. On Monday 1 January he went to an early morning prayer meeting at St George's, Battery Point, praying 'that the new year may be attended by even greater spiritual blessings than those of last year which were many'.[25] On the Wednesday he paid 10/- pew rent at St George's, and on Thursday read a chapter to Martha called 'Do you feel your sins forgiven' and 'had a long talk with her about it'. On Friday he received

---

Harry Garrett was away in Melbourne when Chiniquy came to Tasmania. The relevant dates are completely blank and the next entry tells of his being farewelled from Melbourne by friends.

21. Charles Crosby, a member of a successful merchant company, was an active member of the Davey Street Congregational Church and had marriage and family connections to the main Congregational families in Hobart. Despite their close friendship, Harry Garrett always refers to him as Mr Crosby, Mr C. Crosby, or just Crosby.

22. This was H.B. Macartney, Jr, whose father was the Dean of Melbourne. Macartney, Jr, was the vicar of St Mary's, Caulfield from 1868–98, and a leader in interdenominational evangelical and missionary work. See Darrell Paproth, 'Hussey Burgh Macartney Jr: Mission Enthusiast', 1st Biennial TransTasman Conference on Australians and New Zealanders in Christian Missions, at Home and Abroad, ANU, Canberra, 2004. <rspas.anu.edu.au/pah/TransTasman/papers/Paproth_Darrell.pdf> (accessed 28 March 2005).

23. *The Missionary at Home and Abroad* (March and April 1877). This was a monthly paper edited and circulated by Macartney throughout the Australian colonies and New Zealand.

24. Family information, also Harold Garrett, 'Notes for the Garrett family centenary', 1935.

25. 1 January 1877.

a packet of papers from the Rev. Macartney. On Sunday 7th he went to the People's Hall in the morning, and preached at the Cascades in the afternoon.

During 1877 he sometimes went to church (St John's) with Martha, and she usually went there for the Sunday evening service. In February, he conducted the early morning prayer meeting at St George's, as Mr Smith was away. However, there was a gradual shift in attendance patterns. His sister Kate went to the People's Hall with him for the first time on 25 February, and on 22 April he writes, 'Marth went with me for the first time to the People's Hall.' Later in the year Martha's sister Grace was converted and went with them. Also during this year he started going to a Colonel Shelton's place in New Town with a few others for regular Bible study—working their way through various books, and having long conversations on the walk back to town.

That joining with Christians who were often regarded as rather peculiar had its difficulties may be indicated by a comment later in the year: 'In the evening discovered that a great hindrance to my entering on this life of full trust was fear of the opinion of men. Prayed the Lord to enable me to give up this.'[26] Some sort of milestone was reached in Harry's life on 26 November 1877 when he wrote, 'At St George's prayer meeting at 7.15 had some stirring words from Pitfield on the subject of full trust and reconsecration from Luke 14:33—forsaking ALL. I was much blessed. In afternoon prayer meeting at our home when the same blessed truth was presented'. In the margin he wrote, 'A day of much blessing. "Here I give my all to Thee, In Thy promises I trust,"' and in the corner, diagonally, 'Gave up Imp[atience?], slothfulness, fear of man.'

A gradual transition between denominations was typical of early Brethren in many places. In the 1820s in Dublin, some early leaders went to an Anglican service in the morning, then met with their friends (later labelled Brethren) in the afternoon or on the following evening.[27] As seen in Hobart, the pattern was often dissatisfaction with one's spiritual life, a visiting evangelist or Bible teacher bringing teaching of a fuller life or of trusting fully in Jesus for salvation, a new warmth and desire to evangelize, and a wish to meet with others who felt the same yearnings. In Hobart, as in other places, notably Scotland after the great revivals of 1859–60,[28] these meetings were often non-denominational in character in the beginning, and it is interesting to see how they gradually took the shape of a Brethren assembly—even while still eschewing a 'denominational' name tag.

---

26. 14 November 1877. There is an interesting cognate comment in his son Harold's reminiscences: 'These defections from the church of their ancestors inevitably made a breach in the unity of the family. There was no ill feeling, I think, & they always stood by one another in any time of trouble, yet during my childhood I recall a sense of our being "outcastes" [sic], tempered perhaps by a slightly smug feeling of being the Chosen People. Whether my feeling was shared by my brothers and sisters I do not know.' Harold Garrett, 'Notes for the Garrett family centenary', 1935.

27. F.R. Coad, *A History of the Brethren Movement* (Exeter: Paternoster Press, 1968), ch. 2.

28. F.F. Bruce, *In Retrospect: Remembrance of things past* (London, 1993), pp. 2-7.

In Harry Garrett's case, there was a gradual severing of other ties. In July 1877 he wrote to 'give up his settings in St George's Church', and in the same week wrote to another man 'in reference to evils in Church of England doctrine and practice'. Nevertheless, he still went to the early morning prayer meeting at St George's until at least the end of the year, once or twice leading the devotion at it. But by August he was writing to Canon Davenport,[29] 'telling him I could not subscribe to the new font for Trinity'.[30] Earlier in the year he had written to the secretary of the 'Light of Queenborough, withdrawing from the lodge & from the Order of Good Templars',[31] and in August he had a conversation with a Mr Mather[32] 'as to the inconsistency of Christians remaining amongst the Good Templars', presumably because of being associated with a temperance society similar in organization to freemasonry.[33] He had been active in the Hobart Christian Workers' Association, but in January 1880 he went to this meeting for the last time, 'as I told those present that I felt compelled to withdraw'.[34]

Harry had a growing interest in 1877–78 in believer's baptism by immersion, often seen by more conventional Christians as quaint. In December 1877 he wrote 'we had some talk on baptism when I saw clearly as I had never seen before that it is truly Christ's ordinance and therefore not to be regarded as unimportant'.[35] Then on 11 April 1878, he 'walked home with Mrs Propsting,[36] we spoke together of Baptism, both being desirous of being baptized'. The diary has no reference to his

29. Davenport's vital dates were 1818–1907: 'A leading churchman of the day', G Stephens, *Anglican Church*, p. 105.

30. 23 August 1877. 'Trinity' would be Holy Trinity Church, North Hobart, which dominates the northern skyline of the city.

31. 20 April 1877.

32. A Mr R.A. Mather is listed in *Walch's Almanac* as the manager of the People's Hall in the 1870s. He was probably Robert Andrew Mather (1815–84), a Quaker merchant, the honorary secretary of the Benevolent Society. See Warne, 'Sectarianism in Hobart', 'Biographical Notes', p. 105.

33. 24 August 1877. One of the reasons for an unhappy incident the following year was another person's membership: 'we had a very painful meeting, Mr Lowe behaving in a very violent and insolent manner in reference to Colonel Shelton's action in the matter of Mr Warr's association with Good Templary'. 4 February 1878. The Independent Order of Good Templars still exists: 'The International Order of Good Templars or IOGT...operates worldwide in over 40 countries. As in the original organization, the IOGT admits men and women equally and promotes the ideas of temperance, peace and brotherhood. At this time it stands as the largest non-government run organization working in the field of temperance and has expanded its practice of temperance beyond mere alcohol to include narcotics and other drug dependencies.' <http://www.templarhistory.com/goodtemplars.html> (accessed 13 April 2005).

34. 6 January 1880. No reason is given.

35. 12 December 1877

36. Working from some of Garrett's lists of names and other associations in the diary, this is most likely Elizabeth Propsting (née Davidson, 1830–99), wife of Richard, the Quaker Superintendent of Police.

own baptism, but it has gaps, and, given his preaching on the topic several times, his rejoicing when others are baptized, and his meticulous recording of their names, it would be very surprising if he were not. Baptisms took place at the Domain Baths, an enclosed area on the foreshore of the River Derwent close to the Queen's Domain reserve, often before the Sunday morning service, and usually in quite large groups—several times ten or so names are mentioned.

The meeting for worship and communion was one of the great attractions for early Brethren, and its simplicity contrasted, for them, with the formality and what some perceived as the empty ritual of the Church of England service. Harry Garrett refers warmly many times to his feelings about Sunday and the meeting for worship: 'day of much blessing', 'day of joy and gladness', 'morning meeting with much blessing', 'very blessed meeting for the Lord's supper', 'happy day', 'very blessed ministry in the morning', 'a very happy blessed time', 'a very happy time of worship at the Lord's supper'. There were times when he did not go, when he was overtired, unwell, or (occasionally) was at odds with someone and did not feel it right to participate, but in general it was clearly a happy priority to attend. Towards the end of his life there were some months when a splinter group met at the Garretts' house on Sunday mornings, but they still 'broke bread' together.[37]

Another attraction of the People's Hall was the group's friendship and fellowship. While this had aspects of 'us against the world', it also provided a social outlet for people who felt that worldly pursuits were not for them. There are numerous accounts of picnics and outings—to Brown's River, up the mountain, to the Waterworks, to Long Beach—with one list of names reaching eighty-four, and usually thirty to fifty people listed. These reports are usually accompanied by some reference to the weather and to a 'blessed time of fellowship' or some such phrase. They include occasions when Christians from Hobart would travel down to North West Bay to spend the day with the small group there. That Harry saw these events as opportunities for spiritual as well as physical refreshment is borne out by an entry in 1878, after an outing for boys from the Boys' Home to Beauty Bay: 'Found no refreshment for body or spirit from the trip. I feel more convinced than ever that if we go out in this manner we should go as Christians and if we find the day together without any spiritual communion we do ourselves and those with us much harm. May the Lord give us much grace that we may be more faithful in this matter.'[38] Other times of fellowship were the informal prayer meetings in people's houses, the frequency and regularity of which fluctuated, and meals and informal suppers. The links thus formed were very strong and some of the letters Harry received for his birthdays show the affection, esteem and even love in which he was held. Notes in the diary reveal that he wrote to others on their birthdays also.

One of the testing areas for new fellowships is how they are to be governed. In the first flush of new spiritual life and friendships, it does not appear to be a

---

37. There is no indication as to why Harry was in a 'splinter group'. At this point, probably because of his illness, the diary entries are quite patchy.

38. 9 February 1878.

problem, but soon issues arise which require some sort of judgment. In many cases what later became Brethren assemblies were not established as such in the beginning, and this was the case with those at the People's Hall. At first there was a business meeting to deal with the running of day-to-day affairs. Then, after a serious breach of fellowship in 1878 had been patched up, Harry writes, 'We decided that Colonel Shelton, Mr Lowe and myself should act together as a committee in all matters connected with the Assembly.'[39] Eventually, in 1883, he mentions an 'oversight meeting'[40] and later in that year he writes, 'Searching the Scriptures on subject of Eldership'.[41] It seems that from about that time there was a recognized body of elders, and from the late 1870s there had been contact with other Brethren fellowships and consultation on how matters should be organized.[42] The meetings in the People's Hall were listed as Brethren in *Walch's Almanac* from 1880.

The leadership had to cope with various difficulties over the years. Several times there were major upsets in the meeting—either personality clashes or what they believed to be doctrinal differences. At one stage in the 1880s, thirty or forty people were meeting in the Garretts' home for worship, as the result of some unspecified unhappiness in the wider fellowship. But Harry's bent was for reconciliation. In early problems he talks with the different protagonists and tries to understand each viewpoint: 'Colonel Shelton talks of withdrawing and establishing a new meeting. But I cannot think he is taking a right course.'[43] Some years later he refers to a 'meeting of brethren [that is, males] in the evening with much blessing speaking of unity & division, love & forbearance'.[44]

There were also sad times when some discipline was called for. In 1884 the Hobart meeting received letters from Christchurch and Dunedin about Edward Moyse, the evangelist who had helped stimulate the fledgling fellowship. Harry refers to it as 'the sad matter'[45] and later the meeting wrote to Christians interstate 're Moyse & Dunleavy'.[46] It appears that these two New Zealand Brethren workers had been found to have a scandalous personal relationship. Word went round that they could no longer be received or welcomed to speak in Brethren circles.[47]

Every so often a member of the assembly was discussed by the oversight and told they were to be put out of fellowship. In 1884 a Mr Macrow was told that 'the

---

39. 30 March 1878.

40. 22 March 1883.

41. 16 October 1883.

42. Harry evidently had access to literature about the Brethren, as early in 1878 he 'wrote to Mr Castray enclosing "Accusers of Brethren" and "The Brethren Who are they?"', 22 January 1878.

43. 18 March 1878.

44. 23 October 1885.

45. 20 August 1884.

46. 6 September 1884.

47. Information from Alan Dyer, Sheffield, Tasmania, who interviewed a very old evangelist about the early days of Brethren assemblies in Tasmania.

brethren could not receive him at present into fellowship'.[48] A clue as to why appears the previous year: 'Called with Mr Reeve to see McCrow & spoke to him about the business not being conducted in a godly way. He did not seem to submit himself to our judgement in the matter.'[49] Another situation is indicative of Harry's own approach to delicate situations. In early 1883 a young girl was asked to meet him and three of the women from the meeting. He wrote, 'We had a quiet talk about her sin.'[50] In February he met her again and 'told her her sin had been brought before the church & asked her to attend a meeting of brethren'.[51] A further clue as to what the sin was might be gleaned from the fact that in April 'Lizzie Bolton & Willie Sly [were] put away' [from the Lord's table].[52] There is no mention of them being received back into fellowship.

One of the continuing tensions in Brethren and other similar groups has been that between a desire to welcome all true Christians to the Lord's table, and the aim of keeping the fellowship pure from what was seen as wrong doctrine—the question of reception. It involved what they saw as 'separation'—not just from 'the world' but from ecclesiastical systems which they believed were man-made. Over the years written about by Harry Garrett, there are several references to talking with someone about being received into fellowship, and often this happened after baptism.

In 1883 Brethren meetings in the eastern Australian states divided over the issue of reception. A lady preacher, Mrs Hampson, was staying in Melbourne with Mr Theo Kitchen (himself a leader in inter-denominational activity) and asked to come to the Breaking of Bread. There was concern over how the matter was handled, but the key question was whether this sort of 'occasional fellowship' was part of the biblical pattern. In the end nearly a quarter of the 200-strong assembly meeting in Protestant Hall in Melbourne seceded, believing that this was not right, and one of the leaders of the secession, Gordon Hopkins, toured neighbouring states explaining their position.[53]

Leaders of the Hobart fellowship met with him on 4 December 1883. Always thoughtful, Harry Garrett concluded his brief note with 'Wait on the Lord'. His more detailed note on the meeting, written at the back of the diary, says, 'Talked the matter over. Could see no Scripture to guide us in taking part in the division, decided to wait on the Lord for guidance and light and meet next Sunday.' Sunday's detailed

48. 24 August 1884.

49. 26 October 1883; Charles Frederick Reeve was a freelance evangelist at this stage, loosely attached to the Brethren; later Baptist, and the founder of the Poona and Inland Village Mission.

50. 14 January 1883.

51. 21 February 1883.

52. 8 April 1883, and see 9 April 1883.

53. Hopkins and his brother, Rice T. Hopkins, had some links to the Needed Truth movement, but this incident seems to have been separate from that. The assemblies that seceded, and some planted by them, were colloquially known as the 'Hopkinite' group of meetings—mainly found in Victoria and Tasmania. Most of them rejoined the Open meetings in 1961.

note says, 'Decided that our responsibility was to deal directly with the Protestant Hall meeting, apart from the question of the Division, to ascertain from them the principles they maintain as to reception into fellowship, Clergy and Laity, and fellowship with sects, in the meantime, any coming from the other assemblies in separation from the Protestant Hall to be asked to sit back [i.e. not take communion].'[54] The position of the Hobart assembly eventually crystallized into one of cautious open reception, with letters of commendation from and to other assemblies for people in fellowship. It was well into the twentieth century before these were not required.

The Brethren have been characterized by evangelistic outreach throughout their existence, often linked to some form of philanthropy, and those in Hobart were no exception. Harry Garrett was involved in numerous activities to reach out to those they saw in need of salvation. Firstly, though perhaps he would not have seen it as his main work, was his pastoral visiting. As noted above, he would regularly visit two or three people on the way home, or after tea. He visited people in hospital or gaol, people who were ill, shut-in, or dying, or just people he wished to follow up. In this pre-telephone decade, he frequently called to find someone out, or too ill to see him, or asleep. At one stage (1877–78) he went most weeks to a Miss Gatehouse, evidently a devout invalid, reading and praying with her and also benefiting from her conversation. On one occasion a few of the believers met for communion at her house. He often mentions taking books or tracts to people, including children; at other times, food or medicine.

Most visits were not long. Some resulted in conversations where, to his great joy, the person told him they were 'trusting in Jesus for full salvation' or 'resting in Jesus'. Some long-term friendships formed from these visits, which at times seem to be more than even a minister working full-time could be expected to make. That he was not unaware of the dangers of 'busyness' is borne out by an entry which reads, 'I find I must make some change as I am injuring my own soul for want of spiritual food & time for communion, I must give up going out so much.'[55] Perhaps the simple phrase he read and noted in 1877 best expresses his approach: 'Do the next thing'—which, he writes, would be a very good motto for all Christian workers.[56]

Usually when he mentions a death (distressingly often) he also attends the funeral, or gives the reason why he could not. In February 1883 he went to a baby's funeral: 'Had a very blessed time at the grave, but poor Mrs Bennett was very much broken

54. The leaders met again in January to 'consider the Melbourne matter': 'We decided upon no course of action but to write again and acknowledge their letter, and let them know we were not at all in accord with them in the matters referred to therein', 29 January 1884. On 12 February 1884 he wrote, 'We came to the conclusion that we could not with confidence receive [believers] on letters of commendation from those in oversight in that meeting [i.e. the meeting in secession].'

55. 22 January 1878.

56. 6 February 1877.

down.'[57] Once he mentions trying to reconcile a married couple: 'Called to see Mr & Mrs Knight and tried to make peace between them... Lord give me more wisdom!'[58]

Other avenues of evangelism were the mission at the Cascades, an outreach to cabmen, meetings at the Brickfields for the 'poor old men', meetings at New Town for the 'poor old women' (these last two being institutions for indigent aged ex-convicts), and meetings at Peacock's (the jam factory on the wharf) for workers there. These latter three were more sporadic, but the meetings for cabmen and their associates were quite large (up to 100) at the end of the 1870s, and provided a social service also. On a weeknight, tea was often provided by ladies in the meeting—a welcome respite in winter, one would think. A service would be held, and tracts given out. Some cabmen were converted and joined the assembly, others were helped financially. Charles Crosby left Hobart for Melbourne in 1879 for business reasons, but he left Harry with £100 'to be spent in the Lord's service during his absence'[59] and later sent more.

There were also general evangelistic missions. In 1879 both Mrs Emilia Baeyertz, a converted Jewess from Melbourne,[60] and Henry Varley, a well-known English evangelist with links to the Brethren,[61] came to Hobart. Harry was closely involved with both these speakers, meeting them at the train, and helping to arrange their meetings. Mrs Baeyertz spoke at the People's Hall and Varley at the Town Hall. Harry took his wife, children, and servants, distributed notices of his meetings among the cabmen, and posted '123 notices...to the young men of the town',[62] though he commented on the opening meeting that it was 'very crowded and rather inclined to the disorderly'.[63]

---

57. 19 February 1883.

58. 15 May 1885.

59. 5 September 1879

60. See Elisabeth Wilson, 'Totally devoid of sensationalism: Mrs Emilia Bayertz, the Jewish lady evangelist from Melbourne', *Tasmanian Historical Research Association Papers and Proceedings*, 49 (September, 2002), pp. 153-66; Shurlee Swain, 'In these days of female evangelists and Hallelujah lasses: women preachers and the redefinition of gender roles in the churches in late nineteenth-century Australia', *The Journal of Religious History* 26 (February, 2002), pp. 63-77; Mrs Emilia Baeyertz, the Jewish lady evangelist from Melbourne', *Tasmanian Historical Research Association Papers and Proceedings* 49 (September, 2002), pp. 153-66.

61. See Darrell Paproth, 'Henry Varley and the Melbourne evangelicals', *The Journal of Religious History* 25.2 (June 2001), pp. 173-87.

62. 27 March 1878.

63. 21 March 1878. Varley's style tended to the flamboyant and provocative. Harry had been concerned enough at a 'report of Mr Varley's having denounced Mr Fawns at Launceston' that he talked it over with Charles Crosby and 'decided to send him a telegram at once to ascertain if it is true', 15 March 1878. There is no record of the answer, if any, but he mentions several social meetings with Varley in Hobart, and helped with his meetings, so he must have been satisfied with the result of his enquiries. Varley had publicly named Mr Fawns, a prominent Launceston citizen, as the owner of a building in which a brothel operated.

Mrs Baeyertz's visits raised the knotty question of the position of women in a church. Harry Garrett often talked with some of the older women—in the early days he frequently mentions Mrs Propsting as being at Bible studies and walking home with him, having useful conversations. He visits Miss Gatehouse and also a Miss Sly and her 'girls'—possibly a boarding house. It is evident that he valued their spiritual insights, and many of the active members of the assembly were women. He welcomed Mrs Baeyertz's ministry also. However, in common with almost all Christian denominations in the nineteenth century, public participation by women in normal church services was seen by Brethren generally as not scriptural.[64] Mrs Baeyertz was seen by many as an exception because of the blessing that resulted from her meetings, but not everyone approved. In January 1878 Garrett 'called to see Mr Webster when he explained to me his reasons for not supporting Mrs Baeyertz' ministry, not approving of women preaching'.[65] As Harry took his family to hear her, we may surmise that he did not agree. However, in December 1880 during another visit, he accompanied Edward Moyse 'to speak with Mrs Baeyertz'.[66] As there is no further mention of involvement with her ministry, and other Brethren fellowships in Tasmania stopped welcoming her to speak,[67] it is reasonable to assume that they told her that she could no longer speak at the People's Hall.

The mission at the Cascades occupied so much of Garrett's time that it needs separate attention. Night school and Sunday afternoon or evening meetings were held in the Ragged School,[68] and in June 1891 the committee in charge of the building queried whether the meetings were truly non-denominational and non-sectarian in nature, which was the agreement. A copy of Harry's answer has not survived, but it seems his was a personal concern, with some help from others associated with the Brethren. Harry preached nearly every Sunday evening unless there was a gifted visitor available, or he was unwell, and he usually took a Bible class on Wednesday evenings.[69] The meetings were either educational (night school) or for evangelism or Bible teaching. However, some of the converts were baptized and became members of the Brethren assembly.

Another constant activity was letter writing. With no formal denominational structure, Brethren made the most of their informal networks. Harry Garrett corresponded with a wide range of people: close friends such as Charles Crosby, from

64. Neil Dickson, 'Modern prophetesses: women preachers in the nineteenth-century Scottish Brethren', *Records of the Scottish Church History Society*, 25 (1993), pp. 89-117.

65. 28 January 1878.

66. 27 December 1880.

67 Information from Alan Dyer, Sheffield, Tasmania.

68. The Ragged School was held in a chapel in upper Macquarie Street, opposite Denison Street—later the South Hobart Baptist Church, burnt down in the 1967 bush fires. It was operated by the Hobart Town Ragged School Association. See Ian Terry, *A Thematic History of South Hobart* (Hobart, 1999), p. 57.

69. This must have necessitated consistent preparation and Bible study. Quite often the topics are given, occasionally with short outlines or main headings.

whom he received regular and presumably encouraging letters, visiting speakers and evangelists, Christian literature agents to organize supplies of books, magazines and tracts, Christians in isolated places, young people to whom he was a mentor and who had moved away for work, men and women asking for help in obtaining work or needing a loan. Many letters are from working class people, written with real affection and with gratitude for his pastoral care.

Doubtless because of his profession, and general efficiency and trustworthiness, Harry was constantly being asked to handle money. The diary records money sent for literature, sent and received for Christian workers, lent to and repaid by people in need. It is not clear whether the loans are personal or from the church—probably a combination. They certainly reveal a world in which there was no state welfare to fall back on, and were not only from or to working-class people. Harry was also asked by the wealthy Hobart philanthropist Alfred Kennerley to handle some of his affairs.

By the 1890s the fellowship at the People's Hall had been recognizably Brethren for at least a decade. It had passed from the 'first fine careless rapture' of a group of Christians coming together in renewed faith and life, to an established and somewhat more circumscribed fellowship within the Brethren aegis. Harry Garrett was clearly a major influence in how it evolved, and on his peers and those younger than he. He and others had ensured that it remained within the broad rather than narrow stream of Brethren meetings. However, he did not live to see the meeting continue into the twentieth century. In 1891 he was found to have cancer of the bone in his leg, and went to Melbourne to have it amputated. He and Martha and their youngest child were there for months, living with Charles Crosby and family while Harry was in hospital. His descendants still have the letters he wrote home to the older children, letters we are told are 'full of love and courage and faith in God'.[70] Harry and Martha returned home in 1892 and eventually he resumed work, using crutches and ordering an artificial leg from New York. However, he succumbed to lung cancer in December 1893 at the age of forty-six.[71] The last entry in his diary is a fortnight or so before he died, typically about a visit from a bereaved man: 'The Lord comfort him & sustain him in his sore trial. "If thou wilt believe, thou shalt see the glory of God."'[72] No doubt he was applying this to himself as well.

The assembly must have been bereft, and certainly his family was. In old age his elder son Harold wrote that, 'Father's principle of living by Faith forbade his making provision for the future & he left nothing but a few pounds in his current bank account.' Harold had just started work at the Hobart Savings Bank (of which he later became manager) and the family were largely reliant on his income. They were obliged to move house and 'after much dreary house-hunting [they] found a delightful home at "Remuera", at Lower Sandy Bay'. Another financial consequence of Harry's conscientious application of his Christian commitment was that 'he disapproved of

70. Cramp, *Our Family Homes in Davey Street*, p. 5.

71. His death certificate (AOT reference RGD 35, 1893/810) is dated 6 December 1893, and the cause of death is given as 'pneumonia probably cancerous'.

72. 21 November 1893.

life assurance & had in fact surrendered a policy he previously held',[73] which also lessened the possible family income.[74] It is likely that his attitude to money was influenced by such Brethren leaders as George Müller[75] and Anthony Norris Groves who expounded and lived by the principle of living by faith, and believed insurance showed a lack of trust in God.

The church he had helped to guide through its formative years continued steadily, with a membership of between eighty and a hundred. Hopefully Harry Garrett would be heartened to know it is still in existence. After using a number of rented buildings, in 1917 it moved to the purpose-built Murray Street Gospel Hall, and then in late 2003 to Hope Christian Centre in North Hobart.[76] The assembly has been an 'open' fellowship from Garrett's time onwards, welcoming Christians from other fellowships, albeit in earlier days with some caution and preferring letters of commendation. By and large it has not been characterized by the tendency to split over minor matters, a depressing tendency of Brethren life. Instead it has always had an evangelistic outlook: holding a city open air meeting for many years until the 1950s; having two outreach Sunday schools for several decades; assisting in planting three other assemblies; helping establish a youth camp in southern Tasmania; and having many members involved in inter-denominational or intrastate outreaches such as Scripture Union activities, the Billy Graham crusade in 1959, and the 'Best Thing in Life Team' (a team of men who took gospel weekends in isolated towns in Tasmania in the 1950s and 60s). One can see the legacy of Harry Garrett, among others, in the spirit and outworking of these activities.

---

73. Harold Garrett, 'Notes for the Garrett family centenary', 1935. It seems that Garrett died intestate, as there is no will listed in the AOT index.

74. Many of his descendants are still involved in various Christian fellowships. A grand-daughter, Catharine Burt (née Garrett), served as a Brethren missionary in India from 1929 to 1972.

75. It is likely that Harry met or heard Müller when he visited Tasmania in the late 1880s, but there is no evidence for this—the diaries for the relevant years are missing or blank.

76. The buildings used were: People's Hall to 1897; Gospel Hall, Harrington Street (the old Baptist chapel near Goulburn Street, now the site of Europcar) 1898–1906; the Mariners' Church on the wharf (now the site of the Marine Board building—the actual building was moved to Sandy Bay and became St Peter's Church) 1907–17; Murray Street Gospel Hall, later Chapel, 164 Murray Street, 1917–2003; and Hope Christian Centre (formerly the Sunbeam warehouse), 25 Tasma Street, North Hobart, December 2003–present.

CHAPTER 14

Christian Brethren Assemblies in Jamaica, 1923–2003

Winston G. Litchmore

Jamaica is the third largest of the many islands situated in the Caribbean Sea, ranking behind Cuba and the island of Hispaniola which is shared by Haiti and the Dominican Republic. It has a land area of 4,244 square miles, which is divided into fourteen parishes. It is a very beautiful island with much greenery, several mountains, hills and valleys, rivers, streams, white and sandy beaches, sunshine and blue skies. Only one-seventh of the island is flat and this is mostly along the sea coast. Agriculture, bauxite mining and tourism are the main sources of income.

Jamaica is a stronghold of Protestant witness in the Caribbean. The British seized it from the Spaniards in 1664 and ruled until independence was gained in 1962. The British introduced the English language and as an English-speaking country Jamaica ranks behind the USA and Canada as the country with the most native English speakers in the Western world. The British also established Protestantism. The Moravians, Baptists, Methodists and Presbyterians came in the eighteenth century and waged a relentless struggle for the abolition of the slave trade and the emancipation of the slaves. Slavery was finally abolished officially on 1 August 1838.

Churches of all varieties abound. Jamaica has the largest number of churches per square mile in the world, for a population of 2.6 million. The 2001 census shows that the largest single denomination is the Seventh Day Adventists, with approximately 10% of the entire population. The Adventists have over 281,000 members and 624 churches. However, a combination of four types of 'Church of God' outranks them with a combined total of 617,158. The traditional church, the Anglican, which had the highest membership at the time of Jamaica's independence in 1962 has now plunged to under 100,000. The various Christian cults, including the Rastafarians, have followers numbering under 1%. The same low percentage goes for non-Christian religions such as Bahai, Islam, Black Muslims, Hinduism, and Judaism. Roman Catholicism, the major religion of the Caribbean and Latin America, has under 70,000 members and fewer than 4% of the population in Jamaica.

The work of the Lord among the assemblies known popularly today as Brethren had an early association with the movement that began in the first half of the nineteenth century in the British Isles. This is because two of the influential leaders of the movement passed through Jamaica on their way to Guyana in 1850. The visit of J.N. Darby and G.V. Wigram resulted in the setting up of two Exclusive Brethren assemblies in that year, one in the capital city, Kingston, and the other in rural Clarendon.

However, in 1920 a division arose among the assemblies in Britain that had repercussions in Jamaica. Consequently, several brethren of the Kingston assembly left that fellowship to form an independent gathering known as Christian Brethren. It was to this independent gathering of believers that Leonard and Irene Bewick of Kansas, USA, came in 1923. They started ministry among the group and thus established the first Open assembly of Christian Brethren in the island, which was named Assembly Hall. In 1925 William Gibson, an Irishman who as a boy had settled with his parents in Canada, came to Jamaica with his wife Grace and strengthened the work. They founded and established Maranatha Assembly, which became a large assembly with dynamism for outreach to other parts of Jamaica and the Caribbean.

Today the Closed Brethren continue, having twenty-three assemblies in Jamaica. However, the Open assemblies (Christian Brethren assemblies) number eighty-four, with 6,210 in fellowship as at June 2000. An assembly booklet, entitled the *Address Book—Assemblies of Christian Brethren in Jamaica—2000*, provides a useful profile of each assembly and serves as a communication and prayer tool.

Table 1: Membership of Christian Brethren assemblies in Jamaica, 2000

Size of Membership	Number of Assemblies
400 and over	2
200 and 399	4
150 and 199	4
100 and 149	13
50 and 99	16
20 and 49	36
Less than 20	9

Source: *Christian Brethren Assemblies Jamaica News (CBA Jamaica News)* 2.1 (March, 2001)

Statistical information gathered during 2000 revealed that there was a dip of 261 in membership between 1985 and 2000.[1] It was also established that 44.12% of the membership was concentrated in sixteen assemblies in the combined parishes of Kingston (the capital city) and St Andrew. Membership of the eighty-four assemblies was as shown in Table 1. The smallest gathering had a membership of fifteen in 1985 and eight in 2000. The largest gathering, which had 220 members in 1985, had increased to 590 in 2000. The *Address Book—Assemblies of Christian*

1. *Christian Brethren Assemblies Jamaica News (CBA Jamaica News)* 2.1 (March 2001).

Brethren in Jamaica was due to be updated in 2005, reflecting the anticipated increase in the overall membership of the assemblies.

Evangelistic drive by the Christian Brethren movement generates an influence much beyond their actual membership numbers. This is particularly evident in evangelistic crusades across the island each year, in para-church organizations such as Back to the Bible, Gideons International, Child Evangelism Fellowship, and in the media. Gifted Brethren are popular newspaper columnists, and some are involved in radio and television programmes that emphasize both social transformation and spiritual regeneration. The *Christian Brethren Assemblies Jamaica News* was launched in September 2000, and is recognized as the 'official' Christian Brethren news magazine; it is circulated to each of the eighty-four assemblies and overseas. Two Christian radio programmes, 'Look at Life' and 'His Master's Time', are aired weekly on the national radio RJR. A website is being currently developed for the Christian Brethren assemblies by Christian Missions. This agency, which functions as the legal entity and administrative office of the Christian Brethren assemblies across Jamaica, was established in 1949 as the legal entity and property arm of the Christian Brethren assemblies in Jamaica.

The strong foundation of the work in Jamaica must be highlighted. Missionaries of great ability established the work. Special mention has already been made of pioneer church planters such as Leonard and Irene Bewick, and William Gibson. Others were Arthur Isles Hart of Jamaica, who lived in USA and then returned home; George Hale, a New Zealander who lived in Canada; William Gibson of Ireland; and evangelists such as Harold Wildish of England, who was the greatest reaper of souls we have known in Jamaica and throughout the rest of the Commonwealth Caribbean. Through his team gigantic tents were pitched and thousands of souls were saved and scores of churches established or revived. Harold Wildish's partner in Jamaica was Edwin Willie of Wales. Working alongside him in visitation and pastoral support was Sydney Calcraft of Wales who carried out ministry at the police training school, prisons and hospitals. In their wake came Frank and Florence Fenton, from Bebington, Cheshire, the last of the foreign missionaries who laboured in Jamaica for over fifty years. Frank Fenton was an excellent pioneering pastor, community social worker, evangelist, and Bible teacher, who was instrumental in the planting of the Harbour View Gospel Chapel and the development and growth of several others. He was also the first principal of the Midland Bible Institute (MBI). William and Annie Hately of England came to Jamaica in 1937 and strengthened the work at Elim Assembly. Elim Assembly, where George Markland has been an elder for over forty years, celebrated its seventy-fifth anniversary in 2003 with the theme 'Building a Christ-centred Community'. William and Joan Hynd of Michigan, USA, served mostly in the parish of St Ann from 1933 until 1943, but were later forced to return to the USA due to ill health. Others made a valued contribution, even if for shorter periods, such as Harold Barker and Albert Widdison, senior British missionaries who introduced Harold Wildish to Jamaica in 1928; Richard Hill, George and Maeve Spence, and William and Laurena McCulloch (1933–1939 again mostly in St Ann), all from the USA; and Bill Patterson, Gavin Hamilton, George Tryon of Yorkshire, England, James McLaren, John Rankine, and Jim Davies.

Apart from the wives of the afore-mentioned men there were single women, such as Ruth Desborough of England who faithfully served with distinction in the Christian Literature Crusade from 1962 to the present time. She is currently in fellowship at Mona Heights Chapel and is still serving. Vera Ellis of England, a counsellor, served in Kingston. Laura Thompson of the UK was involved in hospital and Sunday school work, crusade follow-up and visitation. Elisa Scott, also from the UK, who was a nurse, served mainly at Elim Assembly during its early days.

During the transition, and with the departure of the foreign missionaries, the work passed into the hands of local leaders, who rose magnificently to the challenge. Roy Campbell, the son of Scottish parents of Jewish ancestry, became a pioneer of Gospel assemblies to Belize (then British Honduras) from 1949 to 1962, when he returned to Jamaica due to ill-health. He was also instrumental in the launching in 1963 of the Christian Brethren radio programme 'Food for Thought' which was aired by Jamaica Broadcasting Corporation (JBC).

Randall Taylor was the first national full-time worker. Hugh Clacken led in the pioneering of ten assemblies in Jamaica. The Hart brothers, Arthur and Charles, followed by Dr Noel Aiken, have been outstanding church planters and pastors, and regional organizers. Dr Aiken currently serves as an elder at Gideon Gospel Chapel in the parish of Portland and is Chairman of the North Eastern Missionary Conference (NEMCO), among other spiritual, social and public occupations. Kenn D. Fullerton and F. George DaCosta led in the establishing of a literature ministry, Hedley Carter and Zadock Daniels became leading Bible teachers, and men such as Karl Richards, Eli Ho, Bruce Black, Maurice McGann and Charlie Royes (Senior) demonstrated well the qualities of eldership. Emile Turner pioneered institutional Bible training with outstanding exercise of faith in God. The MBI, which was set up by the Christian Brethren, is in the process of reorganization in order to offer degree programmes and to acquire accreditation. It was established in 1971 as a result of Emile Turner's faith, inspiration and drive. A considerable number of MBI graduates are involved in leadership roles in several assemblies. They fill up the ranks which ageing leaders and the great exodus of the 1960s–80s left behind.

The Christian Brethren flourished in the post-World War II years, but in the sixties and seventies, and also in the eighties, they hit a snag when many Jamaicans migrated to the USA, Canada and the United Kingdom. Over these last few decades alone over a million Jamaicans emigrated. Initially post-war emigration was to Britain, but in 1967 the United Kingdom restricted immigration from Commonwealth countries, and since then most Jamaicans have emigrated to Canada and the United States. Among them were hundreds of experienced elders, deacons, Sunday school superintendents, youth leaders, camp directors and counsellors. The movement has not fully recovered from this loss. Rural assemblies in particular have been adversely affected, especially in the areas of leadership, personnel, administration and finance. Various steps are consistently being taken to address the situation through prayer, networking, information sharing, training, including preparation of full-time workers—via MBI and other institutions, promotional activities, sacrificial giving and appeal for funds at home and overseas.

The Christian Brethren assemblies in Jamaica continue to function with a strong emphasis on missions, discipleship and prayer. Hence several gospel crusades are convened throughout the year, as well as Vacation Bible Schools (VBS), a National Easter Convention, a National Children's Convention, camps, and meetings for teaching, revival, rededication, and covenant renewal of the saints. The National Easter Convention has consistently been held since 1955 and provides the opportunity for expository teaching on the Christian life and for fellowship of believers from all over the island as well as from abroad. Up to 2,000 are present at these annual conventions, which are hosted by Maranatha Assembly in Kingston. The National Children's Convention, first held in 2001, runs simultaneously with the National Easter Convention, being held each Easter Monday.

Table 2: Assemblies in each region Brethren administrative region of Jamaica, 2000.

Region	**Number of Assemblies**
NEMCO	32
WEMCO	22
MMC	10
CMF	5
SERCBA	15
Total	84

A commendable effort to support needy assemblies has been a Rural Assemblies Programme (RAP), which was born in 1987 and spearheaded by young people. The involvement of young people in this ministry was as a result of observations made by the youth groups in the Corporate Area Assemblies. They observed that the congregations in the rural assemblies were dwindling and that leaders were not emerging in these assemblies to carry on the work of spreading the gospel and discipling. They also observed that the problem had been made worse through the ageing of the leaders and the migration of youth to urban centres in search of better employment and training prospects. Members of the RAP organize themselves into teams for weekly missions in weaker rural assemblies. The RAP works corporately with selected assemblies in preaching, evangelism, visitation, tract distribution, singing and other community activities, as well as the conducting of follow-up programmes.

In recent years, the assemblies in the island have been divided into five regions, or administrative groupings, in order to maximize spiritual, human and material resources, and to support and strengthen the needy assemblies. These regions are: Northeastern Missionary Conference (NEMCO), Western Missionary Conference (WEMCO), Midland Missionary Conference (MMC), Central Missionary Fellowship (CMF) and South Eastern Region of Christian Brethren Assemblies

(SERCBA). The largest region has nearly 40% of the assemblies. Each region has a Chairman, Executive Board or Elders Council and its own constitution. The number of assemblies per region is given in Table 2. The Christian Brethren Assemblies in Jamaica are cognizant of the teaching that full-time workers in the Lord's service should live by the gospel. However, several assemblies, mostly in the rural areas, are unable to provide adequate financial support for their full-time workers although they are in need of them. There are at present eighty full-time workers including forty-five actively serving congregations in various ministries, five itinerant evangelists, seven itinerant Bible teachers and four overseas missionaries commended from the USA and the UK—Michael and Dianna Aiken from Laurel Bible Chapel, San Diego, California, USA, and the present writer and his wife, Nurkle Litchmore, from Loampit Gospel Hall, Lewisham, London, England. It was therefore considered necessary, and expedient, to set up a fund for the purpose of supporting full-time workers. This fund is known as the National Workers Support Fund (NWSF), and was launched in 1998. The regions and individual assemblies, as well as individual donors, contribute to this fund. The funds are then disbursed to the workers by Christian Missions. This is another way in which assemblies organize themselves to help one another. Thus, although each assembly is autonomous, interdependence is observed among them; this yields many benefits.

Additional Features of Jamaican Assemblies

There are a number of other features of assemblies in Jamaica that are worth noting, as they have been effective in aiding our growth. In our services music and musical instruments are widely used with a healthy emphasis on praise and worship. There is an important accent on training to raise up future leaders and to establish the faith of Christians. The training for leadership has including training by CLIMB International. This acronym stands for Cultivating Leaders to Impact and Multiply Biblically, and it was founded in the late 1990s by its current President, Conway Edwards, who has been training and equipping leaders throughout the United States, Spain and Jamaica for the past eight years.[2] Among the training courses that the assemblies undertake are ones in counselling, child evangelism and a recently introduced one in mentorship. Various Christian groups in Jamaica convene prayer vigils for the nation, and assemblies participate in these. There is a strong sense that Brethren must help to educate the children of Jamaica. Consequently we have about thirty basic schools and six preparatory schools which ready children for secondary education. The work among the youth has been successful and there have been several children's conversions weekly and at special conventions held by the assemblies. There are other ways in which we are involved in improving the lot of the people. Clinics staffed by doctors, nurses and pharmacists from assemblies are run as are Social Outreach Programmes which make available medical aid, food for

2. <http://www.climbinternational.org/about_us.htm> (accessed 16 April 2006).

the poor and literacy programmes. In these ways assemblies seek to establish Christians, reach out to young and old, and aid Jamaicans in their everyday lives.

The assemblies in Jamaica have much to praise God for. There is freedom of public worship. Article 21.1 of the Constitution guarantees

> Except with his own consent, no person shall be hindered in the enjoyment of his freedom of conscience, and for the purposes of this section the said freedom includes freedom of thought and of religion, freedom to change his religion or belief, and freedom, either alone or in community with others, and both in public and in private, to manifest and propagate his religion or belief in worship, teaching, practice and observance.[3]

There has been comparatively good reception of God's word among the people with several fruit-yielding crusades across the island, both amongst adults and children, which have resulted in growth in membership. About a fifth of the Jamaican work force is still engaged in agriculture, and much good work has also been done by the Rural Assemblies Programme and by the Camps. There is also good measure of support from stronger assemblies for the smaller and weaker assemblies, and this is aided by the current measure of cooperation among leaders. It was noted above that many have emigrated to the United Kingdom, Canada and the USA. We are thankful that brethren who have emigrated to all of these countries have a continued interest in Jamaica. However, we are not complacent and there are a number of future needs. Increased cooperation among assemblies' leaders is necessary in order to address issues pertaining to autonomy and diversity. Especially in the rural assemblies we require an increase in the number of leaders, and throughout the assemblies there is a need for more dedicated leaders who are men of faith so that each assembly has a clear direction. Important for the future of assemblies, too, is the systematic training of young people for leadership. In an increasingly materialistic and violent society it is essential that the there is a clear distinction between Christians and the ungodly in attitude and life-style.

What of the Future?

The Christian Brethren Assemblies in Jamaica are very conscious of our Lord's imminent return and are therefore committed to focus on the Great Commission as declared in Matthew 28 and Mark 16. It is recognized that Jamaica is now no longer a 'mission field' but a 'mission force', and this means that we are committed to sending missionaries overseas. Among them are Gordon Soutar and his wife Lolita, commended from Harbour View Gospel Chapel to the work in Belize; Roan and Charmaine Earle who work in a multi-ethnic church in California, USA; Ray and Gloria Hoo who are in Vietnam; Linda Lowe who is in the Pacific region; Nukee and Vie Shim who are with the Navigators in Canada; and Otis Maxwell who is

3. The Jamaica (Constitution) Order in Council 1962, <http://pdba.georgetown.edu/Constitutions/Jamaica/jam62.html> (accessed 16 April 2006).

serving with Youth With a Mission in Surinam—these are all commended by Swallowfield Chapel.

The current thrust is church growth—maintaining and building on what is in place and at this same time increasing the membership in each assembly through the preaching of the gospel. There are street corner crusades, in the square crusades and church lawn crusades—many souls are turning to the Lord and coming into assembly fellowship. The assemblies were challenged by the statistical survey of 2000, which showed the rise and fall of individual assemblies' membership between 1985 and 2000. We have seen much growth among assemblies across Jamaica, but we still hunger for more.

CHAPTER 15

Brethren Missionary Settlers and a Colonial Settler Compared and Contrasted[1]

Pauline Summerton

Walter and Anna Fisher were Brethren missionaries from 1889 until 1937, mainly in Kalene, in north-west Northern Rhodesia (now Zambia). They were part of the Brethren missionary effort pioneered by Frederick Stanley Arnot to evangelize that area of central Africa which became known among them as 'the Beloved Strip'. The missionaries were part of a much wider contemporary European interest in Africa as Westerners carved out careers and lifestyles for themselves as soldiers, politicians, administrators, diplomats, business men, farmers, explorers and adventurers. This migration from north to south is now commonly criticized for being 'colonial': for exploiting the lands and peoples of Africa, often blatantly, sometimes under the guise of paternalism. This paper compares the life of Walter Fisher with that of Stewart Gore-Brown, who settled 600 miles west of Kalene Hill at Shiwa Ngandu in Northern Rhodesia in order to achieve for himself a luxurious lifestyle unaffordable in England. What a different dream or desire Walter Fisher had.[2]

It was in 1889 that Dr Walter Fisher resolved to lay aside all for the sake of the gospel. His biographers present his intentions thus:

> How wonderful to live to be the servant of his fellow missionaries, to heal suffering Africans, and to teach them about the love and power of Christ. It might even be given to him to lay down his life for His sake.[3]

Fisher was a gold medal medical student at Guy's Hospital whose father had wanted him to study for the fellowship of the Royal College of Surgeons.

It is likely that Walter Fisher was influenced by contemporary peer group pressure to explore uncharted areas of the globe; his personal knowledge of, and contact with,

---

1. This paper has been edited by Dr Beth Dickson.

2. The present writer's research on the Fisher family can be found in Pauline Summerton, *Fishers of Men: the missionary influence of an extended family in Central Africa* (Tiverton, 2003).

3. W. Singleton Fisher and Julian Hoyte, *Africa looks Ahead: the life stories of Walter and Anna Fisher of Central Africa* (London, 1948); reprinted as (same pagination), *Ndotolu: the life stories of Walter and Anna Fisher of Central Africa* (Ikelenge, Zambia, 1987), p. 21.

David Livingstone may well have fuelled this enthusiasm. Much of his time as a pioneering missionary was spent travelling: in the first four years of being in Africa, it took a quarter of his time. In *Echoes of Service,* the missionary magazine of the Open Brethren, Fisher described the Africans he knew as migrating people, and because of that concluded that it was advisable for missionaries not to build substantial houses. As well as being able to move with the people, this practice had the advantage of enabling missionaries to retain their pilgrim character.[4] Fisher's journeys proved an excellent means of spreading the gospel. For long periods hundreds of carriers lived in close contact with the missionaries and heard a gospel message each day. Many of those who had on occasions been carriers, when they had concluded their work, carried the gospel to their families and villages.

But soon methods had to change. Modern technology reached Africa, and before long a railway was built, bicycles, motorbikes, and then cars were used. More elaborate mission stations were set up, and other forms of evangelism were used: schools, orphanages and medical services, and, of course, support works for all of these agencies. In 1906 the Fishers moved to Kalene Hill and began to build. Houses were built with bricks in an English garden city style, which was the vogue of the day, and they used western furnishings. The houses were quite large. This was partly because the Fishers had a large family—eight children, six of whom survived childhood—and because of the number of visitors they had to accommodate. Walter Fisher was a much-respected doctor and he and his wife had the gift of befriending Africans and missionaries alike.

When European officials visited the Fishers, they were impressed by them. Colonel Colin Harding, Deputy Administrator based in Lealui, Barotseland, wrote, 'Dr and Mrs Fisher have five small children, nicely dressed and with charming manners, in spite of their association with the many natives who, abusing Dr Fisher's kindness, constantly invade their verandah and house.'[5] On one occasion Dr Fisher was taken by Colonel Harding to dine with King Lewanika after a service in Lealui, where the King had read from the Bible publicly and had said how he knew God took care of him on his journey and desired that people should trust God.[6] Even so their lifestyle seemed to be simple by comparison to Stewart Gore-Browne who came to settle in 1920 at Shiwa Ngandu to fulfil his dream. Fisher continued to keep his sights on the fact that he was there to proclaim the gospel and never thought that they were setting up a personal paradise. Given that as a respected surgeon in England he could have expected a very comfortable lifestyle his self-sacrificing motivation for going to Africa to serve Christ contrasts sharply with Gore-Browne's original self-aggrandizing motivation to achieve a life of luxury for himself.

---

4. W.E. Fisher, *Echoes of Service* (June, 1893), p. 143.

5. Colin Harding, *In Remotest Barotseland* (London, 1904), p. 106.

6. W.E. Fisher MSS, Christian Brethren Archive, John Rylands University of Manchester Library (photocopies of originals lodged in the National Archives of Zambia, Lusaka), W.E. Fisher to 'Mother', Lealui, 4 January 1903.

Stewart Gore-Browne confessed his dream of becoming a country squire in his first diary in 1899 when he was a schoolboy and sixteen years of age.[7] At the back of the diary he sketched out a plan of the house he wanted to live in. At the age of thirty-one he was a humble army officer with little prospect of promotion and only a few hundred pounds a year income, however, he calculated that it would be possible to 'live like an emperor' in Northern Rhodesia.[8] One morning playing golf, he met an old acquaintance who had run an ordinance survey course in the Royal Engineers. He asked if Gore-Browne would like to go to Northern Rhodesia to work on the Border Commission. Gore-Browne agreed and asked where Northern Rhodesia was. 'The chap at the War Office who offered me the post didn't know where it was either.'[9] This was in1911.

Christina Lamb, Gore-Browne's biographer, describes his house as 'a three-storey pink-bricked mansion…like something one might find in Surrey or Hampshire, belonging to a duke or a lord'.[10] Inside the house were many evidences of the opulent lifestyle—the padded-leather visitors books revealed signatures of, among others, Nancy Astor, Kenneth Kaunda, the Montagus of Beaulieu, the Duke and Duchess of Montrose, Elspeth Huxley and Jomo Kenyatta.[11]

Gore-Browne was following his African dream—a better lifestyle than he could have had in England—and as a spin-off he hoped to set an example to the natives of civilized living including 'a table set for tea [with] the Minton china with the family crest'. [12] He thought it had definitely been worth the effort of bringing household goods from England to set a good example to the Bemba people he lived among. He employed them, trained them and supplied the materials—often from Fortnum and Masons, the high-class store in London's Piccadilly—for them to enable him to live as he desired.

Dissimilar in lifestyle, Fisher and Gore-Browne were also dissimilar in terms of personality. Fisher was called 'Ndotolu'—the Doctor—by the local people and was noted for his personal gentleness and quiet wisdom.[13] Gore-Browne was 'Chipembele'—the Rhinoceros, partly because of his courage in killing one early in his career, but also because he had a ferocious temper and used to beat his servants with a stick.[14]

Despite these striking contrasts, Fisher and Gore-Brown, on deeper examination, shared values and attitudes, which were expressed differently because of the different spheres of life in which each was principally engaged. Gore-Browne was sacked from his work on the Anglo-Belgian Boundary Commission in 1913–14 because, unlike

7. Christina Lamb, *The Africa House* (1999), Penguin edn (Harmondsworth, 2000) p. 6.

8. Lamb, *The Africa House*, p. 7.

9. Lamb, *The Africa House*, p. 8.

10. Lamb, *The Africa House*, p. xxiii.

11. Lamb, *The Africa House*, p. xxxii.

12. Lamb, *The Africa House*, p. 75

13. Fisher and Hoyte, *Africa Looks Ahead*, pp. 89, 196.

14. Lamb, *The Africa House* pp. 16, 195.

his superior, he refused to deny the Africans their final wages for the project.[15] This concern that Africans should be treated justly only grew in intensity the longer he lived at Shiwa. Like an English squire, he improved housing and welfare, finally building a school in 1938 and a hospital in 1940. 'I feel like a missionary but without the hymn singing', he wrote, but he was not about to start urging the natives to copy the white man's ways and give up beer-drinking, drumming and polygamy, though he had no qualms about dressing them in European clothes.[16] Gore-Browne was not significantly drawn to religion, though as a professed Christian, he built a chapel on his estate which hosted preachers from a variety of denominations.[17] Like Fisher, he was aware of the power of African beliefs, but, unlike Fisher, on one occasion he visited a witchdoctor in order to procure a charm which would make his wife give birth to a son; his son was stillborn.[18]

Finally Gore-Browne entered politics. He could foresee independence in Northern Rhodesia and was elected to the Legislative Council (LegCo) where he consistently championed 'native interests' and aimed to prepare Africans for the political and civil challenges to the common good which lay ahead:

> All I would ask, as I have half a dozen times before, is the recognition of our common humanity with the African.[19]

He believed that interim arrangements should be undertaken in order to effect a smooth transition as he judged that few Africans were well enough educated to run the country. (At Independence only seventy Zambians were graduates.[20]) His fatal mistake was to enunciate a proposal for home rule by the minority of white settlers. What Gore-Browne intended as a means of wresting powers from colonial officials whom he often found bureaucratic and limited, the Africans construed as a means to enforce discriminatory policies against them as was happening in Southern Rhodesia. At that point, not quite able to rid himself of his colonial attitudes, he lost the support of many African politicians. However, he did understand better than most whites the way in which politics were changing. While his niece, Monica, and her husband Charles Fisher, Walter Fisher's son, were supporting a middle way which wanted whites and blacks to work together, Gore-Browne was coming to the conclusion that any future for the white man in Northern Rhodesia lay in 'assisting blacks'; thereafter he gave unstinting financial and personal support to Kenneth Kaunda.[21] Although Gore-Browne was disappointed not to obtain a position in Kaunda's first administration, Kaunda believed that Gore-Browne 'enabled Zambians to achieve independence without bloodshed':

---

15. Lamb, *The Africa House*, p. 38.
16. Lamb, *The Africa House*, p. 87.
17. Lamb, *The Africa House*, p. 244.
18. Lamb, *The Africa House*, p. 200.
19. Lamb, *The Africa House*, p. 248
20. Lamb, *The Africa House*, p. 321.
21. Lamb, *The Africa House*, p. 309.

> [He was] one of the most visionary people in Africa—he was born an English gentleman and died a Zambian gentleman... I can't think of any settler who made a similar contribution to cutting across the racial boundary anywhere...[22]

Walter Fisher's mission was to preach the gospel and establish churches. He respected the Africans as people for whom Christ died and realized as his ministry developed that 'if Africa is ever to be evangelised it must be done through the native Christians'.[23] He believed that the gospel liberated people from the cruel consequences of their beliefs. People who became ill or old were often accused of bringing an evil spirit into the community. Fisher, therefore, had a number of old women who had been thus accused living on the Kalene Mission. They had little manioc plots (a local staple) which helped them grow enough to eat and they were safe so long as they did not succumb to the blandishments of family members who came to them, telling them that the charges of witchcraft had been withdrawn. At least two women taken in by such deceptions were later murdered.[24]

Because Fisher was making disciples, it was important to establish Christian morality among believers, thus polygamy became an issue which he could not ignore. While men who came to faith who already had more than one wife were not asked to cast off their wives, young men were expected to marry only one wife and remain faithful to her until the death. This different standard of behaviour was not easy to establish.

Fisher was only active politically in so far as political activity seemed to benefit those he served. Thus he did translate orally for the District Commissioner when he came to the area in order to explain why new legislation was being introduced, thus facilitating an informed and orderly response.[25]

Fisher saw medical work and education as 'handmaids' to the gospel. The unintended consequence of this was that these institutions worked towards the common good in ways which parallel Gore-Browne's explicit efforts. Kovina Mutenda, a contemporary Zambian church leader, notes that 'In 1939 Mutembu and Dryden Yikong'a became the first Zambians to pass the Standard Six examinations in North Western Province'.[26] These men were educated at Kalene school. Mutembu's contemporaries, educated at the Brethren mission school in Chitokoloki, entered politics.

In a telling detail, neither Fisher nor Gore-Browne was buried in a coffin. Fisher refused a coffin because throughout his career he had been aware that the apparent riches of missionaries did not reflect as adequately as he would have liked the earthly poverty of Jesus and he was anxious that Africans might not conclude that the coffin

---

22. Lamb, *The Africa House*, pp. 314; 337.
23. Fisher and Hoyte, *Africa Looks Ahead*, p. 123.
24. Fisher and Hoyte, *Africa Looks Ahead*, pp. 176-82.
25. Fisher and Hoyte, *Africa Looks Ahead*, pp. 194-95.
26. Kovina L.K. Mutenda, *A History of the Christian Brethren in Zambia: one hundred years of God's faithfulness and partnership in the gospel (1898–1998)* (Chingola, Zambia, 2002), p.36.

held some sort of charm. He was buried as an ordinary African.[27] At his own request, Gore-Browne was wrapped in mats and buried as an African leader. President Kaunda spoke at the state funeral he ordered for Gore-Browne at which Bemba elders ordered the 'beating of royal drums...and a war dance was performed usually reserved for the death of a Paramount Chief'.[28] While the contrast in wealth is evident even in their death, so too is the comparison of their profound ability to identify with humanity itself, transcending the barrier of race, insurmountable for so many.

Later generations of each family did get entwined. Gore-Browne's niece, Monica Hanford, a doctor, who had come to run the small hospital at Shiwa, met and married Charles, the youngest son of Walter and Anna Fisher. Charles, aged fourteen, was sent to Plumtree School in Southern Rhodesia, then to medical school. He won three scholarships and a gold medal and returned to Kalene where he was a great help to his father who was showing signs of age. However, Charles began to question the ideas that medicine and education were only to be used as 'handmaids' to the gospel. There was no conflict as Walter and Anna accepted Charles' decision to continue his medical career in England and then in Africa, always taking a great interest in missionary work. He and Monica were married at St George's Church on Gore-Browne's estate. Charles was able to fit into the Gore-Browne life style as he played rugby, tennis and golf. His political interests also coalesced with Gore-Browne's: Charles became a member of LegCo in 1945.[29] He was appointed as Chief Medical Officer to the Medical Department of the Roan Antelope Copper Mine in 1936. He served for twenty-three years, achieving his ambitions and receiving an OBE in 1953.

In some ways, the lives of Fisher and Gore-Browne are a commentary on English national identity. Both men are associated, in fleeting references, with knighthood—that aspect of English identity which thinks it is an important and valuable activity to go out into the world in order to right wrongs and improve life. Gore-Browne named his chapel St George's after England's patron saint who slew the dragon. Chipembele slew the rhinoceros, and continued to fight other tough battles throughout his political career—though he also became the rhino for some of his servants. Gore-Browne was proud to be knighted in reality in the 1946 New Year's Honours List. On the other hand, in a sensitive tribute Fisher was described by the Head of the Department of Native Education in Northern Rhodesia as being 'a great missionary in the fullest sense of the word... He was outstanding as an example of the perfect, gentle knight in a country where the daily increasing contact of European and African renders the multiplication of such examples most necessary.'[30] This brief but apt Chaucerian allusion allows others to locate Fisher in that same national tradition.

Did the missionaries manage to avoid the pitfalls of colonialism? Was Charles Fisher seduced by the world? Missionaries brought some western influences where

---

27. Fisher and Hoyte, *Africa Looks Ahead*, p. 206.
28. Lamb, *The Africa House*, p. 338.
29. Lamb, *The Africa House*, p. 309.
30. Fisher and Hoyte, *Africa Looks Ahead*, pp. 206-207.

they thought they would improve the lot of the people. They did not accept the African ways of polygamy and slavery, which were detrimental to the people. They were acutely conscious of their need to be radically distinct from the pagan people to whom they were called—but were they sufficiently aware of their need to be radically and culturally different from their own social backgrounds? With these two examples before you I rest my case and leave you the jury to retire and decide the verdict.

CHAPTER 16

Some Missiological Issues from the Past Facing the Christian Brethren Assemblies in Zambia Today

Kovina L.K. Mutenda

Introduction

The year 2003 marked the 105th anniversary of the Christian Brethren movement in present-day Zambia. More than 1,000 assemblies have been established both in the rural areas and in the cities. During that time a variety of work has been done: mission stations have been built; ministries such as printing, publishing, Bible schools, and Bible camps have been set up; and God has called many national Christians to serve him in full-time in various ministries.[1]

However, despite this rich history of assembly work there are certain problems and issues that have arisen over the years. Two of the missiological issues are dealt with in this article in the form of questions. What is the dependency syndrome and how did it come about? How does it affect the future growth of the national church in Zambia? The second question is: Does Zambia still need missionaries today? Are the conditions which necessitated the sending of missionaries from the West a hundred years ago still valid today?

The above questions, although they seem to address contemporary issues, are discussed, and should be understood, from a historical perspective. It is because of what happened in the past that we seem to have these problems today.

Mission Stations and the Dependency Syndrome

When the missionaries first came to what is now called Zambia, they built mission stations on which they lived. Mission stations not only contained houses to sleep in but other facilities such as hospitals or dispensaries, church halls, schools, farms, bookshops, and in some cases a printing press and orphanage. In a pioneering situation it was necessary to do that or missionary work could not be done. Right from the beginning the missionaries insisted on paying for the services and materials contributed by the nationals to the work of constructing and maintaining the mission

1. Kovina L.K. Mutenda, *A History of the Christian Brethren in Zambia: one hundred years of God's faithfulness and partnership in the gospel (1898–1998)* (Chingola, Zambia, 2002).

stations. Whenever missionaries were given gifts such as chickens, eggs, vegetables, fruit, meat, or other foodstuffs, they gratefully accepted such gifts. But then they always found ways of paying back almost immediately.

The Africans understood reciprocal obligation not as a direct and immediate obligation but as remote and distant. Besides, they gave gifts to missionaries in keeping with African hospitality and generosity commonly practised by the people. By paying back what they received and by paying for the services rendered towards the work of the Lord at the mission station, without knowing it, the missionaries discouraged the national Christians from and denied them the privilege of giving to the Lord. It is not true that Zambian people do not know how to give. On the contrary, Zambians are very generous people. They give for different occasions and causes. They give to relatives needing education, to the orphans, unemployed and other needy people in society. However, many in the Brethren assemblies simply do not give generously to support the Lord's work.

The missionaries wrongly concluded that, 'These people are poor and they will always be that way. We will have to simply need to keep on giving to them—perhaps for a hundred or thousand years.' This was the beginning of the dependency syndrome. When the nationals saw materials, equipment and money come from overseas, without proper understanding, they simply concluded that somewhere in the whiteman's land there is a benevolent source that never dries up. This helped to reinforce the dependency syndrome.

If the missionaries had cared to explain that the things they received were given by ordinary Christians who gave such things as an offering to the Lord, perhaps that would have changed the attitude of the nationals and encouraged them to do likewise. As time went on the missionaries did the giving and the nationals did the receiving. The nationals eventually came to the wrong conclusion that 'we are poor and that is the way it will always be. There is nothing we can do about it.' Unfortunately this attitude has continued in the minds of many even today.

Dependency means that people put in the collection bag less than they are able while allowing others to support their church. Many in Zambia 'confess poverty' and do not give back to God a reasonable portion of what he has given to them. Even the poor sometimes have something to give back to God. In Zambia, if Christians gave just 5% of their income the church could be self-supporting.

The other reason for the dependency syndrome is that right from the beginning missionaries kept the work of the mission station, school, hospital, and other resources separate from the work of the churches they had planted. Strictly speaking, in Zambia the name 'Christian Missions in Many Lands' (CMML) speaks for the missionaries and mission property.[2] The name 'Christian Brethren' speaks for the church and church property. Many nationals were, and some are still, not aware of this distinction. The fact that missionaries used money from their sending churches abroad to maintain the mission stations excluded the nationals from any sense of joint ownership of such work. The nationals have always regarded mission work as

2. For the origin of the term, see Mutenda, *Christian Brethren in Zambia*, p. 15.

the work of the missionaries not the church. This explains the fact that if any building at the mission stations falls into disrepair, the nationals would not fix it. They expect the missionary to do it for it is his property and not the church's.

What is the role of mission stations at this present time? Are they assets or liabilities? Mission stations can be assets if the nationals are able to take over the ownership of the facilities. There are three kinds of ownership. Firstly, there is legal ownership. This occurs when the paperwork is done and the property is transferred. Since most, if not all, of the title deeds for Brethren mission stations were registered under Stewards Company (UK), these properties may have to be re-registered under Stewards Company (Zambia). Secondly, there is functional ownership. This occurs when the positions are filled with local people. These nationals in positions of leadership should be appointed by national Christians themselves and not by missionaries. Lastly, there is psychological ownership. This occurs when people decide that the church programme or mission property is theirs and that it will succeed or fail depending on what they do. Some programmes established by missionaries may simply be too expensive to continue. In some cases it may be wise for church leaders to sell off some old mission property in order to get rid of a major maintenance burden.

When all the three steps of ownership have been achieved the national Christians will feel motivated to support the work of the institutions concerned. Local people should think very carefully before taking responsibility for mission established institutions because such programmes may be too expensive for available local resources. And if they are not ready to take on the responsibility, they will feel no sense of ownership. The nationals may not initially be able to maintain financially the mission stations but they should aim towards self-reliance. If the policy of partnership is rightly practised, then the sending churches and other supporting agencies overseas should help financially and in other practical ways to keep the work of the mission stations running until such time that the national church will take full responsibility for the whole work.

In order for mission stations and other missionary institutions (this includes printing, publishing, bookshops, Bible correspondence work and Bible schools) to run successfully after they have been handed over to the nationals, the handover of such responsibility must be done properly. Missionaries must entrust nationals with a little responsibility at a time and gradually increase such responsibility until nationals prove themselves capable of handling greater responsibility. It is unfair to suddenly entrust nationals with big responsibilities without previous experience and then blame them when they fail.

On the other hand mission stations can be a liability if the national church is not yet ready or able to takeover responsibility at all levels. They may legally and functionally take over ownership but if psychological ownership has not taken place nothing will happen. In that case mission properties will remain 'white elephants'—something that fails to function contrary to its original intention. The nationals must feel that the property is theirs before they can support mission work wholeheartedly. The deeply entrenched attitude of 'theirs' must be radically changed to 'ours' if there is to be a way forward. One factor that can jeopardize self-reliance for the national church is jealousy. Some national Christians will simply not support mission work under Zambian leadership because of the attitude 'Why should he live in an iron-roofed and electrified house when I am living in a grass thatched house?' or 'Why should he have a bicycle when I don't have one?'

What can Brethren missionaries do to eradicate the dependency syndrome? They should stop thinking that Zambians are poor and that they should be given things all the time. Nationals would be capable of supporting their church programmes and their own full-time Christian workers if they gave more money than they are presently doing. Most Zambians in Brethren churches give less than 2% during the Sunday offering. Both missionaries and national church leaders should teach people how to give generously. This may sound new to the ears of many as the subject of giving was neglected by most of the missionaries of the preceding generations. The task of re-teaching the people is not an easy one, but is one thing that must be diligently and systematically done if the Zambian church is to solve the dependency syndrome.

A few Brethren churches which have learnt how to give sacrificially and generously are doing very well. They have built their own assembly halls and have financed all their church programmes without asking for outside help. In addition, these assemblies are helping to support other assemblies. If the majority of assemblies became self-reliant the dependency syndrome would be reduced or even eradicated altogether. And in that case the future of assembly work in Zambia would be positive and would not give any cause for concern.

Does Zambia Still Need Missionaries Today?

This is not an easy question to answer. An honest response would have to be: yes and no. The answer to this question depends on other key questions. Do missionaries aim to work themselves out of a job? Do they make an effort to prepare nationals to take over from them when it is time for them to return to their home country? Are the national believers ready to take over the full responsibility of running the church without assistance from the missionary? Can the nationals build their own church halls and support their own full-time Christian workers, fund church planting programmes and profitably run their Christian literature ministries on their own? Are there enough national Bible teachers and other gifted men and women to serve the church? The question of independence and dependence is very crucial to answering the question as to whether missionaries are still needed today or not.

Many sending churches in Europe and America are asking the same question: 'Should we continue sending missionaries to Africa or not?' Similarly national believers too are asking, 'Should we continue depending on western missionaries to run our church programmes or not? If we need missionaries, what type of missionaries and what should be their role?' Brethren missionaries in Zambia have had different views concerning the preparation of nationals for church leadership and Christian ministry. There have been some who have worked on their own without any nationals working alongside them. The result has been that when these missionaries left for their home countries there was no one to carry on the type of ministry they were involved in.

In some cases these missionaries have had to come back after a few years in retirement or have made periodical visits to their former field of service for a few months at a time in order to 'serve the Lord' because there was no one else to do it. Of course there is nothing wrong with a retired missionary visiting his former mission field to renew fellowship and check on the progress of the work. It is not that there is a lack of nationals who feel genuinely called to the Lord's work but rather a lack of policy and determination on the part of some of the missionaries to encourage partnership with nationals in missionary work. Missionaries should avoid the negative attitude, 'Of course we will give these people authority when they are ready for it—maybe in a hundred years. When we are gone everything will be up to these people. Then we will see what happens.'

In the case of those missionaries serving in specialized professions such as doctors, it is almost impossible for a missionary doctor to train a national to become one (that is the work of university medical schools). However, missionary doctors can encourage some national Christian doctors to consider serving in rural areas as national medical missionaries in fellowship with the local churches. This is not an easy task.

Some missionaries do not fully understand what their role is on the mission field. Missionaries are there to serve and support the ministry of the church. This includes preparing nationals for leadership and ministry, and to discourage a church that is missionary run. It is very important for every missionary to remember that he is not taking God to Zambia, but rather God is taking him to Zambia. This, therefore, means that a missionary should avoid creating the impression that the whole work depends on him. All missionary work depends on God working through the church in reconciling the world to himself. When the missionary realizes that the work he is involved in is God's work and if he is working in partnership with his African brothers and sisters in the same work, he will care to train someone to carry on the work when he is gone. This principle applies to all Christian workers and church leaders whether national or expatriate.

A missionary who returns to his home country after twenty years of service and announces to his sending church that another missionary should be sent to replace him because there is no one else to do the work, only exposes his own weakness and failure. For every one missionary who leaves the field there should be three or more to take over his work. This is a challenge to those churches overseas which are sending missionaries, and organizations and mission boards involved in preparing missionary candidates, to ensure that this policy of partnership is emphasized and included in missionary training.

From the early days of Brethren missionary work in Zambia there have been some missionaries who understood and practised the policy of partnership. They trained national workers as school teachers, evangelists, church planters and Bible teachers. Some of these national workers were given mission stations to look after. A few examples would help illustrate this point—George Suckling of Chitokoloki; Tom Rae of Kamapanda and later of Congo; Herbert Sims of Chavuma; James Caldwell of Chitokoloki, Kabulamema and Mwambashi; Horace Coleman of Samfya—these are but a few of the early missionaries who trained nationals to take full responsibility for the Lord's work in the Zambian assemblies.[3]

In the absence of missionaries is the Zambian church ready to take full responsibility for its own affairs considering that the Zambian church has depended on missionaries for a long time? This question is important in determining whether or not missionaries are still needed. Where there is true independence and determination to manage its own affairs and make its own decisions, a local church would recognize those whom God has called from among its own ranks who have the same spiritual gifts as the missionary—sometimes more fully than the missionary—and commend such workers to the work of the Lord and support them financially.

The question that arises is this: is an average Zambian Brethren assembly in a position to support its own national missionaries? What does the local church do about the sudden loss of roofing sheets, second-hand clothes, medicines, and other materials it is so used to receiving from the missionary? Sometimes the presence of a missionary in a particular area is appreciated or even desired, not necessarily for the spiritual work which that particular missionary does, but for the material things he is able to provide. A missionary should never seek for or accept a position which ought to be filled by a local person. He must be aware of the fact that he may have been invited by the national church to serve in a particular area because of his access to outside funds.

It is obvious that the time for pioneer missionaries, as gospel preachers and church planters, is long gone. After 105 years, the Christian Brethren in Zambia have many able national gospel preachers and church planters. These nationals do not need to learn a new language or adapt to a new culture. However, there are some missionaries who are still needed today. These are a new generation of missionaries with a new approach to missionary work. A modern missionary is one who actively helps to develop local resources and thereby break the dependency which developed in the past. He should be a mobilizer for missions—looking out for the Great Commission national Christians who have the potential to serve among their own people.

What the Zambian church desperately needs are gifted Bible teachers. This is one area in which modern missionaries can play a vital role. Not only should they get involved in teaching God's word, but teaching nationals who would be able to teach others. The training of Bible teachers will not necessarily require the missionaries to learn a new language. Most of the training could be done in English since most of the present generation of church leaders and Christian workers can understand simple English. The importance of Bible schools and Bible training centres cannot be over-emphasized.

---

3. See Mutenda, *Christian Brethren in Zambia*, pp. 47, 55, 51, 53, 61, 64-5.

If there is one area which needs support by way of resources, funds and personnel, it is the ministry of Bible schools. Modern missionaries can be most effective if they are involved in training potential national leaders. In this way a missionary would be more useful to the local church than if he was just manning a mission station simply as a status symbol. This new way of doing missionary work would be more appreciated even by sending churches and mission boards overseas. Where are the new generation of missionaries who are gifted Bible teachers who will be able to pass on their knowledge to a new generation of national workers and church leaders to equip the church to meet the spiritual needs facing the church in the twenty-first century? It is the prayer of many in the Zambian church that God will send into his harvest field the right people from overseas for the right job.

CHAPTER 17

The Brethren Movement in Angola, 1960–2000

José Neto

Introduction

It is quite possible to make an accurate contribution to the history of the Brethren movement in Angola for the period before 1960, because during that period missionaries working in Angola kept a lot of records and also had access to other information about the Lord's work in this part of Central Africa. There are various books and articles with information covering the period from 1885 until 1960.[1]

However, I have chosen a more difficult task, writing about the Brethren movement from 1960 to 2000, because there is not too much written information about Brethren work during this period. Nevertheless, we, as a new generation, need to know more about our roots and our history. In choosing this period I have three challenges in mind: firstly, I would like to see a book written which covers this part of our history in Angola; secondly, I was born in the 1960s, and this is my generation—I have a responsibility to think historically too; and thirdly, this is the period when the Brethren movement began to become more indigenous in terms of its leadership.

The Beginning of the Brethren Movement in Angola

Among those who started the Brethren movement in Central Africa, the name of the Scotsman Frederick Stanley Arnot (1858–1914) is well known. On 15 November 1884 Arnot first arrived at Benguela. The following year, the Berlin Conference began to divide Africa among the European colonial powers anxious to benefit from the opening up of the continent. For 400 years the Portuguese had controlled Angola, and it became part of Portugal after the partition of Africa.

Before the partition, Portuguese officials in Angola did not put a great deal of pressure on Protestant missionaries, the majority of whom were from the British Empire. But when Arnot arrived in Angola, he was in Portuguese territory and

1. Relevant books include W.T. Stunt *et al.*, *Turning the World Upside Down* (Bath, 2nd edn, 1972); F.A. Tatford, *That the World May Know*. Volume 6: *Light over the Dark Continent* (Bath, 1984). Magazines with useful material include *Echoes of Service*, *Echoes Quarterly Review* (for the years after 1948) and *Christian Missions in Many Lands*.

needed to follow Portuguese instructions. He did not have the same facilities that he had had in Zambia, which was controlled by the British, to establish mission stations. The situation became worse when the officials of the Roman Catholic Church forced the Portuguese government to make certain rules for religious groups working in the country, with the goal of controlling their activities.[2] One of these rules, introduced in 1921, was that the language used in education must be Portuguese; vernacular languages were only allowed orally in religious instruction and as a help when teaching elementary Portuguese. 'The use of the vernacular in written form, or of any other language besides Portuguese, was forbidden in the religious teaching of the missions, in their schools, or in their relations with the Africans'.[3] This was the situation when the Brethren movement started in Angola. As a result, Arnot had to adopt a different approach in his strategy in Angola compared with that adopted in establishing mission stations in Zambia.

When Arnot returned to Angola after his first furlough in 1888, some missionaries from America, Canada, and Switzerland, who had been at work before his first period of service, were already establishing mission stations. Arnot and his team received help from them in many ways. It made possible some interaction among missionaries of different evangelical groups in Angola, and at conferences of missionaries they were able to discuss strategic plans to avoid duplicating each other's work in evangelizing the Angolan people, and to defend themselves against the Portuguese colonial authorities and the Roman Catholic Church, which was regarded as the official church by the authorities.

The Portuguese authorities also insisted that they adopt a corporate name in the country. They selected the name of the North American missionary agency Christian Missions in Many Lands (CMML) to identify them as the Open Brethren movement in Angola. Their choice influenced Brethren in Zambia to adopt the same name. But the local assemblies established were simply called evangelical churches.

From 1888 to 1925, seven strategic mission stations were established in Ovimbundu and Luvaleland; this made it possible to open a hundred assemblies in the areas around. Ernest Wilson, who served in Angola from 1924–58, said in one of his reports that in the Chilonda area alone there were twenty-two assemblies and eighty-three preaching points, and that on one occasion 1,200 believers were present at a conference at Chitau. The work was growing so fast that missionaries were involving many indigenous workers. Lunda Norte, in the east of Angola, is one area where the majority of Brethren assemblies were established by indigenous evangelists.

---

2. Catholic officials were suspicious of Protestant missionaries for political as well as religious reasons: Britain had exerted its influence during the partition process to hinder Portuguese expansion (Editors).

3. Stunt *et al.*, *Turning the World Upside Down*, p. 376.

The War for Independence and the Brethren Movement in Angola (1960–1975)

In Africa the 1940s and 1950s saw the start of the movement for independence from the colonial powers, and eventually the majority of missionaries left Angola for security reasons. It happened suddenly, and the missionaries were not prepared emotionally or psychologically for their enforced departure.

Brethren missionaries began to prepare local workers to carry on the work slowly and without any developed strategy. But other evangelical groups, such as the Methodists, Congregationalists and Baptists, in the same period already had a large number of indigenous people well trained in theology and other fields who could continue the work. Brethren missionaries had not made as big an investment in education as had the other evangelical groups. A missionary once told me that one day they had a discussion among the missionaries about starting a good school for native people, and the oldest missionary in the group said that he came to Angola to preach and to teach the word of God and not spend his time opening schools. But the question remained, how could they teach the word of God to a group of illiterate people? The missionaries did open schools among the Umbundu people; in this area you can find the best known schools run by Brethren missionaries, such as Chilonda and Capango.

When these missionaries did begin to develop the right vision for the work, they did not have enough time to continue the project. They wanted to be able to carry on and establish the work with a good foundation. The two reports below enable us to glimpse the situation:

> the Days and the Scotts built up a large educational and Bible school work at Monte Esperança and...in 1955, Dr. Ross Woodward rebuilt and equipped the hospital and also commenced an extensive leper work. After going on furlough in 1964, he and his wife were unable to return.[4]

> In January 1969 Clifford Beggs and his wife, who had served among the Chokwes from 1948 to 1965, were allowed to return to Angola and settle on the coast at the capital. There he has been used to the foundation of an assembly among Portuguese. The area is very unhealthy and they had to return to Canada in 1971...[5]

Clifford Beggs, who served in Angola from 1948, played an important role for Brethren assemblies by starting Emmaus Bible School correspondence courses in Luso (now Luena), and by writing many commentaries on books of the New Testament. This Bible School continues to be the main school among of Brethren movement in Angola to train leaders for local churches.

Persecution of all evangelical and Protestant groups began because the founders and the key persons in the movement for liberation of Angola—including Holden Robert (FNLA), Agostinho Neto (MPLA), and Daniel Chipenda and Jonas Savimbi

---

4. Stunt *et al.*, *Turning the World Upside Down*, p. 384.

5. Stunt *et al.*, *Turning the World Upside Down*, p. 385.

(UNITA)[6]—all studied in the mission stations of different evangelical Protestant groups in Angola and went to universities abroad with scholarships provided by the evangelical churches. Because of this, the Portuguese authorities realized that the missionaries were strong supporters of the indigenous move to seek independence, and so they became a target for the authorities.

Among Brethren assemblies, indigenous political leaders did not rise up to the same extent as happened in other evangelical or Protestant groups. But persecution of all evangelical Protestant workers became more intense; many of the most capable indigenous evangelical Christians had to leave the country for security reasons, and a number were murdered.

Charles Donald Cole, a missionary who worked in Chilonda for eighteen years (1948–66), told of the experience he had with the Portuguese authorities. One day he went to the police station to visit some of the elders who were in prison accused of being terrorists. After a long time of conversation explaining to the police the good work done by the elders in their communities, they said to him, 'All this is happening because you missionaries gave opportunities for the indigenous people to go to school, and taught them the Bible, and now you can see the result of your work.' Cole left the country in 1966, and Portuguese authorities refused him permission to return. In this difficult period some missionaries remained in the country longer than others. Others moved to Zambia and Zimbabwe, hoping to return when the situation improved.

Angola became independent in 1975, and the MPLA took over the leadership of the country with Russian and Cuban support and a Communist ideology. Because of the strong relationships which the majority of key MPLA leaders had with the evangelical churches, they accepted the Communist ideology, but they could not mount a major persecution of Christians because their parents and relatives were active members of evangelical churches. For example, the father of Agostinho Neto, the first President of the country, was a son of a Methodist pastor. He himself worked as secretary to the bishop before going abroad to study, and his mother was an active member of Methodist churches, often the first to arrive at Sunday services. The only ways that the Communists found to be more effective in persecuting the Christian faith were in their speeches, by calling Christians names, and by refusing them privileges because they were not party members.

One of most famous comments made by Agostinho Neto against the Christian faith, in a speech in a sports stadium, was that 'in fifty years from now Angola will have no more churches'. Some people believe that he was forced to say things against Christians in public.

---

6. FNLA is the National Front for the Liberation of Angola (Portuguese: Frente Nacional de Libertação de Angola; the MPLA is the Popular Movement for the Liberation of Angola (Portuguese: Movimento Popular de Libertação de Angola); and UNITA is The National Union for the Total Independence of Angola (Portuguese: União Nacional para a Independência Total de Angola).

Indigenous Leadership to Carry on the Work

Where are the indigenous workers to carry on the work among the assemblies? This was the big question after independence. Elders in local assemblies continued doing what they could, teaching the portions of the Bible that they knew very well and engaging in pastoral work. It is essential to remember that the majority of those elders could not read and write Portuguese very well, and they communicated using the vernacular languages. The way for them to continue teaching and understanding the word of God was only by the interpretation of others.

Many people had close connections with the missionaries, working for them in such capacities as cooks or drivers. A number of them became key leaders in the assemblies because of this, but in reality they did not have enough Bible knowledge to carry on the work; they became influential elders but without adequate Bible knowledge. To make administrative decisions relating to such matters as running the hospital and schools, was more difficult; they did not have any knowledge of whom to contact or how to continue the social work, and so most social work among Brethren ceased.

A contradiction was evident in the role of missionaries on the mission stations, which was like that of the pastor in different evangelical denominations: as the rulers of the community, they gave the majority of the Bible teaching, they solved the majority of problems and dealt with all kinds of issues, as well as made most of the decisions.

The missionaries appointed elders in different local assemblies, and worked with other locals, but they called them 'helpers' or 'catechists', because the Portuguese authorities made it compulsory also to have titles for such helpers; a lot of them were called 'pastors'. Dan Crawford, the Scottish Brethren missionary in Central Africa, once said that the missionaries were forced to be at the same time prophets, priests, and kings, which is why they became important ducks in their private lakes.[7]

But the question remained, who would replace the missionary in the community, travelling around and giving Bible teaching and making decisions?

Teaching was given regarding eldership in the local assembly, but the model they saw and experienced day by day in the practice of the missionaries was different. It gave rise to a lot of discussion. Brethren assemblies in different areas solved the question by doing things the way they felt more comfortable with. It is possible to find different styles of leadership, but the majority of assemblies have a plural leadership. Remember also that the Brethren movement in Angola was also influenced by other evangelical groups, and individuals adopted what worked better in their culture and community. But some missionaries and national workers continued to display the same mentality that Crawford had criticized.

In 1980 the missionaries (now no more than ten in number) made their base Luanda, the capital. As a result, the majority of the work in the mission stations

7. Dan Crawford, *Thinking Black: 22 years without a break in the long grass of Central Africa* (London, 1912), pp. 324-5.

was closed and assemblies were run by national workers, though during this period the work grew extensively around the country. Charles and Elisabeth Shorten played an important role, continuing with the Bible correspondence course from Luanda, selling literature, supporting local workers with Bibles and hymnbooks, and travelling around to give Bible teaching. In Luanda, assemblies began to grow which had a regional flavour; the leadership continued with the same pattern of work as existed in rural areas, and continued to use their vernacular language and not the language of communication for everybody. The big challenge has been to make such assemblies real local assemblies.

Iris Floyd, a visionary lady missionary who arrived in 1955, played an important role in the continuance of medical work in Angola, step by step restoring it in many areas of the country and building physical structures to support this work.

Registration of the Church (IEIA)

The registration of the church was one of the biggest changes to affect Brethren in Angola. When the government informed all churches that they must be registered and have a body which could represent them in dealings with the government, a big conflict broke out among missionaries and national workers. The reason was that the way the missionaries had learned to run Brethren assemblies in their home countries did not allow for any administrative connection between them or any central body to represent them to the British, American, or Canadian governments. They were also afraid that the Brethren movement would become a denominational group that would destroy the autonomy of the local church.

But this was no different from the situation during the colonial period, when missionaries were forced to have a corporate name and to register with the authorities. Then they chose a name and appointed a director of the mission, so Angolan leaders did not understand why they reacted in this way.

Without missionary approval, some courageous national workers, such as Amadeu Maquina Caliata, Antonio João, Segunda Canguia, and Bernardo Alfredo, took the step of registering the church under the name of Igreja Evangélica dos Irmãos em Angola (IEIA), which in English means 'Evangelical Brethren Church in Angola'. The governing body, initially known as the Executive Commission, is now called the National Secretariat.

The main objectives of the elders and deacons appointed to this Secretariat are to represent Brethren assemblies to the government, to give technical support in literature, evangelism, and mission, and to promote the health of local churches among the Brethren. This body does not interfere in the day to day running of local churches: the autonomy of the local church is the one non-negotiable issue among all Brethren assemblies, and we also have a national conference where we discuss issues of common interest and our work together. At the provincial level and sometimes also at the municipal level, we have the same structure. We continue to face many difficulties, but by God's grace we continue to serve him.

Statistics for Brethren Churches in Angola

In 1987 in the areas controlled by the government we had 1,200 Brethren churches or assemblies. Because the war became more intense in rural areas, many assemblies were destroyed and a lot of believers moved to towns where they started to establish big churches, as in Kuito-Bié, where there are 2,000 in fellowship, and Cafunfu, with 1,200 or more.

By 1999 statistics showed that there were 1,550 Brethren assemblies in the area controlled by the government. Brethren churches are the second largest evangelical group in Angola after the Congregational Church. They are still growing, but not as fast as Charismatic and Pentecostal groups.

The Challenge of the Twenty-First Century

Issues facing Brethren in Angola today include the exodus to the cities because of the civil war, developing a new strategy to reach towns and cities, the need for well trained leaders in local churches and well-trained Bible teachers, the need of a residential Bible School, and the need for full-time national workers in the country.

PART 4

The Brethren in International Experience

CHAPTER 18

Anthony Norris Groves in an International Context: A Re-assessment of his Early Development

Timothy C.F. Stunt

Introduction

It was to a packed audience in the Tabernacle in Tottenham Court Road that Edward Irving preached one of his most eloquent sermons to the London Missionary Society in 1824. As he warmed to his romantic ideal of the Christian missionary, he poured scorn on what he called 'the principle of expediency, and...the rules of prudence' which, he claimed, characterized the missionary societies.[1] It was not the sermon that his listeners were expecting, as it seemed to belittle all their efforts of the previous decades. On the other hand their discomfort was probably mild when compared with the reactions of churchmen who read the sermon when it was published the following year. Irving's manifest excitement was giving substance to some of the worst fears that respectable men and women of the establishment had felt for some time about the swelling voice of the missionary movement.

Quite as alarming as the perceived possibility that missionary work might disturb colonial business, was the widespread feeling that although this sort of enthusiastic activity might be expected of Dissenters, it was inappropriate for a churchman or gentleman. These attitudes had been reflected in the early dearth of missionary volunteers suffered by the Church Missionary Society (CMS) and in its heavy dependence during the first quarter of the nineteenth century on German and Swiss recruits—a situation which calls to mind the usefulness of Hessian mercenary troops in the establishment of the earlier British Empire. Indeed, Jon Miller has argued that the CMS Committee preferred 'tough' peasant recruits, with an 'appropriately modest' background, from places like Württemburg, to staff the Society's expanding programme, and considered middle-class recruits in England to be 'a less than desirable solution'.[2] In consequence, during the early part of the nineteenth century

1. E. Irving, *For Missionaries after the Apostolical School, A Series of Orations* (London, 1825), p. xiv.

2. J. Miller, *The Social Control of Religious Zeal: a study of organizational contradictions* (New Brunswick, NJ, 1994), p. 42. Before 1814 (when the prohibition on missionary work in India was lifted) fourteen out of seventeen CMS missionaries were foreigners, and even in the next five years barely two-thirds were English. Only two out

there was a well-worn path, taken by missionary volunteers coming from Germany and Switzerland, by way of the Basel Mission Institute, to London. Here the recruits experienced some months of linguistic, social and even theological adaptation (which after 1825 took place in the CMS College in Islington) before they set sail for what would usually be an English-speaking mission field. The ordination of these continental recruits was normally Lutheran, and this was a potential source of embarrassment, liable to reinforce the perception that missionary activity was not really an occupation for Anglicans, but there was no particular need to publicize the connection and for a while it was largely ignored. It had been quite an unusual event in 1822 when Dr Blumhardt, the Director of the Basel Institute, addressed the annual meeting of the CMS, because foreigners rarely spoke on such occasions.[3] In fact, a year earlier, when members of the CMS were given some details of the Basel Mission Institute, a somewhat better informed Anglican evangelical wrote that it seemed 'like a new discovery, so little is it [the Institute] known in England'.[4] Nevertheless an important link had been forged in the chain of cooperation with the continent—albeit a link deriving from opportunist expediency rather than ecumenical principle and it is in this context that we may look more closely at the neglected career of the missionary strategist Anthony Norris Groves.[5]

Biographical Summary

Any attempt to re-evaluate Groves' career is fraught with difficulties, not the least of which is the aura of sanctity which has gathered around the memory of a man who had decidedly ascetic tendencies and yet seems to have been consistently generous and winsome towards his fellows. The basic outline of his life is not in dispute.[6] Born

---

of the forty-four English missionaries enrolled prior to 1824 were university graduates, [D.T. Barry, (ed.)], *Church Missionary Society Register of Missionaries and Native Clergy* (London, 1896), pp. 1-11.

3. E. Stock, *History of the Church Missionary Society* (4 vols; London, 1899), I, p. 263.

4. Basel, Mission Archives [hereafter BMA], Gemischte Briefe [GB] Q-3-4, F. Cunningham (Vicar of Pakefield, near Lowestoft) to C.G. Blumhardt, May 1821. I am indebted to Mr Paul Jenkins, former archivist of the Basel Mission, for his unfailing help over a period of many years. For C.G. Blumhardt, see D.M. Lewis (ed.), *Blackwell Dictionary of Evangelical Biography 1730-1860* (2 vols; Oxford, 1995), I, p. 110, i-ii.

5. Some of this paper was written before the publication of my *From Awakening to Secession: Radical Evangelicals in Switzerland and Britain 1815–35* (Edinburgh, 2000) which, in some respects, gives fuller details of the following analysis.

6. See F.R. Coad, in Lewis (ed.), *Evangelical Biography*, II, pp. 485-86, and the less accurate article by G.C. Boase in L. Stephen and S. Lee (eds.), *Dictionary of National Biography*, 8 (1885–1900), pp. 742-43 The basic sources for all existing accounts of Groves are his published journals (see below n. 24) and [Harriet Groves], *Memoir of the Late Anthony Norris Groves containing extracts from his Letters and Journals* compiled by his widow (London, 2nd edn, 1857). Sensitive reworkings of this account are to be found in H.H. Rowdon, *The Origins of the Brethren 1825–50* (London, 1967), pp. 38-40,

on 1 February 1795 in Newton Valence, Hampshire,[7] he grew up in London where he studied chemistry, had some experience of walking the wards of a London hospital and trained as a dentist with his uncle James Thompson. In 1814 he established a successful practice in Plymouth but, after marrying his cousin Mary Bethia Thompson, he moved to Exeter in 1818.[8] His first Christian (and indeed missionary) commitment occurred during his time in Plymouth when he was more of a churchman than an evangelical—the latter identification dating from the early 1820s when he was influenced by the poet and curate of Broad Clyst, near Exeter, John Marriott,[9] and by a dissenting lady, Elizabeth [Bessie] Paget. Enrolling with the CMS in 1825, Groves prepared for ordination as a non-resident student at Trinity College, Dublin, where he attended for examinations and where he came into contact with several radical evangelical Christians like John Bellett and John Darby who would later be known as Plymouth Brethren.[10] Abandoning his plans for ordination, he withdrew from the CMS and in June 1829 set out as a freelance missionary, travelling with his family to St Petersburg and then overland to Baghdad. In the course of the journey, at Shushee, they met Karl Gottlieb Pfander with whom Groves discovered an immediate rapport. Pfander joined the party and worked with Groves in Baghdad for over a year.[11] During 1830 a school was established and some apparently useful contacts were made through Groves' medical work, but in March 1831 everything began to change for the worse. Groves now had to endure an epidemic of plague (which eventually carried off his wife and baby daughter), disastrous flooding and finally the paralysis of civil war. By the spring of 1833

188-200; and F.R. Coad, *A History of the Brethren Movement* (Exeter, 1968), pp. 15-24, *et passim.*

7. Details of Groves's youth and family are elusive. Rob Dann (whose *Father of Faith Missions: the life and times of Anthony Norris Groves (1795–1853)* (Waynesboro, GA/Milton Keynes, 2004), I have been privileged to read in proof and whose eagle eye has saved me from several errors in this paper) has used records in the Hampshire County Record Office, Winchester, to establish that the Newton mentioned in Groves, *Memoir*, p. 1, was Newton Valence where he was privately baptized (5 February). His parents were Anthony and Lydia Groves of Lymington.

8. The marriage took place in Fulham Parish Church on 22 October 1816: *Exeter Flying Post*, 7 November 1816. The removal to Exeter is given in Groves, *Memoir*, p. 3, as 'soon after' his marriage, but 1818 is the date given by a writer possessed of good Plymouth sources, J.E. Ryland (ed.), *Memoirs of John Kitto* (Edinburgh, 1856), p. 142.

9. For the evangelical rather than High Church position of Marriott ('one of the most polished and accomplished gentlemen of his time'), see J.W. Burgon's life of Charles Marriott in *Lives of Twelve Good Men* (2 vols; London, 3rd edn, 1889), I, p. 299.

10. Cf. T.C.F. Stunt, 'Evangelical cross-currents in the Church of Ireland, 1820–33', in W.J. Sheils and D. Wood (eds.), *The Churches, Ireland and the Irish: Studies in Church History*, 25 (Oxford, 1989), pp. 220-21.

11. For Pfander, see A.A. Powell, *Muslims and Missionaries in Pre-Mutiny India* (London, 1993), pp. 131-57. Cf. her article in Lewis (ed.), *Evangelical Biography*, II, pp. 879-80.

Groves, deeply depressed, was recognizing an apparently negative response to his self-sacrificial efforts to bring Christ to the inhabitants of Baghdad.

In June Groves set out for India with Sir Arthur Cotton, leaving his two sons in the care of John Parnell (later Lord Congleton) and Edward Cronin, fellow missionaries who had arrived from Britain in June 1832.[12] In India Groves embarked on a lengthy tour of mission stations where he was impressed and thrilled by the work and success of the German missionary Rhenius. However, the decision by the CMS to require all their missionaries to submit to Anglican ordination had given rise to a dispute over the validity of Rhenius' Lutheran credentials—a controversy in which Groves became involved. In 1833 Groves travelled and worked for several months with a Lebanese Christian, Mokayel Trad, who had earlier been associated with other European missionaries like Joseph Wolff and Samuel Gobat.[13] In 1834 Groves sailed for England where he married a second time and gathered another missionary party with whom he returned to India in 1836. Reunited (after more than three years) with his sons, the rest of his life was devoted to independent missionary work, principally at Chittoor not far from Madras. In this he was supported by his German brother-in-law George Müller of Bristol and other Brethren. His health began to fail in 1852 and the last eight months of his life were spent in England where he died in 1853.

Problems of Historiography

Other-worldliness and self-denial meant that Groves wrote very little about himself as a subject that could be considered of interest in its own right. If events in his earlier life had some bearing on, for example, the discovery of biblical truth or the furtherance of the preaching of the gospel, then there was reason for him to mention them, but his own account of his earlier life is singularly devoid of personal detail.[14] During the 1820s Groves came to the conclusion (forthrightly expressed in his booklet *Christian Devotedness* [1825]) that the accumulation of any wealth, beyond the immediate needs of the day, was in conflict with the teaching of Christ. This

---

12. His readiness to leave his sons was undoubtedly facilitated by the loyal care for them given by the Chaldean nurse, Hanie (also Hannai, Harnie) Thomas whose conversion and devotion to the Groves family was one of the few lasting blessings dating from his time in Baghdad. See H. Groves, *Faithful Hanie; or, Disinterested Service: Memoirs of a Ninevite servant* (London, 1866), pp. 37-38. 'Hannah Thomas' was the first named beneficiary in Groves's will, which has recently been located in the archives of the Müller Homes in Bristol.

13. For Mokayel Trad's earlier career, see N.M. Railton, *Transnational Evangelicalism: the case of Friedrich Bialloblotzky (1799–1869)* (Göttingen, 2002), p. 147 n. 50.

14. For instance, there is no mention of the birth of his sons Henry and Frank who were christened in St David's, Exeter, respectively on 18 June 1819 and 17 March 1820 (*International Genealogical Index*). Henry is said to have been born in November 1818, H. Pickering [ed.], *Chief Men among the Brethren* (London, 2nd edn, 1931), p. 98.

conviction, together with the need for minimal encumbrances when travelling, seems to have led to the disposal of much of his substance and with it, presumably, the sort of mementos and memorabilia which would have been useful for a biographer.

Another problem is posed by the personal involvement (and prejudices) of the editor of Groves' *Memoir*, namely his second wife, Harriet, the second daughter of Major-General Edward Baynes of Sidmouth.[15] Her personal acquaintance with Groves dated from 1829[16] when his spiritual development and his independent convictions were fairly well established, so the early part of the *Memoir* is marred by vagueness, inconsistencies and hindsight. For example, the date of Groves' evangelical enlightenment is far from clear and though there are occasional references to his earlier Arminianism, it is only from a very careful scrutiny of the *Memoir* that we begin to realize how comparatively late was his adoption of Calvinist evangelical views and the disintegration of his earlier 'exact' churchmanship.[17] His widow plays down the resilience of Groves' earlier Christian commitment with its involvement in local social welfare and not just missionary dedication. She mentions her husband's adoption of the deaf pauper, John Kitto, in 1824, but makes no reference to the part played in the arrangement by Groves' early 'Christian friend', Robert Lampen, who was a noted opponent of the Calvinist clergy in Plymouth.[18] There is similarly no

15. Edward Baynes (?1765–1829) had been Adjutant-General to the forces in British North America, and Harriet was born in Quebec. Her younger brother, William Craig Baynes, returned to Canada in 1843 where he became Secretary of McGill University, E.A. Collard, *Oldest McGill* (Toronto, 1946), pp. 69-74. Some details of an initiative by Harriet Baynes to promote evangelism at Colaton Raleigh near Sidmouth just after Groves's departure for Baghdad have been published by Gordon Faulkner (see <http://www.faulkner-history.fsnet.co.uk/Passmore_Files/07Biographical Notes.doc>).

16. Groves, *Memoir*, p. 35. Groves proposed to Harriet Baynes by post from Baghdad sometime in 1832—a proposal that was initially refused. Two years later [c.1834] 'hearing that she had been grievously injured and disfigured by a wagon which crushed her face in a narrow Devonshire lane, he renewed his proposal and was accepted', Mrs. F.B. [L.C.] Meyer, *The author of the Peep of Day, being the life story of Mrs. Mortimer* (London, 1901), pp. 65-66. For the postal proposition of marriage from Baghdad, see H. Groves, *Memoir of Lord Congleton* (London, 1884), p. 43. The marriage was celebrated in the Priory Church of St Mary, Great Malvern, on 25 April 1835 (*International Genealogical Index*). For other details of Harriet Baynes and her family, see E.K. Groves, *George Müller and his Successors* (London, 1906), pp. 36, 60-61, *et passim*. This curiously polemical autobiography, by her son, has been regularly ignored by Brethren writers for a number of reasons. The author's adoption of a belief in conditional immortality was unacceptable to many Brethren, as was the fact that he dared to question the infallibility of Müller's judgment. His frank admission that he had suffered mental disturbance was also probably a factor in their disapproval.

17. As late as November 1825, Groves was suggesting to his children's tutor, Robert Nesbit, that 'the high Calvinistic tenets of the Scottish Church were unfavourable to the missionary spirit'. J.M. Mitchell, *Memoir of the Rev. Robert Nesbit* (London, 1858), p. 28.

18. Groves, *Memoir*, p. 3; at the time, Groves's sister 'resided in the Rev. Mr. Lampen's family': Ryland, *Kitto's Memoir*, p. 142; for Lampen's opposition to

allusion in the *Memoir* to his participation at the meeting for the establishment of an Exeter Mendicity Society in 1825[19] for aiding the indigent, nor of the part he played in the work of the local anti-slavery society of which he was the secretary as late as 1827.[20] There are references to his friendship with the Exeter schoolmaster, William Hake, whose question about the lawfulness of war led Groves to question the Thirty-Nine Articles of the Church of England, but one suspects that Hake only earned a mention because of his later association with the Brethren. Harriet Groves makes no mention of the fact that both Bessie Paget (whom Groves regarded as his 'mother, in the things of God'[21]) and Hake had connections with the Society of Friends.[22] These circumstances, taken with the fact that Groves' fellow secretary in the anti-slavery society was another Quaker, George Dymond,[23] suggest not only that Groves' thinking in these years may have benefited from a rather greater input from the Society of Friends than his widow wanted to admit, but that his spiritual development as an evangelical was interestingly unconventional.

Similarly, Mrs Groves' personal attitudes influenced her account of his later career and also her selective use of the *Journals* which Groves kept when travelling to Persia and during his first year in Baghdad—*Journals* which were published in London in 1831 and 1832. A comparison of the original publications with the extracts reproduced in the *Memoir* suggests that Harriet Groves felt free to 'improve' them not only grammatically.[24]

The problem is compounded by Groves' connection with the early Plymouth Brethren. When the great rift developed in the 1840s between the Exclusive Brethren (gathered under the unofficial leadership of J.N. Darby) and the Open Brethren (one of whose most respected figures was Groves' brother-in-law, George Müller) there was

---

Calvinism, see Exeter, Cathedral Archives, ED 11/85 ii. 23-24, 'Bishop Phillpott's Visitation Journal'.

19. *Exeter Flying Post*, 30 June 1825.

20. *Exeter Flying Post*, 2 March 1826; *Exeter Pocket Journal* (1827).

21. Groves, *Memoir*, p. 40.

22. E.K. Groves, *George Müller*, p. 370; Hake's fellow secretary of the Exeter auxiliary of the Society for the Promotion of Permanent and Universal Peace was the Quaker, Jonathan Dymond, *Exeter Pocket Journal* (1827), p. 44. Cf. P. Brock, 'The Peace Testimony of the Early Plymouth Brethren', *Church History* 53 (March, 1984), p. 32.

23. *Exeter Pocket Journal* (1827), p. 44. The Quaker connection is further underlined by Groves' contacts with Sarah Kilham in St Petersburg, A.N. Groves, *Journal...during a Journey from London to Bagdad* (London, 1831), pp. 27, 29-30, 32; A.N. Groves, *Journal of a Residence at Bagdad 1830–31* (London, 1832), p. 36; cf. Ryland, *Kitto's Memoir*, pp. 303-304, 443-44.

24. E.g., although she included some of Groves' comments on the possible dangers of education, Mrs Groves evidently felt, in the aftermath of the Crimean War, that it was wiser to omit a paragraph where her husband had observed, 'I would certainly much rather have to do with a Russian peasant than an English one, and with any one rather than those who are the self-designated learned among the English operatives [referring to an earlier comment on "the spirit from which emanates Mechanic Institutes and such like..."]', Groves, *Journal...during a Journey*, p. 45; Groves, *Memoir*, p. 59.

naturally much argument about what had been the original principles of the 'Brethren'. Almost inevitably, Groves was hailed, by Open Brethren, as the 'prototype' of their less exclusive ideals, while Exclusive Brethren dismissed him as having been only 'on the fringes' of the movement.[25] There is some truth in both statements but Brethren writers have tended to hijack the story of Groves' development to tally with their own particular ecclesiastical preferences. Although his early influence on the Brethren was diminished by geographical distance, the importance of his early role in the movement cannot be disputed and clearly he kept in close touch with Brethren in later years. On the other hand, a later generation of Open Brethren whose ecclesiastical identity was more clearly defined, played down some important aspects of Groves' career, fearing, perhaps, that his easy-going involvement with Christians outside the Brethren orbit was liable to tarnish his credentials among the less liberal of the Open Brethren.

Another aspect of the historiographical problem is that even by the time Harriet Baynes was married to Groves, and certainly by the time she was preparing his *Memoir*, the name of Edward Irving was inextricably associated with the charismatic manifestations of the early 1830s and with the Catholic Apostolic Church of the Irvingites—an ecclesiastical cul-de-sac despised and reviled by most Brethren. There has, therefore, been a reluctance to identify Groves with Irving. Temperamentally, of course, they were very different, but in the later 1820s Groves must have been aware of the similarity of his missionary ideal to that of Irving. The fact that the second and third editions of his pamphlet *Christian Devotedness* were published by James Nisbet, a member of Irving's congregation, and that Groves' *Journals* (also published by Nisbet) were edited by Irving's fellow worker, Sandy Scott, cannot be ignored. Groves continued to regard the possible revival of the pentecostal gifts as an open question for some time after his departure for Baghdad in 1829.

The Church Missionary Society Connection

Groves' first personal contact with the CMS authorities was early in 1825 when the possibility arose of his protégé, John Kitto, working as a printer's apprentice in the missionary College at Islington. This led to Groves' explanation to Edward Bickersteth, the Society's Secretary, of his own long-standing wish to engage in missionary service.[26] So in August, the Secretary was able to report to the Committee that an unnamed individual 'in a respectable situation in life' had offered

25. The two tendencies are well exemplified respectively by G.H. Lang, *Anthony Norris Groves: saint and pioneer: a combined study of a man of God and of the original principles and practices of the Brethren with applications to present conditions* (London, 1949), which contains a sustained critique of some attitudes of the Exclusive Brethren among whom Lang had grown up, and M.S. Weremchuk, *John Nelson Darby, A Biography* (Neptune, NJ, 1992), pp. 66-69.

26. Birmingham, University Library, Church Missionary Society [hereafter CMS] Archive, G/C/1, A.N. Groves to E.H. Bickersteth (25 March 1825) transcribed in CMS Minutes (20 May 1825), 7, p. 517; Groves, *Memoir*, pp. 11-12.

his services to the Society but that circumstances (the expected opposition of Mary's family) 'prevent him coming forward at present to avow his intentions'. The Secretary added that 'both from his conversation with the individual...and from the unanimous testimony of the friends of the Society in the neighbourhood where he lives' it was 'peculiarly eligible [sic] to engage his services'. The Society's minutes record that Groves was acquainted with Latin, Greek, Hebrew, French and Italian and that he wanted 'to know in what quarter it is probable that he may be employed, if eventually accepted'. Although Groves later recalled that the CMS 'accepted my offer, and begged me to change from India to Persia',[27] the minutes make clear that when the committee accepted his offer 'with satisfaction' they indicated that Groves might 'be most advantageously employed in the Mediterranean Mission' recommending him 'more particularly to study Italian, Modern Greek and Arabic and to acquire as much medical knowledge as practicable'.[28] It was only in February 1827 when the inimitable Joseph Wolff, self-appointed missionary to Jews worldwide, gave an account to the CMS Committee of his travels and observations in Persia, that its members were immediately reminded of 'the qualifications of Mr. A.N. Groves...for entering on such a sphere of labour' and recommended that Groves' 'course of study and preparation be directed with a view to his being employed in a mission to Persia in prosecution of the Society's objects'.[29]

Great must have been the rejoicing among the members of the CMS Committee at Bickersteth's discovery of a respected Christian, competent in more than one language, who was willing to serve with the Society—especially when he proved (to begin with at any rate) very ready to comply with the Committee's recommendations and seemed to be blessed with no mean powers of endurance. In his later years, Groves was inclined to hold worldly learning in low esteem, and some of his admirers have been inclined to belittle the importance of study as a preparation for missionary service. Some of his early letters are all the more revealing, therefore, as they indicate just how seriously Groves originally considered the matter of preparation. In the Mediterranean Mission to which he was originally assigned, Groves would have been working with William Jowett whose *Christian Researches*[30] he now read with care. In consequence he gave first priority to his Greek and Arabic studies, 'by way of preparing me for future service'. With the help of the former rabbi, Michael Alexander (later Bishop of Jerusalem), in whose conversion to Christianity he had played a significant part, Groves also aimed to improve his Hebrew, though on his own admission his progress was impeded by professional

27. Groves, *Memoir*, p. 23.

28. CMS Minutes (9 August 1825), 8, pp. 9-10.

29. CMS Minutes (20 February 1827), 9, pp. 29-30. This explains Groves' suggestion in a letter as late as 2 April 1827 that his reader might not 'know our destination is finally fixed for Persia', Groves, *Memoir*, p. 19.

30. W. Jowett, *Christian Researches in the Mediterranean, Syria and the Holy Land* (London, 1820). Groves found himself in agreement with much of what Jowett had written and felt it would be a good basis for 'successful co-operation', Groves to Bickersteth, 15 September 1825 (CMS Archive, G/Ac3/Sept 1825).

responsibilities. It is sometimes supposed that a university degree was required for Anglican ordination, but in fact men could be ordained without such a qualification. It appears to have been Groves' decision, with Bickersteth's approval, to work for a degree and in March 1826, nine months after his original commitment, we learn of his plans to attend regularly at Dublin and possibly to take his degree at Oxford. In the meanwhile, apart from the Bible, his reading was almost totally devoted to Latin and Greek.

> I trust that in the end I may not disappoint your hopes, yet at times when I contemplate the necessary requisites even of a natural kind in the station to which you have thought it best to direct my thoughts, I am almost overcome with the sense of their magnitude.[31]

Remembering that Groves would soon part company with the CMS because he found its requirements too restrictive, the submissive tone of these early letters is noteworthy. And yet Groves was in a very different category from many of the CMS recruits. He was well educated and if not yet a graduate, he soon would be; he was older, in his thirties (barely ten years younger than Bickersteth), with almost a dozen years of professional experience; his income was far from negligible; and he was English(!). Would such considerations affect the way the CMS authorities would view him, if he were to disagree with them? The authoritarian paternalism with which they were inclined to treat their recruits could easily be offensive and more than one of the young continentals who spent time in London has left a record of how insensitive he found the CMS authorities.[32] Tantalizingly, the CMS archives appear to make no reference to Groves' decision to break with the Society and become an independent missionary. In consequence, the only available details are taken from his later recollections.[33] There were several elements that contributed to his abandoning the plans for ordination and his subsequent withdrawal from the CMS. First, there were the doubts raised in Groves' mind by Henry Townley, a retired London Missionary Society (LMS) missionary about the usefulness of studying for a degree.[34] Then, in October 1827, there was the 'providential' theft of Groves' travel money preventing him from going to Dublin.[35] Shortly afterwards

31. CMS Archive, G/Ac3/March 1826, Groves to Bickersteth, 14 March [1826].

32. Cf. T.C.F. Stunt, 'Leonard Strong: the motives and experiences of early missionary work in British Guiana', *Christian Brethren Review* 34 (1983), p. 102; R. First and A. Scott, *Olive Schreiner, A Biography* (London, 1980), p. 31. The problem would become more acute with the retirement of Bickersteth in 1830 and his replacement by the zealous but narrow Dandeson Coates.

33. Groves, *Memoir*, p. 41-42.

34. 'Mr T., of Calcutta' (Groves, *Memoir*, p. 41). Townley was doing deputation work in Devon in the summer of 1827, *Evangelical Magazine* n.s. 5 (1827), p. 498.

35. The account of the burglary in the local newspaper confirms Groves' recollection that the robbery was on a Sunday morning and that other money 'put aside for a particular use' [taxes] escaped the attention of the thieves. More than a year later a tailor, Thomas Salter, was charged with theft committed on Groves who 'declared he would not proceed

when questioned on the subject by Hake, Groves realized that he could not subscribe to the thirty-seventh article of the Church of England in its approval of armed warfare 'at the command of the Magistrate'. Of the CMS reaction to his decision Groves merely tells us that he

> was still so far attached to the Church of England that I went to London to arrange my going out as a layman for the Church Missionary Society; but as they would not allow me to celebrate the Lord's Supper, when no other minister was near, it came to nothing.[36]

Such a suggestion was clearly quite beyond the mind-set of the CMS authorities and one can imagine their sigh of relief when they realized that they would be no longer responsible for a candidate who was turning out to be of a suspiciously radical turn of thought.

Brethren writers, with their anti-clerical perspectives, have understandably seen Groves' break with the CMS as part of a wider ecclesiastical emancipation from restrictive institutional restraints, and certainly it coincided chronologically with his abandonment in 1827–28 of his previously strict churchmanship. But it can also be argued that both developments were logical outworkings of the much more fundamental asceticism and other-worldliness which were central to the case which Groves had argued in his earlier pamphlet *Christian Devotedness*. In passing we should perhaps note that the 'powerful appeals' of this work had contributed to the missionary convictions of Robert Nesbit who, as a tutor, had joined Groves' household in November 1825 but who, less than three months later, was preparing to offer himself for service with the Scottish Missionary Society.[37]

It is evident from a cursory reading of *Christian Devotedness* that Groves' profound fear of anything which might be categorized as treasure laid up on earth or,

---

against a fellow creature in such distress and instantly tendered him pecuniary aid': *Exeter Flying Post*, 24 October 1827, p. 4; 19 March 1829, p. 3.

36. Groves, *Memoir*, p. 42. I can find no reference to this suggestion in the CMS Minutes, though Groves continues to be mentioned in connection with Kitto; see below n. 43.

37. S. Piggin and J. Roxborough, *The St Andrews Seven* (Edinburgh, 1985), p. 98. Cf. Edinburgh, New College Archives, CHA 4.60.5, 7, R. Nesbit to T. Chalmers 17 February and 13 March 1826, where he commends Groves' pamphlet to the serious attention of his fellow students. Characteristically Groves' testimonial for Nesbit in 1826 emphasised his 'simple sincerity of purpose...religious consistency and single devotedness of heart', J.M. Mitchell, *Memoir of the Rev. Robert Nesbit* (London, 1858), p. 34. One of Nesbit's fellow students, Alexander Duff, later wrote to Groves from Calcutta, 'of his first glow of devotedness, as having arisen' from reading Groves' pamphlet, Groves, *Memoir*, p. 295. Duff's biographer makes no mention of this early influence on his subject though he pays tribute to Groves' tireless care of the dysentery-stricken Duff in 1834. Duff's son was named Alexander Groves Duff, G. Smith, *The Life of Alexander Duff* (London, 4th edn, 1904), pp. 121-22.

in his colourful phrase, 'poisonous heaps of gold',[38] was leading him to be increasingly wary of exercising 'worldly' influence of any sort, whether it was financial, educational, social or religious, all of which he treated as aspects of 'the silken age into which we are fallen'.[39] That these implications of his pamphlet had continued to occupy him is apparent from the third edition, published in 1829, in which he refers to the subject of another pamphlet (as yet unwritten[40]):

> I shall endeavour to show, that a grain of the pure gold of Christian influence, which is the exhibition, in truth, of the mind of Christ, springing from the love of Christ in the soul, is no wise increased in value by being beaten out into plates as thin as imagination can conceive, and employed to gild the brassy admixture of earthly influence, the titles, honours, rank, wealth, learning and secular power of this world. It looks indeed like a mighty globe of gold...but the least scratch proves its brassy character. If this simple principle had been perceived, how differently would many public religious bodies have been constituted for the purpose of extending the influence of Christ's kingdom.[41]

In shunning the pedestals of influence provided by clerical and institutional hierarchies, Groves was finding himself at odds with the condescending and arrogant tendencies of his own class towards those whom they regarded as socially inferior—attitudes which often characterized the behaviour of the CMS towards its volunteers, and more specifically their rather high-handed treatment of Groves' intelligent but awkward pauper protégé, John Kitto. In 1826 Kitto had somewhat hastily tendered to the CMS his resignation and then, thinking better of it, asked for readmission. The CMS refused and it was only Groves' eloquent pleadings on Kitto's behalf that caused them to change their minds.[42] Kitto was now sent to

---

38. A.N. Groves, *Christian Devotedness* (London, 2nd edn, 1826), pp. 1-2.

39. Groves, *Christian Devotedness*, pp. 33-34. Cf. the reference in his journal (August 1830) to 'sentimental Christianity' as 'a thing to talk about, on silken sofas with all the refinements of this pampered and luxurious age', Groves, *Memoir*, pp. 57-58.

40. A.N. Groves, *On the Nature of Christian Influence* (Bombay, 1833).

41. A.N. Groves, *Christian Devotedness* (London, 3rd edn, 1829), Preface. An important indication of how Groves' thinking on prophetic matters had recently developed is apparent in this third edition. Here he adopted a premillennial position and excised an earlier suggestion that if Christians were to take the New Testament precepts seriously; 'the day would indeed be dawning when "the knowledge of the Lord shall cover the earth, as the waters cover the sea"' (2nd edn, 1826), p. 51. Although there were three English editions of *Christian Devotedness* there are apparently no extant copies of the first (1825). The on-line catalogue (<www.copac.ac.uk>) lists an edition in New College Library, Edinburgh, which is dated 1828 're-printed at the Church Mission Press, Madras'. If the date is truly 1828 there is a delicious irony in Groves' pamphlet having been issued by the CMS in India in 1828 before he left for Baghdad (and presumably even before he broke off his enrolment with them). It would have been this edition that Daniel Poor passed on to Sir Arthur Cotton, Groves, *Memoir*, p. 273; cf. p. 259.

42. CMS Minutes 9 (6 February, 20 February, 20 March 1827), 17, 30, 55; Birmingham UL, CMS G/Ac3/March 1827, Groves to Bickersteth, 10 March 1827. In a

Malta where he worked in the CMS printing house for more than a year (1827–29) but again he came into conflict with his superiors—this time over a matrimonial proposal—and resigned a second time.[43] On his return to England in February 1829 he was once more *persona non grata* with both the CMS and his former patrons in Plymouth. It was typical of Groves that his concern transcended considerations of class and although he was preparing for his own imminent departure for Baghdad he was again ready to help Kitto find employment with his friend John Synge of Teignmouth. Ultimately Kitto accepted Groves' invitation for him to join his party and come to Baghdad as a tutor for Groves' boys.[44]

The Basel Connection

Some twenty years later Kitto recalled the time he had spent with the CMS at Islington and, in a glowing testimonial, described the continental recruits (to whom he always referred as 'Germans' even though some of them, like Samuel Gobat and Paul Pacifique Schaffter, were French-speaking Swiss):

> [There] were ten Germans from the excellent Missionary Institution at Basle who...were regarded with peculiar interest, and with some curiosity as the first foreigners most of [the students] had ever known... While the German brethren secured respect by their parts, their learning and deep experience in the things of God, they won universal regard by the affectionate tenderness of their demeanour and the Christian simplicity of their character.[45]

It was very probably through Kitto that Groves made his earliest, first-hand acquaintance with the Basel missionaries with whom he felt a natural affinity.[46] That this appreciation was mutual is suggested by the fact that when George Müller came to the Seminary from Germany in early 1829, he soon heard favourable reports of

letter to Robert Lampen, Kitto paid a heartfelt tribute to the patient care and concern of Groves whom he described as his 'guardian angel': see Ryland, *Kitto's Memoir*, p. 231.

43. CMS Minutes 10 (3, 17 June 1828), 563, 579. Kitto's biographer makes no mention of the matrimonial issue.

44. Ryland, *Kitto's Memoir*, pp. 289-93. The CMS Minutes (9 August 1825) indicate that from the outset Groves' younger sister, Lydia, had wished to accompany Groves 'to undertake the children's education'. In fact she had to return home on account of poor health when the party reached St Petersburg.

45. C.F. Schlienz, *The Pilgrim Missionary Institution of St Chrischona*, with introduction by Dr Kitto (London, 1850), p. xxii. Schlienz, for whom Kitto wrote this introduction, was a year older than Kitto whom he had known in Malta where he worked with the CMS from 1827 to 1842 before being appointed as Principal of the St Chrischona Institution in Basel.

46. There is a further parallel here between Groves and Edward Irving who was enthusiastic about the 'German' missionaries, M.O.W. Oliphant, *Life of Edward Irving* (2 vols; London, 2nd edn, 1862), I, pp. 308-309, 352-54.

Groves who was on the point of leaving the country.[47] It is against this background that we may better understand Groves' intense delight at meeting, on his way to Baghdad, Karl Gottlieb Pfander and his German co-workers at Shushee. In contrast to the Moravian colony at Sarepta which he considered 'as a little church gathered together in the wilderness, but not at all as a missionary station, or as having missionary objectives',[48] the Basel missionaries at Shushee shared Groves' concern for identification with the people around them:

> That perfect unity of sentiment which subsists between us as to the importance of laying aside every thing of this world's greatness, and descending to the level of the people, is most grateful [sic. gratifying] to me; and this is not the sentiment of one of these dear brethren but of all.[49]

This emphasis led Groves into a sort of self-contradiction when he was in India. Much has been made by his admirers of his readiness to nurture native leadership and with some reason he has been hailed as a pioneer of 'indigenization'. What is sometimes forgotten is that in his enthusiastic support for Rhenius Groves was siding with a nineteenth-century rejection of an earlier pietist missionary tradition in India that had been far readier to countenance Indian leadership. Herein lay the ambiguity of Groves' position. The Tamil pastors, to whom the earlier German missionaries Ziegenbalg and Pluetschau had given responsibility, had been happy to work within some social and cultural traditions that later Rhenius (and Groves with him) would challenge.[50] In this respect, although Groves strove for identification he seems to have brought to India his own quite radical social agenda. This was apparent on his first arrival in Tinnevelly when he wrote, 'As I desire to break down caste among the Hindoos, to pave the way for the reception of the truth, so do I

47. G. Müller, *A Narrative of Some of the Lord's Dealings with George Müller written by himself* (6 vols; London, 8th edn, 1881), I, p. 44. The CMS College seems to have been shared with the students training with the London Society for Promoting Christianity among the Jews. Cf. Stock, *CMS History*, I, pp. 153-54. It was only later that Müller married Groves' sister and only in 1834 that he met Groves himself.

48. Groves, *Journal... during a Journey*, p. 47.

49. Groves, *Journal... during a Journey*, pp. 80-81.

50. See D.D. Hudson, *Protestant Origins in India: Tamil Evangelical Christians, 1706–1835* (Grand Rapids, MI, 2000), *passim*; H. Liebau, 'Country priests, catechists, and schoolmasters as cultural, religious, and social middlemen in the context of the Tranquebar Mission', in R.E. Frykenberg (ed.), *Christians and Missionaries in India: cross-cultural communication since 1500* (Grand Rapids, MI, 2003), pp. 70-92; I.V. Peterson '"Bethlehem Kuravañci" of Vedanayaka Sastri of Tanjore: The Cultural Discourses of an Early-Nineteenth Century Tamil Christian Poem', in J.M. Brown and R.E. Frykenberg (eds), *Christians, Cultural Interactions and India's Religious Traditions* (Grand Rapids, MI, 2002), pp. 16ff; B. Singh, *The First Protestant Missionary to India: Bartholomaeus Ziegenbalg* (Oxford, 2000).

desire to break down caste in the Christian church to prepare the way for publishing it.'[51]

Although Groves prized most highly his Christian liberty and although his withdrawal from the CMS reflects his deep fear of the institutional shackles which so often accompanied worldly 'influence', we must resist the suggestion that he would have nothing to do with Christians whose opinions on such matters differed from his. Before his departure from England he arranged a meeting with Henry Drummond with a view to obtaining the latest information Joseph Wolff could provide about Persia.[52] At his request the London Society for Promoting Christianity among the Jews provided him with some books for use in Persia[53] and he was similarly glad to make use of the administrative infrastructure of the British and Foreign Bible Society with whose Committee and Secretaries he was regularly in contact from 1829–32.[54] Regular reports of his work appeared in the *Missionary Register* where his explanation of the case for developing a trade route to India by way of the Tigris and Euphrates was surprisingly cognisant of the practical realities of commerce for a man with such other-worldly perspectives.[55] It is similarly refreshing to find that, in spite of the earlier disagreements, Groves had an arrangement with the CMS for forwarding mail to him and was earnestly encouraging the Committee of the Society (in a letter of October 1832) to send someone to Ispahan to whom 'we would be delighted to give...a brotherly help by the way in the language or one of us would go with him till he got a little accustomed to his work'.[56] Of all the missionary societies, however, for Groves the Basel Mission Institute was in a special category of its own and increasingly he began to look in the direction of Switzerland for reinforcements who would share his own concern for a simple life-style and his disregard for social status. After his meeting with Pfander we find Groves writing to Admiral Pearson of the need to establish an Armenian female school:

---

51. Groves, *Memoir*, p. 242; cf. pp. 268, 274, 282, *et passim*.

52. Alnwick, Northumberland Archives, C/1/200, 201, A.N. Groves to H. Drummond, two undated letters [c. February–June 1829].

53. Oxford, Bodleian Library, Dep CMJ, Minutes of the General Committee of the London Society for Promoting Christianity among the Jews, 13 (1829), p. 289.

54. Five letters from Groves—5 June 1829, 28 August 1830, 18 September 1831, 2 May and 20 October 1832—are in Cambridge University Library, BFBS Archives. Cf. *Twenty-eighth Report of the Bible Society* (1832), pp. lviii-lix.

55. *Missionary Register*, 19 (1831), p. 376. The extent to which Groves allowed himself to become involved in the activities of the British Residency at Baghdad is not quite clear. On at least one occasion during the plague epidemic (29 March 1831) he accompanied Dr Montefiore, the medical officer to the Residency, on a visit to the 'Arab infected quarter', London, India Office Records, R. Taylor's Despatch, 17 June 1831, L/PS/9 (Persia 1831), vol. 46, p. 497.

56. Groves, *Memoir*, p. 53; Birmingham UL, CMS G/Ac3/Oct 1832, A.N. Groves to T. Woodroffe, 25 October 1832.

> I wish Mr [Joseph] Greaves and [his wife] your daughter could come here from Basle...or at all events stir up the Basle Committee to send them some one or two faithful men to encourage and strengthen them.[57]

In fact, this was but the start of an important relationship with the continental evangelical movement. Extracts from Groves' *Journal* were published in French in Neuchâtel in 1834,[58] and, in the same year, details of Groves' work in Baghdad with Pfander were reported in the *Journal des Missions Évangéliques*.[59] Groves himself was corresponding with Dr Blumhardt and others at Basel[60] both before and after his visit to Switzerland in 1835 when he gathered new recruits for the Indian mission field. These included the redoubtable Hermann Gundert[61] (a grandfather of Hermann Hesse), Rodolphe de Rodt[62] from Geneva and Ferdinand Gros from Lausanne, as well as two Swiss women from Rolle,[63] one of whom, Julie Dubois, would later become (in spite of the hostility of the second Mrs Groves) the wife of Dr Gundert.[64] Indeed,

---

57. Basel, BMA, GB/Q-3-4, 2 MS copies of A.N. Groves to Admiral Pearson, 14 October 1829. An inaccurate extract from this letter is reproduced in J. Ehret, 'Der Rückzug der Basler Mission aus Russland', *Basler Zeitschrift* 53 (1954), pp. 164-65. For Greaves, see T.C.F. Stunt, 'The Greaves Family: some clarifications', *Notes and Queries* 28 (October, 1981), p. 406.

58. *Extraits du Journal de M. Groves, missionnaire à Bagdad*, traduit de l'anglais par le traducteur de la vie de Mme Judson... (Neuchâtel, 1834).

59. *Journal des Missions Évangéliques* (Paris, 1834), pp. 209-12.

60. By April 1834 Groves is mentioning 'Mr Blumhardt's letters' and his own plans to visit Basel, Groves, *Memoir*, p. 285. Other surviving letters from Groves to Basel include: Basel, BMA. GB/Q-3-4; Personalfaszikell series Q-13 BV235 [Gundert], Groves to Blumhardt, 22 June 1834; Groves to W. Büchelen, 30 November 1835 and 22 March 1836; Basel Staats-Archiv, Pr. Arch. 653.v.11, Groves to C.F. Spittler, 7 April 1835; December 1835. The earlier letter to Spittler is inaccurately quoted in E. Staehlin, *Die Christentumsgesellschaft in der Zeit von der Erweckung bis zur Gegenwart*, volume 2 (Basel, 1974), 506-507.

61. See M. Brecht, 'The Relationship between Established Protestant Church and Free Church: Hermann Gundert and Britain', in K. Robbins (ed.), *Protestant Evangelicalism: Britain, Ireland, Germany and America, c.1750–c.1950* (Oxford, 1990), pp. 135ff.

62. K.W. Bouterwek, *Leben und Wirken Rudolf's von Rodt VDM, Weil, Missionars der Londoner Missionsgesellschaft in Indien* (Elberfeld, 1852), p. 6. Cf. 'Memoir of R. de Rodt', *Calcutta Christian Observer* n.s. 4, o.s. 12 (October, 1843), pp. 561-84; 'R de Rodt's letters', *Calcutta Christian Advocate* 519-31 (9 September–2 December, 1843), *passim*.

63. *Feuille de la Commission des Églises Associées pour l'Évangélisation*, 1 (1836) No. 5, pp. 120-22. This contains a letter from Groves (20 March 1836) written before embarking at Milford Haven. For details (evidently based on unspecified MS material) of Groves' party, see E.B. Bromley, *They Were Men Sent from God: A Centennial Record (1836–1936) of Gospel Work in India among the Telegus in the Godavari Delta and neighbouring parts* (Bangalore, 1937), pp. 14-16.

64. For Harriet Groves' opposition, see H. Gundert, *Tagebuch aus Malabar 1837–1859* (Stuttgart, 1983), p. 34. Gundert's journals and letters edited by Albrecht

for a while Groves' thinking in missionary matters had a discernable impact on the policies of the Basel Mission. In his account of the missionary Samuel Hebich, Gundert indicates that it was Groves' plea for a simpler life style that led to Blumhardt's proposal that the Basel missionaries

> should receive no stated income, but simply draw what was necessary for their subsistence from the society, it being understood that their mode of life was to be as simple as possible, conforming, whenever they could do it, to the habits of the natives of the country.[65]

In his correspondence with the Basel authorities and other societies, Groves' fundamental concern was to mobilize manpower for the gospel and he was not primarily concerned with labels and affiliations. His enthusiastic participation, on his way to Baghdad, in the chapel activities of Richard Knill, the LMS worker in St Petersburg, and his appreciation of the financial help given to him by the members of Knill's congregation are at variance with any sectarian evaluation of Groves.[66] It is true that on a regular basis, Groves was not always the easiest man to work with, as may be seen from the departure of John Kitto from Baghdad in 1833[67] and the later problems of Hermann Gundert in India.[68] However, on the wider front there is very little evidence to suggest that Groves would only co-operate with those who shared his own ecclesiastical ideals. His involvement in the rupture between Rhenius and the CMS was clearly motivated by Groves' concern that the German missionary's work should not be put at risk. The disagreement was over the validity of Lutheran ordination on the mission field—an issue to which Groves sat very lightly—and he was certainly not inveigling Rhenius to 'join the Brethren'.[69] Even

---

Frenz are a useful independent source for Groves' work in India after 1835. See also H. Gundert, *Schriften und Berichte aus Malabar mit Meditationen und Studien* (Stuttgart, 1983); H. Gundert, *Calwe Tagebuch 1859–1893* (Stuttgart, 1986).

65. H. Gundert and H. Mögling, *The life of Samuel Hebich: by two of his fellow-labourers* (trans. J.G. Halliday; London, 1876), pp. 55-56. In another account Gundert makes clear that the Basel Mission's leaders were less enthusiastic about Groves' proposals for fully autonomous missionaries, H. Gundert, *Hermann Moegling, A Biography* (trans. C. Steinweg and E. Steinweg-Fleckner, ed. A. Frenz; Kottayam, Kerala, India, 1997), pp. 75, 77.

66. Groves, *Memoir*, pp. 54-55; *Evangelical Magazine* n.s. 7 (1829), pp. 551-52; cf. London, School of Oriental and African Studies, Council for World Mission Archives A2 [14] 1:3, 'Journal of Richard Knill' 1 (23 June–4 July 1829), pp. 252-55.

67. Rowdon, *Origins*, pp. 193-94.

68. Brecht, 'Relationship', pp. 139-40.

69. The best account of Groves' involvement with Rhenius is Rowdon, *Origins*, pp. 196-97, though he appears not to have used Rhenius' biography. Such was the bad odour in which Brethren were held at the time that Groves' part in the episode is minimized in accounts favourable to Rhenius, e.g. C.J. Rhenius, *Memoir of the Rev. C.T.E. Rhenius* by his son (London, 1841), while Eugene Stock, *CMS History*, I, pp. 283, 320, casts Groves as the villain of the story, but in this respect he cannot be taken too seriously as,

if, in personal practice, he found the principle difficult to implement, Groves believed that missionaries should be free from human restrictions and answerable only to God. His position was clearly expressed in a letter to Blumhardt:

> I wish them [missionaries who might be sent out by the Basel Mission] to look on themselves as only Christ's servants and responsible to him as we are also[.] relative to marrying or not marrying, schools or anything else[,] all we can say is this[:] that as private individuals we might be open to be consulted or applied to for help, yet any expenses arising out of these circumstances shall never in any measure be allowed to be considered expenses connected with which we have anything to do otherwise than as private brothers. In fact our whole desire is not to get dependent servants of ours but free servants of Christ whom our desire is to help. I will not however deny that I do feel the generally expensive plan of missionary establishments in these countries as not only not helping on the cause in proportion to their expense, but in nearly that proportion unfitting them for coming at [sic] the natives in that simple way which I desire. I never shall forget the dear brethren at Shoushee[:] their simplicity edified me and their devotion stimulated me.[70]

Conclusion

In the early decades of the Brethren movement there was a significant element, particularly in Plymouth and the West Country, where the 'missionary imperative' appears to have been lost sight of in a preoccupation with the eschatological details

---

in the same paragraph, he claims that Groves was responsible for the society's loss of Kitto which is a ludicrous suggestion. For CMS anxieties about Groves at the time, see Basel, BMA, CMS correspondence series QK-3, 1D, Coates to C.G. Blumhardt, 12 March 1835. A postscript marked 'strictly confidential', in Coates' own hand, warns the Basel authorities against any co-operation with Groves. For Groves' affectionate account of his 'holy parting moment' with John Tucker, the authoritarian Madras secretary of the CMS, see Groves, *Memoir*, p. 332. Frank Newman's brother John was enthusiastic about Tucker's 'most sensible account of the state of India' (in which Groves was mentioned) thinking that his [Newman's] differences with Tucker 'would in India almost be a matter of a few words'. I. Ker and T. Gornall (eds), *Letters and Diaries of J.H. Newman* (8 vols; Oxford, 1980–), IV, pp. 338, 361-62. Cf my review of J.P. Callahan's *Primitivist Piety* (Lanham, MD, 1990), in *BAHNR* 1.2 (Winter, 1998), pp. 120-21. For further light on the Rhenius affair, see R.E. Frykenberg, 'The Impact of Conversion and Social Reform upon Society in South India during the Late Company Period: Questions concerning Hindu-Christian encounters, with special reference to Tinnevelly', in C.H. Philips and M.D. Wainwright (eds), *Indian Society and the Beginnings of Modernization, c.1830–1860* (London, 1976), pp 187-243. For a disappointingly partisan approach to Groves, see Stephen Neill, *A History of Christianity in India 1707–1858* (Cambridge, 1985), pp. 220, 349, 408, 455. We await with impatience Dr Frykenberg's forthcoming edition of the Rhenius *Memoir*.

70. Basel, BMA, GB series Q-3-4, Groves to Blumhardt, Calcutta, 22 June 1834.

of the Saviour's imminent return. It is, therefore, a little ironic that although Groves has come to be honoured as a founding father of the movement, his lively missiology was at first appreciated by so few of the British Brethren. After a visit to Plymouth in 1840, John Bowes, a former Primitive Methodist preacher, was critical of the Brethren's dogmatism on such subjects as the premillennial advent of Christ and also observed that 'many of them will not support this good man [Groves] because his spirit is too catholic'.[71] There was undoubtedly a 'universality' in Groves' approach to humanity. On one occasion at the beginning of his travels, Groves described his feelings on hearing the British National Anthem being played—'a circumstance which gave that sort of national pleasure, which will steal through the heart [even] of one who wishes to become a citizen of the world, as far as national attachment goes'.[72] It was an honest admission from one who strove, for some thirty years, to be first and foremost a citizen of heaven and not of the world, let alone of Britain. Although Groves was an individualist, he knew that his Christian mission was in this world (albeit not of it), and he constantly delighted in the wide fellowship that he enjoyed with all the children of God wherever he found them. Nevertheless from the evidence adduced in the foregoing paper, Groves seems to have concluded that in his efforts to detach himself from the exercise of worldly influence and to be truly unsectarian in his Christian mission he was more likely to find like-minded fellow-workers in the world of Swiss and German piety than in the wealthier circles of English evangelicalism.

---

71. John Bowes, *The Autobiography or History of the Life of John Bowes* (Glasgow, 1872), p. 236. I am grateful to Tim Grass for drawing my attention to this important source of independent evidence for the criticism and diminishing support from English Brethren alluded to in Groves, *Memoir*, chs xv and xvi, *passim*.

72. Groves, *Journal...during a Journey*, p. 16.

CHAPTER 19

The Place of the Brethren Movement in International Evangelicalism

D.W. Bebbington

In 1905 Alexander Lewis, a boy at a Brethren Sunday school in Hamilton, a few miles south of Glasgow, received a copy of *Boys and Girls*, an eight-page illustrated handout. He saw in it a diagram of a cross carrying the words, 'Who in His own self bare [blank] sins in His own body on the tree.' The editor suggested that, if readers wanted to trust Christ, they should write their own names in the blank space. As the son of a gospel preacher, Alexander knew what was involved and put down his own name. 'Like Paul', he recalled, 'I realised that "the Son of God loved ME and gave Himself for ME " (Gal. 2. 20)'. Jesus Christ, he explained, had made him whole. Now Alexander was carrying posters on billboards through the streets, one of them announcing, 'Christ is coming. Are you ready?' Here is a simple testimony with conversion at its heart. Scripture plays a prominent part: although the account is brief, Alexander wove in two more texts, each with a precise reference. The doctrinal emphasis was on the atonement. 'Just as my sins meant His cross', wrote the lad, 'so His death means my peace.' And in consequence there was the task of 'witnessing a good confession'. Alexander was active in evangelism, and, as he put it, 'I have great joy in His service.'[1] Thus the narrative reveals a fourfold stress on conversion, Bible, cross and activism, characteristics that can be seen as the defining hallmarks of evangelicalism. Alexander Lewis's story illustrates that Brethren were part of the wider evangelical movement.

Two years later a young man in Lisbon, Henriqué Carlos Tavares, was working as an office clerk. A Scottish colleague, Robert Macgregor, invited him to a meeting in Santa Catharina Hall, a Brethren place of worship. Although, after a Roman Catholic education, Henriqué despised religion from the standpoint of a vague materialism, he was impressed by what he heard at the hall. Shortly afterwards, at Macgregor's suggestion, he knelt down, confessed his sinful condition and received Christ into his heart. In recounting the experience, Henriqué adduced two verses from the Bible, both referring to the atoning work of Christ. He explained that Christ had 'died the death of the Cross, so expiating our sins' and that 'the blood of Jesus Christ His Son cleanseth us from all sin'. The young man felt happy and

1. HyP, 'A boy's noble confession', *The Shining Path for Young Folks* (Glasgow, n.d. [1912]).

strong—strong enough to take part in tract distribution that very afternoon. So a life of active Christian service began.[2] Again in Tavares's tale there are the four elements of conversion, Bible, cross and activism, but this time in evidence from outside the British Isles. It seems likely that the clerk was familiar with the English language, but the preacher, C.A. Swan, who had served as a missionary in modern Angola,[3] almost certainly preached in Portuguese. The episode exemplifies the way in which the gospel was carried by Brethren beyond English-speaking lands. The movement helped make evangelicalism a worldwide force.

Brethrenism was international from its inception. Already in the 1830s, when the movement was beginning in the British Isles, it also took root in British Guiana, where Leonard Strong, an agent of the Church Missionary Society, seceded from the Church of England.[4] Switzerland was the focus of a vigorous and many-sided indigenous movement of radical evangelicals that shared many similarities with early Brethren, and, as Timothy Stunt has demonstrated, actually played an important part in the genesis of Brethrenism.[5] Northern Italy also produced, by the 1850s, a home-grown set of Free Italian Churches centred on Count Guicciardini. They received financial help from London Brethren and after Guiccardini's death in 1886 his widow strengthened the alignment with the British movement.[6] Both Switzerland and Italy played a part in spreading similar assemblies in other parts of Europe, but Britain was the chief epicentre of Brethrenism. Businessmen planted their faith in new regions: Philip Robinson, for example, established a Brethren assembly in Singapore in the 1850s.[7] Emigrants carried the gospel with them: converts from the Blackdown Hills in Devon, for instance, were encouraged to leave for America, Canada and Australia as a remedy for rural overpopulation in the 1870s and 1880s.[8] Most of all, full-time workers launched gospel efforts in other lands: from 1879 onwards Alexander Marshall planted congregations in Canada and the United States, and was active in the Faroe Islands, Barbados, Norway, Switzerland, Russia and Estonia.[9] As a result of these methods of propagation, Brethrenism became a

2. H.C. Tavares, 'How God saved a Portuguese', in *The Shining Path for Young Folks.*

3. F.R. Coad, *A History of the Brethren Movement: its origins, its worldwide development and its significance for the present day* (Exeter, 1968), p. 202.

4. T.C.F. Stunt, 'Leonard Strong: the motives and experiences of early missionary work in British Guiana', *Christian Brethren Review* 34 (1983), pp. 95-105.

5. T.C.F. Stunt, *From Awakening to Secession: Radical Evangelicals in Switzerland and Britain, 1815–35* (Edinburgh, 2000).

6. D.D. Ronco, *Risorgimento and the Free Italian Churches now Churches of the Brethren* (Bangor, 1996), pp. 54, 105-107.

7. V. James, 'Evangelicalism and globalization: the Singapore context', in Mark Hutchinson and Ogbu Kalu (eds), *A Global Faith: essays on evangelicalism and globalization* (Sydney, 1998), p. 232; see also Jason Lim, 'The early years of a new assembly: Bethesda Gospel Hall, Singapore, 1864–1914', ch. 11 above.

8. W.J.H. Brealey, *'Always Abounding': or recollections of the life and labours of the late George Brealey, the evangelist of the Blackdown Hills* (Glasgow, 3rd edn, 1897), p.210.

9. H. Pickering, *Chief Men among the Brethren* (London, 2nd edn, 1931), p. 205

significant presence in several parts of the English-speaking world. Although never becoming a major force in the United States, establishing only some 600 assemblies in that vast land at its apogee,[10] in some other countries it developed a strong local culture. In Australia, where there were some 25,000 Brethren in fellowship in the 1990s, a particular area of concentration lay along the northern coast of Tasmania.[11] In New Zealand, where, out of a much smaller population, there were some 20,000 in fellowship, the city of Auckland, with more than thirty assemblies, was subject to powerful Brethren influence.[12] In Canada there was a considerable presence in parts of Ontario, and in Vancouver there were also over thirty assemblies, some of them large and flourishing.[13] Beyond the English-speaking world, furthermore, there was the missionary dimension of Brethrenism. From 1881 onwards F.S. Arnot pioneered work in a region of central Africa that was to become a Brethren bastion. Others opened up new territories, J.R. Olley making a particular impact on Chad from 1926.[14] Consequently by the 1990s there were much stronger centres of the movement outside the English-speaking world than within it. In that decade Argentina was supposed to possess more than 1,000 congregations, India about 1,300 and, most successful of all, Angola about 2,500.[15] Brethrenism was a vigorous branch of evangelicalism that covered the globe.

What, then, was the place of the Brethren in evangelicalism as a whole? The concentration here is not with the Exclusive sections, the followers of J.N. Darby, nor with other groups that separated from the main Brethren movement such as Needed Truth, even though, as the Churches of God, this is now an international network with a remarkable degree of global co-ordination.[16] Rather the focus is on the Open Brethren, by far the most numerous body. What was their identity? Where did they fit into broader patterns? In trying to explore these questions, evidence can be drawn from many parts of the world.

The analysis can begin with the group closest to the Brethren. Like Brethren, but unlike most other Protestant bodies, they began in the 1830s, possessing no prehistory in the Reformation, its aftermath or the Evangelical Revival of the eighteenth century. This group was the section of Christianity variously called the Churches of Christ, the Disciples of Christ or sometimes simply Christians. Their

---

10. Coad, *History*, p. 192.

11. I. Breward, *A History of the Australian Churches* (St Leonards, NSW, 1993), pp. 223-24; K. Newton, 'The contribution of the Brethren to Australian missionary endeavour', in M. Hutchinson and G. Treloar (eds), *This Gospel shall be Preached: essays on the Australian contribution to world mission* (Sydney, 1998), p. 255.

12. P.J. Lineham, 'Tongues must cease: the Brethren and the charismatic movement in New Zealand', *Christian Brethren Review* 34 (1983), pp. 19, 20.

13. R.K. Burkinshaw, *Pilgrims in Lotus Land: conservative Protestantism in British Columbia, 1917–1981* (Montreal and Kingston, 1995), pp. 38, 217.

14. Coad, *History*, pp. 200-203.

15. Newton, 'Australian missionary endeavour', p. 255.

16. [J.J. Park], *The Churches of God: their origin and development in the 20th century* (Leicester, 1986).

opponents often labelled them Campbellites after their founder, Alexander Campbell, a Presbyterian Seceder from northern Ireland who travelled to America in 1809, was baptized as a believer and joined the Baptists. He gradually developed the idea that it would be possible to achieve a restoration of the early church if only Christians would combine on the basis of the New Testament alone. Merging in the 1830s with the followers of Barton W. Stone, who was less committed to believer's baptism, the Campbellites zealously pursued their undenominational ideal. By 1906 they had attained more than one million members in the United States.[17] In Britain they developed as the Churches of Christ, most of which joined the United Reformed Church in 1981. The movement had never enjoyed as much support in Britain as across the Atlantic, partly because the Brethren made so similar an appeal that they drew off potential recruits. The resemblance between the two groups is evident in an address by David King, the chief British leader of the Churches of Christ between the 1850s and 1886:

> Unite with those who congregate, not as a Church of human origin, bearing a name of man's devise [*sic*], but as a Church of Christ, having no Scriptures but the Bible, no Plan of Salvation but that preached by the Apostles, no Order of Worship but that known to the first Churches, no Government but that instituted by Christ, and no Aristocracy but that of Christian Excellence.[18]

One or two words would have jarred on Brethren ears, especially the use of the word 'church' instead of 'assembly', but the substance of the appeal would have been endorsed by members of the sister movement. When in 1847 Alexander Campbell visited Britain, he remarked that the Brethren were more like his followers than any other group he had encountered in the country.[19] It is worth examining the affinities with care.

The parallels can begin with the common belief of the two movements in primitive Christianity, a restoration of the pattern of the earliest church. Both upheld the view that the New Testament represented a distinct mode of divine–human relations that was still in force. The Campbellites even spoke of 'dispensations', though they usually limited them to only three, the patriarchal, the Jewish and the New Testament. The call in the present dispensation, according to one of their American spokesmen, was 'to come out from all party organisations, to renounce all party names and party tests, and seek only for *Christian* union and fellowship according to apostolic teaching'.[20] They were proud of renouncing theological

---

17. D.E. Harrell, Jr, *The Churches of Christ in the Twentieth Century: Homer Hailey's personal journey of faith* (Tuscaloosa, AL, 2000), p. 5.

18. [L. King,] *Memoir of David King* (n.pl., n.d.), p. 209.

19. L. Billington, 'The Churches of Christ in Britain', in M.W. Casey and D.A. Foster (eds), *The Stone-Campbell Movement: an international religious tradition* (Knoxville, TN, 2002), p. 385.

20. Isaac Errett quoted in W.T. Moore, *The Life of Timothy Coop* (London, 1889), p. 115.

systems for the sake of following scripture only. The Churches of Christ freely referred to all other bodies as 'sects'.[21] In all these ways the Churches of Christ were like Brethren in their assumptions. Crucially, they were identical in the most obvious outward expressions of their faith. Both practised believer's baptism, observed the Lord's supper weekly and rejected the distinction between clergy and laity. To outsiders they seemed very much the same. They even appealed to the same social groups, with the Churches of Christ putting down roots in the coalfields in the late nineteenth century just as the Brethren did in the west of Scotland.[22] The resemblances are striking.

It is not surprising, in view of the affinities, that the trajectory of the two movements shows similarities. Many of the inheritors of the Campbellite legacy prospered in the later nineteenth century, and so wanted to have the advantages enjoyed by members of other denominations. In particular individual congregations began to appoint full-time evangelists who, over time, became virtually indistinguishable from ministers. Simultaneously there was a development of denominational structures such as committees for evangelistic campaigns and legal purposes. The commitment to Christian unity gave the more progressive elements, who in the United States were called Disciples of Christ, a pioneering role in ecumenical endeavours. Their magazine, *The Christian Commonwealth*, turned into the leading American interdenominational periodical of the later twentieth century. On the other hand, some members were more committed to traditional ways, opposing the introduction of pastors, the creation of denominational structures and any compromise of principle. In America the central dividing issue was instrumental worship. The more sophisticated wanted organs; the more traditional insisted on nothing but *a capella* singing, which led to their churches being called the 'Non-Instrumental' Churches of Christ. There was a gradual divergence around the opening of the twentieth century into separate bodies.[23] The process was a virtual anticipation of Brethren developments in the later twentieth century. There were the same tendencies to appoint full-time workers, to develop denominational agencies and to co-operate with other Christians. The consequence for Brethren was a process of polarization that is still incomplete. It paralleled what had happened among the Churches of Christ fifty or a hundred years before.

A further, and highly significant, affinity lies in the area of the attitude to the mind in the two movements. An ambiguity has run through evangelicalism on this subject: knowledge was thought to be a good thing, but knowledge might distract from the best thing, the gospel. The resulting tension was specially acute in smaller religious communities. Among the Churches of Christ it has given rise to what has been called 'cerebral anti-intellectualism'.[24] A suspicion of the mind, expressed particularly in awareness of the risks of education, co-existed with hard thinking

21. D.M. Thompson, *Let Sects and Parties Fall: a short history of the Churches of Christ in Great Britain and Ireland* (Birmingham, 1980), p. 57.

22. Thompson, *Let Sects and Parties Fall*, p. 61.

23. R.T. Hughes, *Reviving the Ancient Faith* (Grand Rapids, MI, 1996).

24. I owe this term to Dr Jerry Rushford of Pepperdine University, California.

about the Bible and its application to life. The same phenomenon is apparent among Brethren. John Douglas (1891–1976), for instance, was a Lanarkshire miner turned tomato-grower who left school at thirteen. He did not, according to his obituarist, 'lean heavily on books', and when, late in life, he acquired a concordance, he found it confusing rather than helpful. But as a young man he had habitually studied the Bible into the early hours with the aid of a paraffin lamp and had gained an enormous memory for scripture, preaching regularly without notes.[25] It has been shown that among Scottish Brethren schoolchildren, the attainments of those from a working-class background were roughly equivalent to the higher achievements of those from middle-class homes in the population at large.[26] Brethrenism cultivated verbal dexterity even while it pointed to the dangers inherent in the life of the mind. That characteristic helps explain the differing experiences of the movement by capable men. Sir Robert Anderson, in charge of the Criminal Investigation Department at Scotland Yard in the last years of the nineteenth century, did not remain in fellowship with Brethren because of their unwillingness to provide intellectual ministry except at the Lord's Table.[27] Conversely F.F. Bruce, Rylands Professor of Biblical Exegesis at the University of Manchester, stayed with the assemblies because 'in these churches I have found an atmosphere of spiritual and intellectual freedom so congenial and indeed exhilarating that I doubt if it could be matched elsewhere'.[28] Brethrenism, like the Churches of Christ, exalted words, but they could either loose or fetter the mind. There was certainly in both movements the phenomenon that the French philosopher Jacques Derrida identifies as logocentricity. The word was central to the experience of adherents.

A consequence of logocentricity in the Churches of Christ was the high salience of its journals. In the conservative branch of the movement during the twentieth century, co-ordination could not be by means of denominational agencies because there were none. Instead it was achieved by magazines. The editors of the journals circulating in the movement were the *de facto* leaders, producing decisive answers in controversies, though often disagreeing with other editors and so provoking further controversies.[29] There was a similar position among Brethren. Thus Donald Ross, a late nineteenth-century itinerant worker, guided the early assemblies of North America through the pages of *The Barley Cake*.[30] Likewise the bond of union of New Zealand Brethren has long been *The Treasury*.[31] But the chief example was *The Witness*, for many years the leading British Brethren journal. In some ways, its editor co-ordinated the global movement. In 1919, *The Witness* enjoyed a worldwide circulation of 20,000 and published articles from abroad such as one by the New

25. J. Anderson (ed.), *They Finished their Course* (Kilmarnock, 1980), pp. 66-67.

26. I.G.D. Ford, 'Religious affiliation and educational achievement: a note on the "Brethren" in the West of Scotland', *Scottish Educational Studies* 3 (1971), pp. 20-24.

27. *W*, 48 (December, 1918), p. 100.

28. F.F. Bruce, 'Why I have stayed with the Brethren', *JCBRF*, 10 (1965), p. 5.

29. Harrell, *Churches of Christ, passim.*

30. C.W. Ross (ed.), *Donald Ross, 1824–1903* (Glasgow, reprint, 1987), p. 205.

31. Lineham, 'Tongues must cease', pp. 10, 27.

Zealand veteran C.H. Hinman.[32] The editor from 1914 to 1940, Henry Pickering, acted as a genial archbishop, kindly but firm. Controversial issues were given a thorough airing in his magazine, with several contributors taking different sides of each debate, but Pickering chose the contributors, selected which of their views to publish and reserved the last word for himself. In November 1919, for example, on the question of whether it was legitimate to use individual cups at the Lord's Supper, five opinions were printed. Three were definitely against; one was middling; and the final statement from the editor was a decisive rejection. This declaration virtually had the force of legislation. The directives were not necessarily wholly restrictive, though they were often hedged about with careful qualifications. Two years later, for instance, on the question of whether sales of work were allowable, the editor summed up as follows:

> If control of such 'work' is in the hands of aged godly sisters, the thing is carried through without ostentation, the garments are those befitting Christian homes, fair business prices are charged so as not to undersell those in the trade (often aged sisters in reduced circumstances), and all is done in happy fellowship with the Assembly, such efforts should be encouraged and prayed for as part of the regular work of God.

It was an exercise in systematic casuistry, but the outcome was definite. No doubt some ignored Pickering's deliverances while others preferred different journals. Here, however, was an approximation to government by the word of a magazine, what might be called 'logocracy'. Just as in the Churches of Christ, so among Brethren the printed word reigned.

The range of similarities between the two movements, however, fell short of identity. Differences between the Churches of Christ and the Brethren did exist and are highly revealing. The most obvious distinction was over the doctrine of baptism. The Campbellites, citing Acts 2.38, insisted that baptism was designed for the remission of sins. The resulting theological position was closer to that of the Anglo-Catholics than to that of the evangelicals. Members of the Churches of Christ agreed with evangelicals that regeneration was independent of baptism, but claimed that divine forgiveness came through believer's baptism.[33] Here was a major doctrinal division from Brethren. There was also a difference in worship. Whereas Brethren allowed any brother to exhort at the breaking of bread, the Churches of Christ condemned the practice as 'Plymouthian leaven'. It was absurd, according to David King, for anybody to judge his own fitness to exhort. To do so constituted a breach of church order, for the task should be undertaken by the elders.[34] In the view of the Churches of Christ, furthermore, the office of evangelist continued in the present and it was legitimate for any holder of the post to be paid a regular salary. It was also right for the churches to co-operate in evangelism and so to hold an

32. *W*, 49 (January, 1919), p. 20; 49 (November 1919), p. 165.

33. As explained by Isaac Errett in Moore, *Coop*, p. 117.

34. [King], *King*, pp. 239-40.

assembly to co-ordinate a strategy for outreach.[35] The two movements differed in practice as well as teaching.

What underlay these divergences was a difference in ecclesiology. King held that the laws of God, found in New Testament precept and example, applied permanently to the churches. Jesus was their 'sovereign', the New Testament their 'statute-book' and the apostles their 'legislature'.[36] Such political categories, however, were entirely alien to the Brethren, who talked instead of a personal gathering to the Lord. The New Testament was certainly to be imitated, but its text was not to be treated as a system of positive law and procedure was not to be regulated by rules. There was, for example, normally no definition of membership in a Brethren assembly, and it was expected that elders would emerge naturally, by doing the work of elders. The assembly was an organic community that would grow under the nurturing influence of the Holy Spirit. For the Churches of Christ, ecclesiology was a question of the execution of the laws of Christ the King; for the Brethren, it was a matter of communal response to Christ the Saviour. The difference betrayed contrasting mentalities. The Churches of Christ overwhelmingly reflected the assumptions of the Enlightenment, but the Brethren predominantly accepted those of Romanticism. Alexander Campbell's thought was moulded by the age of reason, and his followers were tinged with a similar rationalism. Thus King justified the weekly observance of the Lord's supper with the argument that, since Christians commemorate the resurrection fifty-two times a year by special recognition of the first day of the week, 'reason requires' that they should mark his death with the same frequency.[37] The Brethren would never have tried to vindicate the same practice by 'reason'. Again, King held public debates with freethinkers including a celebrated contest with Charles Bradlaugh in 1870.[38] Brethren would never be found debasing the faith by arguing its merits in public. The Churches of Christ, children of the Enlightenment, prized human reason in a way that Brethren did not. There was the fundamental distinction between the two movements.

Brethren arose in an age when the values of Romanticism were spreading through society. At the opening of the nineteenth century, the Romantic movement was the property of cultural pioneers—*littérateurs*, artists, musicians. By the 1830s, the new cultural atmosphere was affecting religious leaders: J.H. Newman, who expressed it through the Oxford Movement; Edward Irving, who embodied it in the Catholic Apostolic Church; and J.N. Darby, whose ideas were so deeply absorbed by the Brethren. Premillennial teaching, shared by Irving and Darby, and at first by Newman, was a leading symptom. The world would not grow better towards a millennium of peace and plenty, as optimistic Christians of the Enlightenment era had supposed, but its wickedness merited the judgements of the Almighty, a thoroughly pessimistic view. It could be rescued only by the supernatural intervention of the imminent second coming, which would precede the

35. Thompson, *Sects and Parties*, pp. 31, 64.

36. [King], *King*, p. 119.

37. [King], *King*, pp. 420-21.

38. [King], *King*, p. 28.

millennium.[39] This was the novel worldview adopted by the Brethren, so that a motif shaped by Romanticism was embodied in the eschatology that marked the movement out from the beginning. Other aspects of Romantic influence were evident in Brethren life. There was a characteristic denigration of reason. Thus Donald Ross, the Scottish and North American evangelist, condemned the tendency to replace the word of God with 'wrecked human reason'.[40] In place of reason there was an emphasis on faith, the undergirding principle of Brethren missionary practice. When F. McLaine, a missionary to Mysore in India, began a church roll there in 1909, he headed it, 'Work commenced in simple faith in the living God, our needs for the work being supplied by His loving hand.'[41] Across the world such faith was often rewarded, as when William Sloan, the first evangelist in the Faroe Islands, had no food in the house, but an unexpected gift arrived from New Zealand.[42] The insistence on faith being antithetical to reason, shared by Brethren with Newman and Irving but not with most evangelicals, expressed itself in many ways. It dictated the rejection of structures of support for mission—societies, committees, organized appeals, collections. It meant that missionary agents were not given directives, but followed their own intuitions of divine guidance. Ross and his colleague in North America, Donald Munro, believed it imperative 'to seek their orders direct from the Master, sometimes only getting instructions for a day at a time'.[43] And the privileging of faith meant that it could not be reduced to rational propositions. Brethren did not set out their beliefs in structured form. Although Methodists often suspected Brethren of being Calvinists, the choice between Arminianism and Calvinism was brusquely dismissed in *The Witness* for 1920: 'The wiser way is to hold all that is taught in Scripture.'[44] Brethren were concerned not with systematic theology but with how to be saved. They were exponents of a Romantic version of the evangelical faith.

There were, accordingly, many other Romantic attitudes among Brethren. One was cultural relativism, the belief that different cultures upheld values which, though contrasting with each other, were equally valid. It led, for example, to the ready willingness of many Brethren missionaries to adopt local customs rather than impose Western manners. Hudson Taylor, the founder of the China Inland Mission, is a good example with his use of Chinese dress.[45] Cultural relativism applied over

---

39. D.W. Bebbington, *Evangelicalism in Modern Britain: A History from the 1730s to the 1980s* (London, 1989), pp. 78-86.

40. Ross (ed.), *Ross*, p. 229.

41. K.J. Newton, *Brethren Missionary Work in Mysore State* (Pinner, Middlesex, 1975), p. 11.

42. F. Kelling, *Fisherman of Faroe: William Gibson Sloan* (Göta, Faroe Islands, 1993), p. 138.

43. J. R[itchie]., *Donald Munro, 1839–1908: A Servant of Jesus Christ* (Glasgow, reprint, 1987), p. 98.

44. *W*, 50 (June, 1920), p. 290 (C. F. Hogg).

45. J. Hudson Taylor, *A Retrospect* (London, 2nd edn, n.d.), p. 57. The idea, however, was suggested to Hudson Taylor by a veteran member of the London Missionary Society.

time as well as over space. The understanding of dispensations drawn from Darby, though never universal among Brethren, undoubtedly predominated until long into the twentieth century. Its central principle was that God deals differently with humanity in different ages. There were practical consequences—for example, the belief that although diversities of tongues existed in the early church, the gift was not to be renewed until after the church was translated to heaven.[46] Hence Brethrenism offered stout resistance to the early stages of classical Pentecostalism. Again, Brethren showed a typical Romantic affection for the past. For Sir Walter Scott, it found expression in the evocation of Scottish history; for Brethren, it led to a fascination with the details of the Jewish Tabernacle. Often Brethren preachers carried models of the Tabernacle about with them, leading an exasperated refugee from the movement in the 1960s to urge that a discourse on the Tabernacle was not the simplest method of evangelism.[47] Furthermore the movement was affected by a Romantic sense that exposure to nature brings wholesome benefits, a central theme of the poet Wordsworth. Among Brethren, it sometimes took the form of the belief that through nature its Creator supplies all the bounty necessary for human health. Naturopaths were common in Brethren circles, one example being Will Miller of Howe Street Assembly, Auckland, in the later twentieth century.[48] Health food shops were a classic Brethren species of business enterprise. A Romantic style of thinking had a variety of outward expressions.

The Romantic affinities of the movement meant that it enjoyed a particular advantage in the era when Western societies were swayed by that cultural mood. In the early years of Brethrenism, the 1830s to the 1850s, it specially attracted those who were disposed to look at the world in Romantic fashion: to admire faith not reason, to be drawn to cultural relativism, to love for the remote past and to appreciation of nature. The young, the educated and the prosperous were disproportionately predisposed to have these tastes. Accordingly it was from these categories that the incipient movement gained many of its adherents. It is remarkable how many of the early leaders were young men: A.N. Groves in his thirties, George Müller, Benjamin Newton and R.C. Chapman in their twenties. Because they often joined young, they frequently spent long years in the movement: Müller until 1898, Newton until 1899 and Chapman until 1902. Many were highly educated. Oxford graduates formed one of the early cores of Brethren; and Samuel Tregelles, one scholarly member of the movement, produced a critical edition of the Greek New Testament in 1857–72 complete with copious patristic citations.[49] A large number enjoyed high status and income. The Hereford assembly, for instance, was said to have numbered in its ranks 'professional men of high standing [and] many first class tradesmen'.[50] Even peers were attracted to the movement: Lord Congleton to its heart

46. *W*, 50 (June 1920), p. 281.

47. E.W. Ives, 'On returning to the Brethren', *JCBRF*, 10 (1965), p. 20.

48. Lineham, 'Tongues must cease', p. 23.

49. D.M. Lewis (ed.), *The Blackwell Dictionary of Evangelical Biography, 1730–1860* (2 vols; Oxford, 1995), II, pp. 1117-18.

50. Pickering, *Chief Men*, p. 139.

and Lord Radstock to its fringe. Early recruits were overwhelmingly drawn from the Church of England, whose members were generally of higher status than Nonconformists. They were therefore more exposed to the rising tide of Romantic cultural influence and conversely less embedded in Enlightenment thinking. Brethrenism, it is true, altered its social appeal around the end of the 1850s. From the revival excitement of 1858 onwards it gathered mass support at humbler levels, among fishermen, miners, even agricultural labourers. By this time, however, Romanticism had spread to a wider public, and the Brethren movement was both agent and expression of this pattern of diffusion in the religious sphere. The process was still continuing in the twentieth century. During the inter-war years, for example, the Pilgrim Preachers spread the gospel in a romantic package. Their meetings concentrated on the premillennial message of 'the Return of the Lord'; they operated on the faith principle; and their very title, 'Pilgrim', drew on Romantic imagery.[51] As Romanticism became part of popular taste, so Brethrenism became part of popular religion. It was an expression of the Christian faith well adapted to its period.

A consequence, however, was that the movement encountered difficulties when the vogue for the Romantic began to fade in society at large. On the one hand, the distinctive features of the particular evangelical style associated with Brethren no longer had a special appeal. Sankey's songs, with their sea imagery and sentimental content, had once made an immense impact, but by the 1960s no longer attracted the young. On the other hand, newer cultural forms started to shape Western society. The rejection of Romanticism was linked with the emergence of what in the early twentieth century was called Expressionism or Modernism, a shift of sensibility that allowed free rein to the subconscious in the wake of Freud and accepted with Nietzsche the arbitrariness of the application of language to things. It was later to merge into Postmodernism, reaching a mass constituency in the 1960s through popular culture. In Christianity, it was associated with the rise of charismatic renewal in that decade, exalting the subconscious and downgrading the word.[52] Brethren could avoid the postmodern in the form of popular culture, but they were forced to encounter it in charismatic renewal. It posed a serious challenge to a logocentric movement. In New Zealand, as Peter Lineham has shown, there was a titanic struggle for the soul of the movement. Able young evangelists moulded by renewal, specially Campbell McAlpine and Arthur Wallis, injected a charismatic stimulant into the bloodstream of the assemblies. Traditionalists, insisting on dispensationalist lines that tongues had ceased, resisted the new style, but at the cost of the loss of roughly ten per cent of the movement.[53] Similar events took place elsewhere, though the confrontation in Britain and some other countries was less contentious. By 1988, eight per cent of Brethren congregations responding to a British survey identified themselves as charismatic, allowing prophecy, healing and

51. *W*, 49 (August, 1919), p. 129.
52. Bebbington, *Evangelicalism*, ch. 7.
53. Lineham, 'Tongues must cease'.

sometimes tongues.[54] Such congregations, though hugely growing, usually lost most Brethren distinctives in the process. In a new era, Brethren did not have the natural fit they had enjoyed in the past.

During the phase when they flourished most readily, the period when the Romantic mood influenced evangelicalism to the greatest extent, Brethren were the most Romantic sector of the broader movement. They pushed the Romantic love of the otherworldly further than others, sometimes becoming distinctly odd. During the Second World War a Scottish member of the Brethren, when challenged by a policeman to say where he was going, answered, 'Broxburn, via Edinburgh, sir, but heaven is my ultimate destination.' Perhaps it is not surprising that he was taken to the police station as a suspected spy. The same man, when asked whether he was in the Forces, replied, 'Well, I prepare men for the air every day and will meet the Lord in the air one day.'[55] Such people lived in an atmosphere where supernatural categories swamped those of the everyday world. Consequently their insistence on evangelical priorities was particularly emphatic. George Brealey, the evangelist of the Blackdown Hills in Devon, announced in his last sermon, 'make much of the Cross, make much of the Blood'.[56] Parallel statements could be found in other evangelical bodies, but it would be harder to discover equivalents for the dictum of a Brethren preacher in Wales, 'You are either going to hell on Welsh religion or to heaven by the blood of Christ.'[57] Equally there was single-mindedness in the quest for conversions. Eminent Brethren were celebrated for their subterfuges in bringing the conversation round to 'spiritual things'. Jimmy Black of Bethesda Hall, Falkirk, would ask in a department store the whereabouts of the free gift department. When the bewildered assistant could not help, Black would reply that he knew the free gift of God, which was everlasting life.[58] The experience of Cicely Middleton, a ten-year-old American girl, in 1905 again illustrates the intensity of the call to conversion. Cicely was deeply troubled when a preacher at the gospel hall declared, 'Those who go out of this meeting unsaved are trampling Jesus under their feet.' Returning home, her father remarked that he wished the Lord would return before morning. Cicely realized in despair that she would not go with him, but her father's only comment was, 'It's your own fault, Cicely', reducing her to tears. Through a talk with her mother, she found eternal life. The shame of excluding Christ and the danger of being left behind are commended by the editor of the account as motives for decision.[59] There was no mincing of words when the aim was the salvation of the lost.

Brethren were also extremists about the third evangelical characteristic, devotion to the Bible. They took up Darby's principle of the literal interpretation of scripture

54. Peter Brierley *et al.* (ed.), *The Christian Brethren as the Nineties Began* (Carlisle, 1993), pp. 50, 59.

55. Anderson (ed.), *They Finished their Course*, pp. 144, 143 (Willie Steedman).

56. Brealey, *'Always Abounding'*, p. 236.

57. Anderson (ed.), *They Finished their Course*, p. 154 (L.H. Tranter).

58. Anderson (ed.), *They Finished their Course*, p. 26.

59. HyP, 'How God saved a little girl', *Shining Path* [1912].

with enthusiasm. It was bound up with the vision of a restored future for Israel after the church age. The prophecies of Israel's future in its own land must be understood in a literal sense. This hermeneutic entailed a strong commitment to a high doctrine of inspiration. Henry Pickering insisted in 1921 that not only every word but also every letter and iota of the Bible was inspired.[60] The result was unremitting Bible study. It was said to have been common for David Craig of the Dundonald Assembly, Belfast, to spend six to eight hours a day in 'the study of the Word'.[61] Biblicism could lead to neglect of other books. When preaching on a mission, George Brealey stayed with a Nonconformist minister who offered him the use of his library. The reply of the Brethren evangelist was that he always carried his library with him, more than sixty books, and he produced his Bible. 'I need', he said, 'to carry no other for my work.'[62] Devotion to the Bible could also lead to strange theological sentiments. In the Christmas issue of an evangelistic monthly for children, there was an article on the incarnation. 'If Jesus Christ had not been born into this world as a man', remarked the author, 'we should not have had the Bible.'[63] The reversal of normal priorities bore witness to the exceptional place of the scriptures in the Brethren worldview.

One consequence of the movement's commitment to the Bible was a stout defence of orthodoxy. Brethren, despite their creedlessness, were not to be diverted into the doctrinal vagueness that affected so many who absorbed Romantic spirituality. When belief in hell was starting to wane among broader evangelicals in the later nineteenth century, Brethren knew where they stood. In 1883 a Faroes convert confided his deepest wish about a friend to his diary: may the Lord 'save him from Eternal Fire'.[64] The break between Lord Radstock and Brethren in the 1880s occurred when he renounced the doctrine of eternal punishment.[65] By the 1920s Alexander Marshall was pointing to this teaching as one of the 'fundamentals' over which Brethren could not compromise.[66] In the previous year Marshall had already voiced in *The Witness* his approval of the rise of Fundamentalism in America.[67] In the 1930s the same journal was carrying a review denouncing evolution as a 'soul-destroying error' and an 'awful delusion of the last days'.[68] Brethrenism produced champions of the Fundamentalist cause in interdenominational circles. In New Zealand, for example, William Pettit of Auckland was in the van of the struggle against the Student Christian Movement that led to the establishment of the Inter-Varsity Fellowship in

60. *W*, 51 (September, 1921), pp. 99-100.

61. Anderson (ed.), *They Finished their Course*, p. 48.

62. Brealey, *'Always Abounding'*, p. 249.

63. J.H., 'The mystery of the incarnation', *Shining Path* [1912]

64. Kelling, *Fisherman of Faroe*, p. 152.

65. [A.] Trotter, *Lord Radstock: an interpretation and a record* (London, n.d. [1914]), p. 101.

66. *W*, 50 (March, 1920), pp. 233-34.

67. *W*, 49 (November, 1919), p. 170.

68. *W*, 67 (March, 1937), p. 64.

the dominion.[69] There could be no doubt about the firmness of the Brethren in maintaining a conservative theological stance.

Another result of solid biblicism was long a rigid attitude to the role of Christian women. They should obey and they should keep silence in church—did not the scriptures say so? Women were encouraged in special ministry, what was called 'Dorcas work', in visiting the sick and shepherding their own sex. Yet, according to Pickering in 1921, there was no question of women 'praying in, preaching to, or conducting mixed meetings (for which there is no warrant in Scripture)'.[70] Women might nevertheless serve as missionaries abroad. They could even initiate whole missions, organizing their male workers and participating fully in their teaching ministry. Thus in Queensland, Australia, Florence Young started a Bible class for the South Sea Islanders on her brothers' sugar plantation. From that effort sprang first the Queensland Kanaka Mission in 1886 and then the South Sea Evangelical Mission to the Solomon Islands in 1904.[71] There were also exceptions to the exclusion of women from ministry at home. In 1965 a small village assembly in England permitted sisters to pray, give out hymns and deliver words of exhortation at the Lord's Table.[72] But the second wave of feminism that was then beginning to sweep over the Western world was hard for most Brethren to accommodate. The first formal disownment among New Zealand Brethren during the charismatic controversy came in 1965 because an Auckland assembly allowed women to participate in prophecy.[73] The issue became highly divisive in England. There in 1978 still fifty-nine per cent of surveyed assemblies believed that it was wrong for women to pray audibly in meetings.[74] It was a prohibition that drove many out of Brethrenism altogether. Yet gradually, with more nuanced biblical interpretation, inhibitions were eroded. By the 1990s Counties, the home mission agency supported by Brethren, began to appoint female evangelists.[75] But to the more traditional, this was the question on which the progressives were most clearly abandoning the teaching of scripture. The deep attachment to the Bible of the movement had major consequences.

So did the Brethren commitment to the final evangelical characteristic, activism. 'Himself an active man', it was said of Donald Ross in North America, 'he could not bear to see others who were professedly devoting their time to the Lord's service

---

69. Lineham, 'Tongues must cease', p. 20.

70. *W*, 51 (March, 1921), p. 35.

71. Gordon Griffiths, 'A home grown Australian mission: the formation of the Queensland Kanaka Mission/South Seas Evangelical Mission', in Hutchinson and Treloar (eds)., *This Gospel shall be Preached*, pp. 86-97.

72. Anonymous, 'On returning to the Brethren', *JCBRF*, 10 (1965), p. 22.

73. Lineham, 'Tongues must cease', p. 37.

74. G. Brown and B. Mills, *'The Brethren' Today: a factual survey* (Exeter, 1980), p. 48.

75. B. Mills, *A Story to Tell: evangelism in the twentieth century* (Carlisle, 1999), p. 50.

idle.'[76] Mission was ever a priority. In 1970 the prayer guide of *Echoes of Service*, the Brethren missionary journal, covered 1,120 missionaries, chiefly from English-speaking countries—and that high number excluded those serving with interdenominational societies.[77] It is clear that Brethren played a much larger part in overseas missions than their numbers might suggest. For Australia, figures have been calculated for the proportion of the committed members of the various denominations who were missionaries. Of Wesleyans, there was 1 in 600; for the Church of England, 1 in 400; for the Brethren, 1 in 110.[78] Although there was much involvement in medical and educational ventures, spreading the gospel always caught the imagination most. The primary task, according to Frederick Woods, an Australian full-time worker, in 1932, was 'not to educate or civilize, but to evangelize'.[79] From Groves onwards, Brethren pioneered new areas, the 'regions beyond'. Because they were light on institutional apparatus, they could go where others could not. The considerable impact on Slovakia, for example, was largely the result of the ministry of Fred Butcher and his wife in Bratislava from 1900.[80] For them it was a distinct advantage not to possess a denominational affiliation that could have aroused the suspicions of the authorities. And Brethren were often willing to experiment with new techniques. Thus Ron Russell, a young man who had sailed single-handed from England to New Zealand, invented a fresh missionary method that suited his gifts. From 1969 he travelled the Pacific in a boat called *Dayspring* and its successors distributing Bibles and Christian literature round the islands.[81] The anti-institutional trait so marked among Brethren allowed particular scope for innovation in mission.

The logocentric character of the movement meant that the distribution of literature by *Dayspring* was a typical expression of their activism. Many other efforts concentrated on publications. Tracts were essential equipment for the Christian worker. Thus in the nineteenth century Henry Bewley of Dublin is believed to have paid for between four and five million tracts printed in English, French, Italian, Spanish, German and other languages.[82] Publication could become a large-scale operation. Alfred and Walter Redwood opened a bookshop in Mysore in 1926, soon adding a printing press. By 1938 the venture had thirty employees, published in six languages and issued two magazines in English and two in the local language.[83] Brethren were even more active in distribution than in production. Bible depots run by members of the movement became standard features of towns in the English-

76. Ross (ed.)., *Ross*, p. 213.

77. Newton, *Missionary Work in Mysore*, p. 10.

78. S. Piggin, 'Introduction: the reflex impact of missions on Australian Christianity', in Hutchinson and Treloar (eds)., *This Gospel shall be Preached*, p. 10.

79. Newton, 'Australian missionary endeavour', p. 259.

80. Coad, *History*, p. 195.

81. P.J. Lineham, *Bible & Society: a sesquicentennial history of the Bible Society in New Zealand* (Wellington, 1996), p. 237.

82. Pickering, *Chief Men*, p. 146.

83. Newton, *Missionary Work in Mysore,* p. 32.

speaking world. A successful businessman might see this field as his special evangelistic opportunity. C.J. Morris of Gisborne in New Zealand, for example, operated a bookroom alongside his department store.[84] Colporteurs took the literature out to those who would not buy for themselves. In the Faroes, for instance, D.J. Danielson hawked Bibles and Testaments around the islands at the opening of the twentieth century.[85] In England at the same time Counties evangelism started with the use of horse-drawn Bible carriages and the practice was soon imitated in New Zealand.[86] Nor has the focus on literature disappeared in more recent years. In 1966, for example, Colin Tilsley sent out teams to distribute Christian publications, launching Literature Crusades Australia, a body that turned into a worldwide venture as Gospel Literature Outreach, or GLO for short.[87] Literature evangelism was the way in which the twin Brethren loves of activism and words could be wedded together. Here was another way in which Brethren assumed the role of quintessential evangelicals, often at the cutting edge of the broader movement.

If the Brethren were particularly intense evangelicals, they also showed signs of a form of intensity particularly prevalent in the age of Romanticism. Evangelicals always had a tendency to shun the world as a dangerous threat to spirituality, but the Romantic temper reinforced it. Romantic thought included a motif of withdrawal from the world, an almost eremitical rejection of the values of the day. Brethren displayed this characteristic in many striking ways. John Ritchie of Kilmarnock in Scotland, the editor of *The Believer's Magazine*, once eulogized 'the separation of God's people from the world, alike its sin and pleasures, its politics and religion'. The most remarkable feature on this list is the last item: Brethren, unlike most other evangelicals, saw much religion as worldly. Hence members of the assemblies, or at least those on their more rigid side, were actually hostile to Christian denominations. Thus Ritchie considered the argument that in the absence of an assembly, a brother might 'go in' with the next best thing, 'say a well-favoured Baptist Church'.[88] Should he? The answer was a resounding no. The principle of separation must be observed in its purity.

Likewise in the political sphere Brethren could foster extreme attitudes. *The Witness* decided in 1920 that political participation to the extent of casting a ballot in favour of the prohibition of alcohol was legitimate, but some contributors to the debate thought that was going too far. The only divine method of engaging with social problems, one of them claimed, was the saving of individual souls. 'Society is not to be improved', he contended, 'but left alone.'[89] Around the same time trade unions, the Co-operative Movement and the League of Nations all came in for censure as ways of compromising with the world. A striking expression of the same impulse was conscientious objection—a minority position, but a sizable one. The

---

84. Lineham, *Bible & Society*, p. 193.
85. Kelling, *Fisherman of Faroe*, p. 185.
86. Mills, *Story to Tell,* p. 16. Lineham, *Bible & Society*, p. 90.
87. Newton, 'Australian missionary endeavour', p. 261.
88. R[itchie]., *Munro*, pp. 76, 80.
89. *W*, 50 (September, 1920), p. 325 (Handley Bird).

believer, according to the conscientious objector, was a citizen not of the warring states on earth but of the heavenly city above. This was the view expounded by Hunter Beattie, in fellowship at a Glasgow assembly during the First World War, who wrote a book on *The Christian and War.* He gave a lively account of the trial of Paul Heavenlyman before the tribunal in Twomasters City in the County of Bothworlds.[90] Official figures suggest that in Britain during the First World War Brethren contributed the second largest group of conscientious objectors of any religious body, well behind the Christadelphians, but, remarkably, just ahead of the Quakers.[91] It is a good instance of the desire of many Brethren to avoid any contamination by public affairs.

Their zeal to avoid compromise was evident in many other social attitudes. Worldliness was sniffed out with greater diligence than by most other evangelicals. The present style of female dress, according to a correspondent of *The Witness* in 1919, exposing the bosom and permitting short sleeves, was tempting the devil.[92] Later in the century Harry Bell, a Northumberland full-time worker, was willing to take 'a strong line' about women's hair from the platform.[93] Even the coronation of 1937 was a doubtful affair. There were clear pitfalls, according to Pickering, attaching to involvement in local celebrations. 'When a child of God brings himself into active friendship with unbelievers', he explained, 'it has a hurtful effect upon his spiritual life, and that is when he needs to exercise care.'[94] Football was a particularly serious snare because it united the saved and the unsaved in a single team. Although the game was first introduced into the Faroes when the son of William Sloan arranged a match between islanders and sailors from visiting British battleships,[95] in general football was highly suspect. It might be useful as an inducement for bringing young people together for Bible study, but, as a medical correspondent of *The Witness* once explained, there were preferable alternatives for healthy outdoor exercise in walking or cycling—and the latter had the advantage that it 'enables one to travel greater distances, visit out-of-the-way places, and distribute tracts'.[96] The shunning of worldliness, in whatever form, could generate a certain naivety. After speaking in Lancashire, Harry Bell was told by an excited brother that he had just shaken hands with the mother of Arthur Askey. Which meeting, asked Bell, was the dear brother in?[97] He had evidently never heard of the famous comedian. Detachedness from the world was taken to extreme lengths.

Because it adhered to its own standards so fiercely, Brethrenism was well placed to act as a ginger group in the evangelical world. Over the years it made many

---

90. Hunter Beattie, *The Christian and War* (Glasgow, n.d.), pp. 45-65.

91. J. Rae, *Conscience and Politics: the British government and the conscientious objector to military service, 1916–1919* (London, 1970), p. 250.

92. *W*, 49 (June, 1919), p. 94 (Alfred Page).

93. Anderson (ed.), *They Finished their Course*, p. 20 (Harry Bell).

94. *W*, 67 (February, 1937), p. 39.

95. Kelling, *Fisherman of Faroe*, pp. 136-37.

96. *W*, 52 (July, 1922), p. 227 (E.T. Roberts).

97. Anderson (ed.), *They Finished their Course*, p. 21.

contributions to wider circles. One celebrated invention transmitted to other evangelicals was the Bible reading. Brethren developed the expository technique of choosing a theme from the Bible and exploring as many instances as possible in what Brealey called 'chains of golden texts'.[98] The young Brethren evangelist Henry Moorhouse, on a visit to Chicago in 1868, instructed D.L. Moody in the method, and in turn Moody disseminated it to other evangelicals.[99] An even greater contribution was the idea of faith missions. Hudson Taylor's China Inland Mission, starting in 1865, inaugurated the use of living by faith as the fundamental principle of a whole missionary organization. The example was followed by many other interdenominational bodies—including the Regions Beyond Missionary Union (organized as such in 1900), the Sudan Interior Mission (1900), the Sudan United Mission (1904), the Worldwide Evangelisation Crusade (1913) and even the Christian and Missionary Alliance (1887), which turned itself into a denomination at home in North America.[100] Another Brethren principle that spread widely was dispensationalism—if a scheme elaborated by Darby can be treated as belonging in part to Open Brethren. It was chiefly from Darby that dispensationalism was injected into North America, where it was to become much more influential than in Britain, but Open Brethren had a share in its diffusion. R.C. Morgan, the proprietor of the British interdenominational evangelical weekly *The Christian*, cautiously declared in favour of 'dispensational truth' in 1892, and thereafter the journal did much to bring it to the attention of a wider constituency.[101] Perhaps, however, the greatest Brethren gift of all to broader Christian circles was personnel. The transition to the Baptist ministry, in particular, was an easy one for those who wanted to take up the full-time local service that was long impossible among Brethren. Virtually no sacrifice of principle seemed to be necessary. Thus Harry Young, well known during the 1930s in Cumberland as a Brethren 'Boy Evangelist', eventually became minister of Kingston Baptist Church in Surrey from 1970 to 1987.[102] Likewise women frustrated by the lack of opportunity among Brethren often found service elsewhere. A significant number, such as Jean Coggan in the Church of England and Ruth Beasley-Murray among the Baptists, became dedicated minister's wives. Brethren were generous in what they gave to the wider church.

Many Brethren, however, contributed their time and substance to interdenominational agencies while remaining in their own body. Because they had no minister to pay in the local assembly, it may well be that they could afford to be larger donors to co-operative ventures. Certainly the lack of denominational structures meant that those Brethren who gravitated beyond their locality to a wider stage usually did so through interdenominational channels. Tensions inevitably arose from time to time. In 1944 a reference to the Apocrypha in the New Zealand Bible

98. Brealey, *'Always Abounding'*, p. 250.

99. J. Macpherson, *Henry Moorhouse: the English evangelist* (London, n.d.), pp. 66, 90.

100. K. Fiedler, *The Story of Faith Missions* (Oxford, 1994).

101. *Christian*, 21 July 1892, p. 8.

102. *The Times*, 12 May 2003, p. 24.

Society magazine, for example, induced Brethren supporters to withhold their donations.[103] In general, however, members of the assemblies worked smoothly with other Christians. Their Bible-centred teaching meant that Bible Societies and Scripture Union, the agency designed to encourage Bible study among children, often received their enthusiastic backing. Equally Brethren were prominent supporters of colleges for training Bible teachers and evangelists. The first superintendent of the Bible Training Institute in Auckland, C.J. Rolls, was a Brethren missionary; the Melbourne Bible Institute met during the interwar years in the home of a Brethren couple; and London Bible College depended for its existence on the princely largesse of John Laing, the Brethren housing developer.[104] Regent College, Vancouver, originally conceived as a training school for assembly leaders, was eventually established in 1968 as a 'transdenominational' institution with the doctrinal statement of the World Evangelical Fellowship.[105] Similarly, evangelistic activities in themselves were an interdenominational outlet for Brethren energies. In British Columbia, for instance, members of assemblies backed joint campaigns and participated after the Second World War in the 'Born Again Business Network'.[106] They were specially prominent in agencies targeting young people—Open Air Campaigners in New Zealand, an organization promoting apologetic lectures on Christianity and science in Canada, Crusaders in England and the Inter-Varsity Fellowship throughout the world.[107] Brethren may have held strong reservations about the ecumenical movement for most of the twentieth century, but their part in interdenominational activities that were distinctively evangelical was second to none.

The overall conclusion must be to highlight the evangelical character of the Brethren movement. Members of the assemblies proclaimed a gospel of salvation achieved on the cross, known through the Bible, accepted in conversion and spread by ceaseless activity. Inevitably, with that impetus behind them, they turned into a global movement. Their specific character was very similar to that of the Churches of Christ, who endorsed much the same form of logocentricity. In particular they followed a similar trajectory, tending to divide over time into more and less sectarian groups. Yet Brethren were very different from their closest neighbours because they were wary of applying reason to religious issues, preferring an exclusive exaltation of faith. Brethren were predominantly Romantic in their outlook, prospering as the

103. Lineham, *Bible & Society*, p. 193.

104. Lineham, 'Tongues must cease', p. 11. D. Paproth, 'The Melbourne Bible Institute: its genesis, ethos and purpose', in G.R. Treloar (ed.), *The 'Furtherance of Religious Beliefs': essays on the history of theological education in Australia* (Sydney, 1997), p. 144. I. Randall, *Educating Evangelicalism: the origins, development and impact of London Bible College* (Carlisle, 2000), p. 20.

105. J.G. Stackhouse, Jr, *Canadian Evangelicalism in the Twentieth Century: an introduction to its character* (Toronto, 1993), ch. 11.

106. Burkinshaw, *Pilgrims in Lotus Land*, pp. 217, 241.

107. Lineham, 'Tongues must cease', p. 24. Stackhouse, *Canadian Evangelicalism*, p. 116. *The Story of the Crusaders' Union: these fifty years, 1906–1956* (n.p., n.d.), e.g., p. 21; (e.g.) Burkinshaw, *Pilgrims in Lotus Land*, p. 218.

Romantic mood advanced in the country but facing greater challenges when Western society in general, and the young in particular, began to slip their Romantic moorings. Brethren approximated to the ideal type of Romantic evangelicals—radical, intense, quixotic. Consequently they pressed their views to stronger conclusions than others over the Bible, mission and the rejection of the world. Through the ideas they transmitted to others and through personnel, both those who departed from the movement and those who stayed, they made a huge contribution to the wider evangelical movement. Over the whole world, but especially in a particular era, Brethren played a distinctive role as evangelicals of the evangelicals.

Select Bibliography of the Writings of Harold H. Rowdon

Tim Grass and Graham Johnson

1960

Puritan Church Discipline: a critical analysis and evaluation (Annual Public Lecture of the London Bible College; London: London Bible College, 1960)

1962

'A nineteenth century Nestorius', *Vox Evangelica*, 1 (1962), pp. 60-75

1964

'The congregational view of the church as seen in the writings of Thomas Goodwin', *Christian Graduate*, 17.4 (December, 1964), pp. 13-17

'Disunity, denominationalism and the Brethren', in Anon. (ed.), *Christian Unity: Papers given at a conference of Brethren at Swanwick, Derbyshire, in June, 1964* (Bristol: Evangelical Christian Literature, [1964]), pp. 12-21

'Secession from the Established Church in the early nineteenth century', *Vox Evangelica*, 3 (1964), pp. 76-88

1966

'Unity in the light', *The Witness*, 96 (July–December, 1966), pp. 247-49, 294-96, 336-38, 366-68, 413-14, 450-52

1967

'The early Brethren and the ministry of the word', *Journal of the Christian Brethren Research Fellowship*, 14 (January, 1967), pp. 11-24

'Edinburgh 1910, evangelicals and the ecumenical movement', *Vox Evangelica*, 5 (1967), pp. 49-71

The Origins of the Brethren 1825–1850 (London: Pickering & Inglis, 1967)

1968

London Bible College: the first twenty-five years (Worthing: Henry E. Walter, 1968)

1969

'The historical and political Background to the New Testament'; 'The religious background of the New Testament (pagan)', in G.C.D. Howley (ed.), *A New Testament Commentary* (London: Pickering and Inglis, 1969), pp. 57-66, 67-72

'Preaching—introduction', *Journal of the Christian Brethren Research Fellowship*, 20 (July, 1969), pp. 2-4

1971

'Theological education in historical perspective', *Vox Evangelica*, 7 (1971), pp. 75-87

1972

'A fellowship of minds', *The Witness*, 102 (October, 1972), pp. 369-71

'Law and grace' in *Bible characters and doctrines [Vol. 6]* (London: Scripture Union, 1972); reprinted separately as *Law and Love* (Understanding Bible Teaching; London: Scripture Union, 1978)

1973

'Evangelism in the early church and today', *The Witness*, 103 (June–October, 1973), pp. 213-15, 260-61, 266, 283-85, 338-41, 376-78, 387

'Unity on the basis of the common life in Christ', *Journal of the Christian Brethren Research Fellowship*, 25 (September, 1973), pp. 32-33

'Pilate'; 'Roman Soldiers in the New Testament', in David and Pat Alexander (eds), *The Lion Handbook to the Bible* (Berkhamsted, Herts: Lion, 1973)

1974

'Abernethy, John (1680–1740)'; 'Adalbert of Bremen (c.1000–1072)'; 'Adamites', 'Admonition to Parliament (1572)'; 'Adoptianism'; 'Adrian I (d.795)'; 'Adrian IV (Nicholas Breakspear) (c.1100–1159)'; 'Adrian VI (1459–1523)'; 'Agapemonism', 'Alban (latter third century?)'; 'Alexander V (c.1339–1410)'; 'Antichrist'; 'Anti-Semitism'; 'Bale, John (1495–1563)'; 'Barclay, John (1734–1798)'; 'Barrow, Isaac (1630–1677)'; 'Bereans'; 'Bible Christians'; Coke, Thomas (1747–1814)'; 'Coverdale, Miles (1488–1569)'; 'Elipandus (c.718–802)'; 'Nicholson, William Patteson (1876–1959)', in J.D. Douglas (ed.), *The New International Dictionary of the Christian Church* (Grand Rapids, MI: Zondervan, 1974)

1975

'Ethics of Jesus', in Merrill C. Tenney (ed.), *Zondervan Pictorial Encyclopedia of the Bible* (Grand Rapids, MI: Zondervan, 1975)

1977

'The Brethren'; 'Hudson Taylor', in Tim Dowley (ed.), *A Lion Handbook: the History of Christianity* (Tring, Herts: Lion, 1977)

1979

'The early Brethren and baptism', *Vox Evangelica*, 11 (1979), pp. 55-64

'The interpretation of the Old Testament', in G.C.D. Howley (ed.), *A Bible Commentary for Today* (London: Pickering and Inglis, 1979)

1980

'Co-operate—or Perish', *The Harvester*, 59 (July, 1980), pp. 195-99

1982

'Donald Guthrie: an appreciation', in Harold H. Rowdon (ed.), *Christ the Lord: studies in Christology presented to Donald Guthrie* (Leicester: Inter-Varsity Press, 1982), pp. ix-xi

Turning the Church Inside Out ([London]: BMMF International, 1982)

1984

'Amalgamate or stagnate: second thoughts on the problems of small churches', *Harvester*, 63 (September, 1984), pp. 14-16

1985

'Brethren in North America', *CBRF Newsletter*, n.s. 5 (July, 1985), pp. 8-10

'Preface'; 'The Way Ahead [in World *Mission*]', *Christian Brethren Review* 36 (September, 1985), pp. 7-9, 59-68

'Albert Swift: a social gospeller at Westminster Chapel?', *Vox Evangelica*, 15 (1985), pp. 111-39

1986

'The historical perspective [on full-time ministry]', *Christian Brethren Review*, 37 (April, 1986), pp. 37-47

Who are the Brethren and does it matter? (Exeter: Paternoster on behalf of Christian Brethren Research Fellowship, 1986; first published as a series of articles in *Harvester*, 64 [1985], April, pp. 4-6; May, pp. 8-10; June, pp. 4-5, 7; July, pp. 4-5, 8)

1987

'Is the Brethren movement being reborn?', *Harvester*, 66 (March, 1987), pp. 1-2

1988

'Have the Brethren grown away from their roots?', *Harvester*, 67 (1988), July, p. 7; August, pp. 12-13; September, pp. 13-14

'Darby, John Nelson'; 'Dispensational Theology', in Sinclair B. Ferguson et al. (eds), *New Dictionary of Theology* (Leicester and Downers Grove, IL: IVP, 1988)

'The problem of Brethren identity in historical perspective', in Lorenzo Giorgi and Massimo Rubboli (eds), *Piero Guicciardini 1808–1886. Un Riformatore Religioso nell'europa dell'ottocento* (Firenze: Leo S. Olschki Editore, 1988), pp. 159-74

1989

'Holistic mission', *Christian Brethren Review*, 40 (1989), pp. 32-40

1990

'The Brethren concept of sainthood', *Vox Evangelica*, 20 (1990), pp. 91-107

'Church membership', *Aware/Harvester*, 69 (1990), August, pp. 10-11; September, pp. 10-11

'Hard questions. Church discipline: Is it necessary and does it work?', *Harvester/Aware*, 69 (April, 1990), pp .6-7

'Hard questions. Church membership: leaving and staying', *Harvester*, 69 (January, 1990), pp. 4-5

1991

'Elders and deacons', *Aware*, 70 (1991), May, pp. 12-13; June, pp. 12-13

Contributions to *New 20th Century Encyclopedia of Religious Knowledge* (Grand Rapids, MI: Baker, 1991)

1993

(with Peter Brierley et al.) *Christian Brethren as the Nineties Began* (Carlisle: Paternoster for Partnership in association with MARC Europe, 1993)

'Concentric circles', *Partnership Newsletter*, n.s. 3 (Autumn, 1993), pp. 5-7

'Nicholson, William Patteson', in Nigel M. de S. Cameron (ed.), *Dictionary of Scottish Church History and Theology* (Edinburgh: T&T Clark, 1993)

'The post-war background to Nantwich 1991', in Harold H. Rowdon (ed.), *The Strengthening, Growth and Planting of Local Churches* (Carlisle: Paternoster for Partnership, 1993), pp. 127-41

'Towards new structures for world mission', in V.B. Cole, R.F. Gaskin, and R.J. Sim (eds) *Perspectives on Leadership Training* (Nairobi: Nairobi Evangelical School of Theology, 1993)

'What is going on?', *Partnership Newsletter*, n.s. 3 (Autumn, 1993), pp. 9-11

1994

'The Brethren contribution to world mission', in Harold H. Rowdon (ed.), *The Brethren Contribution to the Worldwide Mission of the Church: International Brethren Conference on Missions held at the Anglo–Chinese School, Singapore, 9-15 June 1993* (Carlisle: Paternoster for Partnership, 1994), pp. 37-46

Contributions to John D. Woodbridge (ed.), *Ambassadors for Christ* (Chicago, IL: Moody Press, 1994)

(edited) *Churches in Partnership for Strengthening and Growth: papers from the Partnership Consultation held at the University of Warwick, 10-12 July 1993* (Carlisle: Paternoster for Partnership, 1994)

1995

'Bellett, J(ohn) G(ifford)'; 'Brealey, George'; 'Chapman, Robert (Cleaver)'; 'Code, J(ohn) M(arsden)'; 'Congleton, (Second) Lord [Parnell, John (Vesey)'; 'Craik, Henry'; 'Cronin, Edward'; 'Dorman, William Henry'; 'Hall, (Captain) Percy (Francis)'; 'Hargrove, Charles (Frearson); 'Paget, Elizabeth [Bessie]'; 'Radcliffe, Reginald'; 'Tiptaft, William'; (with Timothy C.F. Stunt) 'Harris, James (Lampen)'; in Donald M. Lewis (ed.), *The Blackwell Dictionary of Evangelical Biography 1730–1860* (2 vols; Oxford: Blackwell, 1995)

'The church and the churches', *International Newsletter*, 6 (August, 1995), pp. 5-7

'The concept of living by faith', in Anthony Billington, Tony Lane and Max Turner (eds), *Mission and Meaning: essays presented to Peter Cotterell*, (Carlisle: Paternoster, 1995), pp. 339-56

'Getting the gospel across', *Partnership Perspectives*, [1] (November, 1995), pp. 6-7

1996

(edited, with Steve Brady), *For Such a Time as This: perspectives on evangelicalism, past, present and future* (London: Scripture Union, 1996)

1997

'Are all the New Testament gifts still given today?', *Partnership Perspectives*, 4 (January, 1997), pp. 6-8

'Historical reflections on community involvement', *Partnership Perspectives*, 6 (October, 1997), pp. 7-9

'Orientation to the Brethren scene', in Alan Batchelor (intro.), *Don't Muzzle the Ox* (London: Paternoster, 1997), pp. 78-95

'Reflections on the Toronto Blessing', *Partnership Perspectives*, 4 (January, 1997), pp. 13-16

1998

'Beyond mission', *Partnership Perspectives*, 8 (April, 1998), pp. 15-17

'Does it work? [Focus on Children]', *Partnership Perspectives*, 7 (January, 1998), pp. 15-17

'Groves, A(nthony) N(orris)'; 'Kitto, John'; Müller, George'; 'Trenchard, E(rnest) H(enry)', in Gerald H. Anderson (ed.), *Biographical Dictionary of Christian Missions* (Grand Rapids, MI and Cambridge: Eerdmans, 1998)

(edited), *Declare His Glory: congregational worship today* (Carlisle: Paternoster Periodicals for Partnership, 1998) (edited), *Revival in our churches? Report of the Partnership Consultation held at The Hayes, Swanwick, 25-28 September 1998* ([n.pl.: Partnership, 1998])

1999

'Interdependence in action', *International Partnership Perspectives*, 1 (1999), pp. 8-12

'Leadership structures in the New Testament', *Partnership Perspectives*, 12 (October, 1999), pp. 8-9

'Presenting the gospel', *Partnership Perspectives*, 11 (April, 1999), pp. 5-7

'What does it mean?', *Partnership Perspectives*, 10 (January, 1999), pp. 14-15, 18-19, 21-23, 25-26

(edited), *Ten Changing Churches* (Carlisle: Paternoster Periodicals for Partnership, 1999)

2000

'Darby, John Nelson', in Trevor A. Hart (ed.), *Dictionary of Historical Theology* (Carlisle: Paternoster, 2000)

(edited), *Partnership Directory No. 2* (Carlisle: Partnership, 2000)

2002

'Leadership structures', in Harold Rowdon (ed.), *Church Leaders Handbook* (Carlisle: Paternoster Publishing for Partnership, 2002), pp. 2-9

'Local churches', *International Partnership Perspectives*, 4 (2002), pp. 3-7

2003

'Culture and church', *Partnership Perspectives*, 23 (April, 2003), pp. 19-21

'Kirby, Gilbert', in Timothy Larsen (ed.), *Biographical Dictionary of Evangelicals* (Leicester and Downers Grove, IL: Inter-Varsity Press, 2003)

(edited), *Country Reports on the Work of Brethren Churches ... For the International Brethren Conference on Mission 3, held at Selimbar, Romania, 2-7 July 2003* (n.pl.: [Partnership, 2003])

(edited), *Partnership Directory No. 3* (Carlisle: Partnership, 2003)

2004

'Gosse, [*née Bowes*], Emily'; 'Kelly, William'; 'Soltau, Henrietta Eliza'; 'Waldegrave, Granville Augustus William', in H.C.G. Matthew and Brian Harrison (eds), *The Oxford Dictionary of National Biography* (Oxford: Oxford University Press, 2004)

2005

'A review article: reflections on *From Awakening to Secession* by Timothy C.F. Stunt', *Brethren Archivists and Historians Network Review*, 3 (2004–05), pp. 109-14.

2006

'Introduction', in Harold H. Rowdon (ed.), *Serving God's People: re-thinking Christian ministry today* (Milton Keynes: Paternoster, 2006), pp. xiii-xiv

Editorships

Christian Brethren Review (1983–90)
International Newsletter, later *International Partnership Perspectives*, then *International Perspectives* (1990 to date)
Partnership Newsletter, later *Partnership Perspectives* (1991 to date)
Vox Evangelica (1981–91)

General Index

Studies in Evangelical History and Thought

(All titles uniform with this volume)
Dates in bold are of projected publication

Andrew Atherstone
Oxford's Protestant Spy
The Controversial Career of Charles Golightly

Charles Golightly (1807–85) was a notorious Protestant polemicist. His life was dedicated to resisting the spread of ritualism and liberalism within the Church of England and the University of Oxford. For half a century he led many memorable campaigns, such as building a martyr's memorial and attempting to close a theological college. John Henry Newman, Samuel Wilberforce and Benjamin Jowett were among his adversaries. This is the first study of Golightly's controversial career.

***2006** / 1-84227-364-7 / approx. 324pp*

Clyde Binfield
Victorian Nonconformity in Eastern England

Studies of Victorian religion and society often concentrate on cities, suburbs, and industrialisation. This study provides a contrast. Victorian Eastern England—Essex, Suffolk, Norfolk, Cambridgeshire, and Huntingdonshire—was rural, traditional, relatively unchanging. That is nonetheless a caricature which discounts the industry in Norwich and Ipswich (as well as in Haverhill, Stowmarket and Leiston) and ignores the impact of London on Essex, of railways throughout the region, and of an ancient but changing university (Cambridge) on the county town which housed it. It also entirely ignores the political implications of such changes in a region noted for the variety of its religious Dissent since the seventeenth century. This book explores Victorian Eastern England and its Nonconformity. It brings to a wider readership a pioneering thesis which has made a major contribution to a fresh evolution of English religion and society.

***2006** / 1-84227-216-0 / approx. 274pp*

John Brencher
Martyn Lloyd-Jones (1899–1981) and Twentieth-Century Evangelicalism

This study critically demonstrates the significance of the life and ministry of Martyn Lloyd-Jones for post-war British evangelicalism and demonstrates that his preaching was his greatest influence on twentieth-century Christianity. The factors which shaped his view of the church are examined, as is the way his reformed evangelicalism led to a separatist ecclesiology which divided evangelicals.

2002 / 1-84227-051-6 / xvi + 268pp

July 2005

Jonathan D. Burnham

A Story of Conflict

The Controversial Relationship between Benjamin Wills Newton and John Nelson Darby

Burnham explores the controversial relationship between the two principal leaders of the early Brethren movement. In many ways Newton and Darby were products of their times, and this study of their relationship provides insight not only into the dynamics of early Brethrenism, but also into the progress of nineteenth-century English and Irish evangelicalism.

2004 / 1-84227-191-1 / xxiv + 268pp

Grayson Carter

Anglican Evangelicals

Protestant Secessions from the Via Media, c.*1800–1850*

This study examines, within a chronological framework, the major themes and personalities which influenced the outbreak of a number of Evangelical clerical and lay secessions from the Church of England and Ireland during the first half of the nineteenth century. Though the number of secessions was relatively small—between a hundred and two hundred of the 'Gospel' clergy abandoned the Church during this period—their influence was considerable, especially in highlighting in embarrassing fashion the tensions between the evangelical conversionist imperative and the principles of a national religious establishment. Moreover, through much of this period there remained, just beneath the surface, the potential threat of a large Evangelical disruption similar to that which occurred in Scotland in 1843. Consequently, these secessions provoked great consternation within the Church and within Evangelicalism itself, they contributed to the outbreak of millennial speculation following the 'constitutional revolution' of 1828–32, they led to the formation of several new denominations, and they sparked off a major Church–State crisis over the legal right of a clergyman to secede and begin a new ministry within Protestant Dissent.

2007 *1-84227-401-5 / xvi + 470pp*

J.N. Ian Dickson

Beyond Religious Discourse

Sermons, Preaching and Evangelical Protestants in Nineteenth-Century Irish Society

Drawing extensively on primary sources, this pioneer work in modern religious history explores the training of preachers, the construction of sermons and how Irish evangelicalism and the wider movement in Great Britain and the United States shaped the preaching event. Evangelical preaching and politics, sectarianism, denominations, education, class, social reform, gender, and revival are examined to advance the argument that evangelical sermons and preaching went significantly beyond religious discourse. The result is a book for those with interests in Irish history, culture and belief, popular religion and society, evangelicalism, preaching and communication.

***2005** / 1-84227-217-9 / approx. 324pp*

Neil T.R. Dickson

Brethren in Scotland 1838–2000

A Social Study of an Evangelical Movement

The Brethren were remarkably pervasive throughout Scottish society. This study of the Open Brethren in Scotland places them in their social context and examines their growth, development and relationship to society.

2003 / 1-84227-113-X / xxviii + 510pp

Crawford Gribben and Timothy C.F. Stunt (eds)

Prisoners of Hope?

Aspects of Evangelical Millennialism in Britain and Ireland, 1800–1880

This volume of essays offers a comprehensive account of the impact of evangelical millennialism in nineteenth-century Britain and Ireland.

2004 / 1-84227-224-1 / xiv + 208pp

Khim Harris

Evangelicals and Education

Evangelical Anglicans and Middle-Class Education in Nineteenth-Century England

This ground breaking study investigates the history of English public schools founded by nineteenth-century Evangelicals. It documents the rise of middle-class education and Evangelical societies such as the influential Church Association, and includes a useful biographical survey of prominent Evangelicals of the period.

2004 / 1-84227-250-0 / xviii + 422pp

July 2005

Mark Hopkins

Nonconformity's Romantic Generation

Evangelical and Liberal Theologies in Victorian England

A study of the theological development of key leaders of the Baptist and Congregational denominations at their period of greatest influence, including C.H. Spurgeon and R.W. Dale, and of the controversies in which those among them who embraced and rejected the liberal transformation of their evangelical heritage opposed each other.

2004 / 1-84227-150-4 / xvi + 284pp

Don Horrocks

Laws of the Spiritual Order

Innovation and Reconstruction in the Soteriology of Thomas Erskine of Linlathen

Don Horrocks argues that Thomas Erskine's unique historical and theological significance as a soteriological innovator has been neglected. This timely reassessment reveals Erskine as a creative, radical theologian of central and enduring importance in Scottish nineteenth-century theology, perhaps equivalent in significance to that of S.T. Coleridge in England.

2004 / 1-84227-192-X / xx + 362pp

Kenneth S. Jeffrey

When the Lord Walked the Land

The 1858–62 Revival in the North East of Scotland

Previous studies of revivals have tended to approach religious movements from either a broad, national or a strictly local level. This study of the multifaceted nature of the 1859 revival as it appeared in three distinct social contexts within a single region reveals the heterogeneous nature of simultaneous religious movements in the same vicinity.

2002 / 1-84227-057-5 / xxiv + 304pp

John Kenneth Lander

Itinerant Temples

Tent Methodism, 1814–1832

Tent preaching began in 1814 and the Tent Methodist sect resulted from disputes with Bristol Wesleyan Methodists in 1820. The movement spread to parts of Gloucestershire, Wiltshire, London and Liverpool, among other places. Its demise started in 1826 after which one leader returned to the Wesleyans and others became ministers in the Congregational and Baptist denominations.

2003 / 1-84227-151-2 / xx + 268pp

July 2005

Donald M. Lewis

Lighten Their Darkness

The Evangelical Mission to Working-Class London, 1828–1860

This is a comprehensive and compelling study of the Church and the complexities of nineteenth-century London. Challenging our understanding of the culture in working London at this time, Lewis presents a well-structured and illustrated work that contributes substantially to the study of evangelicalism and mission in nineteenth-century Britain.

2001 / 1-84227-074-5 / xviii + 372pp

Herbert McGonigle

'Sufficient Saving Grace'

John Wesley's Evangelical Arminianism

A thorough investigation of the theological roots of John Wesley's evangelical Arminianism and how these convictions were hammered out in controversies on predestination, limited atonement and the perseverance of the saints.

2001 / 1-84227-045-1 / xvi + 350pp

Lisa S. Nolland

A Victorian Feminist Christian

Josephine Butler, the Prostitutes and God

Josephine Butler was an unlikely candidate for taking up the cause of prostitutes, as she did, with a fierce and self-disregarding passion. This book explores the particular mix of perspectives and experiences that came together to envision and empower her remarkable achievements. It highlights the vital role of her spirituality and the tragic loss of her daughter.

2004 / 1-84227-225-X / xxiv + 328pp

Don J. Payne

The Theology of the Christian Life in J.I. Packer's Thought

Theological Anthropology, Theological Method, and the Doctrine of Sanctification

J.I. Packer has wielded widespread influence on evangelicalism for more than three decades. This study pursues a nuanced understanding of Packer's theology of sanctification by tracing the development of his thought, showing how he reflects a particular version of Reformed theology, and examining the unique influence of theological anthropology and theological method on this area of his theology.

2005 */ 1-84227-397-3 / approx. 374pp*

July 2005

Ian M. Randall

Evangelical Experiences

A Study in the Spirituality of English Evangelicalism 1918–1939

This book makes a detailed historical examination of evangelical spirituality between the First and Second World Wars. It shows how patterns of devotion led to tensions and divisions. In a wide-ranging study, Anglican, Wesleyan, Reformed and Pentecostal-charismatic spiritualities are analysed.

1999 / 0-85364-919-7 / xii + 310pp

Ian M. Randall

Spirituality and Social Change

The Contribution of F.B. Meyer (1847–1929)

This is a fresh appraisal of F.B. Meyer (1847–1929), a leading Free Church minister. Having been deeply affected by holiness spirituality, Meyer became the Keswick Convention's foremost international speaker. He combined spirituality with effective evangelism and socio-political activity. This study shows Meyer's significant contribution to spiritual renewal and social change.

2003 / 1-84227-195-4 / xx + 184pp

James Robinson

Pentecostal Origins

Early Pentecostalism in Ireland in the Context of the British Isles

Harvey Cox describes Pentecostalism as 'the fascinating spiritual child of our time' that has the potential, at the global scale, to contribute to the 'reshaping of religion in the twenty-first century'. This study grounds such sentiments by examining at the local scale the origin, development and nature of Pentecostalism in Ireland in its first twenty years. Illustrative, in a paradigmatic way, of how Pentecostalism became established within one region of the British Isles, it sets the story within the wider context of formative influences emanating from America, Europe and, in particular, other parts of the British Isles. As a synoptic regional study in Pentecostal history it is the first survey of its kind.

2005 / 1-84227-329-1 / xxviii + 378pp

Geoffrey Robson

Dark Satanic Mills?

Religion and Irreligion in Birmingham and the Black Country

This book analyses and interprets the nature and extent of popular Christian belief and practice in Birmingham and the Black Country during the first half of the nineteenth century, with particular reference to the impact of cholera epidemics and evangelism on church extension programmes.

2002 / 1-84227-102-4 / xiv + 294pp

July 2005

Roger Shuff

Searching for the True Church

Brethren and Evangelicals in Mid-Twentieth-Century England

Roger Shuff holds that the influence of the Brethren movement on wider evangelical life in England in the twentieth century is often underrated. This book records and accounts for the fact that Brethren reached the peak of their strength at the time when evangelicalism was at it lowest ebb, immediately before World War II. However, the movement then moved into persistent decline as evangelicalism regained ground in the post war period. Accompanying this downward trend has been a sharp accentuation of the contrast between Brethren congregations who engage constructively with the non-Brethren scene and, at the other end of the spectrum, the isolationist group commonly referred to as 'Exclusive Brethren'.

2005 / 1-84227-254-3 / xviii+ 296pp

James H.S. Steven

Worship in the Spirit

Charismatic Worship in the Church of England

This book explores the nature and function of worship in six Church of England churches influenced by the Charismatic Movement, focusing on congregational singing and public prayer ministry. The theological adequacy of such ritual is discussed in relation to pneumatological and christological understandings in Christian worship.

2002 / 1-84227-103-2 / xvi + 238pp

Peter K. Stevenson

God in Our Nature

The Incarnational Theology of John McLeod Campbell

This radical reassessment of Campbell's thought arises from a comprehensive study of his preaching and theology. Previous accounts have overlooked both his sermons and his Christology. This study examines the distinctive Christology evident in his sermons and shows that it sheds new light on Campbell's much debated views about atonement.

2004 / 1-84227-218-7 / xxiv + 458pp

July 2005

Kenneth J. Stewart

Restoring the Reformation

British Evangelicalism and the Réveil at Geneva 1816–1849

Restoring the Reformation traces British missionary initiative in post-Revolutionary Francophone Europe from the genesis of the London Missionary Society, the visits of Robert Haldane and Henry Drummond, and the founding of the Continental Society. While British Evangelicals aimed at the reviving of a foreign Protestant cause of momentous legend, they received unforeseen reciprocating emphases from the Continent which forced self-reflection on Evangelicalism's own relationship to the Reformation.

***2006** / 1-84227-392-2 / approx. 190pp*

Martin Wellings

Evangelicals Embattled

Responses of Evangelicals in the Church of England to Ritualism, Darwinism and Theological Liberalism 1890–1930

In the closing years of the nineteenth century and the first decades of the twentieth century Anglican Evangelicals faced a series of challenges. In responding to Anglo-Catholicism, liberal theology, Darwinism and biblical criticism, the unity and identity of the Evangelical school were severely tested.

2003 / 1-84227-049-4 / xviii + 352pp

James Whisenant

A Fragile Unity

Anti-Ritualism and the Division of Anglican Evangelicalism in the Nineteenth Century

This book deals with the ritualist controversy (approximately 1850–1900) from the perspective of its evangelical participants and considers the divisive effects it had on the party.

2003 / 1-84227-105-9 / xvi + 530pp

Haddon Willmer

Evangelicalism 1785–1835: An Essay (1962) and Reflections (2004)

Awarded the Hulsean Prize in the University of Cambridge in 1962, this interpretation of a classic period of English Evangelicalism, by a young church historian, is now supplemented by reflections on Evangelicalism from the vantage point of a retired Professor of Theology.

***2006** / 1-84227-219-5 / approx. 350pp*

July 2005

Linda Wilson
Constrained by Zeal
Female Spirituality amongst Nonconformists 1825–1875

Constrained by Zeal investigates the neglected area of Nonconformist female spirituality. Against the background of separate spheres, it analyses the experience of women from four denominations, and argues that the churches provided a 'third sphere' in which they could find opportunities for participation.

2000 / 0-85364-972-3 / xvi + 294pp

Paternoster
9 Holdom Avenue,
Bletchley,
Milton Keynes MK1 1QR,
United Kingdom
Web: www.authenticmedia.co.uk/paternoster

July 2005